GREAT AFRICAN THINKERS

Vol. 1

CHEIKH ANTA DIOP

Co-Editor of
This Special Issue:
Larry Williams

editor
IVAN VAN SERTIMA

Transaction Books
New Brunswick (U.S.A.) and Oxford (U.K.)

Second printing, 1987.

ISSN 0270-2495
ISBN 0-88738-680-6 (paper)
Printed in the United States of America

Cover design by Jacqueline Patten-Van Sertima

Great African Thinkers, Vol. 1: Cheikh Anta Diop

Incorporating JOURNAL OF AFRICAN CIVILIZATIONS,
June 1986 (Vol. 8, No. 1)

Contents

Introduction

DEATH SHALL NOT FIND US THINKING THAT WE DIE

Ivan Van Sertima

I felt a strange sense of awe in his presence. It was the aura of nobility and graciousness, perhaps, the quiet air of intellectual authority, the legend of his life and his work that had preceded him. His eyes never left me as he spoke but though his gaze and his grip were firm, his voice was surprisingly soft. The sibilances of his French rose and fell upon my brain like waves of whispers.

"Monsieur Diop," was all I could say, "we meet at last."

It was a cool, blue London day, the light of a premature springtime loitering like a stranger on the streets of a winter morn. January 13, 1985 . . . about a year and a month before his death! We had exchanged long letters, we had spoken on occasion on the telephone, I had read his work in English, he my work in French.[1] He had followed avidly the issues of the Journal of African Civilizations. Yet nearly a decade was to pass before we met face to face. That week in London we talked to packed houses. We dined, we discoursed, we debated. Diop's great friend of many years, Carlos Moore, made us feel at times as though we were conversing in the same language. But in spite of the growing familiarity, my sense of awe and reverence in his presence persisted. I saw him more as a father than as a comrade-in-arms. I felt the long road that I would still have to walk. I could not shake off the impression of being in the shadow of an elder spirit.

It is not for us to say that the death of a man comes too early or too late. Fate is far too complex. But let us venture to say that we in America needed a guide and a teacher like Diop. Africa, above all, needed a leader like Diop. Had he lived to become President of Senegal, he might have piloted some of the nations of West Africa into the first stages of a federated state. His passing, therefore, is a very great blow to us all. Yet history teaches us that men like these do not die at the time of their deaths. Often it is that the fall of a great teacher or prophet is the beginning of the rise of his ideas. So let it be with Diop . . .

He was born on December 23, 1923, in Diourbel, a little town in western Senegal. He was of a Muslim peasant family and attended Koranic schools. His hometown, Spady informs us, was the seat of a strong Muslim sect and brotherhood where collective activity was considered sacred. This was the sect of the Mourides, the only Black African sect, according to Diop, which succeeded in acting independently from the rest of the Muslim world. Diop completed his bachelor's degree in Senegal and then went on to Paris in 1946 to do his graduate studies.

Proud, stubborn, independent, Diop did not take the easy road to his doctorate. Instead, he attempted something that took him straight into the mouth of the guns. He presented a lengthy and closely argued dissertation on ancient Egyptian history. The main lines of his thesis may be summarized and simplified thus: That Egypt was the node and center of a vast web linking the strands of Africa's main cultures and languages; that the light that crystallized at the center of this early world had been energized by the cultural electricity streaming from the heartland of Africa; that the creators of classical Egyptian civilization, therefore, were not the brown Mediterranean Caucasoids invented by Sergi, nor the equally mythical Hamites, nor Asiatic nomads and invaders, but indigenous, blackskinned, wooly-haired Africans; that Greece, mother of the best in European civilization, was once a child suckled at the breast of Egypt even as Egypt had been suckled at the breast of Ethiopia, which itself evolved from the complex interior womb of the African motherland.

Of course, the jury of the University of Paris roundly rejected this thesis, labelling it "unfounded." It ran counter to all that had been taught in Europe for two centuries about the origin of civilization, although the early Greeks themselves, who knew the Egyptians of that time and studied their metaphysics and their sciences would have agreed in the main with Diop. Diop's thesis, after all, was not entirely new. Others had stated this before. What was new was the formidable competency in many disciplines that he brought to bear to establish this thesis on solid, scientific foundations. Although it was rejected by the University, it was published in 1955 under the title *Black Nations and Culture,* earning its author international recognition. It took him ten years and two more doctoral dissertations, both of which were revolutionary in perspective, before he was granted the doctorate. These dissertations were published as *The Cultural Unity of Africa* (1959) and *Pre-Colonial Black Africa* (1960).

Diop was not just a major revisionist historian. He was an extremely promising physicist. He eventually gained entry into a major nuclear research center near Paris. The establishment of this center was made possible through the influence of one of France's most distinguished scientists, Frederick Joliot-Curie, son-in-law of Marie Curie who, with her husband Pierre, won the Nobel Prize for the discovery of radium. Diop spent a lot of time working and experimenting in this laboratory. He became one of the very few Africans, as Spady notes, "with access to the most advanced body of scientific knowledge." At a time when only a handful of people in the world understood Einstein's relativity theory, Diop translated a major portion of it into Wolof, the language of his people.

His scientific background is very important in our assessment of his contribution to historical knowledge. He was able to use it to great effect to refine and develop his earlier Egyptian thesis. For example, Diop developed a chemical process for testing the level of melanin in the skin of Egyptian mummies he studied in the Museum of Man in order to establish their Black African ancestry. His close examination of primary sources and his knowledge of metallurgy enabled him also to establish that the iron artifacts found in the Ancient Egyptian Empire were not intrusions from a higher stratum nor the accidental byproduct of another process, as Profs. Leclant and Mauny had claimed, but very strong evidence of the invention of iron-smelting by the Egyptians long before the Hittites and the Assyrians (see "Iron in the Ancient Egyptian Empire," translated by Darryl Prevost, in this issue).

His greatest strength, perhaps, lay in linguistics. Assisted by the Congolese Egyptologist and linguist, Theophile Obenga, now President of the Center for Bantu Studies in Brazzaville, Diop established at the UNESCO conference on "The Peopling of Ancient Egypt" (January, 1974) that the Egyptian language was African and that it was genetically related to a family of African languages, including his own native Wolof. In spite of the passion and prejudice that marked some of the debates at this conference, the UNESCO report states "the [linguistic] reports of Professors Diop and Obenga were regarded as being very constructive" and "revealed a large measure of agreement among the participants."

A summary of this conference is of interest and value to readers since it reveals the state of Egyptology at the moment and the defensive reaction to the question of "blackness" or "negroness." Professor Ghallab of the Arab Republic of Egypt declared that the human race during the paleolithic era (stone age) was more or less homogeneous and "Caucasian" and that "Negroes" only began to appear much later. A "Negro" culture, he claimed, did not appear prior to the neolithic (age of agriculture). Professor Debono of Malta spoke of a race of pyramid-builders coming into Egypt, a race with Libyco-Asiatic affinities, without even deeming it necessary to show where on this earth stands the proto-pyramid this "race" constructed before it migrated to Africa. Several participants, finding it difficult to demolish Diop, decided instead to demolish all talk about race. Professor Save-Söderberg of Sweden, while demonstrating that the majority of neolithic cultures in the Nile Valley belonged to a techno-complex of Saharan and Sudanic cultures, said the concept of race was outmoded and should now be abandoned. Professor Vercoutter of France, insisting that there was no way to tell how many of the Egyptians were white and how many were black, felt the evidence, nevertheless, showed that Egypt at least was African in its way of writing, its culture, and its way of thinking. Professor Shinnie of Canada said that Herodotus and all the Greeks and Romans who had called the Egyptians "black" were merely being subjective like Dr. Diop. Race was not a scientific concept. Professor Mokhtar of the Arab Republic of Egypt said the problem of race was unimportant. Professor Abdallah of the Sudan, after chiding Diop for adopting an Africanist approach to this problem, went on boldly to assert that the Egyptian language belonged to a family of proto-semitic languages and that there was abundant evidence to prove it. He had not come to the conference, however, with his "abundant evidence." This, in fact, was one of the remarkable revelations of this international conference. In its final report, UNESCO pointed out: "Although the preparatory working paper sent out by UNESCO gave particulars of what was desired, not all participants had prepared communications comparable with the painstakingly researched contributions of Professors Cheikh Anta Diop and Obenga." The Africans, at last, had done their homework, and those theses, which had once seemed formidable, now shook with the fragility of leaves in the new intellectual wind blowing from the continent.

Diop, however, was not merely fighting battles on the intellectual front. He realized that his new conception of history could provide a ground of unity and continuity on the African continent, forging new and powerful political forces to transcend the instability and fragmentation, the lack of real pride and faith and sense of a collective destiny in modern Africa. He founded the *Block of the Masses of Senegal,* a militant political party in 1960. The party was banned and he was arrested and imprisoned. He founded a second political party in 1964, the *Senegalese National Front.* This was declared illegal and he was again arrested. He founded a third political party, the *National Democratic Rally,* in 1976. Speaking of his political experience, in answer to a question posed by Larry Williams in 1985, Diop said: "I'm in the opposition party in Senegal. Senegal is perhaps one country where you can say there is a little more freedom than there is in other places. I can go from one place to another. But this is not a freedom we were given. This is a freedom we took. We paid for this freedom. For 30 years I have paid with my own self. I nearly died in prison, as you know. Things like this are no longer possible in Senegal."

His political vision was both idealistic and practical, radical and yet pragmatic and responsible. In spite of his death, it may have far-reaching consequences. As Charles Finch points out in *Further Conversations with the Pharaoh* "He has worked out a theoretical model for the political, economic and social reconstruction of Africa and has seen many of the programs and projects he has advocated over the last 30 years become public policy in his own country."

Diop was deeply disturbed by the grave instability of modern Africa. In a series of interviews with Carlos Moore in 1977, he spoke of the lack of national leaderships that could set an example, of the swift and inevitable tumble of regimes all over the continent, of the selfish egoism of leaders running ineffectual and anachronistic mini-states. Commenting on the prospects of the newly-formed Economic Community of West African States, Diop warned that all such attempts at economic regional regroupment were likely to fail unless West Africa developed "a supranational umbrella, in the form of a federal executive organ, able to take political decisions binding on all parties." Political unification is a prerequisite, he insisted, to the rational organization of African economies. "We want to create regional economic organizations from which member states can draw maximum benefits, yet we refuse to relinquish even an inch of our respective sovereignties . . . The rational organization of African economies cannot precede the political organization of Africa. [It] must come *after* the creation of a federal political unity."

Political unity . . . a federated structure . . . these were not dreams to Diop but absolute necessities. No other African leader, including Nkrumah, set out with such energy and expertise to discover and to detail what steps should be taken to bring parts of Africa into a federation, none who examined so closely the location, distribution and commercial value of African resources and the way in which these could most effectively be developed and deployed on an African continental basis.

He was no armchair theorist. He worked furiously to build the Radiocarbon laboratory at IFAN in Dakar. This was established in 1966 for the purpose of low-energy radioactivity research and carbon-14 dating. He led the struggle for the formation of an African technology consortium. What has become of this consortium we do not yet know. Not enough information has been passed on to us. Speaking, however, as President of the World Black Researchers Association formed in 1976, Diop declared that the first objective of the Association was to reverse the brain-drain. "The Association will englobe all of the scientific disciplines, both the natural and social sciences. Consequently it will comprise two permanent international secretariats, one for the natural sciences and the other for the social sciences. In both domains scholars and scientists of the black world will be asked to direct their efforts towards solving the most vital scientific and sociological problems presently confronting the black world. This will further solidify the cultural ties binding all black populations of the globe."

Some may find his vision of black global unity uncharacteristically naive for such a preeminently scientific spirit. His idealism, however, went hand-in-hand with a sound critical and commonsensical approach to both ancient and modern realities. Diop attacked the modern African tendency to establish one-party systems. "Experience has overwhelmingly shown that the one-party system has failed to build the type of Africa we desire . . . The building of Africa must be based on freedom of choice. Only what is built on the basis of freedom is durable." Last April, in a question-and-answer session with the Nile Valley Executive Committee, Diop pointed out that although ancient Egypt was elitist and had a hierarchy, it was also democratic. "It has been recorded that workers could sue ministers and governors before the law."

In terms of his vision of Africa as united territory and unifying force, Diop has been placed alongside Blyden, Garvey and Nkrumah. There are certain refinements, however, in Diop's Pan-African philosophy that should be understood. It is not just a matter of semantics. It might be instructive to contrast his complex and dynamic view of what he calls "a cultural personality" and what Nkrumah called "The African personality" or what the poets of Negritude (Senghor and Césaire, for example) would define as "an African identity." Diop feels that an integration of three critical factors constitutes a cultural or collective personality of a people and that the emphasis on *one* can lead to flirtations with the past or an involvement in generalities. An edited version of the exchange between Carlos Moore and Diop on this point will help to explain what I mean.

MOORE: Kwame Nkrumah had opposed his concept of "African Personality" to the concept of Negritude. Are these concepts antithetical or do they converge anywhere?

DIOP: They converge in the sense that they both deal in generalities. We must get down to the facts, to the objective apprehendable realities. When we talk about personality, meaning the personality of collective groups, we can only mean *a cultural personality.* And what is the basis of the cultural personality of a people, African or otherwise, if not a historical, psychic and linguistic self-consciousness? These three elements are the constituent elements of a people's cultural personality or identity. They are not static factors conditioned by man's social and physical environment. . . . My approach has clarified what is called the particular sensibility of the black man, or 'black soul.' I have tried to determine the nature of the black particularity in history and to ascertain the way in which the 'black soul' or 'black sensibility' has influenced the material existence and creativity of black peoples by using the structures evolved by ancient black societies as a basis . . . Rather than deal in generalities we must know what the black soul is because it is our soul. The way I saw it at the beginning was that Africa's soul had been stolen and could only be retrieved through a scientific approach.

It is this approach that has affected the new school of African-American historians. Most of us first came to know of Diop in the seventies through Mercer Cook's brilliant translation and editing of sections from *Anteriorité Des Civilizations Negres: Mythe ou Verite Historique?* and *Nations Negres et Culture* which appeared under the title of *The African Origin of Civilization: Myth or Reality?* James Spady gives us the background to the scholarship on Diop's historical work. Spady has the distinction of being the first person in the English-speaking world to publish an essay on Diop. We have also been fortunate to be able to present reviews on two of Diop's major works in English and an excellent translation of the introduction and first two chapters of his last work, *Civilization or Barbarism: An Authentic Anthropology.* John Clarke and A.J. Williams-Meyers both attempt reviews of *The African Origin of Civilization* Clarke points to Diop's predecessors, African historians like Dr. Danquah, European historians like Massey, Heeren, Volney. Clarke classes Diop among the greatest of African historians and recalls the first time he sought him out in Dakar. The anecdote tells us a lot about the Eurocentric control of African history. Clarke recalls the second meeting of the International Congress of Africanists. It was held about 300 yards from Diop's office and laboratory, yet he was not one of the participants. Reviewing the same work, Williams-Meyers expresses caution about certain aspects of Diop's methodology and terminology but he presents us with a scholarly and balanced analysis, taking account of the critics on the one hand and the body of evidence on the other.

Asa Hilliard introduces us to that difficult but central work in the Diop oeuvre, *The Cultural Unity of Black Africa*. Why this vision and dynamic of cultural unity must be used to weld a "population" into a "people" is eloquently restated by Hilliard: "No people can be liberated who are cultural neuters. 'Individuals' may survive as shooting stars with temporary spurts of speed, but with a curved path that ends in darkness. It is the group (in Diop's terms a *people* rather than a population) that survives as an eternal galaxy."

Runoko Rashidi, co-editor of *The African Presence in Early Asia*, highlights a little known aspect of Diop's work. Diop has taken a very real interest in Asia. A team of Japanese scientists visited his laboratory a few years ago to speak with him on his work. When he founded the World Black Researchers Association he placed particular emphasis on the inclusion of blacks from Australia, Fiji, New Guinea, the rest of Oceania and other parts of Asia, "a zone of the world where black populations find themselves scattered and isolated." Rashidi feels that in this area Diop has also blazed a brilliant trail.

On one point only he takes issue with Diop. That is on the question of the caste system of India. It is not the case, argues Rashidi, that in the caste system as Diop claims, "the criteria of color has a low priority without any ethnic considerations." A fascinating addenda to Rashidi's essay comes in the form of a letter from a black untouchable sect in India, the Dalits, who have named a militant organization of Dalits, *Dalit Panther*, after the Black Panther movement in America. It is refreshing to find young historians who will provide challenges and corrections to the master's work when these are thought necessary. Diop would have welcomed the debate. As he said to me in a letter in 1979 (see Appendix) "You must not abandon discussion out of tact . . . There should be no concession where there is a question of establishing a scientific truth . . . Remember we are focused on a quest for truth and not on a sacrosanct idol whom we must avoid debasing . . ."

Diop's last work has been eagerly awaited in English translation. Several attempts have been made to do it but it is a formidable task. The unusual length of the work, the convolutions and idiosyncrasies of his style (which does not have the same directness as his speaking voice) the technical terminology growing out of his intimacy with many disciplines, daunts the prospective translator. Fortunately, Diop gave his approval to one translation by Edward F. Taylor of Morehouse and cabled us before his death to give the Journal permission to publish it. Readers who would like a sense of what the book is about in its entirety should read the excellent summary of Leonard Jeffries in "The Legacy of Chiekh Anta Diop." This summary has been placed in this issue just before the Taylor translation and should be read as an introduction to it. What is ironic is that Diop died at the very moment that his major thesis—that modern man proceeds from a single African ancestor—found its ultimate scientific confirmation.

We quote now from a document published on the day before Diop's death. It is entitled "Evolutionary relationships of human populations from an analysis of nuclear DNA polymorphisms." It is the work of eleven scientists, most of them from the University of Oxford, England, and it appears in *Nature*, vol. 319 (February 6, 1986). The team of scientists concluded: "The earliest fossils of anatomically modern man (Homo *sapiens sapiens*) have been found in Africa at Omo in Ethiopia, Border Cave in South Africa and at Klasies River Mouth in South Africa. The data from the last site suggest that Homo *sapiens sapiens* was present in South Africa more than 100,000 years ago, and an adult mandible from Border Cave has been dated to about 90,000 years B.P. [before the present era]. Hence, it has been argued that the evolution of modern man took place in Africa. Our data are consistent with such a scheme, in which *a founder population migrated from Africa and subsequently gave rise to all non-African populations*."

A word or two of clarification is needed here for some of our readers to understand the full importance of this breakthrough. What has been in dispute is *not* whether man was born in Africa. This has been universally accepted for some time. Those who argued against Diop (the polygenetic theorists) for a multiple or plural origin of man, could claim that, although man was born in Africa, he migrated to Europe and Asia at a low-level stage (Homo Erectus, say) and then evolved into a more advanced and modern type on those continents. As more and more discoveries were made in Africa, sophisticated revisions could be made to this theory without seriously upsetting their main thesis—of a backward African ancestor evolving elsewhere into an advanced *homo sapiens sapiens* (modern human type). The scientific discovery above proves that this is not the case. What it establishes is that while earlier African types might have migrated and disappeared, the human at its most advanced stage, at the peak of its present phase of evolution, came out of Africa to people other continents and merely underwent mutations or adaptations in other ecological zones. Perhaps, the most lucid layman discussion of this question appears in the lecture "The Beginnings of Man and Civilization" and in his interview with Listervelt Middleton, the only television interview Diop gave during his brief visit to America in April of 1985.

This visit took two years of planning. As Larry Williams says in his overview of the visit "it was the realization of a dream that had germinated in the hearts and minds of African-Americans" since the publication of his books in English. He was invited to preside over the Nile Valley Conference held in Atlanta in September of 1984. An accident with his plane, which Diop vividly describes in an interview with the Nile Valley Executive Committee (see Interviews), aborted a year of laborious planning. Diop finally made it, however, on a maiden flight initiated by Delta Airlines from Paris to Atlanta. His coming was like the arrival of an African President and he was received like one. Morehouse College, which had honored Presidents Kaunda and Mugabe, conferred an honorary doctorate on Diop. Mayor Young, who had issued a proclamation creating a "Cheikh Anta Diop Day" during the Nile Valley Civilizations conference in 1984, now provided him with the city's great hospitality and security. While many individuals and organizations contributed to making the visit possible, special credit should be given to Charles Finch for travelling to London with me in the winter of 1985 to finalize negotiations with Diop, to Larry Williams for his painstaking efforts to develop a valuable library of Diopiana, with the visit to America as focus (tapes, videos, translations, transcripts, slides, photographs) and Dean Lawrence Edward Carter Sr., Dean of the Martin Luther King Jr. International Chapel, for coordinating the visit.

It was indeed fitting that Diop should be hosted at Morehouse College, Martin Luther King's alma mater, and that he should speak in the Chapel dedicated to Dr. King.

"I have come to America to meet with those who are members of my family," he said in the Chapel, "that is to say with you all. In fact, I am convinced that my family has been divided in two and that half of it is here before me now. Just as you Americans who go to Africa feel that you are making a pilgrimage to the lands of your ancestors, I too am making a pilgrimage here in America. The most important thing that we have to do by the end of this century is to reconstruct the links that tie us as communities. I subscribe to the teachings of Martin Luther King, Jr. wholeheartedly. They are teachings that are aimed at unifying and reuniting kindred peoples. What I have to say here today is to reinforce the links that unite us and all people across the world. . . ."

Diop said and did a great deal in a very short space of time. He entered into lectures, discussions, dinners, tours, ceremonies, with the same energy that marked all his endeavors. As he looked back on his American voyage several months later in Dakar, he confided to Charles Finch: "I was very impressed by my contact with the black American community and with Americans in general. I discovered many things of which I was totally ignorant. As I said in the United States, I feel very strongly that this was a sort of pilgrimage for me. I think that all thinking Africans who go to America are, in one way or another, on a pilgrimage. I said before I left that I was going to find half of my family in America. It was just that. We are beginning to feel in a most vital way this biological kinship which ties us to America, the umbilical cord has not been cut. And this is very important. These relations must become much closer in the future. I believe that all of what lies in our common future is in this perspective. America is uniquely brought closer to Africa by historical ties. I was especially aware of this on American soil. . . ."

On this American soil, on this side or plane of time, we shall not meet again, Cheikh Anta. But we have gathered the leaves of this work together because of your presiding spirit, because of the essence and purpose of your work. It is our duty to continue what you have begun since we knew one day we would be forced to continue without your physical presence. Your spirit, after all, is the catalyst. And even if the wings, upon which your body flew, are broken, that spirit has already flown to us. It shall reside with us, it shall be enthroned in the hearts of your people always . . .

Too soon, too soon
the banner draped for you
I would prefer a banner in the wind
not bound so tightly with a scarlet fold
not sodden, sodden, with your people's tears
but borne aloft
down and beyond this dark, dark lane of rags.
Dear Comrade,
if it must be
that I no longer speak with you
no longer walk with you
no longer march with you
then I must take a patience and a calm
for even now the greener leaf explodes
sun brightens stone
and all the river burns
Now from the mourning vanguard moving on
dear comrade, I salute you
and I say
Death shall not find us thinking that we die.[2]

NOTES

1. *Ils y étaient avant Christophe Colomb,* by Ivan Van Sertima (Paris: Flammarion, 1981).
2. Excerpted from the poem "Death of a Comrade" by Martin Carter.

Acknowledgements

The Journal of African Civilizations Inc. would like to thank the following for their services in making this tribute and memorial to the late Cheikh Anta Diop possible:

We thank Larry Williams, co-editor of this issue and Chairman of the Bennu Study Group in Atlanta, for:

- Preparing the transcripts of all but one of the lectures we have selected to publish from the series Dr. Diop gave during his tour of the United States.
- Submission of 27 slides illustrating the most extended of these lectures and preparation also of the question-and-answer session accompanying the lecture.
- Submission of half a dozen of the selected photographs illustrating the Diop visit.
- Negotiating with the Moores and with the magazine *Afriscope* and *Black Books Bulletin* permission to reprint the interviews with Diop by Carlos and Shawna Moore.
- Providing an overview of the Diop visit to America.
- Providing a bibliography of critical essays on, and publications by, Diop.
- Preparing transcripts of the Listervelt Middleton interview and the interview with the Nile Valley Executive Committee.

We thank Dr. Lawrence Edward Carter Sr., Dean of the Martin Luther King Jr. International Chapel, for compiling materials on Diop's visit to America, which was largely sponsored and hosted by Morehouse College in Atlanta. These include:

- Letters of invitation to Diop.
- A dozen of the photographs we have selected to commemorate the event.
- Dr. Gloster's citation to Diop.
- The Mayor's proclamation, making April 4, 1985 "Cheikh Anta Diop Day."
- A selection from one of Martin Luther King's speeches to preface the "Diop in America" section.
- A summary of the highlights of his visit to the United States.

Dean Carter coordinated the work of all the organizations who co-sponsored and financed the visit. A list of these major sponsors is given separately on page 18.

We thank Dr. Charles Finch for providing us with 17 photos used in the French edition of *Civilization or Barbarism* and for travelling to Dakar, Senegal, on behalf of the *Journal of African Civilizations*, to conduct a final interview with Diop in November of 1985.

We thank Marva Griffin Carter for her transcription of Diop's address presented to the All-College Morehouse Assembly on receiving his honorary doctorate.

We thank the translators Elizabeth Clement, Irene d'Almeida, Mary Diallo and Dr. Edward F. Taylor for making most of the lectures Diop gave in America available in English to the readers of the *Journal of African Civilizations*.

We thank Dr. Edward F. Taylor for permission to publish the only authorized English version of the introduction and first two chapters of Diop's last book *Civilization or Barbarism*.

Finally, we thank *Presence Africaine*, publishers of the French edition of *Civilization or Barbarism*, for permission granted to us, at the request of Diop, to publish a substantial section from the book.

Ivan Van Sertima

Sponsors of Cheikh Anta Diop's Visit

Martin Luther King, Jr. International Chapel of Morehouse College

Human Values Program of the Morehouse School of Medicine

Fulton County Arts Council, Dr. Michael Lomax, Chrmn. Fulton Co. Com.

Southern Educational Fund

Office of Mayor Andrew Young, City of Atlanta, Georgia

Delta Airlines, Mr. Ronald W. Allen, President, Mr. John Cox, Vice-President

Southern Christian Leadership Conference, Dr. Joseph Lowery, President

Martin Luther King, Jr. Center for Nonviolent Social Change, Mrs. Coretta Scott King, President

---

CONVERSATIONS WITH DIOP AND TSEGAYE: THE NILE VALLEY REVISITED

Jan Carew

December mornings in Addis Ababa are deceptive. The sunlight sparkles like champagne, but when you venture outdoors, there is a bite in the air and you marvel that in the cold high-altitude atmosphere Ethiopians wear cotton garments that seem much better suited to equatorial climates. I noticed, however, that pedestrians did not exactly saunter. They walked at a brisk pace and sometimes, quite spontaneously, broke into a jog.

The morning I set out to meet Cheikh Anta Diop, I had left my hotel wearing a Guyanese shirtjac and a pair of garbardine slacks. The sunshine on eucalyptus trees, whose glittering leaves seemed to be clapping hands in the wind, had beckoned me from my hotel window to come for a stroll out into warm African sunshine. Ten paces from the hotel entrance, an icy breath of wind sent me hurrying back to put on layers of warm clothing. Once I was appropriately attired to face an Addis winter morning, I set out once more. My rendezvous was with Diop and his student, Tsegaye Medhin Gabre. Tsegaye, one of the foremost contemporary playwrights on the African continent, was also a very knowledgable Egyptologist. He had been Diop's student for years. On the way to meet them, I could not help remembering how Tsegaye had told me that in the 19th century, a British soldier in General Napier's army, had written home to say that before he left England with his regiment they had been briefed that they were about to invade a country of table mountains but after coming to Ethiopia he had discovered that the tables were all upside down, and he always seemed to be climbing up the legs. The Napier invasion had been ordered by the British to overthrow the Emperor Tewodros and conquer Ethiopia. It was a time when Africa was being carved up by European colonizers like the cake at a devil's birthday party. It was also a time when Queen Victoria had penned an insolent letter to Tewodros suggesting that he should invite British missionaries to spread the Christian gospel in his kingdom. Tewodros, along with his icily polite reply, had sent Victoria the copy of a bible that had been published in Ethiopia two centuries before the English had embraced christianity, and, as a footnote, he had pointed out that if missionaries were to be dispatched, perhaps they should be sent from Ethiopia to Britain and not the other way round.

Cheikh Anta Diop was a man of average height, and there was about him an aura of dignity and gentleness that is peculiarly African. These rare twin qualities are the result of a tremendous sense of intellectual and spiritual assurance. That African gentleness, which both Diop, a Wolof, and Tsegaye, an Amhara, epitomized, is a quality that one finds in small pockets of the diaspora, but on the whole it did not seem to travel very well across the Middle Passage. I found Diop's gentleness on the one hand, and intellectual assurance on the other, almost mesmeric. Perhaps a violent uprootment from the homeland and slavery had made a certain aggressiveness and conceit necessary qualities for survival for the folks of the diaspora.

"It is as if the man had rinsed his brain out with clear spring water," an Afro-American friend speaking in awed tones about Diop, had told me.

I remember telling Diop shortly after we had met about one of my Black students at Princeton who had withdrawn into dreaming sanctuaries of the Hindu religion to become a guru; and about a Jamaican friend who, after serving in the Royal Air Force, had left London and gone to Thailand to become a Buddhist monk. African philosophy, Diop had said (and I am paraphrasing all of our conversations, since they took place over thirteen years ago), calls on our folk to enter the arena of life, and not to withdraw from it, to become engaged with life, thought and being and not to retreat into ebony or mahogany towers of eternal meditation.

We were in Addis attending the annual conference of the Association of African Studies. It was being held in the Organization of African Unity building opposite Emperor Haile Selassie's palace. As you walked past the palace, you could see drowsy lions chained at the gates, and tall Danikil guards standing as still as lifesized ebony carvings. The full-grown palace lions ate around forty pounds of meat a day. They were fed choice cuts of steak several times a day, and with appetites surfeited, they stretched, groomed themselves, and looked at passersby with a detached and bored indolence. It was a time when thousands of people were dying from starvation in the Wallo province of Ethiopia; when vultures, gorged with human flesh, were too heavy to fly, when mothers were abandoning the corpses of their emaciated children by roadsides as their legs carried them mechanically into the emptiness of a wider indifference.

Walter Rodney, the internationally renowned Africanist from Guyana, had travelled from the University of Dar es Salaam to attend the conference, and he had no sooner arrived than he became the object of a great deal of attention. His book, *How Europe Underdeveloped Africa,* sections of which had been published in monographs, had made him known everywhere in Africa. He, too, was a quiet man of average height, soft spoken and gracious, but on a political platform or standing at a podium delivering a lecture, he became transformed. He seemed to grow in stature and become possessed with all the fire and passion of an ancient African prophet. He and Diop had the same kind of intellectual honesty and a moral integrity that made toadies and accomodationists wince in their presence. True to the uneasy expectations of the neo-colonial and safari academics attending the conference, he delivered a paper which was considered controversial. In fact, it was outstanding for its lucidity and its original insights into the contemporary African state of affairs.

Rodney and Diop together in Addis, what a historic event! The former was a son of the African diaspora who, despite all the colonial and neo-colonial blandishments and subtle bribes offered him, had devoted his life as a scholar-activist to keeping the flame of African liberation burning. The latter, realizing early in his career that the colonization of the African mind was more dangerous than whips, chains and a repressive state apparatus, had used his formidable intellectual gifts, his courage and his vision of a liberated Africa, to restore that continent and its peoples to their rightful place in world history. As a capricious fate would have it, Diop and Rodney only met in passing at that conference, and that was to be their first and last encounter. Rodney was bombarded with requests from a variety of student groups to speak to them and to advise them. His fame was such that Ethiopians, young and old alike, wanted to see him in the flesh. Rodney and Diop were like intellectual lions in the midst of academic sheep at that 1972 ASA conference.

In that year of the conference, Ethiopia was a medieval kingdom inhabited by a people with twentieth century expectations. A conflict between the two was imminent, and, when the two collided, sparks would rise up to ignite a revolutionary conflagration. The kingdom, with its anachronistic trappings, would be swept aside. The Emperor had tried to move backwards into the future and it would take blood and sweat and untold suffering to bring about this ancient nation's rebirth. Throughout the conference, the university was surrounded by tanks and armoured cars. It was a case of guns being pointed at incendiary ideas of freedom, but, risking death and imprisonment, students were demonstrating daily. The soldiers had to choose between shooting down their own children or disobeying the emperor's orders.

Tsegaye told me that the Emperor censored his plays and other writings personally. When the manuscripts were returned to him by the Security Police, page after page had the notes and comments the Lion of Judah had made in the margins.

The conference droned on. In the midst of a gathering revolutionary storm, academics, with few notable exceptions, read and discussed their irrelevant papers. Tsegaye rescued us from the inanities of scholars reading to scholars, from that peculiar intellectual incest in which academics indulge on these ritual occasions. He took us on day-long excursions into the countryside south of Addis. We went to the hills and the lakes and the rolling landscapes of the Ethiopian heartland. We crossed dry riverbeds, and rested in the shade of solitary acacias that the charcoal-burners had spared. The first lake we came to was in a huge concave basin rimmed by hills bleached to the bone. A combination of profligate woodcutters, rains and erosion had denuded the landscape of vegetation. Beside the lake was a sacred tree like a lonely sentinel gazing at his image in the still water. The bark was stained with sacrificial blood and hundreds of nails had been driven into its trunk. Occasionally we came upon a shepherd with threadbare garments flapping in the wind like torn pennants on gnarled flagpoles. There were flocks of birds grazing amidst the tall reeds that grew in the shallows of the lakes, and clusters of insects boiling above the rippling surface of the water.

On those excursions, our conversations wove themselves endlessly around the theme of the cultural unity of the Black world. Diop, indefatigable scholar and researcher that he was, took pictures, not of landscapes, but of faces. In order to further prove his point that there were unbroken continuities and organic linkages between ancient and modern Nile Valley cultures and the rest of Africa, he was systematically juxtaposing photographs of modern Ethiopian faces, with those sculpted, carved and painted on murals thousands of years ago. It was a technique that Serge Eisenstein, the great Soviet film maker had used so unforgettably in "Time in the Sun", a fragment from a much longer film he had shot in Mexico, but nevertheless a work of genius. In the opening scene in that film, the camera had panned slowly across a relief sculpted on an ancient temple wall. The human figures that the light and shade brought into sharp focus, seemed at once trapped in their granite and basalt background, and very much alive. Then the camera concentrated on the profiles of two Native American men, facing each other. It was as though the ancient sculptor-builder had captured the timeless dreams reflected in those identical twin faces in addition to their precise outer form. Caught in this play of images, your eyes remained rivited to those faces. Then something magical and unexpected happened. One of the faces moved, turned around and faced you. That living descendant of the ancient Olmecs and his distant forebear, had the same features, the same high cheekbones, the same stony, inscrutable look. Ivan Van Sertima, in his trail-blazing and meticulously researched work, *They Came Before Columbus*, also used this Eisenstein technique to refute a spate of nonsense, confusion and racist dissembling that had passed for scholarship before his book appeared. In Plate 27 of the vivid illustrations included in *They Came Before Columbus* he compares the head of a contemporary Nuba Chief from the Nile basin to that of a colossal Olmec Negro stone head found at La Venta in Mexico. The result is equally as startling and magical as those twin faces in "Time in the Sun."

Diop took photographs everywhere we went—on the highways and byways outside Addis, in the countryside, on the city streets and in Addis's vast open market with its turbulent sea of people and its rainbow array of colors and complexions. That was reputedly the largest open air market in Africa. One Ethiopian had told me that I could buy anything there from a pin to a Rolls Royce.

Tsegaye took us to secret hidden places behind God's back, and those were obviously his favourite haunts. The cool groves he occasionally led us into made it easy for us to imagine ourselves living in the age of the Black Pharaohs. If you listened carefully during the silences between the trills and high-pitched fluted melodies of birdsong, you could hear distant echoes of worshippers chanting orisons to Isis with temple gongs booming faintly in the background. But we were not romantics escaping into ebony towers to brood over an idyllic past. The cruelties of the social and political landscapes of Ethiopia during the final years of the Lion of Judah's reign would, in any case, have made this impossible.

One afternoon, when the setting sun seemed to have been impaled on the peaks of distant hills, we came across an old woman who was bent double with the weight of an enormous bundle of faggots. She moved slowly up-hill, balancing her burden and gripping the earth with her bare feet. She was struggling, not only with the weight of her bundle, but against a cold and persistent wind. Quite spontaneously we moved forward to help her. Her face, which had been singed by wind and sun for decades, had deep lines gouged into it by seasons of toil, by bearing and bringing up children and contending with day to day anxieties. For an instant there was a startled look in her eyes. Tsegaye spoke to her softly, but she plodded on, ignoring our offer of help. Diop, persisting, followed her. The darkness swept over us like a silent tidal wave, muffling our voices and forcing us to tread carefully. Diop, with Tsegaye translating, persuaded the proud old woman to accept a gift of money for her children. It was a gesture of love, compassion and friendship from us all, and we were grateful that the old woman had accepted it as such.

One afternoon, sitting on a stranded boulder that overlooked a dry riverbed, we saw a large white flower some distance away. It was moonshaped, luminiscent and the most beautiful wild flower I had ever seen. When I walked up to examine it more closely, Tsegaye warned me not to touch it. That apparently exquisite bloom was full of hidden spikes, and once they lodged themselves in your flesh, you would need surgery to extract them. He pointed out that there was a lot of similarity between that white flower and the white knight in shining armour from Europe who came ostensibly to "civilize" the Africans. Once they buried themselves into the flesh of the African continent, it required the scalpel of revolution to dislodge them.

We had agreed, at the beginning of our excursions and endless conversations, that Diop would speak French (which both Tsegaye and I understood very well) and we, English (which Diop understood and read very easily). In order to give full rein to the complex ideas we were discussing so exhaustively, it was necessary to use a language with which we were completely familiar. There was an underlying, wry humour in Diop's accounts of his fights against racist scholars. Sartre had once said that no great art had ever celebrated bigotry, extolled racial hatred or trumpeted the cause of tyranny and remained genuine art. One can, in fact, say the same thing about scholarship. But over and over again one can hear the fatuous claim that this or that person was a good scholar but they just had a "blind spot" when it came to the question of race and color. Racism and good scholarship, Diop affirmed, are completely incompatible, since racism leads to faulty ideas, and, as the Harvard professor Stephen Jay Gould pointed out in his remarkable work *The Mismeasure of Man*,[1] "ideas can be agents as sure as guns and bombs."

Diop, a brilliant conversationalist, made the past of the pharaohs come to life as he spoke, and it did not take you long to realize that one of his great strengths was that he was a born teacher, that he could not only impart a great deal of significant information to his students, but he could also infect them with a passion to learn more and more about the subject being studied. And like all great teachers he was an infinitely patient listener. It was obvious that, for him, listening and learning were fruits from the same tree. Listening, too, was an intrinsic part of the oral tradition in Africa which was so ancient that the griots claimed that the first stories about the human condition ever told had issued forth from the breath of the Sky-God.

In the midst of our talks about ancient Nile Valley civilizations, Tsegaye regaled us with stories of intrigues that sprung up like mushrooms in the hot and oleous atmosphere of Selasse's court, which, he pointed out, existed as a king of poor man's metaphor for the splendours of the courts of the Pharaohs. Diop, in making the comparison between the ancient and the modern, brought his precise, empirical and scientific mind to bear on the subject, and like so many extraordinarily brilliant people, he could give to the most complex ideas a lucidity that made them readily understood by laymen. He traced for us, sometimes writing on the parched earth with a stick, the origins of ancient Egyptian theology, and showed how the Judeo-Christian religion had borrowed a great deal from, and hence owed a great deal to early Egyptian philosophers and seers. He pointed out that many pseudo-scholars placed an undue emphasis on ancient Egyptian mysticism, magic and religious rituals as part of an exercise in creating false images and fictionalized distortions. This was also the fault of many Eurocentric scholars, who, coming from a liberal arts background, were incapable of understanding the complexities of ancient Egyptian mathematics, science and technology in addition to its sacred philosophy and ritual. One of the most invidious tenets of racism, and many liberals are guilty of upholding it, is to grant to peoples of color exclusive rights to a heaven of emotions, unbridled atavistic impulses, mindless passions, while Europeans and Euroamericans claim for themselves exclusive rights to the world of ideas and the earth's material riches. Countering these fanciful and fallacious white supremacist theories disguised as scholarship, Diop reminded us, in his mildly insistent way, that it was from the Nile Valley in which we were standing, that Black Africans, through their mastery of science, had brought mankind out of prehistory to the first civilization.

Walking in the hills where the parched grass had been flattened by the wind, and Diop never seemed to tire, we would pause to look at pelicans landing gracefully on the sun-splashed surface of a lake. Diop seemed to have achieved a harmony of physical, spiritual and intellectual energy that was enviable. I could not help seeing him in vivid contrast to the many Black intellectuals whom I had to meet constantly at conferences, and who, in their frantic bid to deny their heritage and to win acclaim from their white mentors, were literally tearing themselves to pieces psychologically.

Tsegaye's stories also helped to make these walks a delight. He told us in an aside that he had translated Shakespeare's Hamlet into Amharic, and I could not help thinking that the Prince of Denmark, caught in the web of malevolent intrigues and murder, would have fitted easily into the courts of Ethiopian Kings. Those kings, in order to ensure a smooth succession, banished their sons to monasteries in the far mountains, and only when the ruler died was the heir summoned. How many Ethiopian princes must have suffered from Hamletism! Tsegaye also said that he had helped in the translation of an ancient manuscript (it was over three thousand years old) and must certainly have been the oldest manuscript of a play ever found.

But, as usual, he moved from the academic to the real and the immediate. He said that there were children of powerful figures in Selassie's inner circle of courtiers who were in open rebellion against the suffocating and tyrannical regime under which they lived. Those erstwhile pampered children of the elites were revolting, not only against the regime, but against their sychophantic or quiescent parents. They had abandoned their classrooms to demonstrate time and time again, defying tanks, armoured personnel carriers, bayonets, machine guns, whips and police batons. And the peasants, of the countryside, who had, from the time of the Black Pharoahs, been a special breed of martial cultivators and creators of stupendous monuments, were once again stirring restlessly.

We saw evidence of this awakening protest during our excursions into the rural areas. The shepherds and farmers, protesting against military and civilian motor vehicles that careened up and down with a total disregard for both pedestrians and livestock, were placing huge boulders in the middle of the highways to slow down that infernal traffic.

Sitting in a small inn that was hidden by a grove of trees, we drank honey wine (the mead of medieval times) and listened to Tsegaye talking quietly about events in the corridors of Power at the crumbling center of Selassie's empire:

There were echoes of Diop's voice in many things that Tsegaye said. Tsegaye, like his distinguished teacher, could link the distant past and a troubled present as easily as breathing. What a signal achievement in scholarship! The Carib shamans say that, in the final reckoning, every great man is as much as his shadow and as much as his love. Implicit in this is the affirmation that a great person must train others to walk in his footsteps and to expand the range and scope of his achievements. Meeting Diop and one of his favourite students gave me insights into the man that I would not have been able to glean otherwise. I came away from every encounter with him, marvelling at the inner discipline and dedication he had achieved, the breadth of his creative intelligence and the essential humanity of the man. Tsegaye told me that in Diop's native Senegal the ordinary folk treated that great scholar-man with a reverence bordering on idolatry. As we conversed day after day it was not difficult to picture him in his home setting, standing up resolutely to those misusing their neo-colonial power (and risking imprisonment or worse), and being infinitely kind, patient and compassionate with the lowliest and the most despised.

Diop spoke without bitterness about his fight against racism in scholarship. He had made inexorable choices early in his life, not only to fight against colonialism but to restore Africa to its rightful place on the center stage of world history. He had started out in Pure Science and then concentrated on physics, but as he grew more aware of how profoundly biased European and Euro-American scholarship was when dealing with Africa, he decided to study Egyptology. From this intellectual and academic nexus, he was convinced, he said, that he would be better able to challenge the false tenets of European and Euro-American scholarship that Africa had no history beyond the cruel and monstrous tutelage of slavery and colonialism. His professors at the University of Paris did everything possible to discourage him, but he persisted. His dissertations proving beyond the shadow of a doubt that Egyptian civilization was a Black African one, were thrice rejected. He was only granted his "Docteur des Lettres" after a decade of struggle.

Cheikh Anta Diop, W.E.B. DuBois, Paul Robeson, Malcolm X, and Kwame Nkrumah had this in common: the idea of the cultural unity of the Black world. This was central to their lives and beings. Those opposing this idea have come and gone, vanishing into the oblivion waiting for them, but the idea remains stubbornly reaffirming itself in the midst of the loud clamourings that it is no longer applicable to people of Africa and the African diaspora.

I have not met Diop again since that historic encounter in Addis. But we have remained in touch through friends and students. Diop had left the Conference in Addis to attend another in Cairo. The United Nations Economic Social and Cultural Organization (UNESCO) had organized a special conference of Egyptologists there in 1974 and many of the world's leading scholars in this field had been invited. The Eurocentric scholars who attended, with some notable exceptions, came bent on dismissing Diop's work as that of an "emotional" African scholar dabbling in a field that was theirs by divine right. But after Diop had presented his paper and taken part in the discussions that followed, the ones who had come to overwhelm him with their "superior" scholarship left chastened and defeated.

Very little publicity about that historic conference in Cairo ever filtered out, although the papers presented could provide material for at least a dozen

Ph.D. theses. But what was perhaps most important was that at this conference Cheikh Anta Diop resurrected the living essences of Black Africa's great past in a deadly bout of intellectual jousting with those who had tried to bury them.

NOTES

1. Stephen Jay Gould, *The Mismeasure of Man*, New York, W.W. Norton & Co. 1981, p. 233.

MEETING THE PHARAOH: CONVERSATIONS WITH CHEIKH ANTA DIOP

Charles S. Finch

There was something both unreal and audacious about the impending encounter; we were about to meet the man, Dr. Cheikh Anta Diop, who must be considered the "Pharoah" of Afro-centric or Kamitic* studies, whose daring and inspired scholarship in Egyptology, African linguistics, political theory, African history, and anthropology is certain to reverberate through the centuries. My companion and I, Ron McGee of New York City, felt very much as suppliants must feel when on the verge of meeting an august personage, standing as Dr. Diop does over the entire African world like the proverbial colossus. The anticipation and nervous tension was heightened by our previous failed attempt to meet with him a week earlier because he was still abroad. We weren't waiting in the parking lot of the Institut Fondamental de L'Afrique Noire (IFAN) long when a nondescript, gray-black Peugeot drove up and out stepped a slender, Black man of above-average height with graying hair and the sharply-etched features of the Wolof; like all his people he was a striking man to look at and the immediate impression was one of almost beatific kindness and cordiality as he walked toward us, hand extended, bidding us welcome. It was a simple, open, genuine welcome reflecting the essence of Senegalese hospitality. We conversed for a few moments, I in my broken French and he in his rather better but still halting English. We were ushered into his laboratory, containing a room with scientific apparatus in the rear (Professor Diop is a trained physicist) and a gray but spacious office in the front filled with books, periodicals, and all the paraphernalia of the working scholar. I explained that we wished to conduct a formal interview that we would record, to be published in a new edition of "Egyptian History Revised," the Fall 1982 issue of the *Journal of African Civilizations.* He assured us that his time was ours and that he was amenable to anything we required. Ron McGee had portaged a videotape camera all the way across the Atlantic so that we would have a visual record of this encounter but, predictably, the thing would not function just when we needed it. We had to settle for a series of still photographs and an audio tape recording of the interview. Dr. Diop was very patient as we proceeded with our ministrations, for despite his pains to put us at our ease, we were still a bit nervous.

*I use this word, derived from the Egyptian "KMT" meaning "Blackness" or "Black Land," to designate an Afro-Egyptian frame of reference or world view encompassing an Afro-centric perspective.

At the outset of the interview, Dr. Diop requested that though the questions be put to him in English, he be allowed to respond in French. For reasons which I think are evident, this was clearly the best means of accomplishing the interview, especially since our recorders would capture his remarks for later translation. What was remarkable to us from the beginning—and what is not captured in cold print or even on audio tape—is, when warming to his subject, how a certain charismatic animation grips him and simultaneously reaches out to grip the listener as well. He has the personal force that is characteristic of all great and influential men. For my part, I was not proud of my interviewing style. Though I had written out all the questions I would ask him beforehand, I was still somewhat hesitant and uncertain, sometimes lapsing into a pidgin French. But as I mentioned, Dr. Diop was extremely forbearing and I only needed to introduce a line of inquiry for him to pick it up and expound on it at length. Thus my profound limitations as an interviewer did not seem to be a major liability.

As the interview proceeded, I was struck by what I perceived to be a very special regard for Afro-American Kamitic scholars. Dr. Diop is keenly aware that he has a very substantial following in the U.S., perhaps more so than in any other country outside Senegal itself. It is also evident that, until relatively recently, his has been a solitary battle, contending like a Samson against the phalanxes of academic philistines arrayed against him. And, like Samson, Dr. Diop has carried the day. Those in the French speaking academic world who have not tacitly or overtly come over to his side, have more or less removed themselves from the arena, preferring instead the time-honored ''conspiracy of silence'' so effective in the past against those certain voices ''crying in the wilderness.'' Perhaps because of this, the work and support of Kamitic scholars in this part of the world has been very heartening to him. He reads and liberally quotes from the recent literature out of America: Ivan Van Sertima, John Henrik Clarke, Bruce Williams and James Spady are just a few of the names that dropped from his lips in the course of the interview.

Two of his most important works, *Parenté Génétique De L'Egyptien Pharaonique Et Des Langues Négro-Africaines* (The Genetic Relationship Between Pharoaonic Egyptian and the Languages of Negro Africa) and *Civilization Ou Barbarie* (Civilization or Barbarism) are as yet untranslated out of French. Since the former book has not been reviewed or discussed in the English language literature, whereas the latter has (see Jeffries in this issue), it is essential to point out that *Parenté Génétique . . .* is without question one of the pivotal works in Kamitic studies and African linguistics. In this book, Dr. Diop has produced a glossary demonstrating the identity of 3,000 Egyptian and Wolof words in addition to examining in detail the structural affinities between the two languages. There is hardly anything like it in African linguistics for its depth, scope, and imagination and it very probably signals the beginning of a whole new branch of Afro-Egyptian studies. It is not hard to discern why his adversaries have retired from the field.

Having met Dr. Diop gave us a certain standing among the people of Senegal. He is a household name in his country, even among those without schooling. He is referred to reverently as "Cheikh Anta" by the Senegalese. In the antechamber to his office there were well over a dozen people patiently awaiting an audience while we interviewed him. This is a daily phenomenon; Senegalese come just to bask in his presence.

We have hardly a real glimmer of the full magnitude of his impact on Senegalese and African culture. He inaugurated the process—since taken up by a handful of his countrymen—of turning Wolof into a literary language by his translation of Einstein's Theory of Relativity into Wolof almost 30 years ago. Future generations of Senegalese may well regard him the way Russians do Pushkin, who by turning the vernacular of the people into a language capable of great literature, became the father of literature in his country.

It was we who ended the audience rather than he. We could see that there was a waiting-room full of people who wished to see him and we owed him the courtesy of knowing when to leave. For us, the encounter was one of life's peak experiences. There is a struggle being waged for the mind of Africa; with such field generals as Dr. Diop, none of the odds seem insurmountable.

THE INTERVIEW

Finch: *How did you happen to write Civilization ou Barbarie?*
Diop: *Civilization ou Barbarie* is, for me, a kind of summary of all my works, and in it I try to examine the theme of progress in social scientific studies. And it is for that reason that I took the theme of Anthropology and Cradle of Humanity and showed that the *ensemble* of discoveries give a much clearer picture of the past, that Africa is not only the cradle of humanity but that the other races, particularly the white race, is behind the black race, when one is speaking of developments in early Western Europe.

By the same token, I also took the theme of the evolution of societies to show that even the Roman . . . have something in common. There too, I believe, is a certain rapport on the philosophical plane. I tried to tie together as much as possible, the African element in Greek philosophy with original African philosophy.
Finch: *What has been the reception of the book in academic circles?*
Diop: There is always a qualified silence. Right? Of course, from a technical standpoint, the book, like all scientific works, is not perfect. However, it is difficult to criticize it. I have been truly impressed by the young Black American scholars—Professors Finch, Clarke, Van Sertima, Spady. You are a "pleiade" (group) of Black Americans who are in the process of making an enormous contribution. Also Bruce Williams. We call him "the missing link."
Finch: *Are there plans to translate the book into other languages?*
Diop: That depends. It's a question of finance. I would like as many people as

possible to have access to the book and to understand everything that's been developed, but it is a question of financing it.

Finch: *Can you say a little about your early motivation for studying history?*

Diop: O yes! I was destined for a purely scientific career. I was given information that made me a well-taught (or learned) African, but not cultivated, and I felt a certain cultural emptiness within me. My desire to know my history, my culture, my personal problem (that is, my desire to become fulfilled as a person) led me to history. However, I thought that my friends would have done the job for me but when I realized that nothing was being done, I became more interested. I wanted to become an engineer consultant for airplanes after the war.

Finch: *What were the early obstacles you faced?*

Diop: The usual ones. First of all, a general lack of comprehension at that time because it was a new point of view. Secondly, we knew almost nothing about what was done in the English language. We were completely cut off from the United States and, for the most part, the complete Anglo-Saxon world. You can never imagine the lack of communication when it comes to the reconstruction of Black unity. We knew almost nothing about what was going on on the other side of the Atlantic. There was in the African world at that time the same spirit of revolt as in the U.S. but that was all. From a literary and scientific point of view, we had nothing, as a consequence of this lack of communication.

Finch: *I understand that you are a descendant of a line of Wolof griots. Is that true?*

Diop: No. That's false but I'm not offended by it.

Finch: *Can you explain your "Two Cradle" Theory—The Northern Cradle and the Southern Cradle?*

Diop: At this point in time, Sociology was promoting a theory that Black culture was inferior to Western culture, inferior, in fact, to all cultures. Even the more advanced sociologists subscribed to this concept. For example, the matriarchal family, with the spirit of the mother dominating, was considered inferior to other cultures. However, when we study the different cultures and trace them back to their cradle, we see that this is ridiculous and that is why I had to study the "whole" of African culture, in the African cradle, and study for the first time, with a new penetration and precision, that which the Europeans had not given to us—the ethnology of the West. I believe that it is only through this continued effort of comparison and study that the proper light can be shed on the primary social structures of humanity.

Finch: *What is the relationship between the monogenetic theory and the two-cradle theory?*

Diop: It is certain that man was born in one place. That is a fact. The common belief is that there are several cradles of humanity, but scientific fact opposes this. In prehistoric anthropology one cannot find any evidence which supports the poly-genetic thesis. It is all monogenetic. Had there been several centers of development of humanity, there would have been earlier fossils. Take America, for example. If it passed through all the transitional phases there would have been fossils to attest to this, but the African fossils are far more ancient. You cannot find anywhere else in the world, be it Asia or Europe, evidence supporting the contrary. The most serious of research shows that everything goes back to Africa. Americans are now discovering this fact. All the missing pieces are being found.

Finch: *Can you explain the three factors found in your works—the historique, psychologique and linguistique–in a more detailed manner?*

Diop: Yes, there are several factors which contribute to the cohesion of a people. The first is historical community. The fact is that, although a fraction of the African population was uprooted and transported to the United States, we are rediscovering our common ground today, the broken links of our community. The bonds that we are in the process of establishing go far back, even before the birth of Egyptian civilization. It is that historic bond that unites us and makes the difference. If you visited other countries like Japan, Scandinavia, you will see a historical community. They made their own local history.

The fact of having lived in the same cradle, shaped and transformed us. Instinctively, we have the same sensory response to the same reality. For example, a Black American and an African have similar rhythm and a similar respect for nature. They have the same sense of unity and this potential for unity is a consequence of a shared history.

The third is the linguistic unity. One can lose his language here and there but we can see that the other two unities are fundamental. Even when the language is lost, the other unities suffice in assuring the cohesion of a race. That is why today the laws of the community become a part of the culture. To explain further, let's take a look at the Israelites. They are in the process of learning Hebrew again. If we begin the study of the African languages, we will be overwhelmed by our experience of the ease with which they come. I am sure, from what I see, that something is being started, or will be, in the near future for Black Americans. I think that there are many great languages that Africans are trying to study again, like Swahili, in order to be able to communicate with each other. All these languages have the same root.

Finch: *One of your important theses is the Egyptian or "Nile Valley" origin of West African people. Could you explain the linguistic and cultural evidence and also the comparative mythology that supports this thesis?*

Diop: Yes. When I examine the languages along the Atlantic Ocean, like Wolof. . . (here Diop mentions other languages but they are unintelligible on the tape) the relationship is evident, from the Egyptian language spoken during the time of the pyramids up through the classical period. The Wolof, for example, evolved and unfolded. There is much less evolution with respect to the Romance languages. I explain that by the fact that Africa was (before the slave trade) much less uprooted as a country. She never knew the barbaric invasions which uprooted the European society and introduced Latin, giving to the languages a "roman" flavor. That didn't occur in Africa and that is why language, from a grammatical standpoint, is less complicated as it passed from the Egyptian to other African languages. There is some displacement in the African population which brought about change in the language but not nearly as much as the European.

Finch: *I'd like you also to discuss what you think of the recent discoveries by Bruce Williams of the Ta-Seti kingdom. What do you think of them?*

Diop: By all means. This is very important. What Bruce Williams brought back is "La piece maitresse" (the main piece, the most important) . . . It revealed that there were three generations before the first Dynasty. Even today there are young discoverers, like Vercoutter, who found a new pre-dynastic pottery. Discoveries from the Sudan to the Delta Region show that an effective civilization went up the Valley, from South to North, and it is this element that reinforces the Bruce Williams' discoveries.

Finch: *Have you had any success getting the skins of the mummies from Egypt?*

Diop: No. They didn't give them to me but I saw them. What they gave me was a millimeter. They were *Black, Black*, more black than I. All the plaques that I brought back are mummies I studied in 1974 in Cairo. These are all my preparations, as seen through a microscope. Some of them went back as far as the Third Dynasty. These are the mummies that Mariette brought back with him. They are all in the London Museum. I have found that many other people have done the same research before me but they never published their findings. The reason I know this is because I found that the skin of many mummies had been completely scraped. With the skin, one can make a determination.

Finch: *The Unesco debate in 1974 with you and Professor Obenga—what is the status of that debate? Has there been any progress? There were other professors against you. Gamel Mokhtar, for example. Have they changed their opinions since?*

Diop: They know that they have not been giving an accurate picture. They've been lying. It is a matter of education. It is difficult for them to recognize that officially, because of the cultural domination of one race by another. They will do it as long as they can discriminate against blacks. When we are discussing this issue scientifically around a table, we are in a minority. You have seen the results of the debate. It is very important. It is for that reason we have published the chapter of the second book without any alterations to our findings.

It was necessary to have that conference and it was I who pushed to have it in Cairo. I was responsible. I told them that they were going to write a book that would have international effect. There is no reason to sacrifice the truth. Let's meet in Cairo, I told them, and discuss the questions calmly and one will know the real truth. In case they don't want to do that, I'll be the first one to excuse myself. And you know what followed. Whatever they say when they are together, does not mean anything to me.

Finch: *What are the important directions of future studies? Be it in the Nile Valley, Egypt, Libya or the rest of Africa. Where shall we go with the historical and cultural study?*

Diop: I believe, in developing Egyptology, we must generalize from direct Egyptian knowledge. It is by having the direct knowledge that we can leave the vicious circle, leave these debates behind, and give to Africans the control of their real past. The African is trying to find his soul, his emotions, his way of thinking. He is trying to rediscover himself and eradicate all the complexities and confusion. It is the same for the American Black and all other Black races. It is only through discoveries that one can truly overcome. The West has not continued to address Egyptology in the light of new findings. Too bad for them.

The new ideology can go forward by the further study of Africans and we must push all the way with greater determination for the advancement of these studies . . .

—Dakar, Senegal, August 1983

Diop's responses in French were translated by Ms. Vivian Barron

ORIGIN OF THE ANCIENT EGYPTIANS

Cheikh Anta Diop

The general acceptance, as a sequel to the work of Professor Leakey, of the hypothesis of mankind's monogenetic and African origin, makes it possible to pose the question of the peopling of Egypt and even of the world in completely new terms. More than 150,000 years ago, beings morphologically identical with the man of today were living in the region of the great lakes at the sources of the Nile and nowhere else. This notion, and others which it would take too long to recapitulate here, form the substance of the last report presented by the late Dr. Leakey at the Seventh Pan-African Congress of Pre-History in Addis Ababa in 1971.[1] It means that the whole human race had its origin, just as the ancients had guessed, at the foot of the Mountains of the Moon. Against all expectations and in defiance of recent hypotheses it was from *this place* that men moved out to people the rest of the world. From this two facts of capital importance result:

(*a*) of necessity the earliest men were ethnically homogeneous and negroid. Gloger's law, which would also appear to be applicable to human beings, lays it down that warm-blooded animals evolving in a warm humid climate will secrete a black pigment (eumelanin).[2] Hence if mankind originated in the tropics around the latitude of the great lakes, he was bound to have brown pigmentation from the start and it was by differentiation in other climates that the original stock later split into different races;

(*b*) there were only two routes available by which these early men could move out to people the other continents, namely, the Sahara and the Nile valley. It is the latter region which will be discussed here.

From the Upper Palaeolithic to the dynastic epoch, the whole of the river's basin was taken over progressively by these negroid peoples.

Evidence of Physical Anthropology on the Race of the Ancient Egyptians

It might have been thought that, working on physiological evidence, the findings of the anthropologists would dissipate all doubts by providing reliable and definitive truths. This is by no means so: the arbitrary nature of the criteria used, to go no farther, as well as abolishing any notion of a conclusion acceptable without qualification, introduces so much scientific hair-splitting that there are times when one wonders whether the solution of the problem would not have been nearer if we had not had the ill luck to approach it from this angle.

Nevertheless, although the conclusions of these anthropological studies stop short of the full truth, they still speak unanimously of the existence of a negro race from the most distant ages of prehistory down to the dynastic period. It is not possible in this paper to cite all these conclusions: they will be found summarized in Chapter X of Dr. Emile Massoulard's *Histoire et protohistoire d'Egypte* (Institut d'Ethnologie, Paris, 1949). We shall quote selected items only.

> Miss Fawcett considers that the Negadah skulls form a sufficiently homogeneous collection to warrant the assumption of a Negadah race. In the total height of the skull, the auricular height, the length and breadth of the face, nasal length, cephalic index and facial index this race would seem to approximate to the negro; in nasal breadth, height of orbit, length of palate and nasal index it would seem closer to the Germanic peoples; accordingly the Pre-Dynastic Negadians are likely to have resembled the negroes in certain of their characterics and the white races in others. (pp. 402-3)

It is worth noting that the nasal indices of Ethiopians and Dravidians would seem to approximate them to the Germanic peoples, though both are black races.

These measurements, which would leave an open choice between the two extremes represented by the negro and the Germanic races, give an idea of the elasticity of the criteria employed. A sample follows:

> An attempt was made by Thomson and Randall MacIver to determine more precisely the importance of the negroid element in the series of skulls from El'Amrah, Abydos and Hou. They divided them into three groups: (1) negroid skulls (those with a facial index below 54 and a nasal index above 50, i.e. short broad face and broad nose); (2) non-negroid skulls (facial index above 54 and nasal index below 50, long narrow face and narrow nose); (3) intermediate skulls (assignable to one of the two previous groups on the basis of either the facial index or on the evidence of the nasal index, plus individuals marginal to either group). The proportion of negroids would seem to have been 24% of men and 19% of women in the early Pre-Dynastic and 25% and 28% respectively in the late Pre-Dynastic.
>
> Kieth has disputed the value of the criterion selected by Thomson and Randall MacIver to distinguish the negroid from the non-negroid skulls. His opinion is that if the same criteria were applied to the study of any series of contemporary English skulls, the sample would be found to contain approximately 30% of negroid types. (pp. 420-1)

The converse of Kieth's proposition could also be asserted, namely, that if the criterion were applied to the 140 million negroes now alive in black Africa a minimum of 100 million negroes woudl emerge whitewashed.

It may also be remarked that the distinction between negroid, non-negroid and intermediary is unclear: the fact is that 'non-negroid' does not mean of white race and 'intermediary' still less so.

'Falkenburger reopened the anthropological study of the Egyptian population in a recent work in which he discusses 1,787 male skulls varying in date from the old Pre-Dynastic to our own day. He distinguishes four main groups' (p. 421). The sorting of the predynastic skulls into these four groups gives the following results for the whole predynastic period: '36% negroid, 33% Mediterranean, 11% Cro-Magnoid and 20% of individuals not falling in any of these groups but approximating either to the Cro-Magnoid or to the negroid'. The proportion of negroids is definitely higher than that suggested by Thomson and Randall Mac-Iver, though Kieth considers the latter too high.

'Do Falkenburger's figures reflect the reality? It is not our task to decide this. If they are accurate, the Pre-Dynastic population far from representing a pure bred race, as Elliot-Smith has said, comprised at least three distinct racial elements—over a third of negroids, a third of Mediterraneans, a tenth of Cro-Magnoids and a fifth of individuals crossbred—to varying degrees' (p. 422).

The point about all these conclusions is that despite their discrepancies the degree to which they converge proves that the basis of the Egyptian population was negro in the Pre-Dynastic epoch. Thus they are all incompatible with the theories that the negro element only infiltrated into Egypt at a late stage. Far otherwise, the facts prove that it was preponderant from the beginning to the end of Egyptian history, particularly when we note once more that 'Mediterranean' is not a synonym for 'white', Elliot-Smith's 'brown or Mediterranean race being nearer the mark'. 'Elliot-Smith classes these Proto-Egyptians as a branch of what he calls the brown race, which is the same as Sergi's "Mediterranean or Eurafrican race".' The term 'brown' in this context refers to skin colour and is simply a euphemism for negro.[3] it is thus clear that it was the whole of the Egyptian population which was negro, barring an infiltration of white nomads in the proto-dynastic epoch.

In Petrie's study of the Egyptian race we are introduced to a possible classification element in great abundance which cannot fail to surprise the reader.

> Petrie . . . published a study of the races of Egypt in the Pre-Dynastic and Proto-Dynastic periods working only on portrayals of them. Apart from the steatopygian race, he distinguishes six separate types: an aquiline type representative of a white-skinned Libyan race; a 'plaited-beard' type belonging to an invading race coming perhaps from the shores of the Red Sea; a 'sharp-nosed' type almost certainly from the Arabian Desert; a 'tilted nose' type from Middle Egypt; a 'jutting beard' type from Lower Egypt; and a 'narrow-nosed' type from Upper Egypt. Going on the images, there would thus have been seven different racial types in Egypt during the epochs we are considering. In the pages which follow we shall see that study of the skeletons seems to provide little authority for these conclusions. (p. 391)

The above mode of classification gives an idea of the arbitrary nature of the criteria used to define the Egyptian races. Be that as it may, it is clear that anthropology is far from having established the existence of a white Egyptian race and would indeed tend rather to suggest the opposite.

Nevertheless, in current textbooks the question is suppressed: in most cases it is simply and flatly asserted that the Egyptians were white and the honest layman is left with the impression that any such assertion must necessarily have a prior basis of solid research. But there is no such basis, as this chapter has shown. And so generation after generation has been misled. Many authorities skate around the difficulty today by speaking of red-skinned and black-skinned whites without their sense of common logic being in the least upset. 'The Greeks call Africa "Libya", a misnomer ab initio since Africa contains many other peoples besides the so-called Libyans, who belong among the whites of the northern or Mediterranean periphery and hence are many steps removed from the brown (or red) skinned whites (Egyptians).'[4]

In a textbook intended for the middle secondary school we find the following sentence: 'A Black is distinguished less by the colour of his skin (for there are black-skinned "whites") than by his features: thick lips, flattened nose . . .'[5] It is only through these twistings of the basic definitions that it has been possible to bleach the Egyptian race.

It is worthwhile calling to mind the exaggerations of the theorists of anthroposociology in the last century and the beginnings of the present one whose minute physiognomical analyses discovered racial stratifications even in Europe, and particularly in France, when in fact there was really a single and by now practically homogeneous people.[6] Today Occidentals who value their national cohesion are careful to avoid examining their own societies on so divisive a hypothesis, but continue unthinkingly to apply the old methods to the non-European societies.

Human Images of the Protohistoric Period: Their Anthropological Value

The study of human images made by Flinders Petrie on another plane shows that the ethnic type was black: according to Petrie these people were the Anu whose name, known to us since the protohistoric epoch, is always 'written' with three pillars on the few inscriptions extant from the end of the fourth millennium before our era. The natives of the country are always represented with unmistakable chiefly emblems for which one looks in vain among the infrequent portrayals of other races, who are all shown as servile foreign elements having reached the valley by infiltration (cf. Tera Neter[7] and the Scorpion king whom Petrie groups together: 'The Scorpion King . . . belonged to the preceding race of Anu, moreover he worshipped Min and Set.').[8]

As we shall see later Min, like the chief gods of Egypt, was called by the tradition of Egypt itself 'the great negro'.

After a glance at the various foreign types of humanity who disputed the valley with the indigenous blacks, Petrie describes the latter, the Anu, in the following terms:

> Besides these types, belonging to the North and East, there is the aboriginal race of the Anu, or Annu, people (written with three pillars) who became a part of the historic inhabitants. The subject ramifies too doubtfully if we include all single pillar names, but looking for the Annu written, with the three pillars, we find that they occupied southern Egypt and Nubia, and the name is also applied in Sinai and Libya. As to the southern Egyptians, we have the most essential document, one portrait of a chief, Tera Neter, roughly modelled in relief in green glazed faïence, found in the early temple at Abydos. Preceding his name, his address is given on this earliest of visiting cards, 'Palace of the Anu in Hemen city, Tera Neter'. Hemen was the name of the god of Tuphium. Erment, opposite to it, was the palace of Annu of the south, Annu Menti. The next place in the south is Aunti (Gefeleyn), and beyond that Aunyt-Seni (Esneh).[9]
>
> Amélineau lists in geographical order the fortified towns built along the length of the Nile valley by the Annu blacks.

 }=Ant=(Esneh)

 }=An =the southern 'On' (now Hermonthis)

 }=Denderah, the traditional birthplace of Isis

 }=A town also called 'On' in the name of Tinis

 }=The town called the northern 'On', the renowned city of Heliopolis

The common ancestor of the Annu settled along the Nile was Ani or An, a name determined by the word  (khet) and which, dating from the earliest versions of the 'Book of the Dead' onwards, is given to the god Osiris.

The wife of  the god Ani is the goddess Anet  who is also his sister, just as Isis is the sister of Osiris.

The identity of the god An with Osiris has been demonstrated by Pleyte;[10] we should, indeed, recall that Osiris is also surnamed by (?) the Anou: 'Osiris Ani'. The god Anu is represented alternatively by the symbol and the symbol 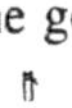. Are the Aunak tribes now inhabiting the upper Nile related to the ancient Annu? Future research will provide the answer to this question.

Petrie thinks it possible to make a distinction between the predynastic people represented by Tera Neter and the Scorpion King (who is himself a Pharaoh even at that date as his head-dress shows) and a dynastic people worshipping the falcon and probably represented by the Pharaohs Narmer,[11] Khasekhem, Sanekhei and Zoser.[12] By reference to the faces reproduced in the figure it is easily perceived that there is no ethnic difference between the two lots, and both belong to the black race.

The mural in tomb SD 63 (Sequence Date 63) of Hierakonpolis shows the native-born blacks subjugating the foreign intruders into the valley if we accept Petrie's interpretation: 'Below is the black ship at Hierakonpolis belonging to the black men who are shown as conquering the red men.'[13]

The Gebel-el-Arak knife haft shows similar battle scenes: 'There are also combats of black men overcoming red men.'[13] However, the archaeological value of this object, which was not found *in situ* but in the possession of a merchant, is less than that of the preceding items.

What the above shows is that the images of men of the protohistoric and even of the dynastic period in no way square with the idea of the Egyptian race popular with Western anthropologists. Wherever the autochthonous racial type is represented with any degree of clearness, it is evidently negroid. Nowhere are the Indo-European and Semitic elements shown even as ordinary freemen serving a local chief, but invariably as conquered foreigners. The rare portrayals found are always shown with the distinctive marks of captitivy, hands tied behind the back or strained over the shoulders.[14] A protodynastic figurine represents an Indo-European prisoner with a long plait on his knees, with his hands bound tight to his body. The characteristics of the object itself show that it was intended as the foot of a piece of furniture and represented a conquered race.[15] Often the portrayal is deliberately grotesque as with other proto-dynastic figures showing individuals with their hair plaited in what Petrie calls pigtails.[16]

In the tomb of king Ka (first dynasty) at Abydos, Petrie found a plaque showing an Indo-European captive in chains with his hands behind his back.[17] Elliot-Smith considers that the individual represented is a Semite. The dynastic epoch has also yielded the documents illustrated in Pls 1.9 and 1.14 showing Indo-European and Semitic prisoners. In contrast, the typically negroid features of the Pharaohs (Narmer, first dynasty, the actual founder of the Pharaonic line; Zoser, third dynasty, by whose time all the technological elements of the Egyptian civilization were already in evidence; Cheops, the builder of the Great Pyramid, a Cameroon type;[18] Menthuhotep, founder of the eleventh dynasty, very black;[19] Sesostris I; Queen Ahmosis Nefertari; and Amenhophis I) show that all classes of Egyptian society belong to the same black race.

Pls 1.15 and 1.16, showing the Indo-European and Semitic types, have been included deliberately to contrast them with the quite dissimilar physiognomies of the black Pharaohs and to demonstrate clearly that there is no trace of either of the first two types in the whole line of Pharaohs if we exclude the foreign Libyan and Ptolemaic dynasties.

It is usual to contrast the negresses on the tomb of Horemheb with the Egyptian type also shown. This contrast is surely a false one: it is social and not ethnic and there is as much difference between an aristocratic Senegalese lady from Dakar and those antique African peasant women with their horny hands and splay feet as between the latter and an Egyptian lady of the cities of antiquity.

There are two variants of the black race: (a) straight-haired, represented in Asia by the Dravidians and in Africa by the Nubians and the Tubbou or Tedda, all three with jet-black skins; (b) the kinky-haired blacks of the Equatorial regions. Both types entered into the composition of the Egyptian population.

Melanin Dosage Test

In practice it is possible to determine directly the skin colour and hence the ethnic affiliations of the ancient Egyptians by microscopic analysis in the laboratory; I doubt if the sagacity of the researchers who have studied the question has overlooked the possibility.

Melanin (eumelanin), the chemical body responsible for skin pigmentation, is, broadly speaking, insoluble and is preserved for millions of years in the skins of fossil animals.[20] There is thus all the more reason for it to be readily recoverable in the skins of Egyptian mummies, despite a tenacious legend that the skin of mummies, tainted by the embalming material, is no longer susceptible of any analysis.[21] Although the epidermis is the main site of the melanin, the melanocytes penetrating the derm at the boundary between it and the epidermus, even where the latter has mostly been destroyed by the embalming materials, show a melanin level which is non-existent in the white-skinned races. The samples I myself analysed were taken in the physical anthropology laboratory of the Musée de l'Homme in Paris off the mummies from the Marietta excavations in Egypt.[22] The same method is perfectly suitable for use on the royal mummies of Thutmoses III, Seti I and Ramses II in the Cairo Museum, which are in an excellent state of preservation. For two years past I have been vainly begging the curator of the Cairo Museum for similar samples to analyse. No more than a few square millimetres of skin would be required to mount a specimen, the preparations being a few um in thickness and lightened with ethyl benzoate. They can be studied by natural light or with ultra-violet lighting which renders the melanin grains fluorescent.

Either way let us simply say that the evaluation of melanin level by microscopic examination is a laboratory method which enables us to classify the ancient Egyptians unquestionably among the black races.

Osteological Measurements

Among the criteria accepted in physical anthropology for classifying races, the osteological measurements are perhaps the least misleading (in contrast to craniometry) for distinguishing a black man from a white man. By this criterion, also, the Egyptians belong among the black races. This study was made by the distinguished German savant Lepsius at the end of the nineteenth century and his conclusions remain valid: subsequent methodological progress in the domain of physical anthropology in no way undermines what is called the 'Lepsius canon' which, in round figures, gives the bodily proportions of the ideal Egyptian, short-armed and of negroid or negrito physical type.[23]

Blood-Groups

It is a notable fact that even today Egyptians, particularly in Upper Egypt, belong to the same Group B as the populations of western Africa on the Atlantic seaboard and not the A2 Group characteristic of the white race prior to any crossbreeding.[24] It would be interesting to study the extent of Group A2 distribution in Egyptian mummies, which present-day techniques make possible.

The Egyptian Race According to the Classical Authors of Antiquity

To the Greek and Latin writers contemporary with the ancient Egyptians the latter's physical classification posed no problems: the Egyptians were negroes, thick-lipped, kinky-haired and thin-legged; the unanimity of the authors' evidence on a physical fact as salient as a people's race will be difficult to minimize or pass over. Some of the following evidence drives home the point.

(*a*) Herodotus, 'the father of history', –480(?) to –425. With regard to the origins of the Colchians[25] he writes:

> It is in fact manifest that the Colchidians are Egyptian by race . . . several Egyptians told me that in their opinion the Colchidians were descended from soldiers of Sesostris. I had conjectured as much myself from two pointers, firstly because they have black skins and kinky hair (to tell the truth this proves nothing for other peoples have them too) and secondly and more reliably for the reason that alone among mankind the Egyptians and the Ethiopians have practised circumcision since time immemorial. The Phoenicians and Syrians of Palestine themselves admit that they learnt the practice from the Egyptians while the Syrians in the river Thermodon and Pathenios region and their neighbours the Macrons say they learnt it recently from the Colchidians. These are the only races which practise circumcision and it is observable that they do it in the same way as the Egyptians. As between the Egyptians themselves and the Ethiopians I could not say which taught the other the practice for among them it is quite clearly a custom of great antiquity. As to the custom having been learnt through their Egyptian connections, a further strong proof to my mind is that all those Phoenicians trading to Greece cease to treat the pudenda after the Egyptian manner and do not subject their offspring to circumcision.[26]

Herodotus reverts several times to the negroid character of the Egyptians and each time uses it as a fact of observation to argue more or less complex theses.

Thus to prove that the Greek oracle at Dodona in Epirus was of Egyptian origin, one of his arguments is the following: ' . . . and when they add that the dove was black they give us to understand that the woman was Egyptian'.[27] The doves in question—actually there were two according to the text—symbolize two Egyptian women who are said to have been carried off from the Egyptian Thebes to found the oracles in Greece at Dodona and in Libya (Oasis of Jupiter Amon) respectively. Herodotus did not share the opinion of Anaxagoras that the melting of the snows on the mountains of Ethiopia was the source of the Nile floods.[28] He relied on the fact that it neither rains nor snows in Ethiopia 'and the heat there turns men black'.[29]

(*b*) Aristotle, –389 to –332, scientist, philosopher and tutor of Alexander the Great.

In one of this minor works, Aristotle attempts, with unexpected *naïveté*, to establish a correlation between the physcial and moral natures of living beings and leaves us evidence on the Egyptian—Ethiopian race which confirms what Herodotus says. According to him, 'Those who are too black are cowards, like for instance, the Egyptians and Ethiopians. But those who are excessively white are also cowards as we can see from the example of women, the complexion of courage is between the two.'[30]

(*c*) Lucian, Greek writer, +125(?) to +190.

The evidence of Lucian is as explicit as that of the two previous writers. He introduces two Greeks, Lycinus and Timolaus, who start a conversation.

> Lycinus (describing a young Egyptian): 'This boy is not merely black; he has thick lips and his legs are too thin . . . his hair worn in a plait behind shows that he is not a freeman.'
>
> Timolaus: 'But that is a sign of really distinguished birth in Egypt, Lycinus. All freeborn children plait their hair until they reach manhood. It is the exact opposite of the custom of our ancestors who thought it seemly for old men to secure their hair with a gold brooch to keep it in place.'[31]

(d) Apollodorus, first century before our era, Greek philosopher.

'Aegyptos conquered the country of the black-footed ones and called it Egypt after himself.'[32]

(e) Aeschylus, −525(?) to −456, tragic poet and creator of Greek tragedy.

In *The Suppliants*, Danaos, fleeing with his daughters, the Danaïds, and pursued by his brother Aegyptos with his sons, the Aegyptiads, who seek to wed their cousins by force, climbs a hillock, looks out to sea and describes the Aegyptiads at the oars afar off in these terms: 'I can see the crew with their black limbs and white tunics.'[33]

A similar description of the Egyptian type of man recurs a few lines later in verse 745.

(f) Achilles Tatius of Alexandria.

He compares the herdsmen of the Delta to the Ethiopians and explains that they are blackish, like half-castes.

(g) Strabo, −58 to about +25.

Strabo visited Egypt and almost all the countries of the Roman empire. He concurs in the theory that the Egyptians and the Colchoi are of the same race but holds that the migrations to Ethiopia and Colchoi had been from Egypt only.

'Egyptians settled in Ethiopia and in Colchoi.'[34] There is no doubt whatever as to Strabo's notion of the Egyptians' race for he seeks elsewhere to explain why the Egyptians are darker than the Hindus, a circumstance which would permit the refutation, if needed, of any attempt at confusing 'the Hindu and Egyptian races'.

(h) Diodorus of Sicily, about −63 to +14, Greek historian and contemporary of Caesar Augustus.

According to Diodorus it was probably Ethiopia which colonized Egypt (in the Athenian sense of the term, signifying that, with overpopulation, a proportion of the people emigrate to new territory).

> *The Ethiopians say that the Egyptians are one of their colonies*,[35] which was led into Egypt by Osiris. They claim that at the beginning of the world Egypt was simply a sea but that the Nile, carrying down vast quantities of loam from Ethiopia in its flood waters, finally filled it in and made it part of the continent . . . They add that the Egyptians have received from them, as from authors and their ancestors, the greater part of their laws.[36]

(i) Diogenes Laertius.

He wrote the following about Zeno, founder of the Stoic School (−333 to −261): 'Zeno son of Mnaseas or Demeas was a native of Citium in Cyprus, a Greek city which has taken in some Phoenician colonists.' In his *Lives*, Timotheus of Athens describes Zeno as having a twisted neck. Apollonius of Tyre says of him that he was gaunt, very tall and black, hence the fact that, according to Chrysippus in the First Book of his Proverbs, certain people called him an Egyptian vine-shoot.[37]

(j) Ammianus Marcellinus, about +33 to +100, Latin historian and friend of the Emperor Julian.

With him we reach the sunset of the Roman empire and the end of classical antiquity. There are about nine centuries between the birth of Aeschylus and Herodotus and the death of Ammianus Marcellinus, nine centuries during which the Egyptians, amid a sea of white races, steadily crossbred. It can be said without exaggeration that in Egypt one household in ten included a white Asiatic or Indo-European slave.[38]

It is remarkable that, despite its intensity, all this crossbreeding should not have succeeded in upsetting the racial constants. Indeed Ammianus Marcellinus writes: " . . . the men of Egypt are mostly brown or black with a skinny and desiccated look".[39] He also confirms the evidence already cited about the Colchoi: 'Beyond these lands are the heartlands of the Camaritae[40] and the Phasis with its swifter stream borders the country of the Colçhoi, an ancient race of Egyptian origin.'[41]

This cursory review of the evidence of the ancient Graeco-Latin writers on the Egyptians' race shows that the extent of agreement between them is impressive and is an objective fact difficult to minimize or conceal, the two alternatives between which present-day Egyptology constantly oscillates.

An exception is the evidence of an honest savant, Volney, who travelled in Egypt between +1783 and +1785, i.e. at the peak period of negro slavery, and made the following observations on the true Egyptian race, the same which produced the Pharaohs, namely, the Copts:

> All of them are puffy-faced, heavy-eyed and thick-lipped, in a word, real mulatto faces. I was tempted to attribute this to the climate until, on visiting the Sphinx, the look of it gave me the clue to the enigma. Beholding that head characteristically Negro in all its features, I recalled the well-known passage of Herodotus which reads: 'For my part I consider the Colchoi are a colony of the Egyptians because, like them, they are black-skinned and kinky-haired'. In other words the ancient Egyptians were true negroes of the same stock as all the autochthonous peoples of Africa and from that datum one sees how their race, after some centuries of mixing with the blood of Romans and Greeks, must have lost the full blackness of its original colour but retained the impress of its original mould. It is even possible to apply this observation very widely and posit in principle that physiognomy is a kind of record usable in many cases for disputing or elucidating the evidence of history on the origins of the peoples . . .

After illustrating this proposition citing the case of the Normans, who 900 years after the conquest of Normandy still look like Danes, Volney adds:

> but reverting to Egypt, its contributions to history afford many subjects for philosophic reflection. What a subject for mediation is the present-day barbarity and ignorance of the Copts who were considered, born of the alliance of the deep genius of the Egyptians and the brilliance of the Greeks, that this race of blacks who nowadays are slaves and the objects of our scorn is the very one to which we owe our arts, our sciences and even the use of spoken word; and finally recollect that it is in the midst of the peoples claiming to be the greatest friends of liberty and humanity that the most barbarous of enslavements has been sanctioned and the question raised whether black men have brains of the same quality as those of white men![42]

To this testimony of Volney, Champollion-Figeac, brother of Champollion the Younger, was to reply in the following terms: 'The two physical traits of black skin and kinky hair are not enough to stamp a race as negro and Volney's conclusion as to the negro origin of the ancient population of Egypt is glaringly forced and inadmissible.'[43]

Being black from head to foot and having kinky hair is not enough to make a man a negro! This shows us the kind of specious argumentation to which Egyptology has had to resort since its birth as a science. Some scholars maintain that Volney was seeking to shift the discussion to a philosophic plane. But we have only to re-read Volney: he is simply drawing the inferences from crude material facts forcing themselves on his eyes and his conscience as proofs.

The Egyptians as They Saw Themselves

It is no waste of time to get the views of those principally concerned. How did the ancient Egyptians see themselves? Into which ethnic category did they put themselves? What did they call themselves? The language and literature left to us by the Egyptians of the Pharaonic epoch supply explicit answers to these questions which the scholars cannot refrain from minimizing, twisting or 'interpreting'.

The Egyptians had only one term to designate themselves:  =kmt=the negroes (literally).[44] This is the strongest term existing in the Pharaonic tongue to indicate blackness; it is accordingly written with a hieroglyph representing a length of wood charred at the end and not crocodile scales.[45] This word is the etymological origin of the well-known root *kamit* which has proliferated in modern anthropological literature. The biblical root *kam* is probably derived from it and it has therefore been necessary to distort the facts to enable this root today to mean 'white' in Egyptological terms whereas, in the Pharaonic mother tongue which gave it birth, it meant 'coal black'.

In the Egyptian language, a word of assembly is formed from an adjective or a noun by putting it in the feminine singular. 'Kmt' from the adjective  =km=black; it therefore means strictly negroes or at the very least black men. The terms is a collective noun which thus described the whole people of Pharaonic Egypt as a black people.

In other words, on the purely grammatical plane, if one wishes to indicate negroes in the Pharaonic tongue, one cannot use any other word than the very one which the Egyptians used of themselves. Furthermore, the language offers us another term, 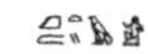 kmtjw=the negroes, the black men (literally)=the Egyptians, as opposed to 'foreigners' which comes from the same root km and which the Egyptians also used to describe themselves as *a people as distinguished from all foreign peoples*.[46] These are the only adjectives of nationality used by the Egyptians to designate themselves and both mean 'negro' or 'black' in the Pharaonic language. Scholars hardly ever mention them or when they do it is to translate them by euphemisms such as the 'Egyptians' while remaining completely silent about their etymological sense.[47] They prefer the expression 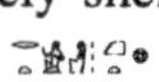 Rmt kmt=the men of the country of the black men or the men of the black country.

In Egyptian, words are normally followed by a determinative which indicates their exact sense, and for this particular expression Egyptologists suggest that  km=black and that the colour qualifies the determinative which follows it and which signifies 'country'. Accordingly, they claim, the translation should be 'the black earth' from the colour of the loam, or the 'black country', and not 'the country of the black men' as we should be inclined to render it today with black Africa and white Africa in mind. Perhaps so, but if we apply this rule rigorously to =kmit, we are forced to 'concede that here the adjective "black" qualifies the determinative which signifies the whole people of Egypt shown by the two symbols for "man" and "woman" and the three strokes below them which indicate the plural'. Thus, if it is possible to voice a doubt as regards the expression =kme, it is not possible to do so in the case of the two adjectives of nationality kmt and kmtjw unless one is picking one's arguments completely at random.

It is a remarkable circumstance that the ancient Egyptians should never have had the idea of applying these qualificatives to the Nubians and other populations of Africa to distinguish them from themselves; any more than a Roman at the apogee of the empire could use a 'colour' adjective to distinguish himself from the Germani on the other bank of the Danube, of the same stock but still in the prehistoric age of development.

In either case both sides were of the same world in terms of physical anthropology, and accordingly the distinguishing terms used related to level of civilization or moral sense. For the civilized Romans, the Germans, of the same stock, were barbarians. The Egyptians used the expression =nahas to designate the Nubians; and nahas[48] is the name of a people, with no colour connotation in Egyptian. It is a deliberate mistranslation to render it as negro as is done in almost all present-day publications.

The Divine Epithets

Finally, black or negro is the divine epithet invariably used for the chief beneficent gods of Egypt, whereas all the malevolent spirits are qualified as desrêt=red; we also know that to Africans this form applies to the white nations; it is practically certain that this held good for Egypt too but I want in this chapter to keep to the least debatable facts.

The surnames of the gods are these:

=Kmwr=the 'Great Negro' for Osiris[49]

=km=the black + the name of the god[50]

=kmt=the black + the name of the goddess[51]

The km (black) qualificative is applied to Hathor, Apis, Min, Thoth, etc.[52] set kmt=the black woman=Isis.[53] On the other hand 'seth', the sterile desert, is qualified by the term desrêt=red.[54] The wild animals which Horus fought to create civilization are qualified as dešrêt=red, especially the hippopotamus.[55] Similarly the maleficent beings wiped out by Thoth are Des=  =dèsrtjw=thr red ones; this term is the grammatical converse of Kmtjw and its construction follows the same rule for the formation of 'nisbés'.

Witness of the Bible

The Bible tells us: '. . . the sons of Ham [were] Cush, and Mizraim [i.e. Egypt], and Phut, and Canaan. And the sons of Cush; Seba, and Havilah, and Sabtah, and Raamah, and Sabtechah.'[56]

Generally speaking all Semitic tradition (Jewish and Arab) classes ancient Egypt with the countries of the blacks.

The importance of these depositions cannot be ignored, for these are peoples (the Jews) which lived side by side with the ancient Egyptians and sometimes in symbiosis with them and have nothing to gain by presenting a false ethnic picture of them. Nor is the notion of an erroneous interpretation of the facts any more tenable.[57]

Cultural Data

Among the innumberable identical cultural traits recorded in Egypt and in present-day black Africa, it is proposed to refer only to circumcision and totemism.

According to the extract from Herodotus quoted earlier, circumcision is of African origin. Archaeology has confirmed the judgement of the Father of History for Elliot-Smith was able to determine from the examination of well-preserved mummies that circumcision was the rule among the Egyptians as long ago as the protohistoric era,[58] i.e. earlier than −4000.

Egyptian totemism retained its vitality down to the Roman period[59] and Plutarch also mentions it. The researches of Amélineau,[60] Loret, Moret and Adolphe Reinach have clearly demonstrated the existence of an Egyptian totemic system, in refutation of the champions of the zoolatric thesis.

> If we reduce the notion of the totem to that of a fetish, usually representing an animal of a species with which the tribe believes it has special ties formally renewed at fixed intervals, and which is carried into battle like a standard; if we accept this minimal but adequate definition of a totem, it can be said that there was no country where totemism had a more brilliant reign than in Egypt and certainly nowhere where it could better be studied.[61]

Linguistic Affinity

Walaf,[62] a Senegalese language spoken in the extreme west of Africa on the Atlantic Ocean, is perhaps as close to ancient Egyptian as Coptic. An exhaustive study of this question has recently been carried out.[63] In this chapter enough is presented to show that the kinship between ancient Egyptian and the languages of Africa is not hypothetical but a demonstrable fact which it is impossible for modern scholarship to thrust aside.

As we shall see, the kinship is genealogical in nature.

EGYPTIAN	COPTIC	WALAF
 =kef=to grasp, to take a strip (of something)[64]	(Saïdique dialect) keh=to tame[65]	kef=seize a prey
PRESENT	PRESENT	PRESENT
kef i	keh	kef na
kef ek	keh ek	kef nga
kef et	keh ere	kef na
kef ef	kef ef	
kef es	keh es	kef ef na
		kef es
kef n	keh en	kef nanu
kef ton	keh etetû	kef ngen
kef sen[66]	keh ey	kef nañu
PAST	PAST	PAST
kef ni	keh nei	kef (on) na
kef (o) nek	keh nek	kef (on) nga
kef (o) net	keh nere	kef (on) na
kef (o) nef	keh nef	kef (on) ef na
kef (o) nes	keh nes	kef (on) es
kef (o) nen	keh nen	kef (on) nanu
kef (o) n ten	keh netsten	kef (on) ngen
kef (o) n sen[67]	keh ney[68]	kef (on) nañu

	EGYPTIAN	WALAF
	=feh=go away	feh=rush off

We have the following correspondences between the verb forms, with identity or similarity of meaning: all the Egyptian verb forms, except for two, are also recorded in Walaf.

EGYPTIAN	WALAF
feh-ef	feh-ef
feh-es	feh-es
feh-n-ef	feh-ôn-ef
feh-n-es	feh-ônes
feh-w	feh-w
feh-wef	feh-w-ef
feh-w-es	feh-w-es
feh-w-n-ef	feh-w-ôn-ef
feh-w-n-es	feh-w-ôn-es
feh-in-ef	feh-il-ef
feh-in-es	feh-il-es
feh-t-ef	feh-t-ef
feh-t-es	feh-t-es
feh-tyfy	feh-ati-fy
feh-tysy	feh-at-ef
feh-tw-ef	mar-tw-ef
feh-tw-es	mar-tw-es
feh-kw(i)	fahi-kw
feh-n-tw-ef	feh-an-tw-ef
feh-n-tw-es	feh-an-tw-es
feh-y-ef	feh-y-ef
feh-y-es	fey-y-es

EGYPTIAN	WALAF
 =mer=love	mar=lick[69]
mer-ef	mar-ef
mer-es	mar-es
mer-n-ef	mar-ôn-ef
mer-n-es	mar-ôn-es
mer-w	mar-w
mer-w-ef	mar-w-ef
mer-w-n-f	mar-w-ôn-ef
mer-w-n-es	mar-w-ôn-es
mer-in-ef	mar-il-ef
mer-in-es	mar-il-es
mer-t-ef	mar-t-ef
mer-t-es	mar-t-es
mer-tw-ef	mar-tw-ef
mer-tw-es	mar-tw-es
mer-tyfy	mar-at-ef
mer-*t*-tysy	mar-at-es
	mar-aty-sy
	mar-aty-sy
mer-kwi	mari-kw
mer-y-ef	mar-y-ef
mer-y-es	mar-y-es
mer-n-tw-ef	mar-an-tw-ef
mer-n-tw-es	mar-antw-es
	mar-tw-ôn-ef
	mar-tw-ôn-es

Egyptian and Walaf Demonstratives

There are the following phonetic correspondences between Egyptian and Walaf demonstratives.

EGYPTIAN	WALAF
	ep→w
=pw	p→b
(ipw)→bw	w→w
=pwy	p→b̄
(ipw)→bwy	w→2
	y→y
=pn bané	p→b̄
(ipn)→	n→n
balé	p→b̄
	n→1[70]
=pf bafe	p→b
(ipf)→	f→f
=pf3→bafa	p→b̄
	f→f
	3→a
=pfy	p→b̄
(ipfy)→bafy	f→f
	y→y
=p3→bâ	p→b
	3→á
=iptw→batw	p→b
	t→t
	w→w
=iptn→batné	p→b
	t→t
Batalé	n→n
	n→1
=iptf	
=iptf→batafé	p→b̄
	t→t
	f→f

These phonetic correspondences are not ascribable either to elementary affinity or to the general laws of the human mind for they are regular correspondences on outstanding points extending through an entire system, that of the demonstratives in the two languages and that of the verbal languages. It is through the application of such laws that it was possible to demonstrate the existence of the Indo-European linguistic family.

The comparison could be carried to show that the majority of the phonemes remain unchanged between the two languages. The few changes which are of great interest are the following.

(a) The correspondence n (E)→l (W)

EGYPTIAN	WALAF
n	l
=na*d*=ask	la*d*=ask
=nah=protect	lah=protect
=ben ben=wellup	belbel=well up
=teni=grow old	talé=important
=tefnwt=the goddess born of Ra's spittle	tefnit='spit out' a human being. teflit=spittle tefli=spitter
=nebt=plait	let=plait nâb=to plait hair temporarily

(b) The correspondence h (E)→g (W)

EGYPTIAN	WALAF
h	g
=hen=phallus	gen=phallus
=hwn=adolescent	gwné, goné =adolescent
=hor=Horus	gor=vir (? male ?)
=hor gwn=the youth Horus	gor gwne=young man (m.ă.m)

It is still early to talk with precision of the vocalic accompaniment of the Egyptian phonemes. But the way is open for the rediscovery of the vocalics of ancient Egyptian from comparative studies with the languages of Africa.

Conclusion

The structure of African royalty, with the king put to death, either really or symbolically, after a reign which varied in length but was in the region of eight years, recalls the ceremony of the Pharaoh's regeneration through the Sed feast. Also reminiscent of Egypt are the circumcision rites mentioned earlier and the totemism, cosmogonies, architecture, musical instruments, etc., of Africa.[71] Egyptian antiquity is to Africa culture what Graeco-Roman antiquity is to Western culture. The building up of a corpus of African humanities should be based on this fact.

It will be understood how difficult it is to write such a chapter in a work of this kind, where euphemism and compromise are the rule. In an attempt to avoid sacrificing scientific truth, therefore, we made a point of suggesting three preliminaries to the preparation of this volume, all of which were agreed to at the plenary session held in 1971.[72] The first two led to the holding of the Cairo Symposium from 28 January to 3 February 1974.[73] In this connection I should like to refer to certain passages in the report of that symposium. Professor Vercoutter, who had been commissioned by Unesco to write the introductory report, acknowledged after a thorough discussion that the conventional idea that the Egyptian population was equally divided between blacks, whites and half-castes could not be upheld. 'Professor Vercoutter agreed that no attempt should be made to estimate percentages, which meant nothing, as it was impossible to establish them without reliable statistical data'. On the subject of Egyptian culture: 'Professor Vercoutter remarked that, in his view, Egypt was African in its way of writing, in its culture and in its way of thinking'.

Professor Leclant, for his part, 'recognized the same African character in the Egyptian temperament and way of thinking'.

In regard to linguistics, it is stated in the report that 'this item, in contrast to those previously discussed, revealed a large measure of agreement among the participants. The outline report by Professor Diop and the report by Professor Obenga were regarded as being very constructive'.

Similarly, the symposium rejected the idea that Pharaonic Egyptian was a Semitic language. 'Turning to wider issues, Professor Sauneron drew attention to the interest of the method suggested by Professor Obenga following Professor Diop. Egyptian remained a stable language for a period of at least 4500 years. Egypt was situated at the point of convergence of outside influences and it was to be expected that borrowing had been made from foreign languages, but the Semitic roots numbered only a few hundred as compared with a total of several thousand words. The Egyptian language could not be isolated from its African context and its origin could not be fully explained in terms of Semitic, it was thus quite normal to expect to find related languages in Africa'.

The genetic, that is, non-accidental relationship between Egyptian and the African languages was recognized: 'Professor Sauneron noted that the method which had been used was of considerable interest, since it could not be purely fortuitous that there was a similarity between the third person singular suffixed pronouns in Ancient Egyptian and in Wolof, he hoped that an attempt would be made to reconstitute a palaeo-African language, using present-day languages as a starting point'.

In the general conclusion to the report it was stated that: 'Although the preparatory working paper sent out by Unesco gave particulars of what was desired, not all participants had prepared communications comparable with the painstakingly researched contributions of Professors Cheikh Anta Diop and Obenga. There was consequently a real lack of balance in the discussions.'

A new page of African historiography was accordingly written in Cairo. The symposium recommended that further studies be made on the concept of race. Such studies have since been carried out, but they have not contributed anything new to the historical discussion. They tell us that molecular biology and genetics recognize the existence of populations alone, the concept of race being no longer meaningful. Yet whenever there is any question of the transmission of a hereditary taint, the concept of race in the most classic sense of the term comes into its own again, for genetics tells us that 'sickle-cell anaemia occurs only in negroes'. The truth is that all these 'anthropologists' have already in their own minds drawn the conclusions deriving from the triumph of the monogenetic theory of mankind without venturing to put them into explicit terms, for if mankind originated in Africa, it was necessarily negroid before becoming white through mutation and adaptation at the end of the last glaciation in Europe in the Upper Palaeolithic; and it is now more understandable why the Grimaldian negroids first occupied Europe for 10000 years before Cro-Magnon Man—the prototype of the white race—appeared (around −2000).

The ideological standpoint is also evident in apparently objective studies. In history and in social relations, it is the phenotype, that is, the individual or the people as that individual or people is perceived, which is the dominant factor, as opposed to the genotype. For present-day genetics, a Zulu with the 'same' genotype as Vorster is not impossible. Does this mean that the history we are witnessing will put the two phenotypes, that is, the two individuals, on the same footing in all their national and social activities? Certainly not—the opposition will remain not social but ethnic.

This study makes it necessary to rewrite world history from a more scientific standpoint, taking into account the Negro-African component which was for a long time preponderant. It means that it is now possible to build up a corpus of Negro-African humanities resting on a sound historical basis instead of being suspended in mid-air. Finally, if it is true that only truth is revolutionary, it may be added that only *rapprochement* brought about on a basis of truth can endure. The cause of human progess is not well served by casting a veil over the fact.

The rediscovery of the true past of the African peoples should not be a divisive factor but should contribute to uniting them, each and all, binding them together from the north to the south of the continent so as to enable them to carry out together a new historical mission for the greater good of mankind; and that is in keeping with the ideal of Unesco.[74]

Note by the Editor of *General History of Africa* (Unesco, 1981): The opinions expressed by Professor Cheikh Anta Diop in this chapter are those which he presented and developed at the Unesco symposium of 'The peopling of ancient Egypt' which was held in Cairo in 1974. The arguments put forward in this chapter have not been accepted by all the experts interested in the problem.—Gamal Mokhtar.

Plate 1. Protohistoric figure of Tera-Neter, a negro nobleman of the Anous race who were the first inhabitants of Egypt.

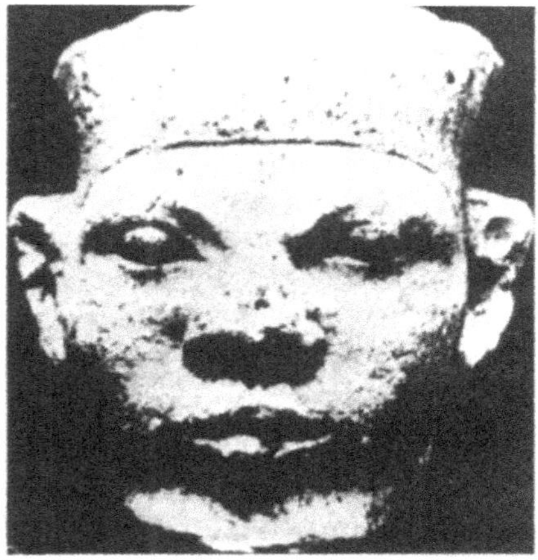

Plate 2. A pharaoh of the First Egyptian Dynasty, said to be Narmer.

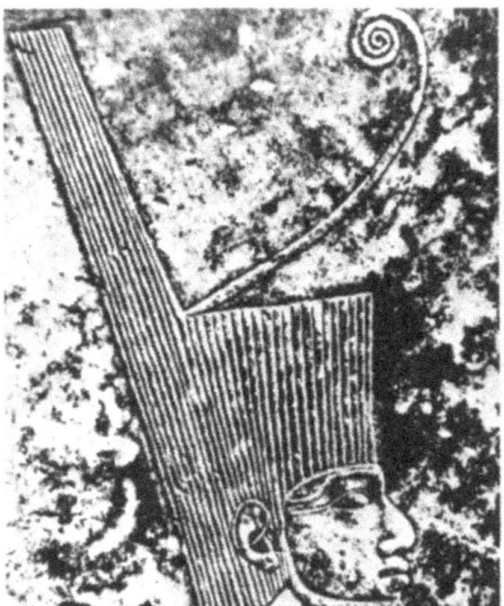

Plate 3. Djeser, typical negro, pharaoh of the Third Dynasty; this ushered in the great age of dressed-stone architecture: the step pyramid and burial complex at Sakkara. By his reign, all the technological features of Egyptian civilization were already developed.

Plate. 4. Door socket from Hierakonpolis, First Egyptian Dynasty.

Plate 5. Libyan prisoner.

Plate 6. Foreigner.

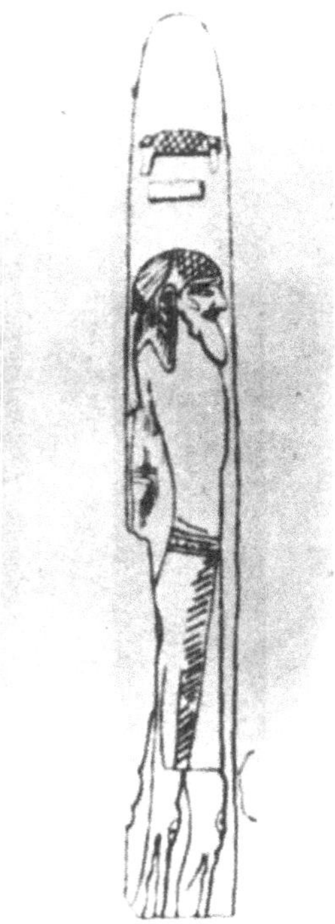

Plate 7. Semitic captive.

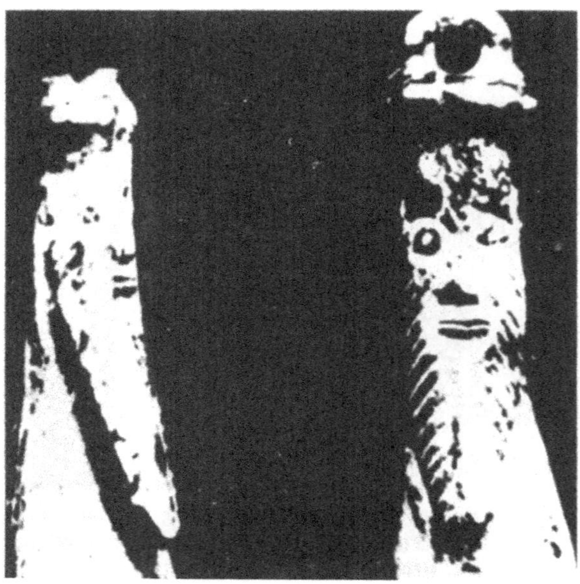

Plate 8. Predynastic figurines.

Plate 9. Indo-European captives.

Plate 10. Indo-European captive.

Plate 11. Indo-European captive.

Plate 12. Cheops, Pharaoh of the Fourth Dynasty, builder of the Great Pyramid.

Plate 13. Semitic captives at the time of the pharaohs; Sinai rock.

Plate 14. Pharaoh Mentouhotep I.

Plate 15. Four Indo-European types (Zeus, Ptolemy, Sarapis, Trajan). Compare with Egyptian groups II and III.

Plate 16. Two Semites. Like the Indo-European type, the Semitic type was totally absent from the Egyptian ruling class, entering Egypt only as war captives.

Plate 17. Ramses II, and a modern Batutsi.

Plate 18. Statue of the Sphynx as found by the first French scientific mission in the nineteenth century. The typically Negro profile is thought to be that of the pharaoh Khafre or Khefren (ca.—2600, IV Dynasty), the builder of the second pyramid of Giza.

Notes

1. *Proceedings of the Seventh Pan-African Congress of Pre-History and Quaternary Studies*, December 1971.
2. M.F.A. Montagu, 1960, p. 390.
3. The study of this race's pigmentation can be carried farther by the method described; actually Elliot-Smith often found patches of skin on the bodies and the mummification eethods which cause skin deterioration were not yet in use.
4. D.P. de Pedrals, p. 6.
5. *Géographie*, classe de 5°, 1950.
6. In his 'Lutte des races' (1883) L. Gumplovicz asserts that the diverse classes making up a people always represent different races, of which one has established its domination over the others by conquest. G. de Lapounge in an article published in 1897 postulated no less than a dozen 'fundamental laws of anthropo-sociology' of which the following are typical: his 'law of distribution of wealth' posits that, in countries of mixed European-Alpine populations, wealth is greater in inverse proportions to the cephalic index; the 'law of urban indices' given prominence by Ammon in connexion with his research on Badener conscripts asserted that town dwellers exhibit greater dolichocephaly than the people in the adjacent countryside; the 'law of stratification' was formulated in the following terms: 'the cephalic index decreases and the proportion of dolichocephalics rises the higher the social class, in each locality'. In his 'Sélections sociales' the same writer has no hesitation in asserting that 'the dominant class in the feudal epoch belongs almost exclusively to the variety "Homo Europaeus" so that it is not pure chance which has kept the poor at the foot of the social ladder but their congenital inferiority'.

We thus see that German racism was inventing nothing new, when Alfred Rosenberg asserted that the French Revolution must be deemed a revolt of the brachycephalics of the Alpine stock against the dolichocephalics of the Nordic race.' (A. Cuvillier, p. 155).

7. W.M.F. Petrie, 1939, Fig. 1.
8. ibid., p. 69.
9. ibid., p. 68.
10. E. Amélineau, 1908, p. 174.
11. Pl. 1.2.
12. Pl. 1.3.
13. W.M.F. Petrie, 1939, p. 67.
14. Pl. 1.11.
15. Pl. 1.5.
16. Pl. 1.8.
17. Pl. 1.7 I know that 'Indo-European' is usually said to be a language, not a race, but I prefer this term to 'Aryan' wherever its use causes no confusion.
18. Pl. 1.12.
19. Pl. 1.13.
20. R.A. Nicolaus, p. 11.
21. T.J. Pettigrew, 1834, pp. 70-71.
22. C.A. Diop, 1977.
23. M.E. Fontane, pp. 44-5 (see reproduction: T).
24. M.F.A. Montagu, p. 337.
25. In the fifth century before our era, at the time when Herodotus visited Egypt, a black-skinned people, the Colchians, were still living in Colchis on the Armenian shore of the Black Sea, east of the ancient port of Trebizond, surrounded by white-skinned nations.

The scholars of antiquity wondered about this people's origins and Herodotus in 'Euterpe', the second book of his history on Egypt, tries to prove that the Colchians were Egyptians, whence the arguments we quote. Herodotus, on the strength of commemorative stelae, erected by Sesostris in conquered countries, asserts that this monarch had got as far as Thrace and Seythia, where stelae would seem to have been still standing in his day (Book II, 103).

26. Herodotus, Book II, 104. As with many peoples in black Africa, Egyptian women underwent excision of the clitoris: cf. Strabo, *Geography*, Book XVII, Ch. I.
27. Herodotus, Book II, 57.
28. Seneca, *Questions of Nature*, Book IV, 17.
29. Herodotus, Book II, 22.
30. Aristotle, *Physiognomy*, 6.
31. Lucian, *Navigations*, paras 2-3.
32. Apollodorus, Book II, 'The family of Inachus', paras 3 and 4.
33. Aeschylus, *The Suppliants*, vv. 719-20. See also v. 745.
34. Strabo, *Geography*, Book I, ch. 3, para. 10.
35. My italics.
36. Diodorus, *Universal History*, Book III. The antiquity of the Ethiopian civilization is attested by the most ancient and most venerable Greek writer, Homer, in both the *Iliad* and the *Odyssey*:

'Jupiter followed today by all the gods receives the sacrifices of theEthiopians' (*Iliad*, I, 422).

'Yesterday to visit holy Ethiopia Jupiter betook himself to the ocean shore' (*Iliad*, I, 423).

37. Diogenes Laertius, Book VII, i.
38. The Egyptian notables liked to have a Syrian or Cretan female slave in their harems.
39. Ammianus Marcellinus, Book XXII, para. 16 (23).
40. Pirate gangs who worked from small ships called *Ćamare*.
41. Ammianus Marcellinus, Book XXII, para. 8 (24).
42. M.C.F. Volney, *Voyages en Syrie et en Egypte*, Paris, 1787, Vol. I, pp. 74-7.
43. J.J. Champollion-Figeac, 1839, pp. 26-7.
44. This important discovery was made, on the African side, by Sossou Nsougan, who was to

compile this part of the present chapter. For the sense of the word see *Wörterbuch der Aegyptischen Sprache*, Vol. 5, 1971, pp. 122 and 127.

45. ibid., p. 122.
46. ibid., p. 128.
47. R.O. Faulkner, 1962, p. 286.
48. Wörter buch der ägyptischen Sprache, p. 128.
49. ibid., p. 124.
50. ibid., p. 125.
51. ibid., p. 123.
52. It should be noted that set=kem=black wife in Walaf.
53. Wörter buch der ägyptischen Sprache, p. 492.
54. ibid., p. 493.
55. Dešrêt=blood in Egyptian; deret=blood in Walaf: ibid., p. 494.
56. Genesis, 10: 6-7.
57. C.A. Diop, 1955, pp. 33ff.
58. E. Massoulard, 1949, p. 386.
59. Juvénal, *Satire* XV, vv. 1-14.
60. E. Amélineau, *op. cit.*
61. A. Recnach, 1913, p. 17.
62. Often spelt Wolof.
63. C.A. Diop, 1977.
64. R. Lambert, 1925, p. 129.
65. A. Mallon, pp. 207-34.
66. A. de Buck, 1952.
67. ibid.
68. A. Mallon, pp. 207-34.
69. By extension=love intensely (hence the verb mar-maral) after the fashion of a female animal licking the cub which she has just borne. This sense does not conflict with the other notion which the determinative may convey of a man raising hand to mouth.
70. See below for the explanation of this important law.
71. See C.A. Diop, 1967.
72. See *Final Report of the First Plenary Session of the International Scientific Committee for the Drafting of a general History of Africa,* UNESCO, 30 March-8 April 1974.
73. Symposium of 'The peopling of ancient Egypt and the deciphering of the Meriotic script'. Cf. Studies and Documents No. I, UNESCO, 1978.

IRON IN THE ANCIENT EGYPTIAN EMPIRE

Cheikh Anta Diop

(Translated by Darryl Prevost)

Editor's Note: The following essay on Egyptian iron metallurgy originally appeared in French in Bulletin de l'Institut Fundamental D'Afrique Noire *(Dakar, 1972). This version is slightly condensed but preserves major technical sections omitted from its first publication in English in* The Daily Californian *(September 18, 1984).*

My goal in writing this article is to prove that, contrary to the point of view of Professor R. Mauny in his book *The Obscure Centuries of Black Africa,* iron metal is an African invention that dates back to the Ancient Empire (2700 B.C.). My embarrassment will be understood if one knows that Prof. Mauny became a friend whom I held in high esteem. Science will learn a great deal from this discussion.

Did the Egyptians know iron metallurgy as early as the Ancient Empire around 2700 B.C., in the pyramid epoch? In order to answer this question, one has to first marshal the facts as revealed by the archaeological research, then go through the different hypotheses.

On Friday, May 26, 1837, when Colonel Howard Vyse was carrying on this archaeological research in lower Egypt, one of his fellow workers, M. Hill, found a piece of iron in the inner joints of the masonry on the south face near the mouth of the air channel of the Great Pyramid built in 2700 B.C. The examination immediately performed by the discoverers showed that the place where the fragment was found had been left intact until then; it was never previously disturbed.

The first precaution during the inventory, which was insisted upon, was to carefully examine the site, which led to setting aside the hypothesis which postulated that visitors after the fourth dynasty introduced the piece. One can never insist enough on this precaution taken from the start. We will see that despite the evidence that the only witnesses gave of the event, today's specialists won't hesitate to omit this fact and to make others (who don't know the details) believe that the piece must belong to a more recent period.

As recently as the Ancient Empire, during which the Egyptians were building the Great Pyramid of Cheops, the metallurgic technique of iron extraction from the ore had already been mastered, and the Egyptians were using it to make, not religious or magical objects, but tools for everyday life. The instrument found in the interstices of the Great Pyramid is a hoe. Whether the discovery of the metallurgic technique was accidental (which would still need to be proved) doesn't matter because of the shrewdness of the Ancient Egyptians. They made use of the technique so that it was not lost.

Professor R. Mauny's objections in regard to the invention of iron metallurgy in the Ancient Empire epoch is partly based upon an article published by Prof. J. Leclant in which the following argument appears: "As to the non-meteoric iron production, it was accidental, during the treatment of auriferous sand in Nubia that contained magnetite."

But if the author's point of view is right, stratum iron with gold pearls should have been found as far back as the fourth millenium starting in 3600 B.C. In addition, most of the gold ores are cold-processed from sand and quartz. Washing stations of auriferous sand have been found on the Nile bank, but no one has found a single oven that would have been used to melt the gold ore. Finally, iron melts at 1520°C, whereas gold melts at 1063°C and copper at 1083°C. The Egyptians as well as today's Africans were only melting gold to beat it out after cold-extracting it from the ore.

Professor Leclant thinks that the perfection that Ancient Egyptians reached in the cutting and burnishing of granite doesn't require the knowledge of iron. He claims that the results obtained can be attributed to the use of copper materials and abrasive powders, especially in light of the endless patience of the ancient artisans.

Let's reply to that. In spite of the immense progress in modern techniques and the infinite diversification of tools, modern people can only scratch granite with steel or diamond, and the technicians who could do it with a copper instrument could patent the process, for they would have achieved a real technical innovation. As for the hypothesis of the abrasive powders, it could be a convenient way to set aside the use of metals by the Egyptians to chisel granite out, but it hasn't been confirmed yet by the archaeological discoveries or by the scenes on bas reliefs showing Egyptians beating out the stone. The author continues, "as for the epoch of the fourth dynasty, one noted a non-meteoric iron fragment at the Great Pyramid of Cheops (ca. 2700 B.C.) found between the stones of the exterior face; it can and *must* have been inserted in a more recent period by those who used the pyramid as an immense quarry of construction materials."

Why "fragment" when it is a tool, a hoe in the present case? Why "non meteoric"? The recognized term is *stratum iron* showing that the extraction technique was very well mastered by the Egyptians as far back as this remote epoch that was the Ancient Egyptian Empire. Finally, the precautions taken in the description of the place by the archaeologists who discovered the instrument forbid one to suggest that the object was an intrusion from a later dynasty. Experienced, these inventors took all the necessary precautions so that posterity could not devalue their discovery in the above-mentioned way. One will notice that the verb "must" in quotes has an almost normative resonance in the above-mentioned sentence of Prof. Leclant.

According to the same author, the lump of stratum iron found at Abydos (6th dynasty) could be a product of accidental fusion. The preceding objections are applicable here too. He enumerates the iron objects found in Egypt from the New Empire: A lump of oxidized iron fixed to an axehead in bronze found by Griffith at Armarna (ca. 1360 B.C.), a few iron objects that belonged to the 18th dynasty, a pair of iron bracelets decorated by dogs' heads on the same site in the tomb of Tutankhamen (ca. 1340 B.C.), a dagger, 16 sharp scissor blades, a small horse, the Eye of Horus in iron. These last objects could have been designed for a magical use. One could even say for a posthumous use, as miniaturized replica of everyday life on Earth.

But I noticed in the funeral furniture of Tutankhamen shown at the Cairo Museum, some objects which would prove that the use of iron was common in everyday life. These are metallic hinges of Tutankhaman's camp bed. As soon as my attention was captured, I asked the question of Dr. Ryad, Cairo Museum curator, who accompanied us during the visit. His answer was positive: *"The pieces are in iron."* Back in Dakar I wrote him two successive letters to ask him to be kind enough to check in his records to see that these pieces are not the result of a restoration of the bed. Alas, these two letters remained unanswered.

Let's go back to M. Leclant's text: Because of the letters of Armarna, it is thought that these objects could have been offered to the Pharoah or to one of his predecessors by some Asian sovereign. It's well known that the Asian metallurgists (more precisely those from the Armenian regions) were the first iron producers *in appreciable quantities.* The Hittites' texts mention arms, iron statues, but it seems as though this metal was destined for temples or royal offerings only.

This language is astonishing! The letters of Armarna are the remains of the administrative archives of the Egyptian chancellery after the conquest of Western Asia by Thutmosis III in the 18th dynasty. More than 110 states, including the Aegean Sea islands, were conquered. At the time of Amenophis III, Phoenicia (Syria) was part of the Egyptian empire as today's Corsica, or the island of Rèunion, to France so that Phoenicians revolted when Egypt was not sending enough troops to protect them. How then can we so glibly talk about an autonomous invention in these regions in that period? The invention of iron metallurgy or the so-called Phoenician writing is an abuse of speech. These archives were centralizing information of all sorts that Egypt collected at this time from these small tribes. The "famous" Hittites were under the Egyptian protectorate. One can hardly imagine today the efficiency of the Egyptian administration of that time in *Eastern* Asia. The system of roads, the inspection tour, the regular couriers with control at the frontier post, *cisterns* and supply posts, the regularly collected taxes, hence these archives named the Letters of Armarna. It was not a vague sovereignty with episodal relations and loose ties, as some scholars pretend.

Finally, in the above-mentioned passage one will notice the expression "iron producers in appreciable quantities." One has to find out if these people have been initiators or not. Well, we know from what came before that they were not even mentioned in history when we have evidence of the process in Egypt and, even more, they all were in varying degrees under Egypt's sovereignty at the time that one makes them inventors. M. Leclant states further: "Under the 19th and 20th dynasties (1320-1200 B.C.), one also notes some iron objects: a sword from Seti's first reign (1318-1298 B.C.), a halberd in the foundation sand of Ramses III's temple at Abydos (1198-1166 B.C.), a divine statue in bia-h-pet (iron) of Ramses III. Under the 21st and 22nd dynasties, bolts that fixed a chest, knives, bracelets, a statuette of the god Horus (ca. 847 B.C.), a postherd and the top of a crown.

Despite these discoveries, some scholars still propagate the idea that the routine use of iron in Egypt dates from the war against Assyria because one found at Thebes in upper Egypt an Assyrian helmet which would date from the Asshurbanipal expedition (663 B.C.). One forgets that this took place under the 25th Sudanese dynasty and that all the campaigns against Assyria were led by the Sudanese pharoahs, notably by Taharka and that iron was already known in Sudan, which would explain its more frequent use in Egypt under the Sudanese dynasty. Indeed, Thebes' capture would have been too recent to explain the diffusion of iron in Egypt. Let's recall that the use of iron was so ancient in Sudan that the Temple of the Lion from the 1st century B.C. was built on one of the crassiers around Meroe, as Paris is built on Lutece's Ruins and Troyes II on those of Troyes I. There is nothing as such around the so-called cities of Asia Minor which would have been first to produce iron in appreciable quantities. Sanam's treasury which dates from Taharka's epoch (689-663 B.C.) included iron ingots and is earlier than the sack of Thebes. One has to really want to see the iron coming from Assyria to suppose (Arkell, *A History of Sudan,* p. 130) that the Sudanese pharoahs introduced the iron of the Assyrians through an exchange, at the very time that they were fighting against them. Note also that this introduction of iron is supposed to be occurring simultaneously in the far end of Sudan and in lower Egypt closer to Assyria.

But as we have seen, the chronology given for this makes the hypothesis indefensible. Iron diffusion in Egypt at that time is tied to the reign of the 25th Sudanese dynasty. The fact that the Egyptians and Sudanese kept bows and arrowheads until this late epoch doesn't prove anything if one understands the reason. Sudan, the principal iron-making country of antiquity, gives its bowmen arrowheads not because of a lack of metal but because the arrow has to be light to fly far. The arrows which are in some ways missiles, that are only used once, were in flint, whereas the arms that one would constantly carry (knives, daggers, swords) were in iron. Flint damages the human body as much as any other metal. We will notice that the principal arm of Africans (Sudanese, Egyptians, rest of Black Africa) is the bow. It is the pharoah's arm in a fight and not the sword, and the whole structure of the Egyptian army was founded on the different bowmen corps. It is remarkable that Egypt armed in such a manner defeated the Sea people (19th dynasty) who had bronze arms and that Egypt has even been the only invaded nation which survived the turmoil because of its technical superiority in general and its national and state organization, in particular.

The second point of Prof. R. Mauny is based upon this passage in Clark's article which I referred to: "Before one found a way to stiffen the wrought metal by constant hammering of the hot iron mass . . . and to put enough carbon in for carburation, the iron was too soft for practical use."

Unfortunately, this passage shows a lack of scientific knowledge. Indeed, in order to introduce through hot-hammering carbon atoms into the iron mass, the blacksmith would have had to make a smelt. This process could only make carbon atoms, which have already been incorporated in the iron at the fusion state, diffuse through the interior of the metal. The cold-hammering tempers the metal and leads to a modification of its crystalline structure, which makes it thinner. The hot-hammering leads to the inverse phenomena, in that the crystalline structure becomes larger. On the other hand, the scoria (impurities) included during the metal fusion are ejected. In both cases (hot or cold-hammering), the actual metal stiffness increases. The Egyptians knew the virtues of the hammering and were already using it for copper as early as the Ancient Empire.

In fact, when one treats iron ore at high temperatures with charcoal, one doesn't get iron at first but cast iron, i.e. a very complex combination of iron and carbon. The carbon is in excess, so the cast iron is brittle. The carbon grade varies from 6.67% to 7%. In order to obtain steel, one has to reduce the carbon proportion down to 1.7%. The carbon grade in steel is between 1.7% and 0.1%. Above that level, we get cast irons and in order to be refined (i.e. to diminish the carbon excess) to decarbonize them, one can use the *comtois* process or the *puddlage* process. In the first case, cast iron is heated in a furnace with charcoal above 1200°. The iron crystallizes and has the shape of that famous lump [the one found at Abydos] but one can see that it is for the opposite reasons to those presented by R. Mauny. The metal decarbonizes, and contains less carbon. In the puddlage process, which is also a process that decarbonizes cast iron, one burns the excess of carbon in the cast iron by the oxygen in the air as well as the oxygen of the ferric oxide that one adds as a melting catalyst. A more elaborate refining could produce pure iron. As a consequence, this one is not the first product obtained nor the easiest to obtain. It is the ultimate stage of the metallurgic operation. The *catalan* process is used for rich iron ores of 70% purity. In this process, the lump appears without noticeable carburation of the metal. We then have relatively decarbonized iron. This technique is very ancient. In order to directly obtain steel without going through the process of cast iron, one would have to diminish the ore (by preventing the pronounced carburation that leads to cast iron) either by using a reducing agent, active under 850°C., or by working in an oxidizing environment to enrich the iron scoria.

On the frescos of the tombs of Rekhmire, vizier of Thutmosis III, (18th dynasty, circa 1450 B.C.), one sees the blacksmiths using the same type of bellows used in Black Africa, a leather bottle over and above a clay bottom that one works with the feet. This technique of bronze casting is closely related to the refining of different metals. One needed the technical discoveries of modern science to obtain, by electrolytic refining, excessively pure iron i.e. incredibly soft, the softest iron ever. Specialists are intrigued by two pure iron samples of Indian and Chinese origins from antiquity, which are later than the Egyptian samples. They wonder how, with the rudimentary techniques of that time, could one get such a result. It is a technical miracle. So, contrary to the belief of Profs. Leclant and Mauny, decarbonized iron is harder to obtain and what they consider an accident is a performance of the Egyptian technique that must be reappraised by a critical examination of the facts that have been systematically misrepresented. It is especially necessary to proceed to a clinical and microscopic analysis of the Egyptian metallic samples. No accidental fusion made by an unskilled metallurgist of the protohistorical period would have led to iron exempt of carbon i.e. soft and mild iron. An accident such as the one that Prof. Mauny and Leclant talk about is technically and scientifically impossible. Voluntarily or involuntarily, one always gets carbonized iron i.e. iron including carbon, and the whole metallurgic technique consists in knowing what to do to diminish the carbon.

The reader who interprets the diagram on iron-carbon in the drawing (Figure 1) can see by the graph that all the iron-carbon combinations have fusion points inferior to pure iron (1535°C.) and this lowering of the fusion points is precisely a consequence of the presence of carbon. As a consequence, the products which are the first to melt in the blast furnaces or in the crucibles are varieties of pig iron (white or gray) and never pure iron. And even if one could get to the fusion temperature of pure iron, this iron, when flowing away would unite with carbon. The obtaining of soft iron is then never the result of an involuntary act and denotes a very high technical stage.

As a consequence, all the objects in soft iron recorded in Egypt are of high importance for metallurgic history and the authors of the above-mentioned articles seem not to have had the slightest idea of this fact.

As one can see, the idea of a soft and mild iron, obtained as a by-product of the preparation of other metals such as gold or copper, cannot be sustained. It is in contradiction to the scientific facts. R. Mauny writes: "The washing of the sands to extract gold was leaving as impurities a large proportion of magnetite. The whole was then melted in the crucible leaving the liquid gold at the bottom, iron scorias at the surface and in the middle pasty iron ready to be wrought. This soft iron had been used to make amulets, tools and jewelry

FIGURE 1

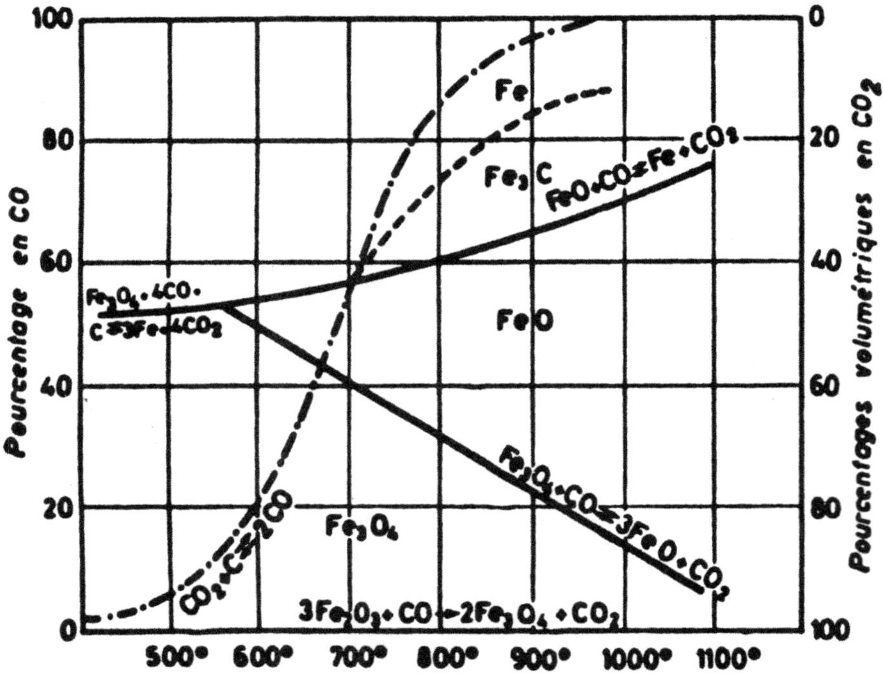

like the ones found in Tutankhamen's and other tombs." This iron was not as soft as one would think for R. Mauny confesses that it was used to make tools and four lines below, aware of the contradiction, he places these tools opposite to tool-making tools.

But the idea of using iron to make tools is sufficient to destroy the theory of accidental metallurgy of iron that was never attested by archaeology even though it is necessary to R. Mauny's theory.

Finally, the process described above by the author can never lead to the production of iron, even soft iron. If one melts gold ore, including magnetic oxide, in a crucible, one gets liquid gold melted before the iron fusion. On the other hand, the heating being on the exterior, only the crucible containing ore, there is no iron oxide reduction agent and this one stays intact. The presence of charcoal in the crucible and more precisely in the oven is necessary in order to get a reduction of the iron ore. But it is the actual invention of iron metallurgy that is the process that the Ancient Egyptians used to extract iron ore that was used to forge the tool found in the Great Pyramid, as attested by the statements and certificates of authenticity written by the inventors so that posterity wouldn't falsify their discovery. The metallurgic process used by the Egyptians of the Ancient Empire as attested by chemical analysis is the one

FIGURE 2

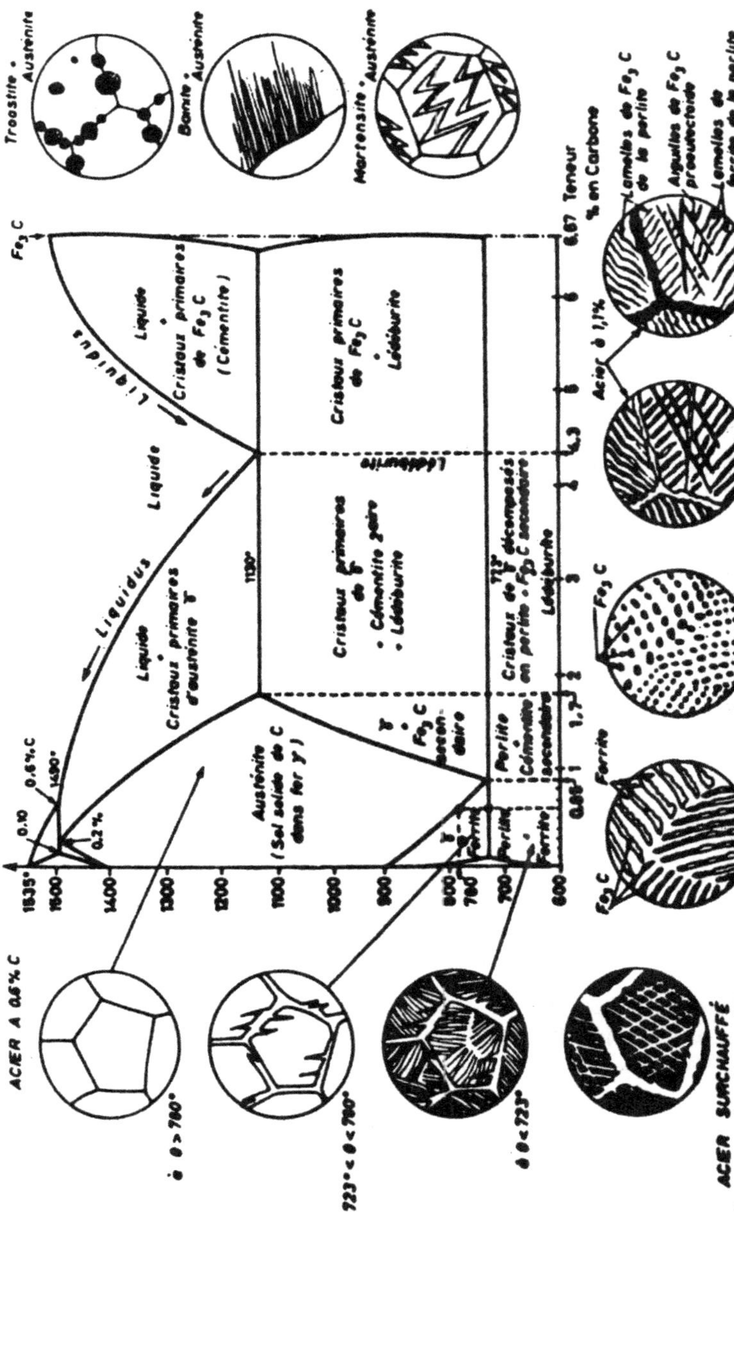

Troostite + Austénite
Bainite + Austénite
Martensite + Austénite
Liquidus
Liquide
Liquide + Cristaux primaires d'austénite γ
Liquide + Cristaux primaires de Fe3C (Cémentite)
Austénite (Sol solide de C dans fer γ)
Cristaux primaires de γ + Cémentite + Lédéburite
Cristaux primaires de Fe3C + Lédéburite
Lédéburite
Perlite
Ferrite
Fe3C
Teneur % en Carbone
Acier à 1,1%
Perlite pure C=0,85
Perlite pure globulisée
Attaque nitrique
Attaque picrale
ACIER A 0,6% C
ACIER SURCHAUFFÉ
Structure de Widmanstätten
Réseau blanc : Ferrite
Aiguilles blanches : Ferrite
Perlite non résolue en noir

that modern science in the industrial era used to extract iron from ore. The author continues: "Hard iron is only obtained by difficult techniques. By a masterly alternation of heating by bellows and hammering, one has to incorporate the necessary amount of carbon. It is by the appearance of iron that one can truely talk about voluntary metallurgy. Tradition attributes this discovery to the Cholybes of Anatolia around 1500 B.C." This passage is directly inspired by the article by Clarke.

Both of them ignore scientific facts as we demonstrated above. It is deplorable to base an argument upon wrong scientific facts and it is the case here. It is also false to talk about "tradition" when in fact one means legends.

But where did the so-called legends take place? For surely not in Egypt where iron metallurgy was invented 1700 years before the existence of the so-called Cholybes of Anatolia (Hittites).

"In many cases, "writes Mauny" such as at Akjouit where copper ore is innately allied to iron ore, metallurgists have obtained iron when they wanted to get copper and didn't know how to get rid of the iron." Wouldn't it be better to say that the so-called Mauritanian copper age could also be an iron age that began in this region of West Africa in the 5th century B.C.? One has to re-examine all the recorded facts much closer within a less aprioristic and more scientific perspective.

The use of iron was already general in the 5th century B.C. in Egypt. However, a review of iron objects of that epoch gives results and Sanfourche is right to write "the rarity of objects doesn't prove anything for such a perishable material like iron." What counts is the mastering of the technique and A.A. Sanfourche notes "it is not sufficient to consider these facts as mere curiosities not implying a common use, when it concerns an alterable metal such as iron. A single sample that lasted centuries implies the existence of a large number of others that underwent alteration."

Besides, if one was excluding from common use the materials one found only rare traces of, would we be led to the paradoxical conclusion that the use of wood at the paleolitic was an exception, a curiosity, since the samples that we know of can be counted on one hand? If the consideration of the alterability of wood warns us against this absurdity, why wouldn't it be the same *mutatis mutandis* for the metals?

Finally, some others (Firth . . .) supposed that it was the Greek mercenaries who campaigned in Nubia at the time of Psammetichus (551 B.C.)[1] who would have introduced the iron arms found in Ilkminfis' tomb, but one notices otherwise that the so-called Greek mercenaries (Carians and Ionians) had bronze arms at that time (26th dynasty, 663-525 B.C.).

In conclusion, one can say that, first, the ancient Egyptians invented iron metallurgy more than 1,000 years before the birth in history of the people the Western scholars persist in attributing the merit of this discovery to, "Cholybes of Anatolia," Hittites.

Second, the use of iron spread or more precisely increased in Egypt under the 25th Sudanese dynasty because Sudan was the great purveyor of that epoch for this metal, the Birmingham of Antiquity in order to use a now classical expression.

To suppose that iron could then have come from Assyria in war against the Sudanese pharaohs is as absurd as to assert that during World War II France was supplying the metal for the construction of its tanks from the German steel of the Ruhr Valley.

Third, the idea of an accidental iron metallurgy, and of an age of "soft iron," has to be set aside as contradicting scientific principles and the archaeological evidence.

References

Clark, J. D. L'Europe préhistorique, 1955, p. 297-298.

Dr. Conteneau, G. Manuel d'archéologie orientale, p. 1890-1891. *Paris,* 1947, Ed. Picard et Cie.

Leclant, Jean. Communication à l'Université de Strasbourg: le fer dans l'Égypte ancienne, le Soudan et l'Afrique.

Lepsius. Les métaux dans les inscriptions égyptiennes 1872, traduit en français par M. Berend, *Paris,* 1877.

Maspero. Pyramide du roi Ounas, Recueil de travaux relatifs à la philolologie et à l'archéologie égyptienne et assyrienne, vol. III, p. 177 et suivantes.

Mauny, R. Les siècles obscures de l'Afrique Noire, *Paris,* Fayard, 1970, p. 65 à 72.

Sanfourche, A. A. La fin du néolithique et l'apparition des métaux, in *Revue de la métallurgie,* nº 8, 1954, p. 521.

Note

1. According to A. Lucas, *Ancient Egyptian Materials and Industries,* a date of 595-589 B.C. is given for the rule of Psammetichus.

AFRICA'S CONTRIBUTION TO WORLD CIVILIZATION: THE EXACT SCIENCES

Cheikh Anta Diop

Since Struve edited the mathematical papyrus of Moscow, the world scientific community knows that Egyptian mathematics was not a mere aggregate of empirical "recipes" but was rather highly elaborate and theoretical. In fact, this papyrus raises two particularly difficult problems involving the surface area of the sphere (problem 10), and the volume of the pyramid's frustrum (problem 14), respectively. Those who have dealt with mathematics, even minimally, know how delicate the treatment of the curved surface is. But the "formula" found by the scribe 1,700 years before Archimedes is rigorously accurate: $S = 2\pi R^2$ for the surface area of the hemisphere. Indeed, to solve the problem it was necessary to calculate what the surface area of the hemisphere was and then multiply the result by two to obtain the surface area of the whole sphere.

The sphere and the circumscribed cylinder, having the same height as the diameter of the sphere are theoretically two inseparable bodies. Their two surface areas are identical and equal to $4\pi R^2$. Being as shrewd as they were, the Egyptians could not have missed this fact. He who can do more can do less. That is why, it was this body of figures that Archimedes considered to be his most remarkable discovery and chose as an epitaph; and it is indeed this epitaph which authenticated the discovery by Cicero of Archimedes grave in Syracuse, Sicily.

But Archimedes could not have been unaware that prior to him the Egyptians had discovered the very same theorem that he probably used, arranged and presented in his own way.[7] His other dealings with Egyptian science testify to that. Speaking exclusively of what is certain, one must say that the Egyptians have passed down to posterity the formula of the exact surface area of the sphere and the exact "formula" of the volume of the cylinder, calculated with the value of $\pi=3.16$.[8] Archimedes did not mention these results at all in his treatise entitled *On the Sphere and Cylinder* written about two thousand years after the Egyptian mathematical papyri.

Problem 50 of the Rhind papyrus provides the exact surface area of the circle having a diameter equal to 9 and a value of $\pi=3.16$ in the following formula:

$$S = \frac{(8 \,.\, d)^2}{9} = \frac{\pi \,.\, d^2}{4} = R^2$$

Archimedes made no mention of this formula in his treatise entitled: *Measurement of the Circle.*

He did the same thing for the calculation of the value π for which he gave the lower and upper limits.

Finally, in his treatise entitled *On the Equilibrium of Planes or Centres of Gravity of Planes,* nowhere did Archimedes show that the Egyptians had already mastered the theory of levers of all kinds, as well as that of the inclined plane, before he did. The scales with annular slides which made it possible to weigh more accurately is the proof of this and it has been confirmed by the works of G. Davies.[9] A further proof is that of the Chadouf[10] which is the current application of the lever with uneven arms. Because he could use this device, Archimedes could say: "Give me a place to stand and I will move the earth."

What was the research method of Archimedes who is regarded as the most ingenious representative of Greek mathematics and intellectualism? Archimedes described it in a letter to his friend Eratosthenes who was a geometrician. Archimedes did not hesitate to tell him how he proceeded. Indeed he first weighed the geometrical figures and only when they were equal did he use mathematics to demonstrate that they were equal. He advised his friend to follow the same method.[11] But Paul Ver Ecke suspects that Archimedes was dishonest and simply wanted to hide the real sources of inspiration and very carefully cover his tracks.[12]

Could this hidden source by anything else than Egyptian? It certainly could not. Indeed, like all the Greek scientists, Archimedes went to study or to further his studies in Egypt. It is only when he came back from Egypt that he "invented" the endless screw that Egyptians had been using for centuries before he was born for the extraction of percolated water.[13]

And so, the method of the most important representative of Greek mathematics is forgotten when gratuitous mention is made of Egyptian empirical methods and scientific recipes.

In studying the method that, in all likelihood, the scribe followed to find the surface area of the sphere, Struve shows that the scribe must have associated the sphere to the circumscribed cylinder of a same surface, of a height equal to the diameter of the big circle of the sphere (as Archimedes did later on). This made it possible for the scribe to deduce a general empirical/theoretical method for the study of curved surface areas and volumes and establish the relationship between the surface area and the volumes of these two bodies. In this way, Struve adds, problem 10 of the Moscow papyrus provided both the formula for the surface area of the sphere and that for the length of the circumference.[14]

In order to understand the significance of this last remark, it is important to remember that the formula $C=\pi D$ is attributed to Dinostratus. This formula which gives the length of the circumference is believed to have been established by the Egyptians 1,400 years before its alledged Greek author. Quoting the works of L. Cron, Struve also points out that in the field of mechanics, the Egyptians had a much wider knowledge than was ever acknowledged. Their planes were as accurate as those of modern engineers.[15]

He concludes that it therefore stands to reason that the Greeks explicitly admitted that the Egyptians were their masters in the field of geometry which came to

Greece from Egypt and not from Babylonia. Struve also insists on the accuracy of Egyptian geometry.

Indeed, an empirical geometry using "recipes" like the Babylonian geometry for instance could never have come to establish formulas approaching the accuracy of Egyptian geometry. This leads us to the second problem, problem 14, of the Moscow papyrus dealing with the volume of the pyramid's frustrum.

The scribe gives the following formula:

$$V = {}^{h}/_{3}\,(a^2 + ab + b^2)$$

where a = the length of the side of the square of the bottom; b = the length of the side of the square at the top; h = height separating the planes of the two squares.

Even Peet who was one of the most vocal detractors of Egyptian mathematics acknowledges the fact that for 4,000 years researchers in the field of mathematics have not been able to improve on that formula.

In fact it is a rigorously accurate formula.

For the same figure Mesopotanian geometry gives the following formula:

$$V = {}^{h}/_{2}\,(a^2 + b^2)$$

This formula which does not even come close to the Egyptian one is wrong. The same situation is observed for the volume of the cone's frustrum:

$$V = {}^{h}/_{2} = (S + S')$$

S and S′ being the surface areas of the circles at the bottom and at the top. Mesopotamian geometry calculated the volume of a cylinder with the value of $\pi=3$ by likening it to a prism, whereas, as was shown above, the corresponding formula in Egyptian geometry is rigorously accurate: In actual fact the whole corpus of Egyptian mathematics does not include a single erroneous formula be it in geometry, in algebra, in trigonometry, in arithmetic or in mechanics: therefore, it can only be a highly theoretical science.

If Egyptian mathematics were simply empirical, one would have to conclude that empiricism outclasses theory, because for centuries mathematicians have been trying in vain to figure out the so-called empirical recipes which resulted in Egyptian mathematics: popular empiricism would then be less accessible than theory.

The So-Called Pythagorean Theorem

Some elements of Egyptian mathematics make it possible to affirm that Pythagoras did not demonstrate the theorem that is attributed to him and a large number of mathematicians who know anything at all about the Egyptian data are conscious of this fact.

Indeed, going back to Plutarch (Isis and Osiris) and to Plato (Politics) one would already know that of all the right triangles, the one whose sides are 3,6,5, respectively, is sacred (problem 6 of the Moscow Papyrus).[17]

And it is readily admitted that the Egyptians certainly had a knowledge of particular cases of the so-called Pythayorean Theorem. But no one wanted to admit that they also demonstrated this knowledge in the general case.

However, it is known that this theorem was certainly discovered along with the irrational numbers, in the general case, without specific numeric value. This can be shown in the case involving the duplication of the square starting from a diagonal.

There exists in relation to this an Egyptian unit of length, the accurate definition of which leaves no doubt that the Egyptians had cognizance of the theorem of the hypothenuse as well as the existence of irrational numbers. This unit of length was known as the "double-remen." The double-remen is the length of the diagonal of a square whose side = a = one (royal) cubit. So $d = a\sqrt{2} = 20.6 \times \sqrt{2} = 29.1325$ inches.[18]

We know that $\sqrt{2}$ is the irrational number *par excellence* but the Egyptians even knew how to extract the square root of fractions. Indeed the Egyptians used this unit of length to draw squares having a surface which was the double of that of the initial square whose side = *a*, or to divide into two an initial double square. It is not possible to find a more obvious application of the theorem of the square of the hypothenuse in the most general case and this was done without mechanical value at least 2,000 before Pythagorus was born.

It also appears that the Egyptians had a thorough knowledge of irrational numbers. This is typically confirmed by the geometrical (not the arithmetical) definition that the Egyptians had for the square root; the phrase was: "to make the (right) angle of a number. For instance: To make the (right) angle of $9=3$. Three is the hypotenuse of the isosceles right triangle whose side is *a:* for instance, to make the (right) angle of $(2a^2) = A\sqrt{2}$; To make the right angle of $(20.6\sqrt{2})^2 = (20.6)^2 \times 2 - 20.6\sqrt{2}$. This geometric definition of the square root is sufficient to show that the Egyptians had mastered the theorem of the square on the hypothenuse and had already made several applications of that.

Quadrature of a Circle

In the history of mathematics, problem 48 of the Rhind Mathematical Papyrus (RMP) is the first one ever to state the problem of the quadrature of a circle. The surface area of a square with a side = 9 was compared to that of a circle whose diameter was also equal to nine.

Trigonometry

The Egyptians were the first to invent trigonometry. Problems 56 and 60 of the RMP all deal with the calculations of trigonometric lines: sine, cosine, tangent, cotangent. Each time, two trigonometric lines are given and the third one is to be determined. Problem 56 involves the calculation of the incline of a pyramid, which is the same as calculating a tangent.

The scribe likened the light of the pyramid to the axis of the sine and, the cosine to half of the parallel of the side of the square at the bottom which passes through the center of the square.

$$\sin = 250 \text{ cubit}$$

$$\text{ws} = {}^{360}/_{2} = 180 \text{ cubits}$$

$$\tan = {}^{250}/_{180}$$

Then the scribe reversed this relation to determine the cotangent:

$$\cot = {}^{250}/_{180} = {}^{1}/_{2} + {}^{1}/_{5} + {}^{1}/_{50}$$

He multiplied this result by 7 to express the final result in palms. Indeed a cubit equals 7 palms. The final result is

$$\cot \alpha = 7 \times ({}^{1}/_{2} + {}^{1}/_{5} + {}^{1}/_{50}) = 5 \text{ palms } {}^{1}/_{25}$$

For the scribe this result had the value of an angle because it enabled him to affirm that the displacement of 5 palms along the axis of the cosine corresponds to a rise of a cubit along the axis of a sine.

It is much later that modern mathematics invented the trigonometric unitary radius.

The Surface Areas of Elementary Figures

Problem No. 49 of the *RMP* deals with the surface areas of the rectangle, $S=1\times1$. Problem No. 5 deals with the surface areas of the triangle, $S = {}^{b\times h}/_{2}$. No. 52 deals with the surface area of the trapezoid, $S = {}^{A+B\times h}/_{2}$. We have already seen that problem 41 deals with the volume of the cylinder, and problem 44 with the volume of the cube. Problem 46 deals with a parallelepiped whose base is square. The volume is given and the three faces must be determined. It is likely that the problem on plate VIII of the Kahum papyrus deals with the volume of the half-sphere with a diameter = 8 units, as Borchardt postulated.[19]

Mathematical Series

The Egyptians were masters when it came to geometric and arithmetic progressions. They knew how to add them or how to find the sequence of terms.

Problem 79 of the RMP deals with a geometric progression whose ratio is $r=7$ and the scribe applied the formula accurately:

$$S = a \frac{R^n - 1}{R - 1}$$

Problem 40 deals with an arithmetic progression. The problem deals with the proportional division of 100 loaves among five people in such a way that the shares would be in arithmetic progression and the sum of the two lowest shares is equal to $^1/_7$ of the sum of the three highest shares.[20]

Problem 64 deals with distributing differences, that is, distributing 10 loaves to 10 people in such a way that the difference between the shares each person and his neighbor is $^1/_8$ of an hekat. One comes to the same result as the scribe by applying the classical formula of an arithmetic progression:

$$1 = a + (n\text{-}l)d \text{ with}$$
$$1 = \text{the last term}$$
$$a = \text{the first term}$$
$$d = \text{the common difference } ^1/_8$$

The Rhind papyrus shows that the Egyptians did invent the arithmetic and geometric progressions. It is interesting to note that the most famous ''alleged'' discoveries of Pythagoras deal with geometric and arithmetic series. All the operations that he made—summations in particular—were commonly made by the Egyptians. For instance, the summation of the terms of the simplest arithmetic progression corresponding to the series of natural numbers (and in which the relation of or difference between the term is equal to the unit) gives the *trigonal* or *triangular* numbers.

In order to find out the tetragonal or square numbers that are 1,4,9,16, and 25, one had to find the summation of the terms of a progression in which the difference of terms was 2, that is a progression of odd numbers like 1,3,5,7,9. Pythagoras believed that the soul was tetragonal and we will come pack to this fact to emphasize that the ideas attributed to Pythagoras are without any doubt of Egyptian origin.

The progressions in which the difference of terms is 3 gives the pentagonal number 1,5,12,22,35. When the difference is 4, one obtains the hexagonal numbers 1,6,15,28. With the same process heptagonal, octogenal and enneagonal numbers can be obtained.

Let us come back to the tetragonal or square numbers. According to Pythagoras they characterize the shape of the soul. They can all be found by means of a series of successive rectangles called "gnomons", from a square unit. One then obtains, as described above, the series of odd arithmetic numbers: 1,3,5,7, etc.

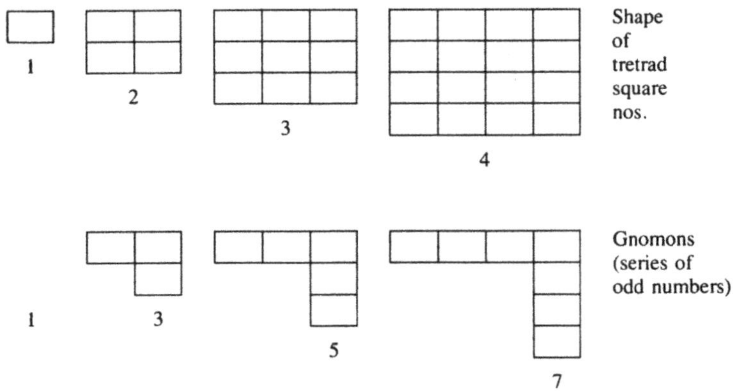

All this explains the importance of the tetrad and the gnomon in Pythagoras' philosophy.

Pythagoras and his disciples have been so much influenced by Egypt that, in spite of the fact that they spoke a different language and had a different writing, they did use the Egyptian hieroglyphic signs in their pre-algebraic mathematical notations. For instance, they used the hieroglyphic sign for water to symbolize the progression of numbers.

The series of odd numbers was represented by a right-angle shaped gnomon (7). The series of even numbers was represented by the sign (=) of the scale. The circle, which was the sign of the Ra, the Egyptian sun God represented eternal motion (O).[21]

We cannot show in a more convincing way that the whole of Pythagoras' philosophical doctrine as well as his theory of numbers were extremely indebted to Egyptian thought.

Algebra

The Egyptians invented algebra. The series of the *RMP* problems described by the Egyptian "Aha," that is, quantity in its most general meaning, are algebra problems in which the unit plays exactly the same role as the unknown factor x is found in modern algebra. The reasoning of all these problems is essentially algebraic as admitted by Eisenlohr, Canton Revillov and even by a detractor like Neugebauer.

The problems studied in the Rhind Papyrus belong to three categories:

1. Problems 26-27 are solved by the method of false assumption. Problem 24. "A quantity and its $^1/_7$ added together become 19. What is the quantity?" Obviously this comes down to the first degree equation:

$$X + {}^x/_7 = 19$$

2. Problems 28 and 29. Problem 28: "A quantity and its $^2/_3$ are added together and from the sum $^1/_3$ of the sum is subtracted, and 10 remains. What is the quantity?" The corresponding first degree equation is:

$$X + {}^{2X}/_3 - {}^1/_3 \,.\, (X + {}^{2x}/_3) = 10$$

3. Problems 30-34.[22] Problem 30: "What is the quantity of which $^2/_3$ $^1/_{10}$ will make 10?" The first degree equation is:

$$X\,({}^2/_3 + {}^1/_{10}) = 10$$

Second Degree Equations

Two problems of the Berlin papyrus deal with a system of simultaneous equations and one of them is a second degree equation. Written in modern form they would be:

$$\text{I}\quad \begin{array}{rcrcr} X^2 & + & Y^2 & = & 100 \\ 4X & - & 3Y & = & 0 \end{array}$$

$$\text{II}\quad \begin{array}{rcrcr} X^2 & + & Y^2 & = & 400 \\ 4X & - & 3Y & = & 0 \end{array}$$

Here is a second degree equation: "How do you divide 100 in two parts in such a way that the square root of one part equals $^3/_4$ of the square root of the other part?" One must write:

$$X^2 + Y^2 = 100$$

$$\text{but } Y = {}^{3X}/_4$$

$$\text{So, } X^2 = {}^9/_{16}\ \ X^2 = 100$$

Gillings thinks that problems 28 and 29 of the Rhind papyrus are the oldest examples recorded in the history of mathematics. They existed well before Diaphantes of Alexandria came to be. They belong to the a category of problems called "think of a number" or "find a number such as." The weighting of quantities: Series of problems called the *"Pesu"* problems in the Rhind papyrus.

In the problems dealing with mass and weight, food quantities in particular were accompanied by a coefficient of utility. These quantities were weighted so as to take into consideration only their useful weight. Example: If the "pesu" of a load is 12, it means that the loaf contains $^1/_{12}$ bushel.

Recto Table of the Rhind Papyrus: Arithmetics

The Recto of the Rhind Papyrus contains the result of the division of 2 by a series of odd numbers from 3 to 101. The results are expressed in unit fractions whose numerator is always equal to one.[23] Today, mathematicians still do not know exactly how to determine the use of this old table. Moreover, they do not know how to figure out the method of decomposition used by the ancient Egyptians. (For further study of this a useful work is Professor Maurice Caveing's dissertation which deals with the history of mathematics in antiquity.)[24]

This table is found in 2000 B.C. and in 600 A.D. Gillings observes that the Greek, Roman, Arabic, and Byzantine mathematicians were never able to discover a more efficient technique to treat a fraction as ordinary as $^p/_9$. In their arithmetic the Greeks have kept the old Egyptian fraction notation of 2200 B.C. Indeed, on the Greek papyrus one can read that $^1/_{17}$ of a silver talent equals 352 $+ ^1/_2 + ^1/_{17} + ^1/_{34} + ^1/_{52}$ drachmas.

Modern mathematicians wanted to know whether the ancient Egyptians proceeded empirically (by trial and error) or theoretically. So, in 1967, a computer was programmed in the U.S. to make all the decompositions that were possible and it produced 22,295 figures. If the scribe's divisions were based on theory, then among the tens of thousands of figures, he had chosen only the 49 simplest and most elegant ones. If this is so, then he will not be bested by the 20th century electronic machine, invented 4,000 years later. That is exactly what happened. "We can conclude that, in this division as elsewhere, the computer did not find a decomposition superior to that given by the ancient scribe."[25] The method that the Egyptians used figures in all the laws of elementary arithmetic, a field that it is not possible to deal with in this paper.

It must be said that, traditionally, philosophers and scientists were persecuted in the Greek Athenian state. On the contrary, the Egyptian State has always encouraged the development of science, philosophy, and arts. Up to the end of the history of the Indo-European state, science and philosophy were as antinomical to the state in continental Greece as they were inseparable from the state in Egypt.

Most of the scientists who gave Greece its scientific fame were persecuted and had to flee from Greece to take refuge in Egypt. Almost all of them went to Egypt for training. Anexagoras, Socrates, Aristotle, Plato were persecuted or had to flee to escape persecution. Aristotle did not hesitate to testify to the fact that if the Egyptian priests reached such a high level in theoretical and speculative science, it was because they were free from material worries. And this was because the state supported them.

The Egyptian Calendar

There have been an impressive number of inventions in Africa between 2000 and 3000 B.C. This was the time period in which indigenous domestication of plants and animals occurred, and this was done by means of indigenous techniques.

It was during that time that metallurgy was invented. The Egyptians of the ancient empire no doubt knew the metallurgy of iron.[26] Also, the recent archeological discoveries made by the Belgium in Burundi confirm our challenging ideas concerning the first iron age in Africa.[27]

Moreover, it is now common knowledge that in 4236 B.C., the Egyptians had already invented a calendar based on the heliacal rising of Sothis or Sirius (the brightest star in the sky) which appeared every 1,460 years. Indeed the Egyptians knew the two types of year: 365 days and 365 days + 1/4. The first one contains 12 months and 30 days = 360 + the five epagomenal days which were dedicated to the birthdays of Osiris, Horus, Seth, Isis and Nephthys, the five Egyptian Gods. So, methologically speaking, Osiris was indeed born the night of December 25 as was Jesus Christ who can be compared to Osiris in this case and in many others.

However, the Egyptians know that the civil year of 365 days was 1/4 of a day shorter than the solar year. This meant that their civil year slipped steadily backwards through the solar year, 1/2 a day every two years and one day every four years. Therefore, as early as the fourth millenium B.C., the Egyptians had already created the leap year. However, it is remarkable that they preferred to choose a time-lag of 1,460 years in order to add a whole year instead of adding one day every four years. Indeed, this time period of 1,460 years is the period which separates the two heliacal risings of Sothis. The latitude of Memphis is certainly not the place where the calendar was invented for reasons which will be too long to develop here.

The heliacal rise of Sothis (a star) coincided with that of the sun. Even Neugebauer, who was a great detractor of Egyptian science, said that "this calendar is indeed the only intelligent calendar which existed in human history."[28] And Gillings added, "it is simpler even than the 'perpetual calendar' which though recommended for world wide use by astronomers seems condemned to remain forever in some official pigeon-holes in all countries" (p. 235).

About the two calendars Gillings concludes: "These two calendars (of 365 and 365 1/4 days) existing side by side from, it is thought, the time of the first pharaoh of upper and lower Egypt, was "the most scientific organization of calendar which has yet been used by man."

We said in our book entitled *Civilization or Barbarism* that "until today, with the Egyptian sideral calendar which could very well be reactivated, humanity or at least Africa has a scale of absolute chronology compared with which the Christian era, the hegira and various landmarks, are completely relative.[30]

At the annual congress on Egyptology, held February 24-26, 1984, at Los Angeles Southwest College, Black Americans of the Diaspora reactivated this calendar using 4,236 (give or take 4 years) as the absolute chronological landmark.

Unlike Mesopotamia which never managed to establish a calendar worthy of the name and which, even at its highest period of development had not gone beyond the stage of drawing up "ephemerides." When the chronological gap became very wide the king simply added a thirteenth or fourteenth month to the year.

Because Rome had no scientists or astronomers worthy of the name, he had an astronomer come from Egypt. Similarly when an eclipse of the sun brought widespread panic in the ranks of the Greek army during Alexander the Great's battle against the Persians, it was not Aristotle, the king's tutor, but a priest, an Egyptian astronomer, who restored calm by giving a scientific explanation of the phenomenon.

The Carlsberg papyrus no. 9 describes a method for determining the phases of the moon deriving from more ancient sources and which were in no way influenced by the hellenistic sciences. The same is true of the Carlsberg papyrus no. 1 which proves that there existed treatises on Egyptian astronomy.

In the Denkmaller III, plate 228(b), Lepsius reproduced a figure which represents a real system of coordinates centered on the observatory to locate the position of the stars according to the time of the day or night. The positions are recorded on a graph accurately squared using coordinates.

Egyptian science was well aware of the concept of coordinates. Ivan Van Sertima[31] published a diagram drawn by an ancient Egyptian architect during the third dynasty which is no more and no less than a descending curve. The descending ordinates are given in hieratic writing according to the divisions into equal values of x (abcissa).

We have seen that the two Egyptian calendars were already in use during the first dynasty. This did not prevent Diagenes Laerces, Thales' biographer (6th century B.C.), from writing that he was the first to divide the year into 365 days.

Mechanics

Much could be said about Egyptian mechanics. Ivan van Sertima[32] published in the *Journal of African Civilizations* the model of an Egyptian glider dating from the fourth or third century B.C. This object was in Room 22 of the Egyptian museum in Cairo and bore the no. 6347. It is 14 cm long. The article is signed jointly by Khalil Messiha and Guirguis Messira. "The model attracted my attention," said Messira, "as it was very much like the aeroplane models I used to make some 20 years ago. It was discovered in Sakkara, in 1898, and is made of sycamore wood."[33]

The two authors quoted above are aeronautical engineers. Dr. Gamal Mokhtar, a former Egyptian minister and former Director of Antiquities in Egypt, is associated with this publication. These are the facts: it was a NASA official who collected the documents. Dr. Gamal Mokhtar writes that the discovery was made during a visit to the museum by the members of the International Aerospace Education Commission. Having regard to the credibility of the authors, we relate the fact although we ourselves are unable to authenticate it. We can have no personal opinion on the matter as we have not yet seen the model itself, only a copy of it. In any case, confirmation of the fact would be of vital importance.

We do not have space here to go into statistics and the mathematical bases of Egyptian architecture, using the values of the series (oudjat) $1/2 + 1/4 + 1/8 + 1/16 + 1/32$ to determine the proportions of the monuments and in particular just how thin to make the columns.

The Egyptians routinely siphoned off liquids using atmospheric pressure and the difference in level.

Again, we do not have the space to speak of the influence of the Egyptian cosomogonies (Heliopolitan and Hermopolitan) on Greek philosophy, particularly pre-Socratic philosophy. However, there is a very close connection between Plato's Timaeus and the heliopolitan cosomogony and the latter would help to clarify many unclear passages in this book.[34] Empedocles merely repeated the theory of the four elements of heliopolitan cosmogny.

Medicine

Opinion is virtually unanimous that in this field, especially in the area of bone surgery, the Egyptians had already achieved the scientific level from the time of the ancient empire. The basis for this belief can be found in the 48 minutely detailed descriptions of cases of brain injury in the Smith papyrus. What we find there is in fact location of the brain functions, 3,000 years before Broca; in fact, the 48 cases of injury all relate to the skull and the neck and in each case to the side effects on parts of the body. Even those furthest away from the brain are noted. "Case 6" describes for the first time the cerebral convolutions that take place when the cranium is pulled away, like "the wrinkles that form on copper when it is being smelted." "Case 8": an injury to the brain causes "an inversion of the eyeballs" and the patient "drags his feet when he walks." "Case 22": a perforated temple causes loss of speech. "Case 31": dislocation of the neck vertebrae causes paralysis of the arms and legs. . . .

For each case, a cure is given if there is one. The Ebers papyrus shows that the Egyptians had discovered blood circulation and the functioning of the heart. The document states that: "the heart speaks in all the organs." the reference is to the heart beat which is reflected in the pulse.

Theophrastus, Dioscorides and Galen all consulted annals of Imhotep in the Memphis Temple Library until the second century A.D. Hippocrates had already done this before them in the fifth century.

The influence of Egyptian medicine on Greek medicine can be observed. For example, the method given in the Carlsberg papyrus no. 4, whether it is true or false, has been copied out verbatim by "the father of medicine": I refer to the clove of garlic method for diagnosing sterility in women.

Like all the other Egyptian sciences, medicine survived in the rest of Africa, but deteriorated as Africa became more and more isolated, and as the continent fell under foreign domination.

Dr. Charles S. Finch quotes the Edinburgh Medical Journal, 1884 where Dr. R.W. Felkin describes a Cesarean operation performed by a Ugandan surgeon using traditional medicine. Both mother and child were saved, something that had never been seen at that time even in Europe, where they were usually content to save the infant at best.[35]

Never has a similar case been recorded in ancient civilizations.

By way of conclusion to this second part dealing with the study of how the values of the civilization of Egypt were transmitted to the rest of the world and to Greece in particular, we can refer to the title of the Rhind Papyrus "Rules for Studying[35] nature, for understanding everything that exists, every mystery, every secret."

Dr. Faustus could have signed this declaration of belief. In fact, it was not until the renaissance that F. Bacon stated a similar lay belief in the almighty power of the number.

The Greeks never went any further in the expression of man's desire or ability to master nature through science and through mathematics in particular. Contrary to a current belief, Egypt was not that land hidebound by a religiosity that prevented it from conquering nature through science. Let it be remembered that it was in fact this country, which through science brought mankind out of prehistory to the real conquest of civilization. The first state organization in the world was in the Nile Valley, in Nubia in Sudan, first at Qustul,[36] then in Egypt with Menes (circa 3,150 B.C.).

Bureaucracy, that is to say, the scientific and scholarly organization of the state, was first of all a tremendous step forward, a technological conquest. It has often been disparaged much more because of Eurocentrism, than because it constituted any real danger: for even today, what State even a revolutionary one has managed to do without it?

It is only true that it was not an invention of the Indo-European city state in the period following the prehistoric era; it was without question an African invention for controlling the organization of the human community on the large scale of the Egyptian nation state from 3,150 B.C.

Furthermore, "the dialogue of a desperate person with his soul" shows that the Egyptians were not satisfied to tame external nature through science but that they made an equally thorough study of human nature.

We perceive the falseness and the danger of the stereotyped opinions advanced by the ideologists of the different schools, who could not accept the idea that civilization began in Africa.

However, this would mean forgetting the opinions that were current until the XIX century. In fact, Lenormant in his study of the first Oriental civilizations reminds us that throughout antiquity the unanimous opinion of the Indo-European and semitic peoples, who were then lagging behind the Blacks, was that the descendants of Kam were particularly adept at taming nature, creating science and material civilization and that they were the first to embark on this course: mankind everywhere owes them its early progress and the first civilizations.

Notes

Since Dr. Diop's paper was published in *Nile Valley Civilizations* (*JAC*, vol. 6, no. 2) as two separate articles to fit the thematic structure of that issue, the notes in this, the second article, begin with note 7.

7. V. Struve. Mathematischer papyrus des Staalichen Museums der Schönen Kunste in Moskau (Quellen und Studien zur Geschiste der Mathematik, Abteilung A: Quellen, Band I) Berlin, 1930.
8. $V=\pi R^2$ h: See the Rhind mathematical papyrus, T.E. Peet, ed. no. 41.
9. N de G. Davies. Rekhmire p. 1L IV.
10. N de G. Davies. The Tomb of two Scupltors at Thebes. P. h 28.
11. Archimedes dedicated his treatise *The Method* to his friend E. Ralosthenes and revealed that his mechanical method (of weighing geometric figures) was the hidden source of his main discoveries.
12. Paul ver Ecke: *Les Oeuvres Completes d'Archimede* (Archimedes Complete Works) Albert Blanchard, Paris, 1960. Introduction p. SLIV-SLV.
13. P. ver Ecke, op. cit. p. XIV-SV. Strabon geography translated by Amedee Tardieu Vol. III book SVII p. 433. Diodore de Sicile: *History.* Vol II Book V. Chapter XXXVII, p. 39.
    Also, Albert Slosman writes: "For let us not forget that it was because of the rampant use of plagiarism among the Greeks that Clement of Alexandria said at the time: "A one thousand page book will not be long enough to cite the names of my fellow countrymen who have used and abused the Egyptian science." Albert Slosman *Le livrede l'au-dela de la vie.* (The book of the Life Beyond) Boudouin, Paris, 1979.
14. "Die Aufgabe Nr. 10 hat uns aber zusammen mit der Formel fur die Kugeloberflache auch die Formel fur den Kreisumfang gebracht," Struve; op. cit., pp. 177-178.
15. "Die agyptischen Werkzeichnungen erweisen sich abenso genau wie die der modernen Ingenieure."
16. P. ver Ecke, op. cit. p. XXXI. That is why an Egyptian priest told Diodores of Sicily that once the Greeks returned home they took credit for all the sciences they learned in Egypt.
17. Pythagoras and Plato, who received their training in Egypt, adopted this method of notation.
18. Richard J. Gillings: *Mathematics in the Time of the Pharoahs.* M.I.T. Press, Cambridge, Massachusetts and London, England. Chapter 20, p. 208.

19. Borchardt: AZ, 35, p. 150-152.
20. Peet RMP. p. 78.
21. Ferdinand Hoefer: Histoire des Mathematiques, Librarie Hachette. Paris, 1984 (4th edition), pp. 99, 129-130.
22. R. J. Gillings, op. cit.
    Peet: RMP - Problems 24 to 34 (op. cit.)
23. R. J. Gillings, op. cit. p. 181.
24. Maurice Coveing: Idealite mathematique grecgue. Paris.
25. R. J. Gillings, op. cit. p. 52.
26. Cheikh Anta Diop. "La metallurgie du fer sous l'ancien Empire" (The Metallurgy of Iron in the Ancient Empire) in *Bulletin B. IFAN,* vol. XXXV, Series B, no. 3, Dakar, 1973.
27. Cheikh Anta Diop. "Vers une remise en question de l'age du fer en Afrique" (Toward a Reassessment of the Iron Age in Africa), in *Notes Africaines* IFAN, no. 152, October 1976.
28. O. Neugebauer. *The Exact Sciences in Antiquity.* New York: Harper, 1962, p. 81; quoted by Gillings, op. cit., p. 235.
29. J.W.S. Sewell "The Calendars and Chronology," in *Legacy of Egypt,* S.R.K. Glanville ed., London: Oxford University Press, 1963, p. 7; quoted by Gillins, op. cit., p. 236.
30. Cheikh Anta Diop. *Civilisation ou Barbarie* (Civilization or Barbarism). Paris, 1981: Presence Africaine, p. 356.
31. Ivan Van Sertima, op. cit., p. 77.
32. Ibid., p. 92-99.
33. *Blacks in Science,* Ivan Van Sertima (ed.), p. 92; Qudjat = Eye of Horus.
34. cf. Cheikh Anta Diop: Civilisation ou Barbarie, chapter 17.
35. Charles Finch, "The African Background of Medical Science," in *Blacks in Science* op. cit. p. 152.
36. Bruce Williams, Chicago Oriental Institute.

Bibliography

P. Lenormant, *Ancient History of the East,* vol. III, p. 100.

UNESCO, Seminar at Athens, March 30 - April 3, 1981. Racism, science and pseudo-science-close relationship between the Indo-Europeans, the Blacks and the Boschmen from the viewpoint of the antigones of seplems. Article by Albert Jacquart, "Science and Racism."

M.H. Day, M.D. Leakey and C. Magore, "A New Hominid Fossil Skull," (L.H.18) from the Ngaloba Beds, Laetoli Northern Tanzania in Nature, vol. 284, March 6, 1980.

David Pilbeam, "From Primates to Man," *Pour la Science,* May 1984.

Proc. Nat. Acad. Sci. USA, vol. 78, no. 4, pp. 2638-2642, April 1981. Popular biology. A. Piazza, P. Menozzi and L.L. Cavalli Sforza, "Synthetic Gene Frequency Maps of Man and Selective effects of Climate."

M.J. Johnson, D.C. Wallace, S.D. Ferris, M.C. Baltazzi and L.L. Cavilli Sforza, "Radiations of Human Mitochondria DNA Types analysed by Restruction Endonuclease Cleavage Patterns."

La recherche, no. 148, October 1983.

Beaujouan, C., "Ancient and Medieval Science," PUF, 1957.

Archaelogical Dictionary of Techniques, vols. I and II. Editions de l'Accueil, 1963.

Gimpel, Jean, *The Industrial Revolution in the Middle Ages,* Editions du Seuil, 1975.

Van Sertima, Ivan, *They Came Before Columbus,* Flamarion, 1981.

Y. Al-Hassan, Ahmad, "Islam and Science," *Research,* no. 138, July 1982.

THE CHANGING PERCEPTION OF C.A. DIOP AND HIS WORK: THE PREEMINENCE OF A SCIENTIFIC SPIRIT

James G. Spady

"C. A. Diop's entire approach is based on a dual assumption—the African nature and Negritude of the Egyptian civilization, a Negritude that only begins to alter with foreign invasions (during the Middle Empire) and the territorial expansions of Egypt to the New Empire. In order to evaluate the scientific validity of this assumption, which is, in fact, the crux of the great debate on Egyptian civilization, every responsible historian must first question the documents and vestiges the Ancient Egyptians left behind, the first hand accounts of travelers and ancient Greek and Roman scientists who knew the Egyptians, the actual civilizations which seem to resemble the civilization of Ancient Egypt the most. This is indeed what C.A. Diop did without exception during the course of his research. As far as methodology is concerned, his procedure is beyond reproach."[1]

Dr. Aboubacry Moussa Lam, who made the above statement, is a member of the Department D'Histoire, Faculté des Letters et Sciences Humaines, Universite De Dakar in Senegal, where Cheikh Anta Diop directs the Radiocarbon Laboratory. The mere fact that we can begin this discussion of Diop's work with a lucid, penetrating assessment of his methodological procedure by a fellow African Egyptologist, a Senegalese colleague with a Ph.D. in Egyptology from the Sorbonne University, is a clear indication of the extent to which Diop has influenced the field of Egyptology as well as pioneered in establishing a firm foundation for the growth and development of an entire cadre of scientifically trained African Egyptologists. Concomitantly, this has led to a changed perception of his work.

When we published, "Negritude, PanBanegritude and the Diopian Philosophy of African History,"[2] nearly 15 years ago, it was the first full essay on Diop to appear in an English language scientific journal. One has to recall that this was a period when the Fages, Olivers, McCalls and others were considered the foremost authorities on African history. Even among Black scholars and publicists in the United States, Basil Davidson was widely read, discussed and taught to the exclusion of African Africanists. It was sometimes agreed that

This article is dedicated to Alioune Diop, Mercer Cook, Harun Kofi Wangara, and Theophile Obenga.

since Diop's writings were written in French, and published in Paris, there was no choice but to turn to the above mentioned. But what about the writings of J.F.A. Ajayi, Bethwell A. Ogot, S. O. Biobaku, G. Olusanya, K. Onwuka Dike, and other highly capable African historians? As a matter of fact, even with the "discovery" of Diop, Afro-American Africanists wantonly ignore the current body of scholarship produced by Africans in the growing discipline of African Studies. Suppose continental Africans decided to rely entirely upon Euro-American writers to learn about the "black experience". What an experience it would be!

Actually, Diop's *"L'Unité Culturelle De L'Afrique Noire* received an English translation—*The Cultural Unity of Negro Africa*—published by Présence Africaine as early as 1962. What one has to wonder is whether the Afro-American's early encounter with Diop in print may have adversely affected their perception of his Ancient Egyptian thesis. During the seething decade of the 1960's one of the most widely read collection of essays by a Black author was James Baldwin's *Nobody Knows My Name.* It appeared in 1961. In a highly evocative essay entitled. "Princes and Powers," Baldwin introduces the name of Cheikh Anta Diop to many for the first time. But how did he choose to do it? In a sweeping *encounter* coverage of *Le Congres des Ecrivains et Artistes Noir* (The Conference of Negro African Writers and Artists held at the Sorbonne in the fall of 1956), Baldwin reveals his inability to grasp the far reaching importance of Diop's message to this assembled body of Afro-American, African and Caribbean scholars. He says: "The evening session began with a film, which I missed, and was followed by a speech from Cheikh Anta Diop, which, in sum, claimed the ancient Egyptian empire as part of the Negro past. I can only say that this question has never greatly exercised my mind, nor did M. Diop succeed in doing so—at least not in the direction he intended. He quite refused to remain within the twenty-minute limit, and while his claims of the deliberate dishonesty of all Egyptian scholars [sic] may be quite well founded for all I know, I cannot say that he convinced me."[3] In, perhaps, the single most revelatory sentence in the paragraph devoted to Diop, Baldwin adds, "He was, however, a great success in the hall, second only, in fact, to Aimé Césaire."[4]

Diop's role in both the first and Second International Black Writers and Artists Conference in Paris, France and Rome, Italy, has already received considerable attention by this author in that very special critical quarterly on Black Culture, *Black Images,* edited and published by Professor Rudy Murrary of Toronto, Canada. "The Cultural Unity of Cheikh Anta Diop, 1948-1964,"[5] is but one essay in this quite unique issue of the journal. Others included "African Sources in New World Black Music"—Laz E. N. Ekwueme, "Ismith Khan and The Theory of Rasa"—R. M. Lacovia, "Afro-Brazilian Culture"—Abdias Do Nascimento, "Frantz Fanon: A Rehabilitation of our Living Dead. (Part I, Section I, "Through European Mirrors")—R.M. Lacovia and "The Swahili Image Today"—Lyndon Harries. Aside from being the first scholarly magazine in Canada to publish an essay on Diop, *Black Images* remains an absolute treasure trove of exploratory, soundly reasoned studies of Africans across disciplines. Finally, we further discussed Diop in the context of other African scholars, based on the continent as well as abroad, in the Afterword to the 1963 reprint of Diop's *The Cultural Unity of Negro Africa*. By this time the title reflected post-1963 Afro American nomenclature. *The Cultural Unity of Black Africa* (1978).[6]

There was certainly no unanimity of opinions on Diop's works. Professors Raymond Mauny, Robert Cornevin and Jean Suret-Canale were among the first to attack Diop's thesis on the origin of the Ancient Egyptian. The summary of that argument is included in *Problems In African History* edited by Robert Collins and also in Diop's own *Anteriorité Des Civilisations Negres: Myth Ou Verité Histoirique?* (1967).[7]

A frontline attack within the African Studies circles of the U.S.A. emanated from a Boston University Professor, Daniel F. McCall. Interestingly, he chose Diop's *Anteriorité* as the basis for his discussion relative to the inappropriateness of accepting the "ethics of the political arena" as opposed to a "single standard" of scholarship. After breaking the long conspiracy of silence which American Africanists had sustained in regard to Diop's previous four books, McCall decided how best to introduce him to his American audience:

"C. A. Diop is, in the typology of Sir Isaiah Berlin, a "hedgehog." Sir Isaiah suggested that many historians could be divided into two categories, the foxes and the hedgehogs. This statement was based on a troublesome Greek text which makes the startling statement that the fox knows many things but the hedgehog knows one big thing . . . Diop 'knows' only one big thing—that Negroes invented civilization."[8]

That one big thing annoyed McCall to the point that he attempts to trivialize Diop's work rather than provide a scientific analysis of *Anteriorité*.

Diop's response to McCall was as follows: "Professor McCall subscribes to the kind of typological classification which allows him to file me in the category of the 'Hedgehog' who knows one important thing as opposed to the 'Foxes' who know many little things. All historians, according to him, are divided into these two categories. Should we laugh or cry? I do not know. But I appreciate the attitude of critics who have the strength to present correctly, without defamation or caricature, the adverse point of view before trying to demolish it. Such was not the attitude of Professor McCall in regard to the thesis which I uphold with arguments, whose consistency he would have felt had he tried to criticize them. He is satisfied with attributing such nonsensical ideas to me that instead of making the reader smile they lead the attentive reader to think of a caricature."[9]

Now that we have examined the background of scholarship on Cheikh Anta Diop's African historiography, we now turn to look at how his own writings and opinions reached the American audience as primary evidence. There were two principal ways: translated excerpts from his work in magazine form and a published transcript of an oral interview.

Mamadou Lumumba, Editor in Chief of *Soulbook: The Revolutionary Journal of the Black World,* based in Berkeley, California, introduced Diop's writings to his readership through an English translation from Chapter 2 of *Antériorité*. This appeared in Vol. 2, No. 4 (Spring/Summer 1969) of *Soulbook*. In the following issue of the Journal (Vol. 3, No. 1, Fall, 1970), there appeared excerpts from the 1962 *Présence Africaine* edition of *The Cultural Unity of Negro Africa.*

In the February, 1974 issue of *Black World* magazine, the first wave in what was to become a flood of interviews with Diop appears. This special issue, devoted to Black History, included "African Perspective on History: Interviews with Cheikh Anta Diop", a most perceptive dialogue with him. The interviewer, Harun Kofi Wangara, is to be credited with providing Professor Diop the first opportunity to speak directly to his American or English speaking audience. Wangara describes it thus:

> For almost an hour we discussed the problems of introducing new African historical themes, the negative influences of some Western historians, Dr. Diop's special areas of research, and my own project, which deals with pre-Columbian West African contacts with the Americas. At the end of our discussion, I asked Dr. Diop if he would consent to a taped interview for possible publication. What he had been saying was so interesting and revolutionary that I thought other English speaking Blacks should also benefit from it.[10]

When asked what sort of preparations young scholars should make to undertake future studies in the field, Diop provides an answer equally relevant in 1986 as in 1973:

> I would like to see above all a greater number of researchers—Afroamericans—young Americans—and even whites. Why not? Because it's the young who are the least prejudiced. As a consequence, they are the most capable of making triumph ideas which frighten the older generation. Also, I think that it will *be necessary to put together polyvalent scientific teams, capable of doing in-depth studies, for sure, and that's what's important*. It bothers me when someone takes me on my word without developing a means of verifying what I say . . . We must form a scientific spirit capable of seeing even the weaknesses of our own proofs, of seeing the unfinished side of our work and of committing ourselves to completing it. You understand? Therefore we should then have a work which could honestly stand criticism, because what we've done would have been placed on a scientific plane.[11]

The Preeminence of a Scientific Spirit

The publishing of Diop's first English translated interviews coincides with Mercer Cook's excellent translation and editing of sections from *Nations Negres et Cultures* and *Anteriorité des Civilisations Negres: Mythe ou Verite Historique?* This work appeared under the title of *The African Origin of Civilization: Myth or Reality?*

It is safe to say that by 1974 the perception of Cheikh Anta Diop as a most significant world intellectual force had greatly changed. It became even clearer to those in the western hemisphere why W.E.B. DuBois and Cheikh Anta Diop were chosen at the first World Festival on Negro Arts in Dakar (1966) as the English-speaking and French-speaking Black intellectuals with the greatest impact on Black-thought in the 20th century.

The presence of well-trained African scholars, the establishment of African research centers in Africa itself, Diop's organization of a modern radio-carbon laboratory, are all contributory factors in constructing a new African Historiography properly linked to the Nile Valley Civilizations. There is far less talk of Africa above and beneath the Sahara. Significantly, the changing perception of Diop coincides with a changing perception of Africans and African History.

How and when did Cheikh Anta Diop initiate his scientific spirit in the continuum so marvelously occupied by Professor William Leo Hansberry, pioneer modern Afro-American scholar interested in Egyptology.[12]

While Hansberry was summarizing his nearly 30 years of studying Nile Valley and other ancient African civilizations, a young African student from Senegal was about to embark on a similar mission—Cheikh Anta Diop. Upon his arrival in Paris in the Fall of 1946, Diop enrolled as a student at one of the elite schools of Math. So that we see right from the beginning Diop demonstrated a remarkable ability by gaining admission to a highly competitive scientific community. Diop has stated, "I began my research in September, 1946; because of our colonial situation at that time, the political problem dominated all others."[13] (How ironic it is that in 1986 the political problem continues to dominate all others.)

This was a period when the French Constituent Assembly had among its members, three Blacks. They were Leopold Sédar Senghor of Senegal, Aimé Césaire of Martinique, and Madame Eugenie Eboué, of Guadaloupe, widow of Felix Eboué and mother-in-law of Senghor.[14] They were later to be joined by Leon Gontran Damas of French Guiana. Damas, Senghor and Césaire were the founders of modern Negritude, a literary movement of the 1930's. Paulus Mohome has defined Negritude as "simply a reaffirmation of Negro Africa's presence and the authenticity of his civilization . . ."[15] Was not Senghor demonstrating the authenticity of his civilization by serving as an active member of the Constituent Assembly's committee designed to write the new constitution in impeccable French?

Much attention was drawn to the presence of the three highly "civilized" Blacks in the French Assembly. Cheikh Anta, too, was associated with an assembly during the same period—the African Democratic Assembly. Just as the battle over the constitution was becoming more engaging, a manifesto was sent to leaders all over French-speaking Black Africa. Eight hundred delegates were in attendance at this pivotal Bamako Congress. The African Democratic Assembly (R.D.A.) was held in Bamako, Mali on 18 October 1946. It became the very first interritorial movement in French West Africa, laying the foundation for political unity among Africans suffering from French colonialism.

Diop was among the student leadership responsible for developing a Pan-African political congress of students.[16] It is most significant to place Diop within the mainstream of political activism of that early period. It is also important to say that it was the political African students who popularized the slogan of national independence from the Sahara to the Cape, from the Indian to the Atlantic oceans. Diop argued that the concept of political unity should be pursued right alongside cultural unity. In fact, cultural unity was the scientific foundation upon which political unity would rest.

Evidence of Diop's concepts and precepts of unity can be found by examining his early environment. He was born in Diourbel, Senegal in the western part of the African continent on December 23, 1923. This little town in western Senegal was the seat of a strong Muslim brotherhood where collective activity was considered sacred. The society was organized on a collective basis. This led to their predominance in the groundnut industry. In pointing out the importance of this nationalized form of Islam, Diop has stated. "It is the only Negro African sect which has succeeded in acting independently from the rest of the Muslim world."[17] He attended Qu'aranic school where the acquisition of knowledge was emphasized. It may prove fruitful to examine the similarities and dissimilarities between the indigenization process utilized by the Nation of Islam in the U.S.A. and the Mourides in Senegal. The contribution of both of these groups to Islamic history and African/Afro-American history has been given minimal consideration.

Before going to France, Diop had passed his baccalaureat in Senegal. What about his activities in Senegal prior to his departure? Were his ideas published there?

To date the first known publication by Cheikh Anta appeared in *Présence Africaine* in 1948 under the title "Origins of the Wolof Language and Race."[18] This two-part essay included extracts from an Etymological Dictionary compiled by Diop. The third publication appeared in November, 1948 under the title "When do we speak of an African Renaissance?"[19] This essay is the unit around which part three of *The Living Museum* monograph is organized and developed.

The very first three essays, all published before he was 25 years old, provide a clear indication of the road he was taking to elucidate the African background. Language, architecture, music (which Diop discusses in relationship to jazz) and visual art were all useful evidences of civilization he employed in this eclectic essay commemorating the abolition of slavery.

Attention should now be drawn to *Le Musée Vivant* (The Living Museum) of November 1948. This special deluxe number was edited by Madeline Rousseau, a French art collector and critic and Cheikh Anta Diop, a young African scholar. The front cover design gives a clear indication of its importance. An African mask graces this cover. In the left bottom corner is 1848—Abolition of Slavery, right bottom corner—1948—Evidence of Black culture. One hundred years after the abolishing of slavery Diop and Rousseau assembled a most unique compendium of thought. The introduction to this volume was by Richard Wright, author of *Native Son* and *Black Boy* and by this time a celebrated author in France.

Richard Wright was called upon by Alioune Diop to assist in founding *Présence Africaine*, a cultural review of the Black World. On November 18, 1948, Wright joined Alioune Diop, Rene Char, Madeline Rousseau, Cheikh Anta Diop and others in opening a special exhibition of rare art objects and books, at the Palmes Bookstore in Paris. Wright captured the essence of this exhibition when he stated: "The vitality, the unconventional bravery, the freedom of invention of these sculptures all testify the power and originality of Negro expression, and in particular of the African artistic expression which is offered to you in this exhibition. What the Negro has accomplished in art is only a measure of what he is capable of, and what he might be able to accomplish in other realms of life, if only he is given a chance. In the meantime, he offers the world tangible images of a life which is nowhere near over, even though often, it must still be led in slavery or oppression."[20]

This *festschrift*, published to coincide with Rousseau's exhibition, included essays on a wide range of topics including, "The Music and Dance of West Africa," "African Philosophy," "The Negro in the Modern World," "New African Architecture." "The Colonial Economy on Black Africa." "Popular creation of Jazz Music" "The Archaeological Diggings in Nigeria and the antiquity of Negro Art." Among the members of the Honorary Committee supportive of this project were: the artist Pablo Picasso (who was strongly influenced by African sculpture. A work by him in 1907 is included.), the architect, Auguste Perret, the architect and urban planner Le Courbusier, the poet Aimé Césaire, André Aymard, who later taught Diop at the Sorbonne, along with the Directors of the Beaux Arts, Natural History Museum and the Bibliotheque Nationale. By 1948 it is safe to say that Diop had already made a decisive impact on French intellectual society. This is quite unusual for one so young, who had only entered France two years earlier.

His relationship with the Popular Association of Friends of the Museums gave him unusual access to a wide range of material cultural objects in both private and public collections. Madeline Rousseau is known to have had one of the finest private collections of African art objects. She was also at the very center of the anti-colonialist support unit among French citizens.

During this period he began to write *Nations Negres et Culture.* Several themes emerged in his research:

1. The Negro origin of Ethiopian and Egyptian Civilization.
2. The spread and antiquity of the Black substratum of humanity.
3. The Primacy of the southern culture over the Mediterranean.
4. The cultural familial linkages of the African peoples.
5. The possibility of these people building a modern culture which would benefit the human race as a whole.

Variations of these themes, with the addition of others, occur throughout his entire *Oeuvre.*

These ideas were first expressed in a formal way in *La Voix De L'Afrique Noir (The Voice of Black Africa)*,[21] a monthly bulletin published by the Student Association of the African Democratic Assembly. The February 1952 issue carried a most important article by Diop called, *"Towards An African Political Ideology."* In the section subtitled, "Wavering of the African Personality", Diop decried the African intellectual's ignoring of his ancestral past along the Nile.

By claiming the Ancient Egyptians as Blacks, Diop argued that "the moral fruit of their civilization is to be counted among the assets of the Black world." To avoid a deformed African personality one must be conversant with the full range of one's ancestral past, not just to establish self pride but to use it as the basis for contructing a modern civilization in the post-colonial and neo-colonial era.

He issued a devastating attack on modern Egyptology. Diop claimed that some were so anxious to meet the needs of imperalist exploitation that an entire process of falsification was developed to serve as an infrastructure for the thesis of white superiority and the concomitant thesis of black inferiority.

Among the Egyptologists cited by Diop as fictionalizing the racial ancestry of the Egyptians was Kurt Sethe, the German Egyptologist, who was George Reisner's mentor.

By 1952 Diop had formulated the cultural unity theory. He had also taken into account the necessity of demonstrating the efficacy of an African language (Wolof) in conveying modern scientific thought. To this end, he translated a portion of Einstein's Theory of Relativity into his own language. This is not gratuitous if one considers that only 15% of Senegal's population can speak or write French while nearly 80% of the population understands Wolof. Although it is mentioned in early 1952, he doesn't publish it until two years later in *Nations Negres et Culture.*

"Negro Nations and Culture" was initially submitted as a doctoral dissertation at the Sorbonne. Its full title *Negro Nations and Culture From Negro Egyptian Antiquity to Cultural Problems of Negro Africa Today* clearly indicates that Diop examined the past with a clear concern for utilizing this knowledge in the present and future African world. This utilitarian usage was not unlike the western world's use of the Greeco-Roman as the basis for a modern western world.

If Blacks had developed the first civilization, as Diop argued, why was it not known? He says: "The desire to legitimize colonization and the slave trade—in other words, the social condition of the Negro in the modern world—engendered an entire literature to describe the so-called inferior traits of the Blacks. The mind of several generations of Europeans would thus be gradually indoctrinated, Western opinions would crystallize and instinctively accept as revealed truth the equation: Negro = inferior humanity. To crown this cynicism, colonization would be depicted as a duty of humanity. They invoked "the civilizing mission" of the West charged with the responsibility to raise the African to the level of other men. From then on, capitalism had clear sailing to practice the most ferocious exploitation under the cloak of moral pretexts.[22] Diop's, Leo Hansberry's and John Johnson's work spanned a hundred years. They all concluded that the economic system of slavery was at the very heart of the "Birth of the Negro Myth." The long deep surge of interest in Egyptology and Nile Valley Civilizations moves in the mind of blacks like a mighty river, like the Nile or the Mississippi. This flow of interest over time, this vital continuum, is very much in evidence.

One of several factors distinguishing Cheikh Anta Diop's work from his worthy precursors, as well as his contemporaries, is his solid grounding in the physical, natural and social sciences. We must be mindful of the fact that it is no mere coincidence that the last 20 years of his professional career has been spent as Director of the Radiocarbon Laboratory at the University of Dakar in Senegal.

Some may already be familiar with the fact that Diop was trained in Anthropology, Archaeology, Sociology, Linguistics, Pre-history and Egyptology during his tenure at the Sorbonne University in Paris. This at least provides some explanation for his solid competency in a range of disciplines. Then, one must consider that, like Hansberry, Diop studied with leading specialists in several areas. Among them were André Aymard, Gaston Bachelard and André Leroi-Gourhan. What is not known and most commonly ignored is his background in Physics.

Perhaps it is necessary to illuminate Diop's early interest and later advanced knowledge of nuclear physics. He worked in the famed research laboratory of Fréderick Joliot-Curie—the leading nuclear physicist in France at the time Diop was studying there. Frederick Joliot-Curie was the son-in-law of Madame Marie Curie, who, along with her husband Pierre, discovered radium. Joliot-Curie like Diop, was trained at one of the premier institutions, the *E'cole Superieure*. He later went to the School of Industrial Chemistry and Physics, where a large portion of the curriculum was devoted to laboratory work. One of his most prominent teachers was Paul Langevin, the man responsible for making known Albert Einstein's Theory of Relativity, as well as contributing to the field himself. Langevin recommended Joliot to study with Mme. Curie and serve as her personal assistant. He joined her daughter Irene, who later became his wife. Together they received a Nobel Prize in Chemistry for "their synthesis of new radioactive elements."

In October, 1945, one year before Diop arrived in Paris, Joliot-Curie had become the high commissioner and organizer of the French Atomic Energy Commission. By 1948 Joliot had persuaded the government to build a major nuclear research center at Saclay, 12 miles south of Paris. In later years he spent most of his time at the College of France, teaching and directing the laboratory. Diop spent a great deal of time working and experimenting in this advanced laboratory open to only a few. Given the close relationship between Langevin, the Curies, the Joliots and Einstein, it is not surprising that Cheikh Anta Diop became one of a very few Africans at home or abroad with access to the most advanced body of scientific knowledge. Viewed in this context, his translation of Einstein's Theory of Relativity is no more unusual for Diop than the comparative philological study of Wolof and Egyptian grammar and vocabulary. In Parts II and III of Diop's *The Economic and Cultural Basis for a Federated State in Black Africa* one becomes even more familiar with how the "Origins and History of the Black World" are linked to the "Compendium of Energy Sources" available to Africa and how "the joint concentration of energy sources and raw materials determines the existence of eight natural zones for industrial development in Black Africa."

There is a back and forth motion between the historian and the physicist. Diop uses one to support the other. He uses his physics laboratory to bring facts to life to support the writing of an indigenous, authentic history of Africa. There is a very intimate relationship between the two. It is the same person giving different images. But they are not completely separate images. Perhaps one can draw an analogy from Quantum Mechanics where you have a particle that can be either a wave or a particle.

Over a three year period 1963-66, Diop worked assiduously to build a much needed laboratory. When he established the Radiocarbon Laboratory at IFAN in 1966, it was for the purpose of low-energy radioactivity research and C14 dating. In reading his latest book, *Civilisation Ou Barbarie*, part of which was presented in Diop's paper submitted to the Nile Valley Conference, one is astounded by his perspective on a wide range of philosophical issues. He makes vital commentary on such philosophical and scientific considerations as the reconciliation of man with himself, the continuing debate on the EPR (Einstein, Podolsky and Rosen) issue among physicists, engineers and philosophers, as well as discussions pertaining to Von Neumann, J. J. Bell and David Bohm.

In *Pre-Colonial Black Africa,* Diop made the quantum leap from a chronos time concept of history to a Sasa or UMUM time philosophical concept of history. Diop demonstrated how one could write a history of Africa without being locked into the chronos time concept or the mere chronology of events. This major philosophical break with traditional African historiography is yet another aspect of his work that cannot be analyzed in this paper.

In Cheikh Anta Diop's work one finds the clearest method of utilizing the vast knowledge of the past to create a vast future world.

Twenty four years ago, Diop proposed the creation of the following institutes in Africa:

1. An institute of nuclear chemistry and physics.
2. An electronics institute.
3. An aeronautics and astronautics institute.
4. An institute of applied chemistry for industry and agriculture (organic synthesis, metallurgy, mineral chemical industry, etc.).
5. An institute of tropical agronomy and biochemistry (soil study, fertilizers, extraction of vegetable products with a view to finding industrial or pharmaceutical applications for certain flora).
6. An institute of health, specializing in the study of tropical diseases.

We would have to conclude, based on a scientific analysis of the full body of Cheikh Anta Diop's work, that his conception and utilization of Nile Valley civilizations is quite unique. He has liberated the use and application of historical knowledge in such a way that it can provide a sound basis for interdisciplinary and transdisciplinary teams of African researchers charged with the responsibility of moving through future millenia.

Nile Valley studies is *not* in need of a Pharoah. As Diop so clearly pointed out: . . . "It is not a matter of looking for the Negro under a magnifying glass as one scans the past; a great people have nothing to do with petty history, nor with ethnographic reflections sorely in need of renovation. It matters little that some brilliant Black individuals may have existed elsewhere. The essential factor is to retrace the history of an entire nation."

It was those years of work in the Gif sur Yvette Laboratory of Radiocarbon in France, those years of probing deep philosophical issues, relating to modern man, experimentations and planning, work, study, organizing, planning and publishing (thanks to Alioune Diop and *Présence Africaine*) all of that energy and activity led to the development of the first radiocarbon laboratory in the Black world, and in 1986 one of three such labs directed by an African. Perhaps, it is Diop the Physicist, as much as Diop the Egyptologist that awaits a clearer understanding. Those radiocarbon 14 dating methods[23] continue to provide scientific data, the melanin tests[24] provide further ammunition in the battle to assure ancient Egypt and Nile Valley Civilizations that continuity of thought and change, that dynamic spirit and mind running throughout the whole world. Cheikh Anta Diop is the axis upon which we must build.

Running parallel to that axis is Diop's comment:

> The oneness of Egyptian and Black culture could not be stated more clearly. Because of this essential identity of genius, culture and race, today all Negroes can legitimately trace their culture to ancient Egypt and build a modern culture on that foundation. A dynamic modern contact with Egyptian antiquity would enable Blacks to discover increasingly each day the intimate relationship between all Blacks of the Continent and Mother Nile Valley. By this dynamic contact the Negro will be convinced that these Temples, the forest of columns, these pyramids, these colossi, these bas reliefs, mathematics, medicine and all the sciences are indeed the work of his ancestors and that he had a right and a duty to claim this heritage.[25]

NOTES

1. This comment appears under the title, "Civilization or Barbarism by Cheikh Anta Diop: Does This Mark The End of A Debate," *Afrique Histoire*, Vol. 2, No. 1, 1985. Professor Aboubacry Moussa Lam presented a paper entitled, "Egypte Ancienne Et Afrique Noire Chez Cheikh Anta Diop" at the Symposium on Diop's work held at the University of Dakar, Senegal, April-May, 1982. See also Aboubacry Moussa Lam, "Quelques Remarques Sur Les Noms De Personnes Dans L'Egypte Ancienne," *Annales de la Faculte des Lettres et Sciences Humaines de Dakar*, No. 13, 1983, pp. 141-153.

2. James G. Spady, "Negritude, PanBanegritude and the Diopian Philosophy of African History," *A Current Bibliography On African Affairs*, Vol. 5, Series II, 1972.

3. James Baldwin, *Nobody Knows My Name*, (N.Y. Dell Publishing Co. In., 1963). p. 46.

4. Ibid.

5. James G. Spady, "The Cultural Unity of Cheikh Anta Diop, 1948-1954," *Black Images* (Toronto, Canada), Vol. 1, No. 3 and 4, 1973.

6. Considerable discussion on the changing of the word from Negro to Black occurred between Paris, Philadelphia, Chicago and New York.

7. Response A quelques critiques (responses au compte rend critique de M. Raymond Mauny para dans le *Bulletin de l'IFAN*, B. Nos 3-4, 1960, relatif A *Nations Negres et Culture* et *L'Afrique Prècoloniale*, A la critique similaire de M. Jean Suret-Canale, para dans *Preuves*, juin-juillet, 1960.

8. Daniel F. McCall, Review of *Anteriorité Des Civilisations Negres: Mythe ou Verité Historique?* by Cheikh Anta Diop, *African Historical Studies*, Vol. 1, 1968.

9. Cheikh Anta Diop, "Project de Response a M. McCall," Dakar, Senegal, 1971.

10. Harun Kofi Wangara, "Interview with Cheikh Anta Diop," *Black World*, Vol. XXIII, No. 4, February, 1974, p. 56.

11. Ibid. 57-58.

12. See: James G. Spady, "Dr. William Leo Hansberry: The Legacy of An African Hunter," *A Current Bibliography* on *African Affairs*, Vol. 3, Nov./Dec. 1970, pp. 25-40, the first full essay on Hansberry to appear in a scholarly publication, and James G. Spady, "Tri-Muse: The Historiography of Joel A. Rogers, Drusilla Dunjee Houston and William Leo Hansberry, in *Black Prehistory*, ed., John A. Wiliams, (Berkeley, California), *Y.Bird*, Vol. 1, No. 2, 1978, pp. 98-115. William Leo Hansberry's "A Survey of Native Documentary Sources Available For the Study of Ancient Ethiopian History," *Howard University Studies In History*, 1913-1973, both offer testimony to the significance of Hansberry to studies in Modern Egyptology and African Historiography generally.

13. Correspondence received from Cheikh Anta Diop, March 21, 1971.

14. Edward A. Jones, "Negroes in the French Constiuent Assembly," *Opportunity*, Vol. XXV, No. 1, Winter, 1947, pp. 4-5.

15. Paulus Mohome, "Negritude: Evaluation and Elaboration." *Présence Africaine*, Vol. 68, 1968, p. 124.

16. Correspondence received from Cheikh Anta Diop, 26 April, 1972.

17. James G. Spady, "Negritude, PanBanegritude and the Diopian Philosophy of African History," *A Current Bibliography on African Affairs*." Vol. 5, No. 1, January, 1972, pp. 11-29.

18. Cheikh Anta Diop, "Etude de linguistique oulove: Origine de la langue et de la race Wolof" *Présence Africaine*, No. 4, pp. 672-684 and No. 5, pp. 848-853, 1948.

19. Cheikh A. Diop, "Quand pourra-t-on parler d'une renaissance africaine?" *Le Musee Vivant*, Special Issue, Vol. 36-37, November, 1948.

20. Michael Fabre, *The Unfinished Quest of Richard Wright*, N. Y., William Morrow and Co., 1973, p. 319.

21. Cheikh Anta Diop, "Vers une Ideologie Politique Africaine," *La Voix De L'Afrique Noire* (Bulletin Mensuer de L'Association Des Etudiants, R.D.A) Fevrier, 1952, pp. 5-24.

22. Cheikh Anta Diop, *The African Origin of Civilization: Myth or Reality*, Westport, Connecticut, Lawrence Hill and Co.,

23. Cheikh Anta Diop, "Radiocarbon Dates I," *Radiocarbon*, Vol. 16, No. 3, 1974, pp. 304-306, "Radiocarbon Dates II," *Radiocarbon*, Vol. 19, 1977, "Centre de datation de L'IFAN: Datation par la methode du radiocarbone, Serie III," *Bulletin de L'IFAN, XXXIV*, Series B, No. 4, 1972, pp. 687-701.

24. Cheikh Anta Diop, "Pigmentation des anciens Egyptiens: Test par la Melanie," *Bulletin de l'Institut Fondamental d'Afrique Noire*, Tome XXXV, Serie B, No. 3., juillet, 1973, pp. 514-531. This article was recently translated, "Pigmentation of the Ancient Egyptians: Test by Melanin Analysis," by Darryl Reynard Prevost of the University of California at Berkeley. This young Afro-American linguist has also translated Diop's, "The Metallurgy of Iron During the Egyptian Ancient Empire," and "Introduction to the Study of Migrations In Central and Western Africa: Identification of the Nilotic Cradle of The Sengalese People."

25. Cheikh Anta Diop, *The African Origin of Civilization: Myth or Reality?*, Westport, Connecticut, Lawrence Hill and Co., 1974, p. 140.

Review

THE CULTURAL UNITY OF BLACK AFRICA: THE DOMAINS OF PATRIARCHY AND OF MATRIARCHY IN CLASSICAL ANTIQUITY

(By Cheikh Anta Diop. Chicago: Third World Press, 1978. First published in France in 1959 under the title *L'Unite Culturelle De L'Afrique Noire*)

Asa G. Hilliard III

> *I have tried to bring out the profound cultural unity still alive beneath the deceptive appearance of cultural heterogeneity . . . Only a real knowledge of the past can keep in one's consciousness the feeling of historical continuity essential to the consolidation of a multinational state.*
>
> —Cheikh Anta Diop

The power of the scholarly and political contributions of Dr. Cheikh Anta Diop to African redemption has been so vast that it will be many years before the real extent of it and its full meaning will be understood. As scientist, Dr. Diop has lived to witness the initial crumbling of an international intellectual order that has been rooted in error, distortion, racism, falsehood and superstition. It is an intellectual order that has denied to Africans a place in human history.

> The native's challenge to the colonial world is not a rational confrontation of points of view. It is not a treatise on the universal, but the untidy affirmation of an original idea propounded as an absolute. The colonial world is a Manichean world. It is not enough for the settler to delimit physically, that is to say with the help of the army and the police force, the place of the native. As if to show the totalitarian character of colonial exploitation, the settler paints the native as a sort of quintessence of evil. Native society is not simply described as a society lacking in values. It is not enough for the colonist to affirm that those values have disappeared from, or still better never existed in, the colonial world. The native is declared insensible to ethics; he represents not only the absence of values, but also the negation of values. He is, let us dare to admit, the enemy of values, and in this sense he is the absolute evil. He is the corrosive element, destroying all that comes near him; he is the deforming element disfiguring all that has to do with beauty or morality; he is the depository of maleficent powers, the unconscious and irretrievable instrument of blind forces. (Fanon, 1968 p. 42.)
>
> Africa is the continent which Hegel and the modern ideologues who came after him excluded from history. Even Karl Marx did it. Frederich Engles

> thought that if whites were more intelligent than blacks, it was only because they were shepherds and ate meat and drank milk! (Diop, 1984)

The restoration of Africa's place in world history is now moving ahead by quantum leaps, thanks to Dr. Diop and others. The November, 1985 issue of *National Geographic* (Weaver, 1985) sums up the present state of the art on information about human beginnings with the confirmation of Dr. Diop's long held thesis that Africa is the birthplace of the human race. Earlier, as a partial result of Dr. Diop's leadership and with a major contribution to the work by him, the United Nations Educational and Cultural Organization (UNESCO) published a set of edited volumes to set forth state of the art information on a comprehensive history of Africa (see *General History of Africa*, vols. 1 and 2). In these volumes, what is almost as important as Dr. Diop's brilliant chapter outlining the categories of data which can be used to rewrite the history of Kemet (Ancient Egypt) is the production of a collection that challenges an entire body of distorted scholarship on African history, some of it written by well known contributors to these very UNESCO volumes.

Dr. Diop is no newcomer to the struggle for scientific truth in the reconstruction of Africa's story. Born in Diourbel, Senegal, West Africa, on December 23, 1923, he was nurtured in the womb of African culture. His people are Wolof. This equipped him with a background of experience, unlike his graduate school professors in the 1950's. It allowed him to see Africa, and Europe for that matter, *through African eyes*. Therefore, with his African consciousness fully awake, it was not possible for him to sit as a passive recipient of the culture bound teachings of his professors in Graduate school at the Sorbonne in Paris.

In 1953, we find Diop as a student in Paris holding the office of Secretary-General of the Student RDU (African Democratic Assembly). Later he called the first Pan-African Student Congress of English and French Students. His scholarship led him to activism in the political arena. Clearly he did not fall victim to the trap of viewing African imperatives through the linguistic and political categories and frameworks of Europe. This conceptual and political freedom has been a major basis for his creative contributions to African liberation on all planes.

Today, we have the benefit of Dr. Diop's latest works, such as his book *Civilization or Barbarism*, as well as the important works of a whole host of important African and African diasporan scholars who are involved in the rescue of African history and the liberation of African people world wide (ben Jochannan, 1972, Dubois, 1965, Carruthers, 1984, Clegg, 1985, James, 1954, Jackson, 1974, Williams, 1974, Van Sertima, 1977, Houston, 1985, Rashidi, 1985, etc.) Collectively they have created an intellectual revolution among many leaders with the likelihood of a massive spread of consciousness among the masses. Therefore, we have a unique vantage point from which to view his earlier works.

By now there is a well known story about how Cheikh Anta Diop was forced to write three separate dissertations before being awarded the doctorate from the Sorbonne in Paris. His first attempt was made in 1955 with *Nations Negres et Culture*, later published as a book by that title. His last attempt was in 1960 when, with the help of African scholars, he successfully defended his excellent work *L'Afrique Precoloniale*. It was between these two efforts that he submitted his second dissertation, *L'Unite Culturelle de L'Afrique Noir*, the subject of this essay.

The *Cultural Unity of Black Africa* was translated into English and published by Third World Press in 1978, many years after its first appearance. While Diop's *African Origin of Civilization* (1975) appears to be the best known of his works, the *Cultural Unity of Black Africa* is at least as important. This is mainly because few other writers have attempted to make the argument for an African continental cultural unity based upon a clear description of cultural phenomena, a methodologically sound scientific approach, or by reference to empirically verifiable data.

The Third World Press edition of the *Cultural Unity of Black Africa* is sandwiched between the foreword by the noted historian, John Henrik Clarke, and an afterword by another noted historian, James G. Spady (originally published as a review in a 1975 volume of *Black Books Bulletin*, 3, 28-35 and 80-84). Both the foreword and afterword stand as valuable history on their own. Together they illuminate the politics of history, the political and intellectual climate within which the book was developed, important biographical information on Dr. Diop and, in the case of Spady's Afterword, a brilliant treatment of critical struggles to develop the idea of an African cultural reality. Spady also articulates clearly the meaning and above all the *function* of that cultural reality in African liberation struggles.

Mention must also be made here of a review by Jacob Carruthers (1977) and of a definitive interpretive essay by Vulinedela Wobogo (1976), both on the *Cultural Unity of Black Africa*. These are important additions to the body of serious comment on Diop's book.

The *Cultural Unity of Black Africa* is divided into seven chapters. In Chapter One Dr. Diop tackles head on a powerful European intellectual hegemony led by J.J. Bachofen, L.M. Morgan, and F. Engels. The fundamental idea common to these gentlemen that Diop attacked was that there was a *universal* evolutionary pattern of social structures, particularly that of the family. In their view matriarchy was seen as an intermediate stage in the development of the family. Patriarchy was seen as the natural and mature end toward which family development led.

Two forms of white supremacy thinking could be and were derived from such a position. On the one hand, the *general supremacy of white people* was indicated because the Patriarchy was more typical of the Indo-European than the Matriarchy. At the same time, the *supremacy of the white male* over the female was indicated. (Hodges, Struckman, Trost, 1975) Patriarchy was thought to represent spirituality, light, reason, delicacy, and activity. By contrast, matriarchy represented the cave-like depths of the earth, material things, the night, the things of the left, and passivity. We have seen the remnants of such thoughts in the analysis by leading Euro-American scholars of African-American family life. The black family has been attacked as being matriarchal.

Engels relied on the theories of Bachofen and Morgan to prove the historicity, or temporary nature of all forms of political and social organizations. While Diop did not challenge the notion of the historicity of political and social institutions, he was devastating in his critique of the arguments about *universal stages* or sequences of development, especially since the existence of these stages was not demonstrated by empirical data.

In Chapter Two, Dr. Diop presented his own "two cradle" theory or hypothesis and launched into a full scale critique of the classical European theory that there was originally a universal matriarchy. For Diop there were *parallel developments*, rather than sequential hierarchial developments.

> . . . instead of a universal transition matriarchy to patriarchy, humanity has from the beginning been divided into two geographically distinct 'cradles', one of which was favorable to the flourishing of matriarchy and the other to that of patriarchy, and that these two systems encountered one another and even disputed with each other in different human societies, that in certain places they were superimposed on each other or even existed side by side. . .(p. 26)

Diop then goes on to show that there is a lack of evidence, literary, mythological, historical or otherwise to show that the "northern cradle" has ever even had a matriarchy. This would destroy the argument about stages. Diop saw that the "northern cradle" possessed the material conditions favorable to nomadic life, or at least a highly mobile way of life. By contrast the "southern cradle" had material conditions that were more favorable to a sedentary agricultural life. It is these two conditions and ways of life, hypothesized Diop, that could be shown to lead in the former case to patriarchy, and in the latter case to matriarchy.

Diop appeals to a wide array of data. For example, linguistic analysis showed that,

> as far as one can go back into Indo-European history, especially by means of comparative linguistics, only one form of patriarchal family can be found which seems to be common to all tribes before their division (Aryans, Greeks, Romans). Verbal expressions relating to nomadic life are common to all these people, unlike those terms which concern the political and agricultural way of life. (p. 28)

For Diop, it was strange that matriarchy could have existed without evidence of its existence being reflected in the ancient languages. Diop then contrasts the orientation of the two cradles toward other aspects of their cultural life such as ancestor worship, including cremation (northern cradle) vs. burial (southern cradle), and the use of fire worship—""eternal flame" (northern cradle) and its absence in the southern cradle.

Most impressive of all is Diop's empirical evidence for the antiquity, pervasiveness and continuity of the matriarchy in the southern cradle. Diop developed the history of the patriarchy and the matriarchy in the northern and southern cradles in greater detail in Chapter Three. This included its manifestations in Egypt, Libya, "Black Africa," Crete, Greece, Rome, Germania, and Synthia. It also included the history of patterns in zones of confluence of culture such as Arabia, Phoenicia, Indus and Mesopotamia, and Byzantium. The exceptions to the rules in the three zones are identified and explained in Chapter Four.

In Chapter Five, Diop extended the "two cradle" analysis to still further aspects of culture, including contrasting ideas on the state and patriotism, royalty, religion, literature, and world view.

Chapter Six is important in showing that present day basic or traditional African culture is *derivative* of southern cradle antecedents, the records of which are best preserved in KMT (Ancient Egypt). This analysis connects KMT firmly to its inner African roots.

In the seventh and final chapter, Diop points to a number of things that require closer examination or further research if his theory of matriarchy and patriarchy is to be understood.

1. The Indo-European term "gens" or "genos" for the *paternal* clan needs to be researched in order to establish its origin.
2. Wolof, a West African language, may have existed in deep antiquity, connecting West African culture to KMT (Ancient Egypt).
3. Evidence of cultural unity between Wolof and ancient KMT is very strong in many respects.
4. The nature of the Mediterranean vocabulary needs to be examined more closely in order to clarify its origins.

In his conclusion to the book Diop provides a succinct and useful summary description of southern cradle culture.

> The Meridional cradle (southern), confined to the African continent in particular, is characterized by the matriarchal family, the creation of the territorial state, in contrast to the Aryan city-state, the emancipation of women in domestic life, xenophillia, cosmopolitanism, a sort of social collectivism having as a corrolary a tranquillity going as far as unconcern for tomorrow, a material solidarity of rights for each individual, which makes moral or material misery unknown to the present day; there are

> peoples living in poverty, but no one feels alone or in distress. In the moral domain, it shows an ideal of peace, of justice, of goodness and an optimism which eliminates all notion of guilt or original sin in religious and metaphysical institutions. The types of literature most favored are the novel, tales, fables, and comedy. (p. 195)

The identification of these parameters opens the door to the possibility for further and more refined empirical tests of the "two cradle" theory.

The Cultural Unity of Black Africa is important because it creates an independent African centered conception of Africa which restores its people to their rightful role as *participants and creators* in the historical process, *not as mere spectators*. Moreover, it exposes the incapsulated European mind that seeks, in its immature and childish egocentrism, to limit its conception of human experience in the world to the limited and incomplete experiences that is known by him or her. It also exposes the inherently political nature of scholarship.

Most of all, the *Cultural Unity of Black Africa* should make it easy for any sensitive reader to understand the fact that culture is neither a mere cosmetic in human life nor is it a dead remnant of some ancient past. Culture serves an indispensible social and political function as a living and growing manifestation of a people's creativities (Cabral, 1973). No people can be liberated who are cultural neuters. "Individuals" may survive as shooting stars, with temporary spurts of speed, but with a curved path that ends in darkness. It is the group (in Diop's terms a *people* rather than a population) that survives as an external galaxy.

The political and social *function* of culture is well understood by those groups that have become viable. Cultural disintegration is also seen in groups that are weak. Sometimes these things are manipulated by colonizers with cold calculated intent. Students of culture may be aware of the fact that it serves as a kind of glue that binds individuals into a group. Shared culture is the indispensible basis for group unity. Group unity is the prerequisite to liberation. Therefore, African and African diasporan people have an economic and political interest in the development of a cultural understanding of themselves.

Diop understood these things well. He saw that colonial powers advanced views that would highlight the unity of northern cradle culture. They also argued for its evolutionary superiority. At the same time, they sought to prove that the southern cradle, Africa, had no cultural unity. Moreover, they asserted that such identifiable culture as may have existed was merely underdeveloped. Diop's *Cultural Unity of Black Africa*, even in its incomplete form certainly shows the illegitimacy of such a position.

Diop explains clearly why observers and investigators have overlooked the cultural unity of African people. They have, according to Diop, confused levels of data, the superficial with the deep. Years later Noam Chomsky (1972), the Harvard linguist, would offer precisely this type of analytical approach for the study of language. He refers to surface structure and deep structure in language. It is the deep structure that carries the human meaning. Yet it is also that part of the structure that is most inaccessible to unsophisticated observers.

Diop has done here what he has done in so many of his other works. He has displayed a genius for *asking the right questions* and for developing models for analysis. By so doing he has left trails that trace out our basic direction. Others can now widen these trails into super highways, confident that the brilliant scout has done his work well.

The Cultural Unity of Black Africa is highly meaningful to all African diasporans. Recent investigations into African culture in the diaspora show varying degrees of cultural retentions at the deep structural levels. The main body of those studies cannot be presented here. However, the reader can follow this line of investigation in such areas as the study of the language of African Americans. (Hilliard, 1983), (Hilliard, 1980), (Smith, 1978), (Smitherman, 1977), (Turner, 1979). Perhaps a new group of scholars will place greater priority on the study of "the cultural unity of the African diaspora."

The Cultural Unity of Black Africa is a difficult book to read. It presumes that the reader is grounded in such fields as European classical mythology, ancient world history, linguistics, anthropology, economics, and other fields. Yet the patient and thorough reader will be richly rewarded by introduction to original insights that remain fresh, vital, and profoundly challenging nearly three decades after they were first presented. *The Cultural Unity of Black Africa* is a cornerstone in the structure of mental and physical liberation. As Diop states in the Preface: "Only a real knowledge of the past can keep in one's consciousness the feeling of historical continuity essential to the consolidation of a multinational state."

References

ben Jochanan, Y. (1972) *Black Man of the Nile*, New York: Alkebulan Books.

Cabral, A. (1973) *Return to the Source*, New York: Monthly Review.

Carruthers, J. (1984) *Essays in Ancient Egyptian Studies*, Los Angeles: Timbuktu Publishers.

Carruthers, J. (1977) "The Cultural Unity of Black Africa," *Black Books Bulletin* 5, 4, 46-48.

Chomsky, N. (1972) *Language and Mind*, New York: Harcourt, Brace.

Clegg, L. (1985) "The First Invaders" *Journal of African Civilizations* 7, 2, 23-35.

Diop, C.A. (1984) Africa's Contribution to World Civilization, Prepared address for the Nile Valley Conference, Morehouse College, Atlanta, Georgia.

Diop, C.A. (1975) *The African Origin of Civilization* Westport Conn: Lawrence Hill.

Diop, C.A. (1981) "The Origin of the Ancient Egyptians" in Mokhtar, G. (ed) *General History of Africa: Volume II* Berkeley: University of California Press.

DuBois, W.E.B. (1965) *The World and Africa* New York: International Publishers.

Fannon, F. (1968) *The Wretched of the Earth* New York: Grove Press.

Hilliard, A. (1980) Language Culture and Assessment, National Institute of Education Conference on Ann Arbor Decision, Ann Arbor, Michigan; Invited Paper.

Hilliard, A. (1983) "Psychological Factors in Language in the Education of the African American Child." *Journal of Negro Education* 52, 1, 24 -34.

Hodges, J.L., Struckman, D.K., & Trost, L.D. 1975) *The Cultural Bases of Racism and Group Oppression* Berkeley: Two Riders Press.

Houston, D. (1985) *The Wonderful Ethiopians of the Ancient Cushite Empire* Baltimore: Black Classics Press.

Jackson, John (1974) *Introduction to African Civilization* Secaucus, New Jersey: The Citadel Press.

James, G.G.M. (1954) *Stolen Legacy* San Francisco: Julian Richardson.

Ki-Zerbo, J. (1981) (Ed) *General History of Africa: Volume I.* Berkeley: University of California Press.

Mokhtar, G. (Ed) (1981) *General History of Africa: Volume II* Berkeley: University of California Press.

Rashidi, R. (1985) (Ed.) "African Presence in Early Asia" *Journal of African Civilizations* 7, 1.

Smith, E. (1978) *The Retention of the Phonological and Morphophonemic Functions of Africa in Afro-American Ebonics* Seminar Series Paper Dept. of Linguistics California State University Fullerton.

Smitherman, G. (1977) *Talkin and Testifyin* Boston: Houghton Mifflin.

Spady, J. (1975) "The cultural unity of Cheikh Anta Diop" *Black Books Bulletin, 3*, 28-35 and 80-84.

Turner, L. (1979) *Africanisms in the Gullah Dialect* New York: Arno Press.

Van Sertima, I. (1985) *Nile Valley Civiliations* Journal of African Civilizations Ltd., Inc.

Weaver, K.F. (1985) "The Search for Our Ancestors" *National Geographic, 168*, 5, 560.

Williams, C. (1974) *The Destruction of African Civilization* Chicago: Third World Press.

Wobogo, Vulindela (1976) "Diop's Two Cradle Theory and the Origin of White Racism" *Black Books Bulletin, 4*, 4, 20-29 and 72.

CHEIKH ANTA DIOP AND THE NEW CONCEPT OF AFRICAN HISTORY

John Henrik Clarke

I first became aware of the writings of Cheikh Anta Diop by reading the proceedings of the First and Second Conferences of Negro Writers and Artists.[1] His work was a revelation to me personally because I had not encountered in print African scholars who were so forthright in challenging prevailing misconceptions about African History and putting forth a new, creative view with documents. When I read his contribution to this First Conference, "The Cultural Contribution and Prospects of Africa,"[2] I began to inquire about his other writings. I discovered later that the contents of the article was part of a chapter of a future book. In reading the proceedings of a Second Conference held in Rome, my curiosity grew concerning this new voice in the African wilderness of historiography. I later enquired about his work and discovered that Presence Africaine had published a comprehensive work of his on African History.[3] I later corresponded with him as one of the founding members of the black Academy of Arts and Letters, and when I was asked to compile a list of the 20 most important books on Africa written by Africans, his book, already referred to, was listed.

When I attended the second meeting of the International Congress of Africanists, which met at the University of Dakar, I sought out Cheikh Anta Diop. I was surprised to know he was not one of the participants at the conference. His office and laboratory were located on the campus of the university, 300 yards from the assembly hall where the Congress was being held. The organization was then predominantly white-dominated and has not yet to this day recognized the scholarship of Cheikh Anta Diop and his contribution to a new concept of African History.

I visited him in his laboratory while attending the Conference and discussed the long effort in which Afro-Americans and Caribbean-Americans have engaged, in the writing and preservation of African history.

I returned to the U.S. and spent the next seven years trying to convince American publishers that the books of Cheikh Anta Diop should be translated into English and published in the U.S.

I first mentioned this to my friend and colleague, the late Alioune Diop, who encouraged me to continue in spite of repeated disappointments. It was not until 1974 that an American publisher, Lawrence Hill, saw fit to publish his book *African Origin of Civilization: Myth or Reality.*

The book was translated by Professor Mercer Cook, former head, Department of Romance Languages, Howard University. At the same time I was still an associate editor of *Freedomways Magazine* and wrote an essay review of the book. I felt its publication was a personal achievement. The following is part of that review.

Cheikh Anta Diop, one of the most able of present day scholars writing about Africa, is also one of the greatest living African historians. His first major work, *Nations, Negres et Culture* (1954) is still disturbing the white historians who have made quick reputations as authorities on African history and culture. In this book Dr. Diop shows the interrelationships between African nations, north and south, and proves, because in this case proof is needed again and again, that ancient Egypt was a distinct African nation and was not historically or culturally a part of Asia or Europe. More myths about Africa are put to rest in another one of his books, *The Cultural Unity of Negro Africa* (1959). The publication of his first book in the United States, *The African Origin of Civilization: Myth or Reality*, is a cause for celebration. This book and others of recent years, all by African writers, have called for a total reconsideration of the role that African people have played in history and their impact on the development of early societies and institutions.

Cheikh Anta Diop was born in the town of Diourbel, in Senegal, on the west coast of Africa in 1923. His birthplace has a long tradition of producing Muslim scholars and oral historians. This is where his inspiration and interest in history, the humanities and social sciences, from an African point of view, began. After the publication of his first book, *Nations, Negres et Culture*, which had been rejected as a Ph.D. thesis at the Sorbonne in Paris, he became one of the most controversial of present day African historians. *Nations, Negres et Culture* is both a reassessment of the African past and a challenge to Western scholarship on Africa. He refutes the myth of Egypt as a white nation and shows its southern African origins. It is his intention to prove that, through Egyptian civilization, Africa has made the oldest and one of the most significant contributions to world culture. This is not a new argument that started with Cheikh Anta Diop's generation of Africans. The Ghanaian historian, Joseph B. Danquah, in his introduction to the book *United West Africa at the Bar of the Family of Nations*, by Ladipo Solanke, published in 1927 (three years after Cheikh Anta Diop was born), said exactly the same thing. His statement reads:

> "By the time Alexander the Great was sweeping the civilized world with conquest after conquest from Chaeronia to Gaza, from Babylon to Cabul;

> by the time the first Aryan conquerors were learning the rudiments of war and government at the feet of the philosopher Aristotle; and by the time Athens was laying down the foundations of European civilization, the earliest and greatest Ethiopian culture had already flourished and dominated the civilized world for over four centuries and a half. Imperial Ethiopia had conquered Egypt and founded the XXVth Dynasty, and for a century and a half the central seat of civilization in the known world was held by the ancestors of the modern Negro, maintaining and defending it against the Assyrian and Persian Empires of the East.
>
> This, at the time when Ethiopia was leading the civilized world in culture and conquest. East was East, but West was not, and the first European (Grecian) Olympiad was yet to be held. Rome was nowhere to be seen on the map, and sixteen centuries were to pass before Charlemagne would rule in Europe and Egbert become first King of England. Even then, history was to drag on for another seven hundred weary years, before Roman Catholic Europe could see fit to end the Great Schism, soon to be followed by the disturbing news of the discovery of America and the fateful rebirth of the youngest of world civilizations."[2]

Here Dr. Danquah is showing that African history is the foundation of world history. In the present book by Cheikh Anta Diop, and in most of his other works, his objective is the same. In his first major work on history, Dr. Diop said:

> "The general problem confronting African history is this: how to reorganize effectively, through meaningful research, all of the fragments of the past into a single ancient epoch, a common origin which will reestablish African continuity. . . if the ancients were not victims of a mirage, it should be easy enough to draw upon another series of arguments and proofs for the union of the history of Ethiopian and Egyptian societies with the rest of Africa. Thus combined, these histories would lead to a properly patterned past in which it would be seen that (ancient) Ghana rose in the interior (West Africa) of the continent at the moment of Egyptian decline, just as the Western European empires were born with the decline of Rome."

While using Africa as the vantage point and the basis for his thesis Dr. Diop does not neglect the broader dimensions of history. He shows that history cannot be restricted by the limits of ethnic group, nation, or culture. Roman history is Greek as well as Roman, and both the Greek and the Roman history are Egyptian because the entire Mediterranean was civilized by Egypt; and Egypt in turn borrowed from other parts of Africa, especially Ethiopia.

Africa came into the Mediterranean world mainly through Greece, which had been under African influence. The first Greek invasion of Africa was peaceful and scholarly. This invasion brought in Herodotus. Egypt had lost its independence over a century before his visit. This was the beginning of the period of foreign domination over Egypt that would last, in different forms, for two thousand years.

The African Origin of Civilization: Myth or Reality is a one-volume translation of the major sections of the first and last of the books by Cheikh Anta Diop, i.e. *Nations, Negres et Culture* and *Anteriorite des Civilizations Negres.* These two works have challenged and changed the direction of attitudes about the place of African people in history in scholarly circles around the world. It was largely due to these works that Cheikh Anta Diop, with W.E.B. DuBois, was honored as "the writer who had exerted the greatest influence on African people in the 20th century," at the World Festival of Arts held in Dakar, Senegal, in 1966.

The main thesis of the present work is a redefinition of the place of Egypt in African history in particular and in world history in general. Dr. Diop calls attention to the historical, archeological, and anthropological evidence that supports his thesis. The civilization of Egypt, he maintains, is African in origin and in early development. In his book Dr. Diop says, "The history of Africa will remain suspended in air and cannot be written correctly until African historians connect it with the history of Egypt."

Dr. Diop approaches the history of Africa head on, with explanations, but no apologies. In locating Egypt on the map of human geography he asks and answers the question: who were the Egyptians of the ancient world?

The Ethiopians say that the Egyptians were one of their colonies which was brought into Egypt by the deity Osiris. The Greek writer Herodotus repeatedly referred to the Egyptians as being dark-skinned people with wooly hair. "They" he says, "have the same tint of skin which approaches that of the Ethiopians." The opinion of the ancient writers on the Egyptians is more or less summed up by Gaston Maspero (1846-1916), when he says, "By the almost unanimous testimony of ancient historians, they, (the Egyptians), belong to an African race which first settled in Ethiopia on the Middle Nile [and] following the course of the river they gradually reached the sea."

"The Greek writer, Herodotus, may be mistaken," Cheikh Anta Diop tells us "when he reports the customs of a people, but one must grant that he was at least capable of recognizing the skin color of the inhabitants of countries he visited." His descriptions of the Egyptians were the descriptions of an African people. At this point the reader needs to be reminded of the fact that at the time of Herodotus's visit to Egypt and other parts of Africa (between 480 and 425 B.C.) Egypt's Golden Age was over. Egypt had already suffered several invasions, mainly the Assyrian invasion from Western Asia (called the Middle East) starting in 671 B.C. If after years of invasions by other people and nations it was a distinct African nation at the time of Herodotus, shouldn't we at least assume that it was more so before these occurred?

If Egypt is a dilemma in Western historiography, it is a created dilemma. The Western historians, in most cases, have rested the foundation of what is called "Western Civilization" on the false assumption, or claim, that the ancient Egyptians were white people. To do this they had to ignore great masterpieces on Egyptian history written by other white historians who did not support this point of view, such as Gerald Massey's great classic, *Ancient Egypt, the Light of the World* (1907) and his other works, *A Book of the Beginnings* and *The Natural Genesis*. Other neglected works by white writers are *Politics, Intercourse, and Trade of the Carthaginians, Ethiopians, and Egyptians* by A.H.L. Heeren (1833) and *Ruins of Empires* by Count Volney (1787).

In the first chapter of his book, Dr. Diop refers to the Southern African origins of the people later known as Egyptians. Here he is on sound ground with a lot of support coming from another group of neglected white writers.

In his book *Egypt,* Sir E.A. Wallis Budge says: "The prehistoric native of Egypt, both in the old and in the new Stone Ages, was African and there is every reason for saying that the earliest settlers came from the South." He further states: "There are many things in the manners and customs and religions of the historic Egyptians that suggests that the original home of their prehistoric ancestors was in a country in the neighbourhood of Uganda and Punt." (Some historians believe that the biblical land of Punt was in the area known on modern maps as Somalia.)

European interest in Ethiopia and the origin of civilization dates from the early part of the nineteenth century and is best reflected in a little known, though important, paper in Karl Richard Lepsius' *Incomparable Survey of the Monumental Ruins in the Ethiopian Nile Valley in 1843-1844.*

The records found by Lepsius tend to show how Ethiopia was once able to sustain an ancient population that was numerous and powerful enough not only to challenge, but, on a number of occasions, to conquer completely the populous land of Egypt. Further, these records showed that the antiquity of Ethiopian civilization had a direct link with civilization of ancient Egypt.

Many of the leading antiquarians of the time, based largely on the strength of what the classical authors, particularly Diodorus Siculus and Stephanus of Byzantium, had to say on the matter, were exponents of the view that the ancient Ethiopians or, at any rate, the African people of remote antiquity, were the earliest of all civilized peoples. Also, that the first civilized inhabitants of ancient Egypt were members of what is referred to as the Black race, who entered the country as emigrants from Ethiopia. A number of Europe's leading writers on the civilizations of remote antiquity have written brilliant defenses of this point of view. Some of these writers are Bruce, Count Volney, Fabre, d'Olivet, and Heeren. In spite of the fact that these writers defended this thesis with all the learning at their command, and documented their defense, most of the present-day writers of African history continue to ignore their findings.

In 1825, German backwardness in this respect came definitely to an end. In that year, Arnold Hermann Heeren (1760-1842), Professor of History and Politics in the University of Gottingen, one of the ablest of the early exponents of the economic interpretation of history, published the fourth and revised edition of his great work *Ideen uber die Politik, den Verkehr und den Handel der Vornehmsten Volker der Alten Weld.* This was a lengthy essay on the history, culture, and commerce of the ancient Ethiopians and had profound influence on contemporary writers for its conclusion that it was among the ancient Black people of Africa and Asia that international trade was first developed, and that, as a by-product of these international contacts, there was an exchange of ideas and cultural practices that laid the foundations of the earliest civilizations of the ancient world.

The French writer Count C.F. Volney, in his important work, *The Ruins of Empires*,[3] extends this point of view by saying that the Egyptians were the first people to "attain the physical and moral sciences necessary to civilized life." Volney further states that "it was on the borders of the Upper Nile, among an African race of men, that was organized the complicated system of worship of the stars, considered in relation to the productions of the earth and the labors of agriculture; and this first worship, characterized by their adoration under their own forms and national attributes, was a simple proceeding of the human mind."

Over a generation ago African-American historians, such as Carter G. Woodson, W.E.B. DuBois, Willis N. Huggins, J.A. Rogers, and Charles C. Seifort, read the works of these radical historians and began to expand on their findings. This tradition continued and is reflected in the works of present-day Black historians, such as John G. Jackson (*Introduction to African Civilizations*, 1970) Yosef ben-Jochannan (*Black Man of the Nile,* 1972) and Chancellor Williams (*The Destruction of Black Civilization: Great Issues of a Race from 4500 B.C. to 2000 A.D.*, 1971).

Until the publication of James G. Spadys' article "Negritude, Pan-Banegritude and the Diopian Philosophy of African History" in *A Current Bibliography on African Affairs*, volume 5, number 1, January, 1972, and the interview by Harun Kofi Wangara, published in *Black World* Magazine, February, 1974, Dr. Cheikh Anta Diop was known to only a small group of Black writers and teachers in the United States. For over seven years his books were offered to American publishers with no show of interest. Then, two of his books were published in the United States within one year. The Third World Press in Chicago brought out his book *The Cultural Unity of Negro Africa.* All of his books were originally published by Presence Africaine, the Paris-based publication arm of the International Society of African Culture.

Egyptology developed in concurrence with the development of the slave trade and the colonial system. It was during this period that Egypt was literally taken out of Africa, academically, and made an extension of Europe. In many ways Egypt is the key to ancient African history. African history is out of kilter until ancient Egypt is looked upon as a distinct African nation.

The Nile River played a major role in the relationship of Egypt with the nations in Southeast Africa. During the early history of Africa, the Nile was a great cultural highway on which elements of civilization came into and out of inner Africa. Egypt's relationship with the people in the South was both good and bad, depending on the period and the dynasty in power.

In his chapter, "Who were the Egyptians?", Dr. Diop explains the rise and fall of Egypt's Golden Age and the beginnings of the invasions, the first from Western Asia which turned this nation's first age of greatness into a nightmare. This was the period of the Hyksos, or Shepherd Kings. During this time seventy Jews, grouped in twelve patriarchal families, nomads without industry or culture, entered Egypt. These Jews left Egypt four hundred years later 600,000 strong, after acquiring from African people all of the elements of their future religion, tradition, and culture, including monotheism. Whosoever the Jews were when they entered Africa, when they left, four hundred years later, they were ethnically, culturally, and religiously an African people. In this part of his book, Cheikh Anta Diop leaves no room for argument.

In the chapter called "Birth of the Negro Myth," Dr. Diop shows how African people, whose civilizations were old before Europe's first great civilization was born, were systematically read out of the respectful commentary of human history. This examination is continued in the chapter called "Modern Falsification of History." Here, Cheikh Anta Diop deals with how Western historians, for the last five hundred years, wrote or rewrote history glorifying the people of European extraction and distorting the history of the rest of the world. Those who read this book seriously are in for a shock and a rewarding experience in learning. This is a major work by a major African historian.

NOTES

1. *The Ideology of Blackness.* Edited by Raymond F. Betts. D.C. Heath and Company, Lexington, Massachusetts, 1971, pp. 127-133.

2. *United West Africa (or Africa) at the Bar of the Family of Nations.* By Ladipo Solanke. First published 1927, reprinted 1969 by African Publication Society, London, England.

3. *The Ruins; or, Meditation on Revolutions of Empires: And the Law of Nature,* by C.F. Volney. Peter Eckler, New York, 1890.

***

Addendum

Since the publication of *The African Origin of Civilization: Myth or Reality,* by Cheikh Anta Diop his career is better known in the U.S. and he has already made one visit and has planned another. *Journal of African Civilizations* has emphasized his work in several volumes and this present issue is devoted to an appraisal of the work of Cheikh Anta Diop by African-American colleagues. His last major work, *Civilisation ou Barbarie*[5] is presently being translated into English for publication in the United States. In my opinion the work of Cheikh Anta Diop is Pan-Africanist, nationalist and socialist with an intellectual balance between all three. His book *Black Africa*[6] was not understood when it was first published and it is now being reconsidered for publication in this country because it is so timely in its concern for the preservation of African resources, not only for this generation of Africans but generations still to come. His two essays in a special issue of the journal, *Nile Valley Civilizations*,[7] points a new direction for African scholarship and reminds us that the Nile Valley was the beginning of our ancient culture and the beginning of so much of the world's culture. I do not think it is too much for me to say that Cheikh Anta Diop is a resource for the whole of the African world and his contribution to a new concept of African History is universal. We must preserve him in order to preserve ourselves.

NOTES

1. "African Cultural Unity," Cheikh Anta Diop. Présence Africaine, No. 24-25. Feb.-May 1959, Paris.
2. "The Cultural Contributions and Prospects of Africa," Cheikh Anta Diop. Présence Africaine. No. 8-9-10, June-Nov. 1956, Paris.
3. *Nations Negres et Culture*, Cheikh Anta Diop. Deuxieme edition. Présence Africaine. Paris, 1955.
4. *The African Origin of Civilization: Myth or Reality*, Cheikh Anta Diop. Edited and translated by Mercer Cook. Laurence Hill and Company. New York and Westport, Conn., 1974.
5. *Civilisation ou Barbarie*, Cheikh Anta Diop. Présence Africaine. Paris, 1981.
6. *Black Africa*, Cheikh Anta Diop. Laurence Hill and Company. Westport, Conn., 1978.
7. "Africa: Cradle of Humanity," Cheikh Anta Diop. *Nile Valley Civilizations*, ed. Ivan Van Sertima. Transaction. New Brunswick, N.J., 1985.

REVIEWS

The African Origin of Civilization: Myth or Reality, by Cheikh Anta Diop. Edited and translated from the French by Mercer Cook. Westport: Lawrence Hill & Company, 1974, Pp v + 317. $9.95 (paper).

When *The African Origin of Civilization* appeared in 1974, the reaction to its publication was mixed: from utter surprise, astonishment, allegations of nationalism and afrocentrism, to questionable scholarship, too polemical, and downright effrontery.[1] Given the overwhelmingly acceptable, but powerful, role of Egypt in this historical development of the West (and it has been one that has remained quite formidable throughout the centuries), the publication of Diop's African Origin, with its afrocentric approach, was viewed by many as part of an attempt to create an all black African history for Africans. Using an abundance of material drawn from various disciplines, no doubt compiled by some of the more noted and respected writers on Egypt, Diop directs his attention at what he considered to be gross misinterpretations of Egyptian history: misinterpretations that were fostered by western writers whom he alleges, in their eagerness to "whiten" ancient Egypt, "perpetrated 'the most monstrous falsification in the history of humanity.'"[2] As a Sengelese historian, Diop's multidisciplinary approach brings together what he considers to be evidence that supports the idea "that Egyptian civilization was produced by black Africans, and that Egyptian civilization played a major role in the shaping of classical Mediterranean civilization and, therefore, lies at the root of much of what is worthwhile in European history."[3]

Now in spite of what appeared to be some favorable remarks by reviewers, such as "the concept of ancient Egypt as a black civilization is developed with an attractive line of reasoning and a massive synthesis of evidence . . .,"[4] and " . . . the author provides an original—though controversial—synthesis of the relationship between ancient Egypt and the western world on the one hand, and the Egyptian customs and contemporary African practices on the other . . .,"[5] the general consensus about the book was that it was too polemical,[6] and more political than historical.[7] One reviewer even went so far as to question the integrity of the writer's scholarship by intimating that "the complex relations between Egypt and other parts of the world, black or otherwise, cannot be explained by the techniques employed."[8]

No doubt there are things in the book that many readers should handle with caution. For one, readers are cautioned against Diop's use of the term "white" to describe the early intruders into the Nile Delta from among the Libyans and those people to the east of the Delta. Although *Choice* elected to describe its use as the author's "careless identification of race with skin color," one wonders whether or not the translator purposely employed the term because of the ideas that "white" evoke in the western mind. Another caution is with the author's persistence in giving the impression that ancient Egyptian appears to have more affinities with Wolof (?).[9] Perhaps here one might question the author's methodology: but then again all of this could be explained in terms of the dualism detected in Diop's writing: a dualism that is perhaps a mark of most historians. On the one hand here is Diop the historian attempting to remain as objective as possible with his material, yet on the other hand he is a victim of his environment and inevitably a feeling of nationalism creeps into his style. There is this constant reminder that regardless of the copious accounts of a probability of Indo-European roots for Egyptian culture and civilization, the pathway along which future generations of black historians should direct their research is towards creating a "rectification of human history" for black Africans and others as well.[10]

To rectify human history is the task that Cheikh Anta Diop has set for himself. In addition to acknowledging that the ideas contained within *The African Origin of Civilization* are only "a progress report," Diop also encourages scholars around the world, both black and white, to exert themselves in unfolding the ancient pages of Africa's past. With respect to this, in both his preface and conclusion to the book, Diop is quite emphatic about the fact that future generations of black African scholars can rest assured that true salvation lies at the end of such a task, and that in the final analysis the American contribution towards this end could be decisive.[11] It is with this in mind that I wish to give reconsideration to the book through an assessment of some of the techniques Diop employed by drawing upon some recent material which could lay a basis for corroborative evidence. However, it must be made perfectly clear from the very beginning that for most people in the west, *The African Origin of Civilization* encroaches upon beliefs about the origins of western civilization that have withstood centuries of cerebral erosion. Given the West's command over "advanced mechanical and social technology"[12] as opposed to Africa's lack of such a command, it would appear only natural to assume that such a condition springs from historical roots of primacy. The copious evidence that is now available in the West points in this direction, and until scholars, both black and white, begin to take up Diop's challenge to seek "the true African past," then his argument for an African primacy can only be hypothetical at the least and speculative at best.

In reading *African Origin*, and despite the questions raised by reviewers over the techniques employed, one is struck by the persuasiveness of Diop's argument. If one is trained or has some knowledge of the various disciplines employed in the work, then much of what is attempted begins to make sense. For example, recent archaeological research tends to corroborate or at best to give an indication that Diop's Black African population-base for Egyptian civilization is possible. Diop's contention is that the Nile Delta was not originally settled by pharaonic Egyptians coming from the east but was an expansionist move into the Delta from the southern plateaus, most likely from within the heart of present-day Sudan (Nubia?). In a fairly recent article by J.E.G. Sutton, "The Aquatic Civilization of Middle Africa," archaeological data has reconstructed what was a viable culture in existence throughout most of what is now the southern part of the Sahara desert.[13] The dates for this culture are 9,000 to 2,000 B.C. Further details on the culture can be found in the article,[14] but what is of importance here are the time span of this aquatic culture and economy, and the linguistic and physical type of the population. With regard to the physical type Sutton writes: ". . . any population in Middle Africa during the post-Pleistocene times is likely to have been more or less Negroid."[15] Relying on the work of Joseph Greenberg,[16] Sutton indicates that there is the possibility that the family language which linked the aquatic population together was Nilo-Saharan.[17] But as the Sahara began to dry up some time around four thousand B.C., much of Middle Africa was invaded by other cultural and linguistic groups (agriculturalists and pastoralists) whose lifestyles all but completely replaced that of the aquatic population. The time span is of interest because of the extent and duration of the aquatic civilization: existing for almost four and a half to five thousand years before the rise of pharaonic Egypt. The decline of this aquatic world appears to have coincided with the ever widening and increasing dessication of Middle Africa, and the encroachment of other linguistic and cultural groups. An interesting question which might have some bearing on Diop's thesis, is whether or not the movement of a significant number of people further north, and away from the drier regions of Middle Africa, in any way contributed to the rise of what eventually became Nubia in later pharaonic Egypt?

Perhaps in support of this are the revelations in an article which appeared in the *New York Times*. Based on preliminary observations of artifacts excavated fifteen years ago in the southern Sudan, the writer of the article acknowledges that the University of Chicago could have evidence for a Nubian monarchy which existed "as long ago as 3300 B.C., several generations before the earliest documented Egyptian king."[18] If the eventual publication of the findings indicate in any way the possibility of an ancient monarchy in Nubia, then a gradual settlement of the Nile Delta by peoples from the south enters into the realm of fact rather than remain totally dependent upon mere speculation.

Diop's argument for a southern origin as well as a northern push into the Delta by "black Africans" is quite similar to the material on the same topic presented by Henri Frankfort. In his book *Kingship and the Gods*, Frankfort refers to the fact that the population of the Delta takes its origins from the south: "The evidence of the fauna and flint tools suggests that the inhabitants descended in early neolithic times from the surrounding desert plateaus. The change of climate which turned these wide pasture lands into deserts at the same time made the marshes of the Nile Valley fit for human habitation . . . ."[19] Not only is Frankfort adamantly against a northeastern origin totally for the first inhabitants of the Delta, but he stalwartly defends the position that cultural traits of dynastic Egypt (social, political, and religious) lay up the Nile rather than in the Delta.[20] Diop's position is that the southern city of Abydos was the font of the Egyptian gods such as Osiris, Isis, and Horus, and that the African tradition of ancestor veneration (worship) is the historical precedent from which the cult of Osiris and the Great Procession derive.[21] In defense of this position Diop states: "Thus, contrary to Moret's[22] affirmation, authentic Egyptian tradition, as old as recorded time and written into the Texts of the Pyramids and The Book of the Dead, teaches us in unequivocal terms that the Egyptian deities belonged to the Black Race[23] and were born in the south. Furthermore, the myth of Osiris and Isis points out a cultural trait characteristic of Black Africa: the cult of ancestors, the foundation of Negro religious life and of Egyptian religious life as Amelineau[24] reports."[25] Perhaps mirroring Diop, Frankfort had this to say of Abydos:

> The most important of the Osiris relics, the head, was assigned to Abydos by tradition; and it was there that later times recognized the tomb of Osiris in the grave of one of the kings of the First Dynasty and that the Great Procession took place. From the Middle Kingdom onward, Abydos was the main center of the Osiris cult. We may well ask what were the grounds for this association of an unimportant town in Upper Egypt with the cult of the god. There is considerable, though circumstantial, evidence to suggest that the association was an original one. It seems that Osiris (as the dead king) was acknowledged and worshiped by the house from which Menes[26] derived and which owned the province of This where Abydos lies. If this is true, the worship of Osiris, not as a god of the dead, but as the mythological form of the dead ruler, was already established at Abydos before the rise of Menes . . . . One would expect, however, that the specific forms which that worship assumed (such as the Great Procession) and the name under which the dead kings were worshiped (Osiris) would derive from the region whence the royal house came. And this is precisely what the evidence seems to suggest.[27]

It is possible through the use of historical linguistics to make inferences about the cultural and linguistic traits that might historically connect two people as having been one in the past. The fact that the historian can resort to the use of linguistics to reconstruct the past makes one somewhat hesitant about *Choice's* 1974 statement that "the complex relations between Egypt and other parts of the world, black or otherwise, cannot be explained by the techniques employed in the book." First of all, language and culture are one and the same, i.e. (1) the use of linguistics gives the historian a wealth of evidence for the remote past that is beyond the reach of oral tradition, and (2) linguistics gives identity to cultures for which archaeology can only describe the material possessions.[28] Diop's use of linguistics in his work is in pursuit of these very things. In addition, "while an affinity of language provides insufficient grounds for assuming ethnic affinity, one can, however, sometimes deduce that behind a genetic relationship between several languages lies an ethnic relationship."[29] Again, one of the things demonstrated in *African Origin* is the affinity between Egyptians and the Africans to the south. Frankfort intimates this in his work. Although he uses linguistic terms that smack of the C.G. Seligman school,[30] he nevertheless links the origins of the Egyptians to the south. According to Frankfort:

> We know that the physique of the inhabitants of this valley [the Nile] from the Delta deep down into Nubia remained much the same from predynastic to late historic times. They also shared a common material culture in predynastic times. There are indications that this culture, the Amratian,[31] extended well into Libya and reached the Red Sea in the East. And somatic and ethnological resemblances, and certain features of their language, connect the ancient Egyptians firmly with the Hamitic-[Cushitic-] speaking people of East Africa. It seems that Pharaonic civilization arose upon this Northeast African Hamitic substratum . . . .[32]

According to Greenberg's classification of African languages, Ancient Egyptian is a daughter language of AfroAsiatic; and it would seem that all daughter languages subsumed under the mother (proto-) language could demonstrate a common font of cultural and linguistic characteristics. Essentially, what is inferred here is that through genetic relationships of languages it is possible to say something about the people who spoke the proto-languages (ancestral), as well as whether or not these people were one group in the remote past. Cognates (words with common origins) can indicate that relationship, as well as the reconstruction of vocabulary can tell us about the culture. And further, the use of linguistics can tell the historian the historical location of the proto-language.[33] Echoing the above, Herbert S. Lewis has stated:

> One conclusion suggested by the present distribution of the subgroups and languages of the Hamito- [i.e. Cushitic] semitic family is that when they began differentiating from the proto-Hamitic-Semitic they were located in Northeastern Africa, probably in Eastern Sudan. Such an inference derives from methods of analysis of linguistic distribution suggested by Sapir, Voegelin, Dyen, and others.[34] This hypothesis is of great importance for African historical reconstruction, for it maintains that there were no waves of Hamitic invaders from Asia . . . On the contrary, it would appear that the Semites migrated to Asia. Such conclusions have been suggested before, usually on other evidence by some Orientalists [here he refers to the book by G.A. Barton, *Hamitic and Semitic Origins* (Philadelphia, 1934)] . . . If this hypothetical reconstruction of the origins of these two families has any validity, then some cultural and physical similarities between these two groups might well be the result of their common share in an Eastern Sudanic culture area several thousand years ago . . . .[35]

Now the relevations in The New York Times article raise further questions as to the basis of *Choice's* remark that "even the data on the origin of writing are not well understood by the author." An important point that the article brings out is that this ancient Nubian civilization was on its way to literacy." . . . some of the Nubian artifacts bore disconnected symbols resembling those of Egyptian hieroglyphics that were readable . . . They [(Nubians) were . . . probably quite close to accomplishing what in fact became a base for Egyptian success with writing].''[36]

In light of the above, a reconsideration of Diop's basic thesis seems warranted: if not to establish conclusively that Pharaonic Egypt's origins were ''black,'' then at least to reconsider the validity of his basic ideas and the worth of his methods. It definitely offers historians a challenge; and if the recent revelations from the University of Chicago are any indication of Diop's remark that the American contribution could be decisive, then we have, without a doubt, begun the final phase.

Review by A.J. Williams-Myers

Notes

1. Cf. *Book Review Digest* 1974 (March 1974-Feb. 1975), New York, p. 295; *Choice*, (July-August 1974), Vol. 11, p. 810. Science Books, Vol. 10, no. 4 (March 1975), p. 971; *Booklist*, 70, 24 (July 1, 1974), p. 1178; Publisher's Weekly, 204, 24 (December 10, 1973), p. 34.

2. *Publisher's Weekly*, op. cit.; *Library Journal*, 99, (April 15, 1974), p. 1129.

3. *Choice*, op. cit.

4. *Booklist*, op. cit.

5. *Library Journal*, op. cit.

6. Ibid.; *Publisher's Weekly*,. op. cit.

7. *Choice*, op. cit.

8. Ibid., my emphasis.

9. Wolof is classified under West Atlantic languages, a sub-family of Congo-Kordofanian. If the genetic relation is with Ancient Egyptian, then it is rather distant. Perhaps what is suggested are lexical elements in Wolof as proof of contact and influence, but a generic relationship would be wrong.

10. Diop, *The African Origin of Civilization*, p. 276. It is interesting to note that Ancient Egyptian does not appear in the genetic diagram of ''The Indo-European family of Languages'' as listed in *The American Heritage Dictionary of the English Language, New College Edition* (Houghton Mifflin Company, Boston, New York, 1975), diagram on back cover. I suppose what needs to be explained is the lack of a linguistic influence from Egypt in light of a cultural and political impact on the West.

11. Diop, op. cit., p. xvii.

12. Cf. E.A. Britt, "Dependency and Development: Some Problems involved in the Analysis of Change in Colonial Africa," in *Cahiers d'Etudes Africaines*, XI, 44 (1971), p. 538.

13. J.E.G. Sutton, "The Aquatic Civilization of Middle Africa," *Journal of African History*, XV, 4 (1974), pp. 527-546. The area would not only include the southern reaches of the Sahara but the Sahel and countries adjacent to the Sahel stretching from west to east as far as the Great Lakes of East Africa.

14. An interesting point is Sutton's evidence for the existence of pottery in this part of Africa as early as 6,000 B.C., with the understanding that there is the possibility that pottery developed independently in different parts of the world. "Aquatic Civilization," pp. 529-531.

15. Ibid., p. 535.

16. J.H. Greenberg, *The Languages of Africa* (Indiana and The Hague, 1963).

17. Sutton, "Aquatic Civilization," pp. 536-537. Cf. Herbert S. Lewis, "Ethnology and African Culture History," in Creighton Gabel and Norman R. Bennett (eds.), *Reconstructing Africal Culture History* (Boston 1967), p. 43.

18. Boyce Rensberger, "Nubian Monarch Called Oldest," *The New York Times*, 128, 44, 143 (March 1, 1979), pp. A1, columns 2-3, and A16, columns 3-5. For a view that plays down the Nubian role see G.A. Barton, *Semitic and Hamitic Origins. Social Religious* (Philadelphia, University of Pennsylvania Press, 1934). The book definitely suffers from the weight of Eurocentrism. Barton had this to say about the Nubians: " . . . One must recognize the possibility that Nubians, the creators of the Badarian civilization, and even palaeolithic elements entered into the composition of the Egyptian people, but if so they were so absorbed by the Hamites and Semites that these became the dominant elements . . . linguistic evidence makes it clear that the dominant strains in the fusion of these elements were Hamitic and Semitic. The Egyptian language which emerged was a Hamitic language Semitized;" pp. 93-94. If one takes note of what is said (i.e. the use of Semites and Hamites), it is possible to see that unknowingly Barton, and others, is putting the precursors, although somewhat distortedly, of Egyptian culture up the Nile River and not in the Delta. For a fuller explanation of this point see below with respect to the use of Cushites rather than Hamites, note 30.

19. Henri Frankfort, *Kinship and the Gods* (Chicago University Press, 1948), p. 16. Cf. Barton, op. cit., pp. 89-91. Barton acknowledges settlement from the higher regions to the south but distortedly, through the association of Hamitic and Semitic with "white," links the settlers with areas far to the northwest and in the northern litoral of the Mediterranean.

20. Frankfort, op. cit., pp. 348-349, notes 3 and 4.

21. Diop, op. cit., pp. 75-77, 88-89. Cf. Frankfort, op. cit., pp. 202-207. Barton, *Semitic and Hamitic Origins*, is of the opinion that Osiris was a Semitic god and was imported into Egypt from the east. In classic Bartonian: "The Egyptians were not possessed of philosophic power . . .;" pp. 132-133, 176.

22. Cf. Alexandre Moret, *Le Nil et la civilisation egyptienne* (Paris, 1926), p. 118; cited in Diop.

23. This is perhaps what *Choice* had in mind when it remarked in its review of the book that "part of the problem rests in the careless identification of race with skin color"(?). Yet, how different is this from what Barton does in his book? Cf. Science Books, Vol. 10, no. 4 (March 1975), p. 971.

24. Abbe Emile Amelineau, *Prolegomenes a l'etude de la religion egyptienne* (Paris: Ed. Laroux, 1916), p. 104; *Nouvelles Fouilles d'Abydos* (Paris: Ed. Laroux, 1899), p. 248. Both cited in Diop.

25. Diop. op. cit., p. 91.

26. Menes is acknowledged as the first "black" Pharaoh of Egypt who united Upper Egypt with Lower Egypt. Also, he is referred to as Narmer. Barton calls him Mena on pages 94, 184, and 198. Diop's evidence points to Upper Egypt as the font of Egyptian culture, and that it was under Menes' rule that the construction of a dike was begun to divert the waters of the Nile in the Delta. The purpose of the dike was to make the Delta region habitable; and the city of Memphis was built upon the area that had been drained. Prior to this, the Delta was "universally recognized as the permanent home of the plague in the Near East." *African Origin*, p. 93. For more on the idea of "black" Pharaohs see Edith Sanders, "The Hamitic Hypothesis: Its Origin and Function in Time Perspective," *Journal of African History*, X, 4 (1969), pp. 521-32.

27. Frankfort, op. cit., pp. 201-202.

28. Christopher Ehret, "Linguistics as a Tool for Historians," *Hadith I*, (Dar Es Salaam 1968), pp. 199-133; B.A. Ogot (ed.).

29. Jan Vansina, *Oral Tradition: A Study in Historical Methodology*. Translated from the French by H.M. Wright, (Chicago, 1965) p. 180.

30. Terminology, such as Hamites and Nilo-Hamitic, rather than Cushites, are terms used in the works of C.G. Seligman, especially his *Races of Africa* (rev. ed.; London 1957). For an argument against the use of the terms Hamite/Nilo-Hamitic see C. Ehret, "Cushites and Highland and Plains Nilotes." in B.A. Ogot (ed.), *Zamani*: A Survey of *East African History* (Longman Group Ltd., 1973), pp. 150-169); J.E.G. Sutton, "The Settlement of East Africa." *Zamani*, esp. pp. 95-97, "Appendix: 'Hamites' and the Hamitic Myth." Cf. E.E. Evans-Pritchard, "Sources with Particular reference to the Southern Sudan," in *Cahiers D'Etudes Africaines*, XI, 42 (1971), pp. 130-131. On these pages the author gives the impression that he repudiates his earlier support for some of the distortions found in the Seligman's work.

31. According to Diop, "an early predynastic culture of Egypt characterized by finely worked implements of bone and stone." Cited in Diop, op. cit., p. 297. (Could this Amratian culture have anything to do with Sutton's "Aquatic Civilization?").

32. Frankfort, op. cit., 16. Cf. J.E. Greenberg, "The Negro Kingdoms of the Sudan," *Transactions of the New York Academy of Sciences*, XX: Ser. II (1949), pp. 126-135. In this paper Greenberg alludes to the fact that the origins of Pharaonic Egypt appear to be up the Nile; p. 135. Also, Herbert S. Lewis in his "Ethnology and African Culture History," op. cit, seems to take the same position. He intimates on page 39: "... It is clear, for example, that Moslem influences on the states of the Sudan were historically later and secondary to the processes of State formation. The same could be true (hypothetically) of Egyptian influences on the Nubian states."

33. Ehret, "Linguistics," p. 125. Cf. H.S. Lewis, "The Origins of the Galla and Somali," *Journal of African History*, VII, 1 (1966), pp. 27-46. It was formerly thought that the Galla and the Somali had their origins in southern Arabia, but Lewis, through linguistic analysis, establishes the origin for both in southern Ethiopia with other Cushitic-speakers. Even the Afars and Issas of Djibouti region are related to these southern Ethiopian Cushitic-speakers.

34. Cf. E. Sapir, *Time Perspective in Aboriginal American Culture: A Study in Method* (Ottawa, Geological Survey, Department of Mines, Memoir 90, 1916). C. Voegelin, "The Dispersal Factor in Migrations and Immigrations of American Indians," in R. Thompson, *Migrations in New World Culture History* (University of Arizona Social Science Bulletin No. 27, 1958, pp. 47-52. Both cited in Herbert S. Lewis, "Ethnology and African Culture History," note 38.

35. Lewis, "Ethnology and African Culture History," p. 43. See Barton, op. cit., for an argument that postulates an eastern movement into Egypt of bearers of civilization that gave rise to Pharaonic Egypt; pp. 92-93, 176. Cf. *Science Books*, op. cit. " . . . As the linguist Greenberg has made clear, the now extinct ancient Egyptian language is a branch coordinate with the African based Cushitic, Berber and Chad languages (which are sopken today by dark-skinned peoples) as well as Semitic. Their geographical distribution gives substantial reason to assume a common (linguistic) origin in the Nile valley. At this level Diop's argument is fascinating to follow . . . ."

36. Boyce Rensberger, op. cit., p. A16, column 4. Rather than "on its way to literacy", it is perhaps appropriate to say that the Nubians were on the threshold of literature.

DR. DIOP ON ASIA: HIGHLIGHTS AND INSIGHTS

Runoko Rashidi

Dr. Cheikh Anta Diop has been justly called the pharaoh of Nile Valley studies, and we are well aware that the African origin of Egyptian civilization has been the major focus of his more than thirty years of research. It is impossible, however, as Diop makes clear, to isolate the populations and civilizations of early Africa from the rest of the world. Asia must also be taken into consideration in this respect, if only to be examined as an extension of the African cradleland. Diop, as usual, has done this remarkably well. Indeed, his work on Asia has blazed as brilliant a trail as his more comprehensive work on continental Africa. If he is not the pharaoh of Afro-Asian studies as well, he is the author, at least, of some of the most profound explorations of the subject.

Diop's concern is not only with Africa as the cradle of civilization but as the cradle of humanity as well. For a long time the cradle of humanity was actually placed in Asia. This was done for three reasons: (1) the ancient presence in Asia of all three major human races: Black, White, and Yellow; (2) the discovery of Homo Erectus in Java at a time when Africa had not become a target for archaeological and palaeontological excavation; and (3) the Biblical tradition which puts the cradle of humanity in Western Asia, with the creation of Adam and Eve. With new discoveries, however, the cradle of humanity has become ever firmly entrenched in Africa and seems more and more destined to remain there.

In addition to Homo Erectus, who was the first hominid to journey into Asia (the arival of Homo Erectus in Europe is a much later development), the Great Lakes region of East-Central Africa also produced the first modern human populations (Homo sapiens sapiens) yet identified, which, as a result of migrations, came to populate Asia.

Both Homo Erectus and Homo sapiens sapiens, born originally in Africa, were undeniably Black:

> The man born in Africa was necesssarily dark-skinned due to the considerable force of ultraviolet radiation to the equatorial belt. As he moved toward the more temperate climes, this man gradually lost his pigmentation by a process of selection and adaptation.[1]

There were different routes with varying degrees of difficulty that the Africans could have taken as they left the Great Lakes region. These routes

Bust of a Black warrior from Afghanistan. C. 100-200 A.D. Stucco. (Photo courtesy of James E. Brunson)

include the Nile Valley, the Suez Isthmus, Palestine and from there to far Asia, Oceania and Europe. "It is in the light of this route that the human presence in Palestine can be traced. No one was born there. They came from elsewhere."[2]

THE ORIGIN AND EVOLUTION OF MONGOLOID ETHNIC GROUPS

As a working hypothesis Diop postulates that the "Yellow race" is probably the result of extensive co-mingling between Whites and Blacks at an extremely early age in human history. He argues that the melanin content of "Yellow peoples," as well as physical characteristics, such as prognathism, lips and nose, are those of "mixed breeds." Of course these characteristics would become further distinguished by centuries and millennia of forced adaptation to environmental factors, among the most critical of which are wind currents.[3]

Certainly, traces of Blacks have been found in both the prehistoric and historic periods throughout the latitudes of Northeastern Asia, and Diop calls our attention to a Japanese proverb: "For a samurai to be brave he must have a

Africoid representatives of China's first historic dynasty—the Shang, 1523-1028 B.C. Bronze. According to the Chou, the Shang were distinguished by "black and oily skin." (Photo courtesy of James E. Brunson)

bit of black blood."[4] We also have knowledge, in Japan, of Sakanouye Tamuraro (c. 800 A.D.) the Black general who led the Japanese armies into battle against the Ainu, who were the neolithic inhabitants of Japan, and whose name harkens back to the ancient Anu of Nile Valley fame. Tamuraro's successful generalship ultimately won him the Japanese shogunate.[5]

In China an Africoid presence is visible from the Paleolithic through the Mesolithic periods. The recent work of Afro-centric art historian James Brunson is critical here, because it substantially adds to Diop's own work in the area. Brunson, in fact, has gone considerably farther than anyone else in exploring China's early Black presence. He shows that China's historic period was alive with an active Black participation. The Shang, for example, China's first dynasts, apparently had a Black background, so much so that the conquering Chou described them as having "black and oily skin."[6]

COULD EGYPTIAN CIVILIZATION BE OF ASIAN ORIGIN?

Mesopotamia

Diop argues that it is important to distinguish between what can be deduced from a strict examination of historical documents and what is claimed beyond those documents. To assign Egyptian civilization an Asian origin, or, for that matter, any foreign origin, it is necesssary to be able to show a prior cradle of civilization outside of Africa. Diop establishes that there is no tangible evidence of this, and points out that the world's oldest recorded date, 4236 B.C., is from Africa, when the calendar was already in use in Egypt. If there was a contemporary or simultaneous high-culture in Western Asia, Diop argues, the material basis for it is vague and uncertain, suggesting that the most ancient civilization of West Asia (Sumer) has been artificially embellished and given an unsubstantiated precedence over Egypt.

> Egypt's pyramids, temples, and obelisks, its abundance of columns at Luxor and Karnak, its avenues of Sphinxes, the colossi of Memnon, its rock carvings, its underground temples with proto-Doric columns (Deir el-Bahri) at Thebes, are an architectural reality still palpable today, historical evidence that no dogma can blow into thin air. In contrast, what did Iran and Mesopotamia produce prior to the eighth century (epoch of the Assyrians)? Only shapeless clay mounds.[7]

Even conservative Sumerologists date the beginnings of Sumer's initial dynastic period at not earlier than 2750 B.C., whereas Egypt's dynastic history was in motion, at the latest, by 3100 B.C., and thus it is small wonder that Diop regards the synchronization of Egyptian and Mesopotamian history as a political necessity "resulting from ideology, not from fact". The goal behind this game is to successfully explain Egypt through Mesopotamia, that is Western Asia, thus denying Egypt its African roots. "If we remain within the realm of authentic facts, we are," he says, "forced to view Mesopotamia as a belatedly born daughter of Egypt."[8]

Diop does not end his discussion of Mesopotamia at this point but seeks to examine, though briefly, the ethnicity of the Sumerians themselves, whose thousand-year existence is essentially one of city-states, and only seldom that of large kingdoms and empires. Who were these Sumerians of Mesopotamia, Diop asks, who occupy such a prestigious, if disputed, position in world history?

On the Nile Valley origin of the Sumerians, Diop draws attention to several points of corroborative evidence, which are listed below:

1. The Hebraic traditions support the idea that the Sumerians were Black migrants from the Nile Valley. Genesis states that "Cush (Ethiopia) begat Nimrod: he began to be a mighty one in the earth. . .And the beginning of his kingdom was Babel. . .in the land of Shinar (Sumer)."[9]
2. The evidence of *The Epic of Gilgamesh*, a passage from which Diop cites: "Father Enlil, Lord of the countries, Father Enlil, Lord of the True Word, Father Enlil, Pastor of the Blacks. . ."[10]
3. The statue of Anu, "the primitive god, father of Ishtar, has the same Negro name as Osiris the Onian." Anu was the great father of the gods, including Ishtar and Enlil, in Sumerian religious mythology.[11] Anu was also a name frequently associated with the early Blacks of the Nile Valley and related areas. The Anu Seti, for example, lived on the banks of the Upper Nile, in the Sudan. The Anu-Tehennu were the early Black inhabitants of Libya. The ancient people of Arabia Petraea were called the Anu. According to Diop, "These Blacks [the Anu] were probably the first to practice agriculture, to irrigate the valley of the Nile, build dams, invent sciences, arts, writing, the calendar. They created the cosmogony contained in *The Book of The Dead*, texts which leave no doubt about the *Negroness* of the race that conceived the ideas."[12]
4. (A) The Egyptian traditions, as reported to Roman historian Diodorus Siculus, c. 40 B.C., on the origins of the Chaldeans, who were the descendants of the Sumerians. The Egyptians considered the Chaldeans a transported colony of Egyptian astronomer-priests.[13] (B) The close resemblance of the ancient ziggurats in Mesopotamia and Iran to the step-pyramids of Africa. Diop notes, for example, that the Tower of Babel, also known as "Birs-Nimroud" and the "Temple of Baal," was probably the astronomical observatory of the Chaldeans. He then raises the question, "What, then, would be more normal than the existence of step pyramids in Saqqara, in Babylon (Kushite city of Bel), in the Ivory Coast (in the form of bronze weights), and in Mexico where Negro emigration across the Atlantic is attested by Mexican authors and archeologists themselves?"[14]

Diop illustrates the Sumerians visually with a striking photograph of Gudea, c. 2300 B.C., the Africoid ruler of the kingdom of Lagash.[15] Interestingly enough, Gudea, in spite of the general scarcity of stone, which Diop makes abundantly clear, had numerous, almost life-size statues of himself carved from hard *black* diorite, as though he could have actually anticipated the historical dilemna his descendants would find themselves in, and thus left his personal calling cards that would shout to the world his Nile Valley roots.

Diop points to the Africoid presence in early Iran (Elam), focusing especially on the region's artistic and sculptural remains identified by Dieulafoy from his late 19th century excavations at Susa. He also cites supporting statements on the physical characteristics of the people, as noted by Contenau fifty years later. On the basis of this, he concludes his discussion on Western Asia with the following remarks:

> Millions are spent on excavating clay mounds in Mesopotamia, in the hope of finding evidence to pinpoint with certainty and finality the birthplace of civilization in Western Asia.[16]
>
> Although those who undertake this have very slim hope of ever attaining their objective, they nonetheless continue, as if the routine had become a permanent habit.[17]

Phoenicia and Arabia

Next in importance for Diop, after the early Asian civilizations of Mesopotamia and Iran, is Phoenicia. This was the name given by Greeks in the first millennium B.C. to the coastal provinces of modern Lebanon and northern Palestine, although occasionally the term seems to have been applied to the entire eastern Mediterranean seaboard from Syria to Palestine. Phoenicia was not considerred a nation, in the strict sense of the word, but rather as a chain of coastal cities, of which the most important were Sidon, Byblos, Tyre and Ras Shamra. To the Greeks, the term Phoenician, from the root "Phoenix," had connotations of "red," so presumably the name was derived from the physical appearance of the people themselves.

The Phoenicians were a coastal branch of the Canaanites who, according to Biblical tradition, were the brothers of Cush (Ethiopia) and Mizraim (Egypt), members of the Hamite, or Kamite, ethnic family. The Bible says that the Canaanites, Ethiopians and Egyptians were all Black and of Nile Valley origin.[18] Diop claims that "Phoenician history is therefore incomprehensible only if we ignore the Biblical data according to which the Phoenicians, in other words, the Canaanites, were originally Negroes, already civilized, with whom nomadic, uncultured white tribes [as represented by Abraham] later mixed."[19] From this period, towards the middle of the second millennium B.C, the term Leuco (White) Syrians came to be applied to the newly arived populations. Ultimately, says Diop, the people of Abraham and the already settled Canaanites fused to become the historical Hebrews.

While acknowledging the Biblical data, Diop cautions that the economic relations shared by Egypt and the Phoenicians should not be minimized in explaining the strong sense of solidarity which generally existed between them. There was frequently an Egyptian presence: military, diplomatic, religious or commercial, both in the Canaanite hinterland and the Phoenician city-states themselves, and Diop goes on to state that, "Even throughout the most troubled periods of great misfortune, Egypt could count on the Phoenicians as one can count more or less on a brother."[20]

Looking at Phoenician religious mythology, Diop finds himself almost peering into a mirror of Egypt. He highlights, for example, the importance of

Jewish captive from Lachish, Palestine, c. 700 B.C. Assyrian. "Ultimately, says Diop, the people of Abraham and the already settled Canaanites fused to become the historical Hebrews." (Photo courtesy of James E. Brunson)

Taaut, who was none other than the *Thoth* (thought), or *Tehuti*, of the Egyptians. In both cultures he was the inventor of sciences and letters. This information may be found in the fragments of Sanchroniatho and, in the texts of Ras Shamra, we find that the original home of the national heroes of Phoenicia is placed in the south, near the borders of Egypt.

Spurred on by increasing population pressures, the Phoenicians, who were becoming increasingly mixed racially, had by the middle of the second millennium B.C. developed a prowess on the seas, and were in the process of establishing a network of colonies and trading posts that not only brought them fame and prosperity, but introduced in some cases, and reinforced in others, vital elements of the cultural attributes of the Southern world. "It seems impossible" says Diop "to exaggerate the essential role played by Negroes and Negroids at a time when the European races were still uncivilized."[21]

Of course the most famous colony of the Phoenicians was Khart-Haddas (new town) later known as Carthage. Khart-Haddas was established in 814 B.C. on the North African coast, in what are now territories embracing portions of both Tunisia and Algeria. The colony was supposedly founded by Dido, who was a queen of the Phoenician city of Tyre, although the name itself may have actually been a title indicating female royalty, as opposed to a proper name.

Arabia

Arabia too, Diop notes, was once an exclusively Kushite domain with a high civilization in the south, upon which was imposed nomadic white ethnic elements from the north and east. In elaborating this theme, Diop relies significantly upon the research of 19th century French historian Francois Lenormant, whose works have constituted, for Diop and others, a rich source of information on the Black presence in early Western Asia.

One of the effects of the invasions of these white nomads into Arabia was the flight of blacks, who streamed across the Red Sea back into Africa, creating inseparable links linguistically and ethnographically between South Arabia and Ethiopia.

Of the great Black personalities of Arabia, Diop hightlights *Bilqis*, or Makeda, the famous Queen of Sheba (Saba); *Lokman*, the supposed architect of the stupendous Marib Dam and a great sage of the east, on whose life Aesop's is thought to have been modeled; and *Antar*, the fabulous hero of pre-Islamic Arabia. It was upon this base that the religion of Islam as proclaimed by Mohammad, who also appears to have had a prominent Black ancestry, arose to stir humanity and shake the world.

The Indus Valley Civilization

The riverine civilization of the Indus Valley (in the area now known as Pakistan) is included by Diop in the Zone of Confluence. It marks its eastern limits. The Harappan civilization, named after one of its largest and most studied sites, Harappa, flourished from about 2200 B.C. to 1700 B.C. The complex actually had extensions reaching from the river Oxus in Afghanistan in the north to the Gulf of Gambay in India in the south. At its height, the Harappans engaged in regular commercial relations with Iraq and Iran. This much we know with certainty. We are equally certain that the founders of the Harappan civilization were Black. This is verifiable through the available physical evidence—skeletal remains, the eye-witness accounts preserved in the Rig Veda, artistic and sculptural remains, the regional survival of Dravidian languages (including Brahui, Kurukh and Malto) and the essential role of these languages, which are now being used in the decipherment of the Harappan script. We should also take into account the prominence accorded the mother goddess in the Harappan cities and the sedentary nature of the Harappan people themselves. Fairservis claims that the Harappans cultivated cotton and may have domesticated the chicken.[22]

The decline and fall of the Indus cities has been linked to several factors. The most important of these are: the reduction of agricultural productivity due to over cultivation; an escalation in local flooding, as a result of tectonic fluctuations in the area of the Lower Indus; a proliferation of human and cattle populations; and the increasingly frequent incursions of Indo-Aryan patriarchal, nomadic clans from Central Asia and later Iran. The name Iran, in fact, means the "land of the Aryan."

Two Cradles and the Zone of Confluence

Western Asia, some of whose civilizations we have briefly surveyed, and Byzantium as well, are placed by Diop in the Zone of Confluence, which for him is the middle ground between the Southern or Black Cradle and the Northern or White Cradle. In addition to each cradle's racial distinctions, there were cultural patterns peculiar to each.

For Diop, and this is critical in his view of the evolution of the world, the Zone of Confluence, or overlap, was a cradle in itself, out of which emerged the Semitic world. He states that, "Anthropologically and culturally speaking, the Semitic world was born during protohistoric times from the mixture of white-skinned and black-skinned people in Western Asia."[23] At this juncture, Diop asserts, we go beyond the point of working hypothesis into the realm of

Head of an unknown Africoid male from the Indus Valley. Found at Harappa, Pakistan; one of the two major Indus Valley sites, c. 2000 B.C. The Indus Valley complex marks the eastern boundaries of Diop's Zone of Confluence. (Photo courtesy of James E. Brunson)

provable fact, which is where we want to go, and where we must go for a serious understanding of the ethnic composition and evolution of a geographical region encompassing probably the most complex and confusing collection of physical types in the world.

The Southern Cradle, confined to Africa, was characterized by the matriarchal family and the emancipation of women in domestic life; the creation of the territorial state; an attraction to things foreign, whether manners, styles or peoples; an international or worldly, as opposed to a local or provincial, outlook; and a "sort of social collectivism having as corollary a tranquility going as far as unconcern for tomorrow and a material solidarity of right for each individual." In the moral sphere, the Southern Cradle reflects ideals of peace, justice and goodness, with an optimistic view devoid of a concept of guilt or original sin.[24]

Regarding matriarchy, Diop notes that it is a well-balanced and harmonious dualism, defended and protected by both sexes, where irrespective of sexual distinctions "each and everyone could fully develop by following the activity best suited to his physiological nature."[25]

The Northern Cradle, on the other hand, was characterised by the patriarchal family; the city-state, "outside of which a man was an outlaw"; a fear and hostility towards things foreign; individualism, moral and material solitude; and what could only be called a pessimistic view of existence itself. The Northern Cradle introduced cremation, while the Southern Cradle utilized burial as a method of disposing of the dead.[26]

The Dispersal of the Nomads

> Behold, he shall come up as clouds, and his chariots shall be as a whirlwind: his horses are swifter than eagles. Woe unto us! for we are spoiled.[27]

Who were these people of the Northern Cradle, these nomads, and how did they come to wreak such havoc and destruction upon the civilized world, especially the long established agricultural settlements of the Blacks? This was, first of all, not an isolated phenomenon and the movements of the Aryan tribes into Iran, Pakistan and India reflect a major turning point in the history of mankind and the overall ascendancy of the Indo-European speakers in the world at large. The Kassite rulers of Babylon, for example, in power for roughly 500 years beginning about 1600 B.C. had Indo-Aryan names. So did the rulers of the kingdom of Mitanni (1500 B.C. to 1370 B.C.) on the Upper Euphrates. There were Indo-European elements amongst the Hyksos invaders of Egypt, c. 1720 B.C. Such elements could also be found within the Hittite aristocracy of Turkey and northern Syria of the same period.

A western branch of Indo-European speakers, the Achaeans, who were cousins of the Aryans, violently attacked the settled populations of early

Greece, besieged and sacked Troy, and conquered the centuries-old civilization of Minoan Crete around 1450 B.C. Two centuries later appeared the Dorians, also Indo-Europeans, even more violent than their Achaean predecessors. The Dorians rapidly proceeded to assault the surviving cities of Crete, and either exterminated, reduced to vassalage, or chased away many of the former inhabitants of Greece itself. We see some of the results of the Dorian conquests in the brief rise of the Sea Peoples, who, fleeing from the encroachments of other nomads even more aggressive than themselves, shattered the Hittites, conquered the Libyan populations, and invaded Egypt three times in the reigns of Merenptah (19th dynasty) and Ramses III (20th dynasty).

Since the late 19th century the Indo-European homeland has been placed somewhere in the vast Eurasian steppes between the frontiers of China on the east and the plains of Central Europe on the west. This veritable sea of grass was the true breeding ground of nomads. By the fifth millennium B.C. these steppes were peopled by scattered tribes united by common cultural traditions and a proto-Indo-European language which separated ultimately into local dialects with a common root.

The Eurasian steppes was also the home of the wild ancestors of the horse, which was rapidly domesticated, and with the development and evolution of increasingly sophisticated and elaborate harnesses, saddles, stirrups and related gear, effectively exploited by the region's nomadic populations. Whether this occurred first among the Indo-Europeans themselves or the Mongoloids further to the east is not known, but there is no question that the Indo-Europeans made the first significant impact in their application of this development. The same can be said for the spoked wheel chariot which the Indo-Europeans may or may not have invented, but certainly perfected.

Whether in the hunt or in war, the steppe dwellers made use of the powerful compound bow, strengthened with bone and sinew in a manner designed to increase its resilience. The compound bow and the light, spoked-wheel chariot constituted the ultimate military weaponry of their era, making those that possessed and effectively utilized them highly formidable, if not absolutely irresistible, on the battlefield. Metallurgy was exposed to the Indo-European tribes north of the Caucaucus no later than 2500 B.C., which enabled them to acquire a wide range of copper and bronze weapons and tools.

Now armed wth military technologies second to none, by the end of the third millennium B.C. the Indo-European tribes, including the Aryans, were in full motion, carrying their families and all worldly possessions on their backs and in their wagons. Whether motivated by drought, excess populations, or forces and factors that have not been fully explained, these northern nomads were heading like a great human juggernaut towards new and unknown lands, uprooting whole peoples in their path. The Southern world, ill prepared to defend itself against the onslaught, was rocked to its foundations.

What sort of people were these Indo-European intruders from the steppes? What kind of mentality did they have and how did they see themselves and the world? Diop is so brilliant on these issues that it is necessary to quote him at length:

> The ferocity of nature in the Eurasian steppes, the barrenness of those regions, the overall circumstances of material conditions, were to create instincts necessary for survival in such an environment. Here, Nature left no illusion of kindliness: it was implacable and permitted no negligence; man must obtain his bread by the sweat of his brow. Above all, in the course of a long, painful existence, he must learn to rely on himself alone, on his own possibilities. He could not indulge in the luxury of believing in a beneficient God who would shower down abundant means of gaining a livelihood; instead, he would conjure up deities maleficent and cruel, jealous and spiteful: Zeus, Yahweh, among others.
>
> In the unrewarding activity that the physical environment imposed on man, there was already implied materialism, anthropomorphism (which is but one of its aspects), and the secular spirit. This is how the environment gradually molded these instincts in the men of that region, the Indo-Europeans in particular. All the peoples of the area, whether white or yellow, were instinctively to love conquest, because of a desire to escape from those surroundings. The milieu chased them away; they had to leave it or succumb, try to conquer a place in the sun in a more clement nature. Invasions would not cease, once an initial contact with the Black world to the south had taught them the existence of a land where the living was easy, riches abundant, technique flourishing.
>
> Man in those regions long remained a nomad. He was cruel. The cold climate would engender the worship of fire, to remain burning from the fire of Mithras (in Persian mythology, Mithras was the god of the light and truth, later of the sun) to the flame on the tomb of the Unknown Soldier under the Arch of Triumph and the torches of the ancient and modern Olympics. Nomadism was responsible for cremation: thus the ashes of ancestors could be transported in small urns. This custom was perpetuated by the Greeks; the Aryans introduced it to India after 1450 B.C., and that explains the cremation of Caesar, and of Gandhi in our own epoch.
>
> Obviously, man was the pillar of that kind of life. Woman's economic role was much less significant than in Black agricultural societies. Consequently, the nomadic patriarchal family was the only embryo of social organization. The patriarchal principle would rule the whole life of the Indo-Europeans.[28]

If we have quoted the author at length here, it is because we regard these passages as representative of Cheikh Anta Diop at his finest: incisive, succinct, uncompromising, almost brutally direct.

The Aryan tribes may have begun to make their presence felt in the Harappan complex as early as the end of the third millennium B.C. and their increasingly bold and frequent raids added, with the progression of time, the finishing touches to a civilization already well into its late period. The invaders seemed to have been well aware of their impact on the Blacks and were quite conscious of the destruction around them:

> The people to whom these ruined sites, lacking posts, formerly belonged, these many settlements widely distributed, they, O Vaisvanara, having been expelled by thee, have migrated to another land.[29]

> Through fear of you (Agni) the dark people went away, not giving battle, leaving behind their possessions, when, O Vaisvanara, burning brightly for Puru, and destroying the cities, you did shine.[30]

The Aryans may have deliberately shattered the dams and reservoirs of the Blacks, and Indra is said to have freed the waters by rolling stones like wagon-wheels. As Purandara, the "fort-destroyer," Indra gave the Aryans victory over the Blacks in their strongholds, walled towns and now fortified cities.

Raiding now gave way to settlement. By 800 B.C. the Aryans had extended their conquests from Pakistan to the entire Gangetic plain of India east to the river Jamuna. Their new dominions they called Aryavarta (the Aryan Land). This era, which is called the Vedic Period by historians, reflects the consolidation of Aryan power and institutions in North India, and the extermination of many of the conquered Blacks, the subordination of many others, and untold numbers of other Blacks who simply left the region, to establish, for example, the Dravidian kingdoms of South India.

Two of the most interesting institutions we find in Aryavarta, and later in South India with the spread of Aryan ideas, are the *suttee* and *jati*. Diop has effectively pointed to the patriarchal character and the practice of cremation among the descendants of the Northern Cradle, and nowhere is this seen more vividly than in the *suttee*, one of India's most awesome and awful rituals. The suttee was the self-immolation of the devout Hindu widow on the funeral pyre of the deceased husband. The suttee rite accomplished two goals: the wife could continue to serve her husband-lord in the next life, and would save both souls for thirty-five million years! If she can not burn herself, she must at least remain chaste. If not, she will go to hell. If the deceased died on a distant battlefield, the widow might take an article of his clothing, and with this in her possession successfully burn herself. If the widow were pregnant or had an infant child, she might be honourably spared the suttee.[31]

Jati pertains to what is in the West called caste, which is actually a Portuguese term and concept based on what they saw in India. Caste however, Diop argues, is actually an indigenous African institution, which was also in existence in the Black dominated civilizations of Western Asia, and Pakistan and India. When the Aryans entered these areas they found this system, which was based on labor, already intact and functionally operational. Diop says that, "the caste system of social organization assures a greater permanence and equililbrium to a society than does the system of classes created by the

Aryans in Rome and Greece," and the "criteria of color has a low priority indeed without any ethnic connotations."[32] On this latter issue however, Diop is in sharp disagreement with a number of Afro-centric researchers, including myself. The Aryan aristocracy did adopt certain elements of the prevailing social system. One has to recall that the Aryans were essentially nomads, and after hundreds of years of interaction with the Blacks and an adjustment to settled life, this seems only natural. But the caste system was modified with a cold blooded racist logic, with the Whites on top, the mixed races in the middle and the mass of the conquered Blacks at the bottom. This is not to deny that there were Black priests and tribal or provincial leaders who managed to gain prominence in the essentially Aryan but still evolving social structure. The masses however, the vast multitude of the Blacks, were placed at the bottom and were called the Sudras. As early as the Rig Veda, 1500 B.C. to 1000 B.C., we find in Aryavarta the notion that the Sudras sprang from the feet of Brahman (God) and were predestined to serve the upper castes in any capacity required, most often as landless agricultural laborers. In religious mythology the Sudras were regarded as untruth itself, and were always identified with the color Black. Caste in early India was inseparable from race. Indeed, the term *jati* was closely connected with *varna*, a Sanscrit word which literally means "color" or "complexion."[33]

This was the rigid and ugly reality for the Black masses in conquered India. Servitude became the basis of their lives for generation after generation after generation. Their reward for perfect service: a higher birth in the next life. This chain of subordination was not broken until the reign of Mahapadma Nanda in the fourth century B.C. who was known as "the exterminator of the Kshatriya race." In the Mauryan dynasty, which was again of Sudra origin, social gains were also made by the Sudra caste, but this is a much later period of Indian history. By this era, 300 B.C., a physical amalgamation of sorts had taken place, but it had not been a total synthesis, and the original racial distinctions had only been blurred, not completely forgotten. They still have not been forgotten today, although the original four castes have now proliferated into thousands of sub-castes and outcastes, or "untouchables."

The social structure of Iran (the land of the Aryan) seems to have paralleled that of the Indian Aryavarta in its racial element. The Iranian upper caste was composed of the *Airyamen*, who were divided into priests, chariot driving nobles, herdsmen and artisans. Apparently the lower caste was recognized as distinct in race for the name of this caste was *pishtra*, literally color.[34]

When Buddhism finally emerges in the sixth century B.C. it comes in the form of a protest against Hinduism. The significance of caste is relatively minor in Buddhism, and it therefore comes as no surprise that it developed such a large and rapid following in the sectors of India where the Blacks existed in large numbers. Diop points out that "it would seem that Buddha was an Egyptian priest, chased from Memphis by the persecutions of Cam-

Young Dravidian male from early 20th-century South India (Dravida). Venetian traveller Marco Polo called Dravida "the greatest India," and assures us "that the darkest man is here the most highly esteemed and considered better than the others who are not so dark!"

byses. This tradition would justify the portrayal of Buddha with wooly hair. Historical documents do not invalidate this tradition. . . .There is general agreement today on placing in the sixth century not only Buddha but the whole religious and philosophical movement in Asia with Confucius in China, Zoroaster in Iran. This would confirm the hypothesis of a dispersion of Egyptian priests at that time spreading their doctrine in Asia."[35] It is worth noting, as a final note in this regard, that the Chinese sage Lao-Tze, c. 600 B.C., who, along with the Buddha, is said to have been of a virgin birth, was "black in complexion." He was described as "marvelous and beautiful as jasper." Magnificient temples were erected for him, inside of which he was worshipped like a god.

APPENDIX

C4-C/75, Janakpuri
New Delhi, India
September 26, 1983

Runoko Rashidi
4140 Buckingham Rd.
Los Angeles, CA 90008
U.S.A.

Dear Mr. Rashidi:

It is really fascinating to have your letter of September 15, 1983. We are equally anxious to develop relations and mutual cooperation with Blacks in general and American Blacks in particular.

It is undoubtedly true that Dalits (oppressed and suppressed) who were abused to the extent of being called *untouchables, have a black background.* But we are sympathetic towards American Blacks because they have no identity in American society. American Blacks are also second class citizens in practice as we are in ours. This is more harmful than foreign rule. Battle against foreign rule, and you have sympathies and support all over the world, whereas you are totally missing this when you fight against discrimination that you are facing in your daily life. Do you not think the Blacks in various newly independent countries are honourable and enjoy better status in the eyes of whites, including American Whites, than the Blacks in America?

This is how we are always sympathetic towards American Blacks. When American Blacks showed militancy and started talking about Black Power, we were highly impressed and we named a most militant organization of Dalits at present, as Dalit Panther. Undoubtedly, the word Panther is taken from Black Panther. I do not know whether you are aware or not that Dalit literature, is also influenced very much by the protest literature being written by the Blacks.

So, we have very much in common. And, if we realise, that we have to fight back the situation, which is the worst type of exploitation, we can at least build strong world opinion against this. Similarly exploited class such as Burakumen in Japan, can also join us.

More when I hear from you. Meanwhile please accept my warmest greetings. Yours in struggle,

Bapurao Pakhiddey,
Dalit Panther of India

NOTES

1. Cheikh Anta Diop, "Africa: Cradle of Humanity," *Nile Valley Civilizations*, ed. Ivan Van Sertima *Journal of African Civilizations*, vol. 6, no. 2, 1984, p. 27.
2. Diop, p. 26.
3. Diop, *African Origin of Civilization*, trans. Mercer Cook (New York: Lawrence Hill & Company, 1974) pp. 280-281.
4. Diop, p. 281.
5. Beatrice J. Fleming and Marion J. Pryde, *Distinguished Negroes Abroad* (Washington, D.C.: The Associated Publishers, n.d.) pp. 3-9.
6. James E. Brunson, *Black Jade: African Presence in The Ancient East* (DeKalb, Illinois: KARA Publishing, 1985).
7. Diop, *African Origin of Civilization*, p. 101.
8. Diop, p. 106.
9. Genesis 10: 8-10.
10. Diop, *African Origin of Civilization*, p. 105.
11. Diop, p. 105.
12. Diop, p. 77.
13. Diop, p. 101.
14. Diop, p. 102.
15. Diop, p. 42.
16. Diop, p. 123.
17. Diop.
18. *Genesis* 9.
19. Diop, *African Origin of Civilization*, pp. 107-108.
20. Diop, p. 108.
21. Diop, p. 119.
22. Walter Fairservis, "The Script of The Indus Valley Civilization," *African Presence In Early Asia*, eds. Ivan Van Sertima & Runoko Rashidi (New Brunswick, New Jersey, 1985) pp. 64-79.
23. Diop, *African Origin of Civilization*, p. XV.
24. Diop, *Cultural Unity of Black Africa* (Chicago: Third World Press, 1978) p. 195.
25. Diop, p. 120.
26. Diop, p. 195.
27. *Jeremiah* 5:13.
28. Diop, *African Origin of Civilization*, pp. 112-113.
29. *Hymns of The Rig Veda*, quoted by T. Burrow, "The Aryan Invasion of India," *The Encyclopedia of Ancient Civilizations*, ed. Arthur Cotterell (New York: Mayflower Books, 1980) p. 184.

30. *Hymns of The Rig Veda.*

31. "It must not be imagined that the Brahmans have legally possessed the means of dragging the devoted victim to the pile, by any other chains than those of superstition. . . .The main crime of the Brahmans then has been the fabrication, from these flimsy materials, of the soul-enfeebling chain of superstition, and decking it with flowers of heavenly promise. There is, besides these, another powerful motive which operates in conjunction with them. Among the Hindus a woman, after the decease of her husband, loses entirely her consequence in his family, and is degraded to a situation little above that of a menial. She is told that if she become a Suttee, she will not only escape from that life of assured debasement and contempt, but will ascent to a state as preeminently exalted; and will thus (whatever the crimes of the parties may have been) save both her own soul, and the souls of her husband and her husband's family from purgatory and future transmigration. I now turn me to a different picture. . .which various other authorities before, as well as my own local inquiries, oblige me to say is not infrequent. . . . 'Bancha-ramu, a native of Mujil-poora, a place about a day's journey from Calcutta, dying, his wife went to be burnt with the body. All the previous ceremonies were performed: she was fastened on the pile, and the fire was kindled; but the night was dark and rainy. When the fire began to scorch this poor woman, she contrived to disentangle herself from the dead body, and creeping from under the pile hid herself among some brushwood. In a little time it was discovered that there was only one body on the pile. The relations immediately took the alarm and searched for the poor wretch. The son soon dragged her forth, and insisted that she should throw herself on the pile again, or hang or drown herself. She pleaded her life at the hands of her own son, and declared that she could not embrace so horrid a death: but she pleaded in vain. The son urged that he should lose his caste, and that, therefore he would die or she should. Unable to persuade her, the son and others present then tied her hands and feet, and threw her on the funeral pile, when she quickly perished.'" Charles Coleman, *The Mythology of The Hindus* (London: Parbury, Allen, and Co., 1832) pp. 166-173.

32. Diop, *L'Unite culturell de L'Afrique Noir* (Paris: Presence Africain, 1960).

33. One of the very best discussions of this subject is Vulindlela Wobogo's "Diop's Two Cradle Theory and The Origin of White Racism," *Black Books Bulletin*, ed. Haki R. Madhubuti (Chicago: Institute of Positive Education, 1976) vol. 4, Winter, pp. 21-29.

34. T. Olmstead, *History of The Persian Empire* (Chicago: University of Chicago Press, 1948) p. 22.

35. Diop, *African Origin of Civilization*, p. 287.

CIVILIZATION OR BARBARISM: THE LEGACY OF CHEIKH ANTA DIOP

C.A. Diop, *Civilisation ou Barbarie: Anthropologie sans complaisance*, Presence Africaine, Paris, 1981

Reviewed by Leonard Jeffries Jr.

In his latest work, *Civilization or Barbarism* (1981), Dr. Cheikh Anta Diop presents us with an extraordinary intellectual achievement, the culmination of thirty years of multidisciplinary scholarship. His analytical and scientific presentation of the history of African peoples from an Afrocentric perspective cuts across various disciplines yet it provides us with conceptual and comparative frameworks needed to see the parts as well as the whole of history. The book reconfirms the controversial concepts and ideas of his earlier works with a critical analysis of the latest historical and scientific discoveries. As a result, he has made another outstanding contribution to the intellectual process of rethinking and rewriting African and world history which he helped initiate many years ago. *Civilization or Barbarism* is appropriately subtitled, *Anthropology without Compromise*. The value of the work, however, is not limited to Anthropology, it is also an invaluable treasure for the sociologists, the scientists, the biologists, the archeologists, the political scientists, the linguists, the mathematicians and above all the historians.

Without a doubt, *Civilization or Barbarism* is a monumental culmination of a life long scholarly effort. A primary objective of Diop's work has been to provide a catalyst to further the cultural and political revolution of African people. His investigations convinced him that the West has not been objective enough to teach Africans history correctly without crude falsifications. As a result, he would like to see the formation of teams of African researchers who will be committed to work long and hard to explore and substantiate his ideas.

In the Introduction, Diop states that his major objective was raising of the idea of a Black Egypt to the level of an Operative Scientific Concept. Others have recognized the importance of Egypt in world history, but have failed to reach this scientific level. He attacks the idea of a 'white' Egypt and links its recent development to grotesque falsifications by modern Egyptology, which was born at an opportune time, around the 1820's, and was subsequently linked to the ideology of imperalism and racism. The new Egyptology reinforced the theoretical bases of the imperialist ideology. Diop makes a monstrous charge of falsification of the history of humanity. In previous works, he explains his charge of falsification of history by attacking the creation of the Negro Myth. He links these efforts to a Euro-American process of cultural and intellectual genocide of African and Asian peoples.

In the introduction to the outstanding English publication of his works, *The African Origin of Civilization: Myth or Reality* (1974), Diop explains the meaning of his years of intensive research and scientific investigations. He began his research in September 1946, when the political problems of colonialism dominated all others. While continuing his scholarly work, he became the Secretary General of the student wing of the RDA, the post World War II French speaking African political movement, from 1950 to 1953. In February 1953, he published an article entitled "Toward a Political Ideology in Black Africa," in the first issue of RDA student publication.

This article contained an outline of ideas and concepts he had already completed in the manuscript of his earliest major publication, *Nations negres et cultures* (1955), Diop describes the comprehensive nature of this work as follows:

> All our ideas of African history, the past and future of our languages, their utilization in the most advanced scientific fields as in education generally, our concepts on the creation of a future federal state, continental or subcontinental, our thoughts on African social structures, on strategy and tactics in the struggle for national independence, and so forth, all those ideas were clearly expressed in that article.

He notes that there are three factors which compete to form the collective personality of a people: (1) a psychic factor, susceptible of a literary approach often called national temperament; (2) an historic factor and (3) a linguistic factor, both of which are susceptible of being approached scientifically. Diop's life-work over the past 30 years has concentrated on the historic and linguistic factors through a rigorous scientific approach.

The ideas and key concepts developed and substantiated in Diop's work include:

1. *Ancient Egypt was an African Civilization.* He feels very strongly that the history of Africa will remain suspended in air and cannot be written correctly until African historians dare to connect it with the history of Egypt. It is impossible to build a body of African human sciences so long as that relationship does not appear legitimate. The African historian who evades the problem of Egypt is neither modest nor objective, nor unruffled; he is ignorant, cowardly and neurotic. The ancient Egyptians were Africans. The moral fruit of their civilization is to be counted among the assets of the African World. Instead of presenting itself to history as an insolvent debtor, the African World is the very initiator of the "Western" civilization flaunted before our eyes today. Pythagorean

Mathematics, the theory of four elements of Thales of Miletus, Epicurean materialism, Platonic idealism, Judaism, Islam and Modern science are rooted in Egyptian cosmogony and science. In a word, Diop feels that we must restore the historical consciousness of the African people.

2. *Anthropologically and culturally speaking, the semitic world was born during proto-historic times from the mixture of white-skinned and Black-skinned people in Western Asia.* This is why an understanding of the Mesopotamian Semitic world, Judaic or Arabic, requires constant reference to the underlying Black reality.
3. *The triumph of the Monogenetic Thesis of Humanity (supported by the work of Dr. Leakey) even at the stage of "Homo sapiens-sapien"*, compels one to admit that all races descended from the Black race, according to a filiation process that science will explain one day.
4. In *L'Afrique Noire precoloniale (1960),* Diop developed a research design based on socio-history not on ethnography. Many scholars have since utilized his method. His major objectives were: (a) Write a history free of mere chronology of events; (b) Define the laws governing the evolution of African socio-political structure, in order to explain the direction that historical evolution has taken in Africa.
5. In *Black Africa: Economic and Cultural Basis to a Federated State (1974)*, he defines the image of modern Africa reconciled with its past and preparing for its future.
6. Once perspectives accepted by official science have been reversed, the history of humanity will become clear and the history of Africa can be written. Essential factor is to retrace history of the entire nation.
7. Modern Black literature has focused on minor aspects of life's drama. Diop believes some Black writers should pose the question of mankind's fate.
8. In *L'Unite culturelle de L'Afrique Noir (1960)*, Diop tried to pinpoint features common to African Civilization.
9. In *Nations negres et cultures (1955)*, Diop demonstrated that African languages could express philosophic and scientific thought.
10. Diop called for more research into the pre-Columbian relations of Africa with America in his work, *L'Afrique Noire Pre-Coloniale*. This area of research was earlier taken up by Professor Harold G. Lawrence in an article. A major contribution, however, has been made by Professor Ivan Van Sertima in his book, *They Came Before Columbus*.

Dr. Cheikh Anta Diop opens his new work by stating clearly that this material is intended to raise the idea of an African Egypt to the level of an *Operative Scientific Concept*. He points out that for the classical European writers (Herodotus, Aristotle, Diodorus, Strabon . . .) who were contemporaries of the ancient Egyptians, the Africaness of the Egyptians was visible and evident and did not call for any special reference. About 1820, on the eve of the birth of Egyptology, Count C.F. Volney, the French scholar, reminded the world that the recent slavery of Africans had created an amnesia concerning the glorious past of these people. Not long thereafter, however, Egyptology emerged as an instrument for scholars who used it to achieve a grotesque crime against science with the conscious falsification of the history of humanity. Egypt became "white," a European creation, and Africans were pushed systematically beyond the pale of history. Unfortunately, this false science was supported by the governments of Europe and merged with the new ideology of imperialism and racism that dominated the 19th Century. As a result, Egyptology and imperialism were easily able to drown out the voice of science by covering historical truth with a cloak of falsification.

Diop continues his indictment of European scholarship and science with an analogy. He equates imperialism with the prehistoric hunter who first kills spiritually and culturally before trying to kill physically. He then follows this with his strongest charge that "the negation of the history and intellectual realizations of African people is a cultural and mental death which proceeded and prepared genocide here and elsewhere in the world."

Dr. Diop points out in his Introduction that there is a gap that separates himself and others from some Africans who are content to flirt with Egyptian culture. He states very clearly that "for us, the return to Egypt in every domain is the necessary condition to reconcile African civilization with history, to build a body of modern human sciences and to be able to renew African culture." He adds that, "Egypt will play the same role in the rethinking and renewing of African culture that ancient Greece and Rome plays in the culture of the west."

In so far as Egypt is the distant Mother of the science and culture of the West, Diop points out that this book will reveal that the major proportion of the ideas we consider foreign are often only the modified, turned over and perfected images that were the creations of our ancestors: Judaism, Christianity, Islam, the Dialectic, the theory of being, exact sciences, arithmetics, geometry, mechanics, astronomy, medicine, literature (novel, poetry, theatre), architecture, arts, etc.

He predicts that, "When this historical legacy is understood we realize how false is the notion of importing foreign ideologies into Africa," He feels that this stems from a profound ignorance of the African past.

He concludes by stating that:

> Universal knowledge runs from the Nile Valley toward the rest of the world in particular toward Greece which served as an intermediary. As a result, no thought, no ideology is foreign to Africa which was the land of their birth. Consequently, Africans must draw from the common intellectual heritage of humanity, guided only by the notions of what is useful and effective.

Finally, Diop cautions us that no thought and particularly no philosophy can develop outside its historic land.

> Our young philosophers must understand this and develop as rapidly as possible the necessary intellectual means to re-establish themselves with the home of philosophy in Africa instead of becoming involved in a false combat of ethno-philosophy. In re-establishing a connection with Egypt we will dis-

> cover one day an historic perspective of 5,000 years which makes possible diachronic study on our own land of all the scientific disciplines that we can integrate into modern African thought.

Part I includes the first 4 chapters and focuses on an approach to paleontology. Professor Diop presents a scientific analysis of facts from an absolute chronology based on pre-historic archeology and physical anthropology which established Africa as the birth place of humanity at the ''Homo sapiens'' stage of development. Chapter 1 provides a general summary of these ideas on the origin of humanity. Chapter 2 presents material of a more detailed nature, concentrating on paleontologic evidence and critically reviewing the most recent thesis on the origin of mankind. Diop presents the scientific evidence for the monogenetic and African origin of the human race, and rejects the polycentric theories of separate human development in several centers on different continents. In chapter 3, Diop shows how archeology, using the radio carbon methods, has helped clarify the myth of Atlantis by applying science and comparative historical methodology. He provides the factual evidence linking Atlantis to Crete, and Minoan civilization to the 18th Dynasty of Egypt. He uses Atlantis to establish the Egypto-Nubian presence in the Mediterranean during the outward expansion and empire building of the Kings of the 18th Dynasty when a volcanic explosion of the Island of Santorin gave birth to the myth. He points out that the Egyptian presence also explains the appearance of the Linear A & B writing systems in the Mediterranean area. In Chapter 4, he analyzes the latest archeological discoveries from Nubia by a team from the University of Chicago which provides further evidence that Egyptian civilization has its roots in the heart of Africa and moved from South to North. Furthermore, these finds clearly established the Nubian monarchy as older than that of Northern Egypt, and adds additional support to Diop's efforts to raise Black Egypt to the level of an Operative Scientific Concept.

Part II of this monumental study covers chapters 5 througn 13. Diop describes the laws which govern the evolution of societies through their different phases of development—the clan, the tribe and the nation. He identifies four different types of Nation-States and provides a special study of the ''Motor of History'' in African-Asian States described as MPA—''Mode of Production among African and Asians'' and compares their development with that of the Greek City-States, specifically ancient Athens and Sparta. He concludes this section with a general law that applies to the transformation of societies and is a significant addition to the theory of revolutions. In Chapter 5, he initiates his analysis by focusing on Clan and Tribal Organizations. He states that ''Clan organization based on the incest taboo marks the beginning of civilization.'' At this stage man was no longer a simple biological animal. Future sexual relations were regulated by very strict social rules and regulations, which accelerated the development of clans and tribes. In Chapter 6, he analyzes the kinship structures of the clan and the tribe as part of the processes of nation building. In Chapter 7, he shows that race and social class are effected by certain ethnological laws which are an important determination on race relations. Chapter 8 provides an outline of four different types of states that have evolved. In Chapters 9, 10, and 11, Diop analyzes Key Revolutions in history, their causes, their successes and their failures. He focuses on the MPA States in Africa and Asia and the Greek City-States and presents a significant challenge to Marxist theories on revolution and the development of society. In Chapter 12, he provides a study of the particularities of African political and social structures and their impact on history. He presents a special case study of royalty in Senegal in the Kingdom of Cayor where the designation of the Damel or King illustrates the relationship of the African monarchy to the pharaonic model.

In Part III, Diop includes a short two-chapter section dealing with cultural identity. In Chapter 14, he defines cultural identity and relates the individual to his people. He notes that there are three factors which go to make up the collective personality of a people:

1. historical factor.
2. linguistic factor.
3. psychological factor.

These factors are undergoing constant change, particularly the psychological aspects, while the linguistic and historic aspects provide coordination of relationships. The linguistic and historic factors are the most important for Diop. He points out that the Blacks in the Diaspora have had the linguistic ties cut but the historic factor remains as strong as ever, perpetuated by memory. Similarly, the cultural heritage of Africa is obvious in the Americans and attests to the continuity of cultural customs. The historic factor is the cultural cement which unites the disparate elements of a people to make a whole.

Historical consciousness is the most solid rampart of the cultural security of a people. Historical continuity is the effective cultural arm of a people against outside cultural aggression. Diop had said earlier that a people without an historical consciousness is just a population. He believes that loss of historical continuity can lead to stagnation and retrogression, as was the case of the Egyptians under the Romans.

The linguistic factor is important in cultural identity. Africans should seek the unifying elements of their many languages. The Egyptian-Nubian language group may provide a unifying underlying factor as has the Indo-European language.

Part IV is entitled, "The Contribution of Africans to Humanity in the Sciences and in Philosophy." In Chapter 16, Diop reviews the scientific contribution the African Egyptian world has made to Greece and shows that Egyptian science was extremely theoretical. He proceeds to reveal in the next chapter how enormous was the debt owed Egypt by the Greeks in science and philosophy. He illustrates how exact and theoretical was Egyptian mathematics and geometry, particularly in comparison with the empirical geometry of Mesopotamia.

In Chapter 17, Diop defines the main currents of Egyptian philosophy and shows its relationships with developments in Greece and the world. He delineates the African philosophies and shows how Egyptian philosophical thought throws new light on the heritage of African peoples. His work also underlines the historical relationships of the three revealed religions of Judaism, Christianity and Islam to Egyptian religious thought.

The final chapter is a short appendix of Greek words that have an African origin. Diop attempts to show the early influence of Egypt on Greek thought and culture.

In the first Chapter of Part I, "Prehistory: Race and History, and the Origin of Humanity and Racial Differentiation," Cheikh Anta Diop presents the scientific and historical data for the *concept of the monogenetic and African origin of humanity*. Based on the latest paleontological research and particularly the work of Dr. Leakey, it is clear that humanity's birthplace was in East Africa in the Grand Lakes region around the Omo Valley. As a result of these developments two conclusions are evident.

1. Humanity born at the latitude of the Great Lakes near the Equator is by necessity pigmented and African. This is substantiated by *Gloger's Law* which states that warm blooded animals are pigmented in hot and humid climates.
2. All races are issued from the African race by direct relationships, and other continents were peopled from Africa at the *Homo Erectus* stage as well as the *Homo Sapiens* stage which appeared about 150,000 years ago. Earlier theories that have Africans coming from elsewhere are not valid.

The author further develops his thesis by stating that the first Africans peopled the earth by migrations through the Straits of Gilbraltar, the Isthmus of Suez and perhaps Sicily. He cites the extensive existence of cave painting of the Upper Paleolithic period in Europe and Africa as confirmation of these developments. He refers to the early migration to Europe and Asia by the African Grimaldi Man and the Aurignacian industry of painting and materials that can be radio carbon dated for an absolute chronology. Diop insists that Europe did not see the birth of *Homo Sapien Sapiens* until the African appeared by migration. The first so-called "whites", the Cro-Magnon Man, did not appear until around 20,000 B.C., probably as a result of the mutation of Grimaldi Man neccesitated by adaptation to the cold environment. Diop also cites the existence of the pre-Hellenic Black Virgins around the Mediterranean as evidence of an earlier African presence.

The ancient Cult of the Black Virgin which the Catholic Church has sanctified in modern times is derived from the Cult of Isis that preceeded Christianity in the Mediterranean Area. Diop notes that although we are missing the scientific proof linking the pre-historic Aurignacian Venus to this later Cult, their existence confirms the southern origin of the Civilization.

At the end of the first chapter he provides a Chronological Table of the Evolution of Humanity in general and the African World in particular. This table includes dates from pre-historic times through to the Arab invasions of Egypt in 639 A.D. with parallel events and commentaries

In Chapter 2, Diop presents a "Critical Revue of Recent Theses on the Origin of Humanity." He is highly critical of the utilization of the new science of molecular biology which supports a polycentric thesis of human development. Diop maintains the monogenetic and African origin of humanity and rejects ideas that this evolution stopped at *Homo erectus* stage and that sapienization took place at the level of each continent. He believes that the work of Dr. Leakey and other experts has resulted in the triumph of the monogenetic theory of humanity in Africa which was by necessity Black before becoming white through mutation and adaptation at the end of the last glaciation in Europe in the Upper Paleolithic.

In defense of the monogenetic concept of the origin of humanity, Diop criticizes the use of the molecular biology which has revealed the genetic polymorphism of populations and has led specialists more and more to deny the existence of race. Diop points out that hemotypology which is the flower of molecular biology provides evidence for the existence of "racial markers" through the system of blood groupings. These blood markers translated into three factors that reveal racial differentiation. These three factors are: the Kell Factor found predominantly among Caucasoids, the Diego Factor found predominantly among Mongoloids, while the Sutter Factor predominates among Africans. These "racial markers" support the Diop thesis on the Africaness of the ancient Egyptians.

To clarify his concept of racial differentiation, Diop presents a simplified scheme of the probable processes of development under the effects of physical factors. He traces mankind's development through Australopithecus (5,500,000 to 2,000,000 years); Homo Habilis (2,500,000 years); Homo Erectus (1,000,000 years); Homo Sapiens Sapiens (150,000 to 130,000 years); Grimaldi Man appearance in Europe (40,000 years); Cro-Magnon first appearance (20,000 years); Yellow Man's appearance (15,000 years).

Part II of this monumental work is entitled, "The Laws Governing the Evolution of Societies: Motor of History in Societies with MPA and in the Greek City-States." In these chapters Diop presents several key concepts concerning human and societal development in the African-Asian and Indo-European worlds. He analyzes these concepts from various perspectives and provides special insight into the Afrocentric view of these developments. He makes a major contribution by providing an Afrocentric critique and enlargement of Marxist and revolutionary theory. He demonstrates how the African-Asian system of societal development contrasts with that of the Indo-European City-State, pointing out the capabilities of the differing systems and their historical results. His analysis of revolutionary and evolutionary history clarifies the processes that developed to produce clans, tribes, city-states, nation-states and empires.

In Chapter 5, a key concept and process is outlined. Diop points out that Clan organization is founded on *Incest Taboo* which marks the beginning of civilization. He notes that in the Clan, man is no longer a simple biological animal. He must regulate his sexual and social relations by very strict rules. As a result, Clan formation developed clear notions of parenting, property, inheritance, and individual and group responsibilities. Marrying outside of the Clan, exogamy, produced neighboring clan relations and led to a sense of ethnicity and tribe. Environment played a major role in determining whether a Clan became patrilineal (father's lineage) or matrilineal (mother's lineage). The nomadic environment inevitably produced a patrilineal system while a sedentary agricultural environment produced a matrilineal system. Diop states that the division of work at the Clan stage produced processes of social stratification and primitive accumulation which engendered a "clan" system and a tribal structure. As the tribal structure expanded and became complex it developed processes that led to monarchy. At the end of the chapter, Diop presents a clan chart which contrasts the characteristics of the African Matrilineal Clan that developed around agricultural society and the Indo-Aryan Patrilineal Clan that emerged from the nomadic life of the Euro-Asian Steppes. This environment was difficult and under constant attack from the outside enemies which put a premium on the strength of the warriors, resulting in the processes that caused the emergence of a military aristocracy. The easier agricultural environment developed forces of production that created a surplus and led to the emergence of a monarchy and priesthood to control the society. These clan structures have remained at the base of African and European societies.

Some of the contrasting characteristics of the African system and the Indo-Aryan systems are:

African Matrilineal Clan	**Indo-Aryan Patrilineal Clan**
SEDENTARY	NOMADIC
AGRICULTURAL SUBSISTENCE	PASTORAL SUBSISTENCE
CLAN EXOGAMY	CLAN EXOGAMY
RELIGION ANCESTOR WORSHIP	RELIGION ANCESTOR WORSHIP
BURIAL FUNERAL RITES	CREMATION FUNERAL RITES
MAN BRINGS DOWRY	WOMAN BRINGS DOWRY
MATRILOCAL MARRIAGE	PATRILOCAL MARRIAGE
MATRILINEAL SUCCESSION	PATRILINEAL SUCCESSION
WIFE KEEPS LEGAL STATUS	WIFE LOSES LEGAL STATUS
WIFE KEEPS FAMILY NAME	WIFE LOSES FAMILY NAME
INHERITANCE FROM MATERNAL UNCLE	INHERITANCE FROM FATHER
WIFE CAN DIVORCE	WIFE CANNOT DIVORCE
LAND IS COLLECTIVE PROPERTY	LAND IS PRIVATE PROPERTY
COMMUNALISM SPECIAL VIRTUE	INDIVIDUALISM SUPREME VIRTUE
ALL CHILDREN RAISED	EXCESS BABIES KILLED
MATRIARCHAL SOCIETY	PATRIARCHAL SOCIETY
COSMOGICALLY OPTIMISTIC	COSMOGICALLY PESSIMISTIC
NO NOTION OF ORIGINAL SIN	ORIGINAL SIN FAULT OF WOMAN
PACIFIST MORALITY	WARRIOR MORALITY

In his analysis of the kinship structure at the clan and tribal stage in Chapter 6, Diop notes that kinship, inheritance and naming are not fixed but part of a transitional process which is not racial as much as environmental. He cites Irish family relations to make his point. He summarizes this process of development by restating the importance of incest taboo.

> The passage from clan to monolinguistic tribe or ethnic groups to the nation or nationality is a consequence of the exogamy of the clan. Mankind's prohibition against incest marks a starting point toward civilization. Since endogamy of the clan is prohibited, several neighboring clan establish marriage arrangements which became over time kinship ties through alliance. Several clan groups began to share language and culture and develop into ethnic groups and nationality. The individual will even carry the clan name after detribalization.

In his chapter on "Race and Social Classes," Diop discusses the laws which regulate ethnic relations throughout history. The first law is the law of percentage. When a minute percentage of foreigners are among an indigenous population, there is often curiosity and sometimes sympathy. However, when the percentage increases substantially and represents 4 to 8% as in the case of immigrant workers, then racial aspects become predominant. The greater the increase, the more the class struggle is transformed into social confrontation. The second law is the law of assimilation. If the majority and minority are part of the same ethnic group and share the same culture, assimilation will take place progressively. If the ethnic and cultural differences are too great, then the racial tensions will increase over time. The third law is the law of distance. Two ethnic groups who are not struggling over the same space or markets, and occupy clearly separate territories, can maintain normal relations and alliances as did Germany and Japan during World War II. The fourth law is the law of phenotype—based on physical distinction. The laws of class struggle of historical materialism only apply after a society has been made ethnically homogeneous by violence. The same analysis ignores the preceding phase of Darwinian or bestial struggle. This is a stage experienced by many nations today. Throughout history conquerors often build their domination on ethnic bases thus the exploitation of man by man takes on an ethnic framework with social class status linked to the dominant group.

Diop cites the example of Sparta as the classic example of this form of economic exploitation founded exclusively on ethnic difference. The Spartans were probably of Doric origin and invaded and conquered the region of Lacontia inhabited by the Hilotes. In order to maintain this ethnic dominance, Sparta developed the most ferocious military regime in history, living in separated army camps, building the education system around the military from birth to death, organizing programs periodically against the Hilotes to maintain the ethnic balance of the conquered and conqueror. Fortunately Sparta had only 9,000 citizens and could not exercise absolute control over an extended territory. It is important to note that although the Spartans and Hilotes were of the same race, their ethnic difference cannot be overlooked or forgotten and overshadowed by the difference of economic class. It would be historically incorrect to deny the ethnic origin of the class struggle and the violent Darwinian forms it initially took. Diop describes the relationship of Rome and Carthage, the Franks and the Gauls, and most recently the Hutus and Tutsis in Rwanda and Burundi as examples of this pattern of ethnic dominance and destruction.

Diop's discussion of race and class leads into his analysis of the birth of different types of states in Chapter 8. He claims that there are at least four types of states.

1. *States called "Asiatic" or Mode of Production in Asia and Africa (M.P.A.)* These states were described by Marx and Engels as emerging from the grand hydraulic works of river valley societies. Diop points out that the most outstanding model of this state was Pharaonic Egypt, so it really should be called, "the African State Model or Type."
2. *States resulting from Resistance to an Enemy.* This type of state is born out of struggle to defend a common territory and often welds together separate entities. The importance of the military functions inevitably produces a supremacy of the warrior clans which form the basis of an aristocracy.
3. *States represented by the Ancient Athenian City-State.* Diop states that this model is a consequence of the dissolution of the ancient mode of production in which the state is nothing more than a legal instrument for the domination of one class over another. In Athens, the dominant class was centered around the initial property owners.
4. *States resulting from Genocidal Conquest—Spartan and Tutsi Model.* This type of state is the result of domination of one ethnic group over another in which the conquering groups maintain genocidal practices institutionalized around the state structure. The ancient Spartan and the more recent Tutsi State in Rwanda and Burundi were excellent examples of the domination and elimination of the indigenous people.

In Part II, Diop makes a major contribution to an analytical understanding of the development of societies from the clan-tribe stages to the city-state and nation. He further clarifies the laws which govern this evolution, and effect race and social class structure. He presents a general concept of clan development as a key motor of history and analyzes this development from an Afrocentric perspective that allows him to compare the characteristics of the African Matrilineal Clan with the Indo-Aryan Patrilineal Clan. Through this framework he shows how distinct African-Asian and Indo-European societal and state systems emerge out of different sedentary and nomadic environments. Each system is maintained by internal and external processes dictated by its environment. These include processes of socialization (clans), production (division of labor), accumulation (surplus), and militarization (classes). Out of these processes have come certain value systems and laws which effect race and social structure. As a result of the total historical process, different types of state systems have evolved.

In the second half of Part II Diop provides a comparative analysis of different types of state systems, concentrating on states of African-Asian M.P.A. Model and the ancient Greek City-States. In Chapters 9, 10, 11, he discusses in detail revolutions in history, their causes and conditions of success and failure. He points out the limitations of Eurocentric and Marxist analysis of African-Asian state systems and proceeds to correct and expand Revolutionary and Developmental theory.

In these chapters, Diop makes a major theoretical breakthrough in analyzing history from a non--Eurocentric perspective and establishing the analytical value of the African-Asian world view. He points out the limitations and errors of Marx and other European theorists who were not able to thoroughly analyze African-Asian societies. Marx characterized African-Asian formations (M.P.A.) as "ephemeral," transitory societies outside of the pale of historical revolutionary movement. Diop corrects this view but this error has been repeated by theoreticians over the years. After studying the failure of revolutions in Africa, China and Greece he demonstrates how insights into these processes will add new elements and greater clarity to theories of sociology and revolution. Marx and others incorrectly analyzed the African-Asian state system and misunderstood the collective consciousness, the communal benefits and the cooperative production, land use, and ownership. As a result Marx referred to African-Asian production as "generalized slavery" in contrast to the private slavery of Greco-Latin states. He also believed that the closed village communities of African-Asian states (M.P.A.) were the reasons for the stagnation of these societies.

Diop corrects this erroneous analysis of African-Asian societies and points out that revolutions and revolutionary conditions did occur in these states but several inherent factors prevented indigenous movements from being successful. After analyzing the failure of revolutionary activities throughout history, Diop notes that one is brought back to the historic-economic factors which produced territorial unification in one place (Egypt-China) and not in others (Greece).

He concludes that the creation of the state apparatus of African-Asian (M.P.A.) societies allowed for the coordination of social, military, and political actions on a grand scale, forging chains that could not be broken except by modern progress which makes education and information available to the masses, and facilitates coordination of the struggles of the working class. As a result, revolution becomes impossible when the state takes the ancient African-Asian form, whether in Greece, Rome or Persia. In spite of the fact that these states developed the conditions and fundamental contradictions needed for revolutionary activity, the socialization process, the complexity of the state and the bureaucracy, and the size of the territory, inevitably prevented the success of revolutionary movement. These conclusions represent an important development and transformation of society.

In Chapter 9, Diop analyzes revolutionary processes in the history of the African-Asian (M.P.A.) States as well as in the Greco-Latin City-States. He outlines the characteristics of the African-Asian (M.P.A.) States and explains the special relationship of the civil bureaucracy and the people. This relationship was necessary in order to organize the great irrigation and construction projects that benefited the whole society. As a result of the nature of the (M.P.A.) States and its capacity for problem solving, he concludes that the public role of the bureaucracy and its ability to intervene made the people less revolutionary and less desirous of change. In contrast, the Greek City-State of the Athenian individualistic type and the Spartan militaristic type were subject to constant revolutionary activity because they were based on slave dominated populations with limited territories and bureaucracies.

In Chapter 10 and 11, Diop provides several examples of significant unsuccessful revolutions. He points out that although the fundamental contradictions in these societies existed and revolutionary conditions were wide spread, other factors were at work that produced failure. He gives extensive details about the first large scale revolution in history which occurred in Egypt about 2100 B.C. at the end of the VI Dynasty during a period of chaos. Miserable conditions in Memphis, the capital, led to the sacking of the town and the spread of popular revolt along the Nile River. Diop calls this mass movement, the ''Osirian or Proletarian'' Revolution. It failed, however, because of the complexity of the state apparatus and the size of the nation. Clearly, it lacked the force and coordination of other similar movements in modern times.

Another major example of unsuccessful revolutionary activity occurred in China during the 9th Century A.D. at the time of the T'ang Dynasty. Problems of land use and expropriation created conditions of impoverishment for the peasantry and produced a veritable agricultural proletariat. This violation of their inalienable rights to land led to widespread revolt which forced the Royal Court to flee to the neighboring Turks who intervened, crushed the revolt and restored the Emperor to power.

In this case, although the revolution was defeated by outside intervention, the complexity of the State and size of the territory were nevertheless major factors. Diop also looks at the failure of the Islamic revolution in Africa, which could have been a true revolutionary movement but coalesced with the aristocracy and did not become a force for change. By looking at the failure of revolutionary movements in history, Diop has been able to make a significant addition to the theory of change in societies.

In Chapter 16, Diop presents a detailed analysis of the African contribution to science and provides documentation to illustrate the theoretical basis of Egyptian mathematics, particularly its geometry. Utilizing the Egyptians' own scholarly works, which came down to us through various papyri, Diop makes very revealing comparisons between what is attributed to Greeks, such as Archimedes, Pythagoras, Hippocrates and Aristotle, and what was actually achieved by Nile Valley specialists thousands of years previous. He refers to the work of Paul Ver Eecke, *The Complete Works of Archimedes* (1960), and notes that he accuses Archimedes of dishonesty because he did not acknowledge the theoretical mathematics he borrowed from the Egyptians.

Diop cites other scholars, such as V.V. Struve whose volume, *Study of the Mathematical Papyrus of the Moscow Museum* (1930) shows that the Egyptian Mathematicians had established a vigorous formula for the surface of a sphere. Similarly, mathematical knowledge which has been attributed to Pythagoras can be found in the Rhind Papyrus, which contains the calculation of problems that affirm the Egyptian knowledge of geometry and trigonometry. This ancient document was completed two thousand years before the Greek intellectual efforts and is analyzed by T.E. Peet in his book, *The Rhind Mathematical Papyrus* (1923). The Medical Papyrus of Adwin Smith contains the first known mention of the brain, acknowledging its importance to the body. This document is a recording of part of the extensive knowledge the Egyptians possessed concerning medicine, particularly anatomy. The Eber Papyrus and other ancient documents recording scientific development, also revealed the high level of achievement in chemistry and metallurgy, Diop gives various illustrations of the mathematical basis for the art and architecture of the Egyptians and the significance of the sacred square in their artistry. Similarly, the calendar development in pre-historic times provides evidence of the importance of astronomy.

In Chapter 17, Diop asks the question, does African Philosophy exist? He then proceeds to detail the Egyptian contribution to World Philosophy. He points out that in the classic sense, philosophical thought must have at least two fundamental criteria:

1. It must be conscious of itself, and exist as thought.
2. It must realize, to a satisfactory degree, the separation of myth and concept.

He points out that the Egyptian cosmogony was centered around three great systems of thought:

1. Hermopolitan System.
2. Helipolitan System.
3. Memphite System.

He adds a fourth school of thought referred to as the Theban System.

In the presentation of the evidence for the existence of African philosophical thought, Diop relates the concepts of the universe's existence as chaotic matter and the creation of order by Ra to the materialist and idealist schools of Greek thought. He notes that the Osirian Drama, Resurrection and Renewal, the Trinity and the *Book of the Dead* all relate to the Judeo-Christian philosophical tradition. He continues to develop this analytical approach to Egyptian philosophical thought by making comparisons with the Dogon cosmogony and the significance of their knowledge of the star Sirius. He maintains this approach as he analyzes Bantu philosophy as well as the Medieval philosophy of Timbuktu.

Finally Diop raises the question as to whether the African philosophical tradition can help provide the means for a new philosophy that will aid humanity in its search to reconcile man with himself. Diop's *Civilization or Barbarism* is truly an extraordinary scientific and scholarly masterpiece, which represents a challenge to all scholars, particularly those Africans who accept the call to create a new social science, a new humanity and a new society. This work will undoubtedly become a classic of Afrocentric scholarship. It has been published in France by Presence Africaine. We must do all we can to make sure it is published in English, Spanish, and Portuguese so that it can be a creative unifying force in the African World.

CIVILIZATION OR BARBARISM: AN AUTHENTIC ANTHROPOLOGY

Cheikh Anta Diop
(Translated by Edward F. Taylor)

I dedicate this book to the memory of Alioune Diop, who died on the battlefield of African culture. Alioune, you knew what you came on earth to do: A life devoted entirely to others, nothing for itself, everything for others, a heart filled with kindness and generosity, a soul imbued with nobility, a truly serene intellect, the embodiment of simplicity: Did the Creator wish to offer us an example, an ideal of perfection by bringing you into existence? Alas, he took you away too soon from the earthly community to which you knew how to convey better than any other this message of human truth which springs forth from the innermost recesses of existence. But death will never be able to extinguish your remembrance from the memory of the African people to whom you devoted your life. It is because of this that I dedicate this book to your memory, as testimony to a brotherly friendship more lasting than time itself.

—Cheikh Anta Diop,
Dakar, October 29, 1980

This introduction is intended to facilitate the reading of the work and to emphasize what it offers new with regard to our previous publications.

This is moreover a body of work which has permitted raising the idea of a black Egypt to the level of an operative scientific concept. For all the authors who preceded the grotesque and vicious falsifications of modern Egyptology, and who were contemporaries of the ancient Egyptians (Herodotus, Aristotle, Diodorus Siculus, Strabo . . .) the black Egyptian presence was an obvious fact which was apparent to the eye, that is to say, could be seen at a glance. Therefore, it would have been superfluous to prove it.

Around the 1820s, on the eve of the birth of Egyptology, the French scholar

This translated excerpt—the dedication, introduction, and first two chapters from Cheikh Anta Diop's *Civilisation ou Barbarie*, copyright 1981 by Présence Africaine, Paris—is published with permission. The complete English version of *Civilization or Barbarism* will be published by Lawrence Hill & Co., who control the English language rights.

Volney, an objective and widely known intellect, if ever there was one, tried to revive the *memory* of humanity concerning the past of Black people, which their recent slavery had rendered amnesic.

Since then, the succession of dishonest Egyptologists, armed with a very determined scholarship, have perpetrated a crime against science which is known, by subscribing to a deliberate falsification of human history. Upheld by all of the western countries, this ideology based on intellectual and moral fraud easily won out over the true scientific tenets developed by the opposing group of honest Egyptologists, whose intellectual integrity and even courage one cannot emphasize too much. The new Egyptological ideology, born at the opportune moment was used to support the theoretical bases of the imperialist ideology. That's how it was able to muffle the voice of science so easily; by veiling historical truth with falsehood. It was propagated with the aid of extensive publicity and taught globally. It had both the material and financial means necessary for its own propagation.

Thus imperialism, as the hunter of prehistory, killed the being first spiritually and culturally, before seeking to destroy it physically. The negation of history and of the intellectual accomplishments of black African people is the cultural and mental murder which has already taken place and has paved the way for genocide here and there in the world. So that between the years 1946 and 1954, when our project of restoring authentic African history and of reconciling African civilizations with history was developed, the distorted perspective caused by the blinders of colonialism had so thoroughly altered the vision of intellectuals concerning the African past that we experienced the greatest difficulties, even with Africans, in having ideas accepted which today are about to become commonplace. One can scarcely imagine what must have been the level of alienation of Africans of the past.

Therefore, for us, the considerable new feat, is less having stated that the Egyptians were a Black people in accordance with the ancient writers, one of our principal sources, than having contributed to making this idea a fact of African and world historical consciousness, and especially, a working scientific concept: this is what our predecessors had not succeeded in doing.

Resistance from old-timers, that will always be, but one is currently seeing even Africans strut on conquered new ground now that the battle is virtually won, all the while causing minor annoyances and giving us "lessons in scientific objectivity."

The black race of Egypt does not exist! But we know that Europe is inhabited by Whites, Asia by people of yellow and white skin who are all responsible for the civilizations of their countries and their respective places of origin. Only the race of the ancient Egyptians must remain a mystery. Western ideology thought that the matter could be settled thus. Today, data from molecular biology are used to try to deliberately complicate the controversy. But indeed, the procedures of this new discipline can shed a special light on the ethnic identity of the ancient Egyptians, if ever one dared to apply them sensibly. It is acknowledged that a biased anthropologist can whiten a Black man or "negroidize" a White man by a biased interpretation of measurements and by well chosen one-sided analyses.

In spite of the genetic polymorphism of populations, revealed by molecular biology, and which has led humanist and sympathetic scholars, like J. Ruffie, A. Jacquard and others to deny race, bloodtype, which is the flower of this science, teaches us the existence of "racial indicators": The system of blood groups "A B O" is common to all races and precedes the racial differentiation of humanity. The "Rh" factors also exist in all races, but with a variable frequency; thus the chromosome "r" is present in all Whites and "achieves its greatest frequency" in the Basques; "Ro" is found everywhere, but its frequency is particularly high in Blacks south of the Sahara.

A third category is even more specific, it concerns "racial indicators": the Diego factor is characteristic of the yellow race and is found only in Amerinds, the yellow-skinned people of the far east and in certain inhabitants of Nepal (probably of mixed blood.) "The Sutter and Henshaw factors are almost solely detectable in Blacks."[1] The Kell factor is particularly noticed in Whites.[2]

Therefore, those who still wish to be enlightened on the ethnic group of the ancient Egyptians should research the factors cited (above) in the true native ancient population and not in the foreign mummies, Greek Ptolemaics or others . . . The team charged with this task, in order to be credible, should understand African scholars. The pure race exists nowhere, but one speaks readily of the Whites of Europe and the Yellow men of Asia; it is for the same reason that we speak of the Blacks of Egypt.

If the city of Dakar became a new Pompeii following a cataclysm, in two thousand years, on analyzing the petrified ruins of William Ponty[3] Avenue, one could boldly affirm that Senegal of 1981 was a multiracial community whose civilization was created by a white element heavily represented in the population and that Blacks were only the slave element. Today, Africans have become immune with regard to falsifications of this type, so common around the time of the birth of Egyptology. We have purposely had the table of all the known races of the Egyptians, portrayed by themselves, reproduced. On referring to it (Figure 17), one will see that the only ones who can still doubt are those who have shameful reasons for doing so, be they Africans or others.

At this point one must emphasize the abyss which separates us from those Africans who believe that we can content ourselves with flirting with Egyptian culture. For us, the return to Egypt in all domains is the necessary condition for reconciling African civilizations with history, in order to build a body of modern human sciences, and thus revive African culture. Far from being a diversion centered around the past, a look toward ancient Egypt is the best way to conceive and to build our cultural future. Egypt will play the same role in the rethinking and renewing of African culture that ancient Greece and Rome play in the culture of the West.

Inasmuch as Egypt is the remote mother of western science and culture, (and how well that will emerge from the reading of this book) the majority of the concepts which we designate foreign are often just distorted, turned around, modified, improved ideas from the creations of our ancestors: Judaism, Christianity, Islam, dialectic, the theory of being, exact sciences, arithmetic, geometry, the science of mechanics, astronomy, medicine, literature (novel, poetry, drama), architecture, arts, etc.[4]

One considers then, how basically improper is the notion, so often repeated, of the importation of foreign ideologies into Africa: it comes from a total ignorance of the African past. Just as modern science and technology come from Europe so, in antiquity, universal knowledge flowed from the valley of the Nile toward the rest of the world, and in particular toward Greece, which served as an intermediary link.

Consequently, no thought, no ideology is essentially foreign to Africa, which was the land of their birth. Therefore, Africans must draw freely from the common intellectual heritage of mankind, letting themselves be guided only by the notions of utility and efficiency.

At this juncture one should also state that no thought, and in particular no philosophy, can be developed outside of its historic terrain. Our young philosophers must understand this and quickly equip themselves with the intellectual means necessary to renew contact with the source of philosophy in Africa, instead of being sucked into the false combat of ethnophilosophies.[5] On reuniting with Egypt we will discover very quickly an historic perspective of five thousand years which renders the diachronic study possible, on our own soil, of all the scientific disciplines which we are trying to integrate into modern African thought. The history of African thought becomes a scientific discipline where the "ethnophilosophical" cosmogonies occupy their chronological place like the mummy in its sarcophagus. The Gods will be appeased. Hegel and Marx did not pick a "German quarrel" with St. Thomas or with Heraclitus the Obscure; because without the rambling of the latter, they would never have built their philosophical systems. We must therefore break with the atemporal structural study of the African cosmogonies, because on separating ourselves thusly from the historical framework, we exhaust ourselves, without knowing it, slicing the air with cutting blows of the sword. Without the historical dimension, we would never have had the possibility to study the evolution of societies,[6] to move to and fro from the ethnological level to the sociological level. Of course, it is not a question of that ethnology whose description would cause a monkey to blush. In our report at the symposium on "Lenin and Science," organized by UNESCO in 1971 in Helsinki, to commemorate the centennial of Lenin's birth, we underlined the particular difficulties which the African sociologist encounters: he is often obliged to take into account the two levels mentioned above, as Engels did somewhat, either by using the works of Morgan on the Indians, having remained at the ethnographic era, or by studying the social structures of the Germanic tribes. Works are more quickly stamped with decrepitude if the ethnological material is poorly analyzed. In general, the ethnological stage is absent in the works of the western marxists who study the contradictions of European societies of the industrial period.

What does this book contain?

A current ideological tactic consists in modifying, altering the conceptual apparatus in order to make only concessions in structure not in substance, in dealing with new scientific discoveries. A similar tendency is becoming apparent, slowly, concerning the thesis which places the cradle of mankind in Africa. They are beginning to say and to write, that Africa is the cradle of mankind only at the stage of "Homo erectus" and that the "intellectualization" took place following the adaptation of this primitive African stock to the geographic conditions of different continents.

It seemed indispensable to show just how untenable this new point of view is scientifically. The reader who is interested in it can follow the details of our reasoning in chapter 2.

Basing our research on absolute chronological data, on physical anthropology and on prehistoric archeology we believe that we have shown that Africa is the cradle of mankind both at the stage of "Homo erectus" and that of "Homo sapiens sapiens."

Chapter 1 gives an easily read general summary of this idea and chapter 2 discusses it in depth. Thus, it is possible to go from the first to the third chapter or to read the second if one wishes to be enlightened.

The so-called "itinerant" cradle of mankind is not as mobile as they pretend. For thirty years it has passed from Asia, on a whole to Africa, and has never been placed either in Europe or in America.

Chapter 3 shows the way in which archeology, placing emphasis on the radiocarbon method, introduced the myth of Atlantis into the domain of science and history.

It is also a question in this chapter of showing that the XVIIIth Egyptian dynasty, contemporaneous with the explosion of the island of Santorin in the Cyclades, which gave birth to the myth of Atlantis, had actually colonized Crete and the whole eastern Mediterranean during this same epoch. This permits an understanding of the appearance of linear "A" and "B" and a great many other facts still puzzling till now because one had not wanted to link them to their historical background.

Chapter 4 treats, so to speak, the main archeological part, proving that Egyptian civilization is indeed part of the very heart of Africa, from south to north, and that the Nubian royalty precedes that of Upper Egypt and gave birth to her.

Chapters 5 to 13 are devoted to the description of laws which govern the evolution of societies in their different phases: clans, tribes, nations; to the identification of different kinds of States and to that of the mover of history in the States with an M.P.A.; to the study of different revolutions in history, especially revolutions which apparently failed and which classical theory has never taken into account.

In chapter 12, in a short part, we have furnished the theoretical elements which permit additional consideration, based on knowledge of the caste system in the region of the Sahel.

The study of these revolutions is important, at the moment when the African society is going to enter the phase of true class struggles in the modern sense of the word. In fact, the process of accumulation, of the confiscation of riches is very advanced; the latter, in an unequal distribution, have passed from the hands of the former colonists to those of the new African middle classes which, for the moment, are investing in the parasitic sectors: construction . . . But the first strike of African workers against a boss in an African factory will mark the beginning of the new era of class struggles.

Chapters 14 and 15 give respectively a definition of cultural identity and a rapprochement of intercultural relations.

Chapter 16 reviews the scientific contribution of the black Egyptian world to Greece in particular and shows that Egyptian science, in spite of a persistent legend, was highly theoretical. It permits, like the following chapter, an evaluation of the numerous unacknowledged borrowings which Greek scholars made from Egyptian science and philosophy.

One will see that a rigorously exact mathematics is necessarily theoretical: this is the case of Egyptian mathematics, and of Egyptian geometry in particular. On the contrary, a grossly incorrect mathematics is necessarily empirical: this is the case of the Mesopotamian geometry in particular.

Chapter 17 defines the Egyptian philosophical currents and their apparent rapport with those of Greece. It emphasizes the historical relationship of the three revealed religions with Egyptian religious thought.

It attempts to sort out the premises of a new philosophy largely founded on the sciences and scientific experience and which could, perhaps, one day, reconcile man with himself.

Finally, chapter 18 is a kind of appendix, which defines a method suitable for identifying items in Greek vocabulary of Egyptian origin even if the few terms cited lack relevance.

The existence of an African Egyptology, alone, will permit, thanks to the direct knowledge which it grants, genuinely going beyond the disappointing and destructive theories of obscurantist or agnostic historians who, in the absence of solid information drawn from the source, seek to save face, by proceeding with a hypothetical variety of influences, as if they were dividing an apple.

Only the rooting of such a scientific discipline in Black Africa will lead one day to grasping the novelty and the richness of the cultural conscience which we wish to create; its quality, its scope, its depth, its creative power.

The African who has understood us is that one who, after the reading of our works, will have felt another man born within him, moved by an historical conscience, a true creator, a Promethean bearer of a new civilization and perfectly aware of what the whole world owes to his ancestral genius in all domains of science, culture and religion.

Today, each race armed with its rediscovered or reinforced cultural identity, arrives at the threshold of the post-industrial era. An atavistic but vigilant African optimism leads us to wish that all nations join hands in order to build the planetary civilization instead of foundering in barbarism.

PART I: THE PALEONTOLOGICAL APPROACH

CHAPTER I: THE PREHISTORY; RACE AND HISTORY; ORIGIN OF MANKIND AND RACIAL DIFFERENTIATION

The research pursued in human paleontology by the late Dr. Leakey, in particular, permitted placing the cradle of mankind in east Africa, in the region of the Great Lakes, around the valley of Omo.

Two consequences, which haven't been emphasized till now, proceed from this discovery:

1. Mankind born under the latitude of the Great Lakes, almost under the Equator, is necessarily pigmented and Negroid; Gloger's law requires that warm blooded animals be pigmented in a warm, humid climate.
2. All other races are descended from the black race by more or less direct relationship, and the other continents were populated from Africa, as much at the time of "Homo erectus" as at that of "Homo sapiens," who appeared around 150,000 years ago: the earlier theories which made the Black man come from somewhere else are no longer valid.

The first Negroids who proceeded to populate the rest of the world left Africa through the strait of Gibraltar, through the Isthmus of Suez and perhaps also through Sicily and southern Italy.[7]

The existence of an African art inscribed on walls and rocks of the high Paleolithic period appears to confirm this view (Figures 1, 2, 3).

Figure 1. Art typical of the African high Paleolithic period. Stone engraved image, Arybourg, the country of Botswana, South Africa. (L. Frobenius: *Histoire de la civilisation africaine*, Figure 44.)

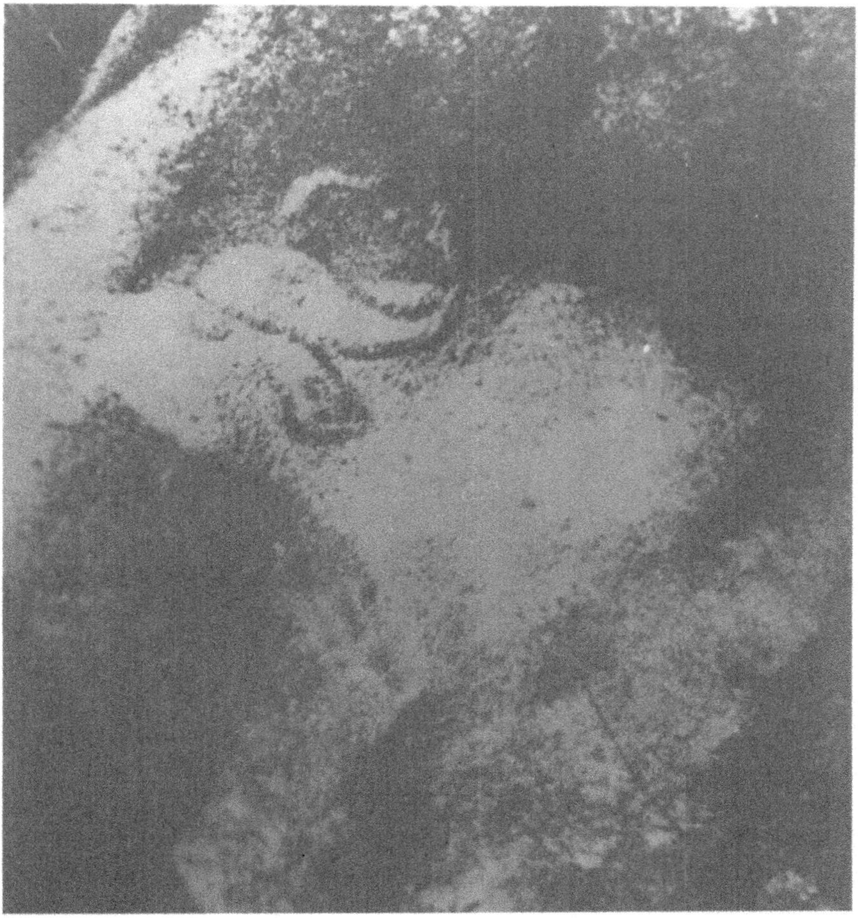

Figure 2. Prehistoric African painting. Cape elk, stone painting, Khotsa cave, Basutoland, South Africa. (L. Frobenius: *Histoire de la civilisation africaine*, Figure 45.)

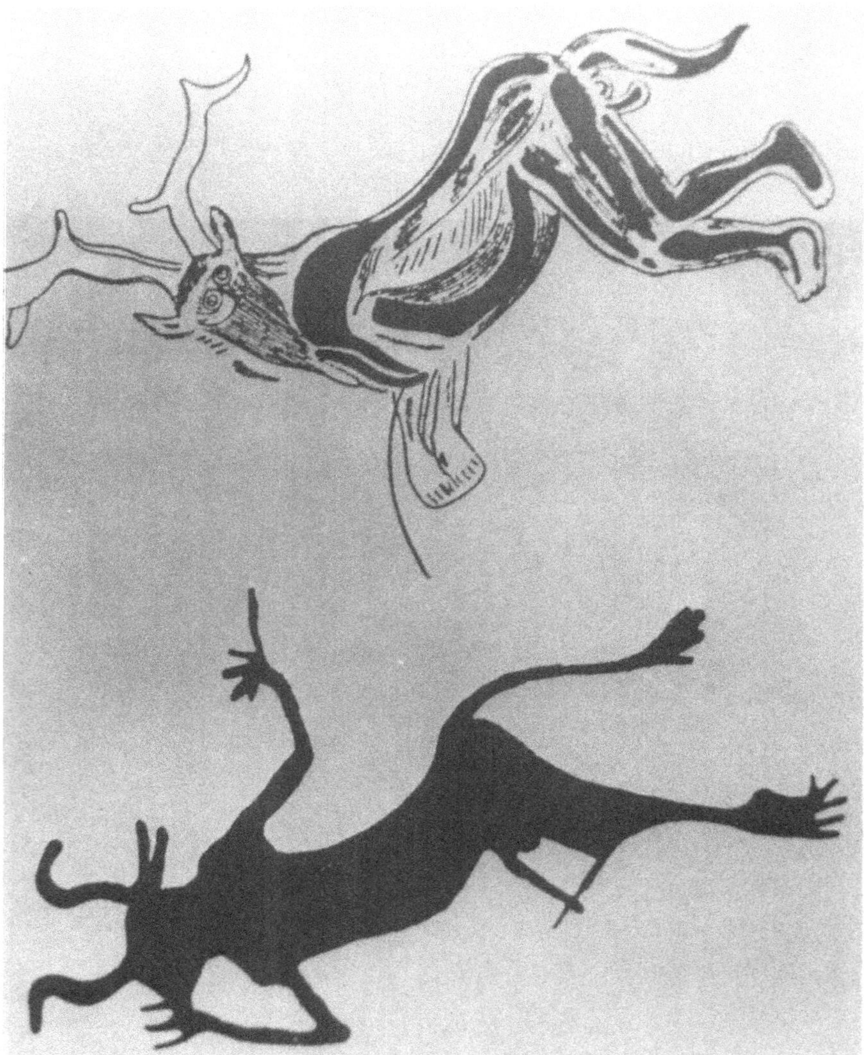

Figure 3. On the left: Dancing sorcerer of Afvallingskop, South Africa (according to L.S.B. Leakey). On the right: Dancing sorcerer in the Three-Brothers Cave, France (according to Count Begoven and Abbot Breuil). The resemblance between these two figures separated by more than 10,000 km is striking. Even today, these "skillful" disguises of men into animals, suggestive of initiations into secret societies, help to support even in African universities, the superstitious belief according to which human beings can change themselves into animals and vice versa, like the "Neuri", which according to a legend gathered by Herodotus, changed themselves into wolves: survivals from prehistory. (R. Furon: *Manuel de préhistoire générale*, 4th ed. Payot, Paris, 1959, Figure 57, p. 213 and Figure 105, p. 316.)

The engravings at Djebel Ouenat in Libya probably date from the Upper Paleolithic period, according to Abbot Brewil. In Egypt the oldest engravings probably are from the Upper Paleolithic period. In Ethiopia, near the site of Dire Daoua, the paintings of Porcupine Cave are of the same type as those of Egypt and Libya. According to Leakey, the oldest art in east Africa is probably from the Upper Paleolithic period. The presence of the Still Bay art in the districts rich in paintings (west banks of Lake Victoria, Eyasi, the central part of Tanzania) attests to their antiquity. The archeological strata at a depth of more than 5 meters contain coloring material and palettes of color. In Swaziland, men of the Upper Paleolithic period worked an iron mine 30,000 years ago in order to extract the red ocher.[8] This is the oldest mine in the world.

This is the advent of absolute chronology, that is to say of radioactive methods of dating, in particular that of Potassium/Argon, which permits science to achieve this progress and to batter in the dogmatism which formerly reigned in this domain. In fact, the stratigraphic methods did not permit scholars to choose. Thus one knew fundamentally, that the first inhabitant of Europe was a Negroid migrant, "Grimaldi Man." But an important authority, the late French scholar Vaufray, had decreed that Africa was lagging behind. From then on, African prehistoric facts appeared too new in the eyes of scholars to be able to explain those of Europe. Plainly, neither the Grimaldian, nor the man of Combe Capelle, both Negroids, could possibly be indigenous to Europe; however, a chronological difficulty, tied to the limitations of the stratigraphic methods, did not permit having them come from Africa.

The racial differentiation was achieved in Europe, probably in southern France and in Spain, at the end of the last Würmian Glacier, between −40,000 and −20,000 years (Figure 4). We understand now in the light of the above-mentioned facts, why the first inhabitant of Europe was above all the Negroid of Grimaldi,[9] responsible for the first stone industry in the Upper European Paleolithic Period, called the Aurignacian industry. Certain people believed that they saw in the Lower Perigordian a thoroughly European industry, prior to the preceding work, whose creator would be the truly indigenous Man of Europe, as opposed to the Grimaldian Negroid invader: this refers to the Man of Combe Capelle. They ignored the fact that he is as typically a Negroid as Grimaldian Man himself and that the two individuals indeed belong to the same anthropological type; that is why the Lower Perigordian man and the Aurignacian man were considered at first as making one and the same industry. It is not possible to present all of the reasons which led to making these distinctions outdated. We refer to our article cited above[10] and to the discussion below.

The Negroids of Grimaldi left their countless traces on the whole area of Europe and Asia, from the Iberian Peninsula to Lake Baïkal in Siberia, pass-

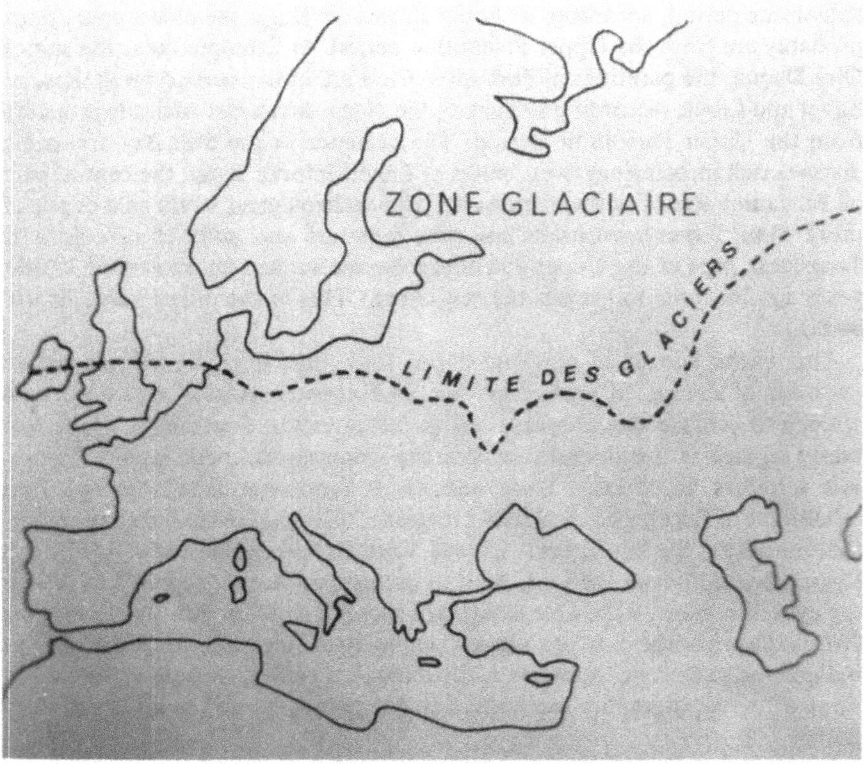

Figure 4. The boundaries of habitable Europe during the Würmian Glacier. (On the map (a) ZONE GLACIAIRE = Glacial Zone, (b) LIMITE DES GLACIERS = Boundary of the Glaciers).

ing through France, Austria, Crimea, the Don River basin, etc. In these last two regions, the late Soviet professor Guerassimov, a scholar with a rare objectivity, identified the Negroid type of the skulls found in the middle Mousterian Period. M. Boule and H.V. Vallois insist on the fact that the localization layers of the Grimaldians are always in direct contact with those of the Mousterian Period when vanishing Neanderthal Man lived. Otherwise stated, there is no other variety of "Homo sapiens" who could be a predecessor of Grimaldi Man in Europe and in Asia.

The first white man will not appear for about nearly − 20,000 years, if one judges using morphology: this is Cro-Magnon Man. He is probably the result of a mutation of the Grimaldian Negroid during an existence of 20,000 years under the excesssively cold climate of Europe dating from the end of the last glaciation.

The Basques, who live today in the Franco-Cantabrian region where Cro-

Magnon was born, would correctly be his descendants; in any case these people are numerous in the south of France.

Chancelade Man, who probably is the prototype for orientals, appeared in the reindeer age, about 15,000 years ago, during the Magdalenian Period. Is he a cross-breed, born under a cold climate, of the two stocks of Grimaldian Man disappearing in Europe and of the new Cro-Magnon Man?

In any case, account taken of his dolichocephalism, he could only be a Paleosiberian and not a true Oriental (like the Chinese or the Japanese), because the latter is generally brachycephalic, and we know that this morphological trait did not exist in the Upper Paleolithic Period; mesocephalism appeared in the Mesolithic Period (around −10,000) and the brachycephalism much later.

The brachycephalic yellow races, and the semites (Arabs or Jews) appear only within the confines of the Mesolithic Period, probably following great migratory currents and the cross-breeding which followed it.

Thus, humanity originated in Africa and would be diversified into several races in Europe, where the climate was sufficiently cold at the end of the Würmian glaciation.

If humanity had originated in Europe it would have been first white in order to have become later blackened under the equator, by the appearance of a screen of melanin in the epidermis, protecting the oganism from the ultraviolets rays.

Now, to avoid a false value judgement, there is no particular glory to be drawn from placing the cradle of mankind in Africa, because this is only a fact of chance; if physical conditions of the planet had been different, the origin of humanity would have been elsewhere.

Thus, the interest of this account consists solely in the necessity of knowing, with the greatest possible degree of scientific accuracy, the unfolding of facts related to the human past, in order to give their true meaning back to them and also to free the very foundations of science and civilization.

One can then measure the extent of the evil perpetrated by the ideologists who knowingly falsify this data.

In light of the facts pointed out above, it seems natural that Africa, which witnessed neither the birth of Cro-Magnon Man nor that of Chancelade Man, is ignorant of their respective industries: the Solutrean and the Magdalenian cultures. On the contrary, she is familiar with an industry of the Aurignacian type (Egypt, Kenya, etc. . . .) whose age will have to be reexamined in the light of new techniques of dating.

But as one can imagine, physical anthropology, utilizing the latest acquisitions of genetics, molecular biology, and linear analysis, denies race and admits only the reality of populations. This is the lofty science enshrined in ideology! As soon as it's a question of the transmission of an hereditary defect, of sickle-cell anemia in this case, the notion of race reappears: sickle-cell anemia strikes only Black people, genetically speaking, says the same science which denies race. Concerning thalassemia, another hereditary defect which strikes the alpine race, or white mediterraneans, physical anthropology explains itself euphemistically; this disease affects only "inhabitants" of the periphery of the Mediterranean.

Race doesn't exist! Is this to say that nothing permits me to distinguish myself from a Swede, and that a Zulu can go demonstrate to Botha that they have the same genetic stock and that consequently, on the level of the genotype, they are almost twins, even if accidentally their two phenotypes, that is to say their physical appearances, are different?

Certainly the mixing of the genes of the human species in the course of prehistoric times is very important, but to deny race when in fact it intervenes in history and in social relations, particularly at the phenotype level (which is what interests historians and sociologists) is to deny the reality of daily life itself.

Why does a certain physical anthropology use this scholarly manner to drown the fish? Does it feel repugnance in drawing rigorously all the consequences from the monogenetic origin of mankind and therefore in taking into consideration the real process of the appearance of races? But a western vanguard is already beginning to courageously spread these ideas; and it's an American White who writes: "I proceed to explain that the first human beings were black, and that light skinned people developed later, by natural selection, to survive in temperate climates; it made us all feel much closer."[11]

The paleolithic industry, being affirmed in the Nile Valley, it appears therefore that this region was necessarily inhabited solely by Negroids from the origin of mankind till the appearance of other races (−20,000 years to −15,000 years), and till some infiltrations dating near the end of the IVth millenium, whites were absent in Egypt and would remain so practically until 1300 B.C., period of the great invasions of the Sea People in the XIXth dynasty, the Hyksos invasion disregarded.[12]

The generic table of the races represented in the tomb of Ramses III (XIIth century B.C.) shows that the Egyptians perceived themselves as Blacks (Figure 17). In fact, the Egyptian artist does not hesitate to portray the Egyptian generic type as a typical black, a Nubian; Lepsius, who made this statement, was astonished and wrote: "Where one expected to see an Egyptian they depicted a genuine black person".[13] This destroys all of the misleading studies of the ideologists and shows that the Egyptians established no difference between themselves and the other Africans; it was a question of the same ethnic universe.

What happened in detail, on the anthropological plane, after the appearance of Cro-Magnon in Europe? This question will be long debated. But there is reason to assume that the alpine race is indigenous to Europe and therefore descends from Cro-Magnon, whose survivor would be the Basque.

Thus, the Basque language could possibly be the oldest language in Europe.

A group of these Cro-Magnons probably moved toward the north, with the retreat of the cold, around the end of the glaciation, that is around −10,000. This stock would give birth to the Scandinavian and Germanic branch.

A first group will become separated from this Nordic branch at an undetermined time, but certainly well after −10,000, and will occupy the eastern part of Europe, then will descend to Scythia, to the confines of the southern cradle: the Slavs.

Other branches will probably descend by means of the Rhine and the Danube to the Caucasus and into the Black Sea: from there the secondary migrations of the Celts will set out, Iberian and other Indoeuropean tribes, which in no case came from the heart of Asia. One sees thus how this illusion was created.

Around 2200 B.C., the Greeks became separated from the Nordic branch and, in a north-south migration, arrived in Greece.

The Latins, more slowly perhaps, took possession of Italy where they found the descendants of the alpine race (the Umbrians) probably mixed with the disappearing Grimaldians; just as the Greeks found on the spot the Siculi, the Scythians, and the Pelasgians, who must have been of a type closely related to that of the pre-Latins.

In 1421 B.C. the explosion of the Santorin Island of the Cyclades must have had migratory consequences which one has neglected to study until now. Perhaps this event could explain the great migration of the Nordic peoples toward India: from whence comes the appellation of Indo-Europeans, or Indo-Aryans? This is the explanation, perhaps, of the myth of Atlantis (see my work: *L'Unité culturelle de l'Afrique Noire*, Présence Africaine, Paris, 1959).

One will notice that the portion which went toward India, and which must have passed between the Black Sea and the Caspian Sea, had necessarily lived very near the Greeks previously, as the study of manners and customs bears witness (see *L'Unité culturelle*).

Even in modern times, Goethe will celebrate this irresistible attraction of the South on the Nordics:

> Do you know the country where the lemon trees blossom,
> Where the golden oranges shine in the dark foliage,
> A gentle wind blows in the blue sky,
> The myrtle is always tall and still and the laurel upright,
> Do you know it well?
> Over there! Over there!
> I must take you, O my beloved.[14]

The last Nordic migrations are those of the Vikings in the middle period; Thule, Iceland, the polar circle are indeed the mythical countries of the ancestors and of the Gods: Ossian, Woden, etc.

The Saxons were separated from the continental Germanic stock in order to inhabit England. Thus, the Nordics and the Germans were probably born in the North following an on-the-spot adaptation of Cro-Magnon. They did not come from Asia or the Caucasus; it is the opposite which was produced, and the secondary gyratory migrations born of these regions have complicated facts and give the impression, at times, of an initial movement from west Asia.

England of the megalithic era was subjected greatly to the Negroid Egypto-Phoenician influence; in fact, the first Phoenician navigations, Sidonian, of the bronze age are contemporaneous with the XVIIIth Egyptian dynasty, the Phoenicians, subjects and agents of the Egyptians, went to look for tin in the Scilly Isles, that is in England. Today they have rediscovered the galleries of the mines, so long that they extend under the sea. It was in this epoch that a whole pre-christian African vocabulary passed into what was going to become the English language, old saxon. The population of the island was very small then and that facilitated the southern cultural penetration: less than 3 million until the One Hundred Years' War.

It is interesting to note that according to Marija Gimbutas[15] there existed an ancient civilization, christened "ancient European," directly sprung from the Upper Paleolithic and the Mesolithic periods, and which was characterized by the sedentary life, agriculture, the cult of the fertility mother goddess of nature and other feminine deities, the matriarchy, the urban egalitarian society, peaceful; it must have lasted three millennia, from 6500 to 3500 B.C. and was totally unaware of war: thus a society which, in all respects, recalls the sedentary, agrarian matrilineal African societies.

It was developed in central Europe and from the southeast, in the Balkans, along the Danube and tributaries in the fertile and agriculturally suitable valleys. It gave birth, at different epochs, to the cultural cycles known by the names: Karanovo (Bulgaria), Stracevo (Hungary), Sesklo (Greece), Cucuteni (Rumania), Vinca (in the north of Macedonia) . . .

It must have been destroyed by proto-Indo-European nomads, (named "Kurgans" by the author), come from the Russian Eurasiatic Steppes, between the Caspian and the Black Sea. These latter very primitive populations had a culture characterized by nomadism, the patriarchy, the worship of warlike dieties, the domestication of the horse, and arms unknown until then in ancient Europe. The newcomers literally erased the ancient European civilization created by the cro-magnoids who remained in the South (Alpines and others) and to the vanishing Negroids who were still present as far as Switzerland.[16] There must have been three Kourgan invasions spaced out between 3400 and 2900 B.C., the last waves reaching the confines of the Baltic through the Danube basin. The excavation of the tumuli, left by the invaders, and the C14 dating provide precious information on this stratification of civilization in Europe. These facts provide a solution to a problem in social evolution: there had not been, as Bachoffen supposed, internal passsage from matriarch to patriarch, within the course of an evolution of the same society by the simple play of endogenous factors. It was really a patriarchial nomadic group which surprised a sedentary society and introduced, by force, the patriarchy and all of its corollary practices there. This shows also that the patriarchy and the matriarchy do not depend on race, but follow consequentially the material conditions of life, as we have always affirmed. There were more of them (patriarchies) than in the Iron Age. With the arrival of the Dorians in Greece, the patriarchy triumphed definitively in the Indo-European societies: Greece, Rome, aryan India, Persia, etc.; it is inconceivable to suppose a former matriarchial past among the people who transport the patriarchy, especially among the Dorians: it was a question of people who, according to all likelihood, passed from hunting to the nomadic life, without ever knowing the sedentary phase; it was only later, with the conquest of agrarian regions, that they became sedentary.

Nevertheless, let's express clearly some reservations concerning the thesis of M. Gimbutas. As she recognizes herself, the culture of the coiled pottery method, which was developed from that of the globular jars, at the beginning off the 3rd millennium B.C. is considered as the first typical Indo-European culture of the north: "Germans, Celts, Illyrians, Baltics and perhaps Slavs."[17] It is not absolutely certain that the hypothetical Kurgan invaders, to whose influence she attributes the transformation in the north of Europe, from the culture of funnel-shaped goblets into the culture of globular jars, were Indo-Europeans or proto-Indo-Europeans. One notices that the invaded area, principally that of the Balkans, shelters the most remote European branch of the Nordic type, often presenting Negroid traits which go back to the Grimaldian type, or Asiatic traits due to Asiatic invasions of which those of the Huns and the Hungarians were probably the last. In fact, the author writes: "Analysis of the skeletons of the Budakalasz and Alsonemedi cemeteries (famous for the four wheel chariot clay miniature)[18] near Budapest, revealed the presence of populations linked to the type of the Steppes[19] as well as to the Mediterranean type."[20]

The author believes that there already existed a beginning of writing with a body of more than two hundred linear and hieroglyphic symbols, in the cultures of Vinca and Karanovo. "This writing precedes by three thousand years the Minoan linear and seems to have a certain relationship with it."[21]

In reality, it concerns symbolic drawings which present in no way the coherence of writing, otherwise this would be the first in the world and one would not understand why Crete and the Aegean, situated in the zone spared by the destructive invasion of the "Kurgans," did not know writing three thousand years sooner. Nothing of the kind! Crete, in spite of this alleged cultural heritage, will not leave Protohistory and will not know writing until under the Egyptian colonization of the XVIIIth dynasty (see chapter 3); and this writing she will owe to Egypt, as all the facts cited below attest. One has taken note particularly in the writing tablets of the linear writing of Pylos, in continental Greece, during the Mycenaean epoch, of two symbols of metrology, typically revealing of the Egyptian influence: the "talent", a weight equivalent to 29 kg., is noted by the Egyptian scale picture symbol 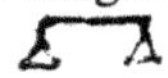 , just like the weight equivalent to the capacity of a fourth of a litre, the "Kotyle," is indicated by the Egyptian picture  = nb = basket = half-sphere, etc.[22] Likewise, the name in the genitive case for Dionysos, a replica of Osiris, has been noticed in the tablets. Finally, the Aegean civilization, instead of moving from the north toward the south, as one would expect, spread rather in every direction from the extreme south toward the north of Greece, which remained semi-barbarian even at the time of Thucydides.

R. Furon recalls that Ch. Autran particularly insisted on the role of the Dravidians in the diffusion of the prearyan myths in the west.[23]

The former predominance of the black civilization around the Mediterranean is attested to by the unexpected existence of pre-hellenic black virgins, like "the prehellenic black goddess, the black Demeter of Phigalia in Arcadia, the black Aphrodite of Arcadia and of Corinth, finally the black virgin of Saint Victor of Marseille and the black virgin of Chartres, which was formerly honored under the name of Our Lady Underground."[24]

Finally, M. Boule and H.V. Vallois, citing Schreiner,[25] insist on the recent nature of "Homo nordicus," which probably resulted from the superimposition, at the beginning of the Neolithic Period, in the south of Denmark, of a local element formed by the descendants of men from the Upper Paleolithic Period and of a complex of invaders from the south: diverse dolichocephalics with, to a certain point, small neolithic brachycephalics.[26]

On the other hand, these authors considered that the mesocephalics of Ofnet evolved in the Neolithic Period in order to give the first brachycephalics of the world at a time when the latter existed neither in Russia nor in the Near East, nor in North Africa: they existed even less in the Upper Paleolithic Period which knew only dolichocephalics and mesocephalics, more or less.[27]

The third "Kurgan" invasion ("jamna" in the Soviet terminology) is placed around 2900 B.C. and "is confirmed by hundreds of tombs in Rumania, Bulgaria, Yugoslavia and central Hungary. These tombs ressemble, to the smallest detail, the Kurgan tombs of the lower Dnieper and the lower Don called "Jamna" (shaft tombs, in Russian)."[28]

These invasions could well have contributed, in no small degree, to the formation of the slavic branch or to a separation into two groups: the Slavs of the north (Russians, Poles) and the Slavs of the south (the Balkan peoples).

It is important to underline that these "Kurgan" people of the lower Dnieper and the lower Don had themselves recently come into this region, probably at the beginning of the Neolithic period. Their presence there is not confirmed during the Upper Paleolithic period. It is only after the retreat of the cold, at the end of the last Würmian glaciation, that cro-magnoids must have advanced more to the east and occupied these regions in order to set out again later toward the west, after an adaptation to the conditions of nomadic life, thus giving the signal to the so-called Kurgan invasions.

On the other hand, in spite of the assumptions of Gimbutas, ancient Europe did not know writing and transmitted no evidence by this means to posterity, not even a single legible sign; also the "matriarchy" of this ancient society, although probable, remains a pure hypothesis, not demonstrable today for lack of documents.

Finally, this ancient culture founded on agriculture was completely destroyed and replaced by a nomadic patriarchal culture from outside, that very culture which Europe finally passed on to history dating from the Dorians, 1200 B.C.

The cult of the black virgins, which the Church finally sanctified in modern times, is derived directly from the cult of Isis, which preceded Christianity in the northern Mediterranean.[29] We lack scientific proof in order to connect them to the Aurignacian Venuses. But their existence confirms the southern origin of civilization.

Finally, Gimbutas could have given the raw value of the C14 dates beside the calibrated values, that is to say corrected according to highly technical procedures, but they are still discussing it. The calibration, in conformity with the raw age found, can render a date recent or remote without restriction, so that many laboratories are satisfied for the moment with providing non-calibrated dates.

CHAPTER 2: CRITICAL REVIEW OF THE MOST RECENT THESES ON THE ORIGIN OF HUMANITY

The monogenetic and African origin of humanity becomes each day a more tangible fact. What then remains to be done to the ideology? Face to face with scientific progress, the ideologists, instead of renouncing the lost terrain, the indefensible positions, tax their ingenuity by altering their conceptual devices: this is a current practice. They think that they can thus integrate all of the recorded material facts without having to abandon the sacred ideas which are dear to them, since this would be equivalent to moral suicide.

Hence the trend, according to which the monogenetic and African origin of humanity would stop at the stage of "Homo erectus." They are hypothesizing that "sapientizing" would be produced at the level of each continent, dating from this African "Homo erectus," but in a paleo-environment and in conditions of "cultural" adaptation which safeguard the necessary specificity of the races, and consequently their desirable hierarchization, which very subtle socio-biological studies would be able to demonstrate.

These are the infinitely varied nuances of this position which we briefly describe here, in order to show that the ideologists are not at the end of their torment, because the logical coherence remains with science.

Let us recall historically that this unrest had already affected the preceding generation of eminent anthropologists, at a time when the methods of absolute chronology had not yet cast a singular clarity on the prehistoric archeology of each continent. What they knew then was quite disturbing.

The first "homo sapiens" which inhabited Europe is unquestionably a Negroid migrant, having come from outside, about 40,000 years ago,[30] just as R. Verneaux[31] demonstrated. The first "white", the Cro-Magnon, appeared in the same region 20,000 years afterwards. What is his ancestor, if he is not derived from the Negroid by mutation? Because neither he nor the Negroid comes from the Neanderthal Man which preceded them and lived 80,000 years ago, in the Würmian Period.

Thus was born, as a necessity, the theory of the pre-"Sapiens" on the strength of three fossil discoveries, of which the main one is known to be false. These furnished the ideology with an illusion of evidence since real facts failed to appear. It concerns the all too famous "Piltdown Man" (Figure 5), discovered—actually fabricated—in 1912 by the British geologist Charles Dawson.[32] Everything considered, it's wrong that they have dismissed this talented forger, a true scholar, as a simple joker, having had no other intention but that of misleading the specialists, in order to amuse himself or to take revenge. His plan was quite different, because for 50 years, scholars of good faith, such as Henry V. Vallois, all the while clearly expressing reservations, adhered to the theory of the "pre-Sapiens" of which cultural and political Europe had such great need. It's in this regard that the latter writes: "The documents of Piltdown Man are unfortunately incomplete. Their interpretation, extremely difficult, is still doubtful concerning some essential points. One cannot however deny especially now that we know that the jawbone indeed belongs to the skull, that it represents one of the most instructive and extremely important discoveries. It informs us of the existence of a man with a brain-pan very closely related to that of 'Homo sapiens' at a time which, being less remote than one had believed at first, dates no less from the Lower Pleistocene Period. And in this way is connected much more clearly to the ascent of this same 'Homo sapiens' than to that of 'Homo neandertalensis.' The origins of our ancestors must be thus very remote in the past. Until the present, one had cited, with the support of this hypothesis, a certain number of discoveries without geological assurance, and consequently, without demonstrative value. The skull of Piltdown has put us face to face, for the first time, with a well examined fact, whose significance appears clear and precise in spite of the uncertainties which continue to exist concerning its age."[33]

Thus, even a scholar of the quality of Vallois was able to believe that the monkey-like jawbone of Piltdown and the skull belonged to the same individual and emphasized the geological assurances which surrounded the discovery

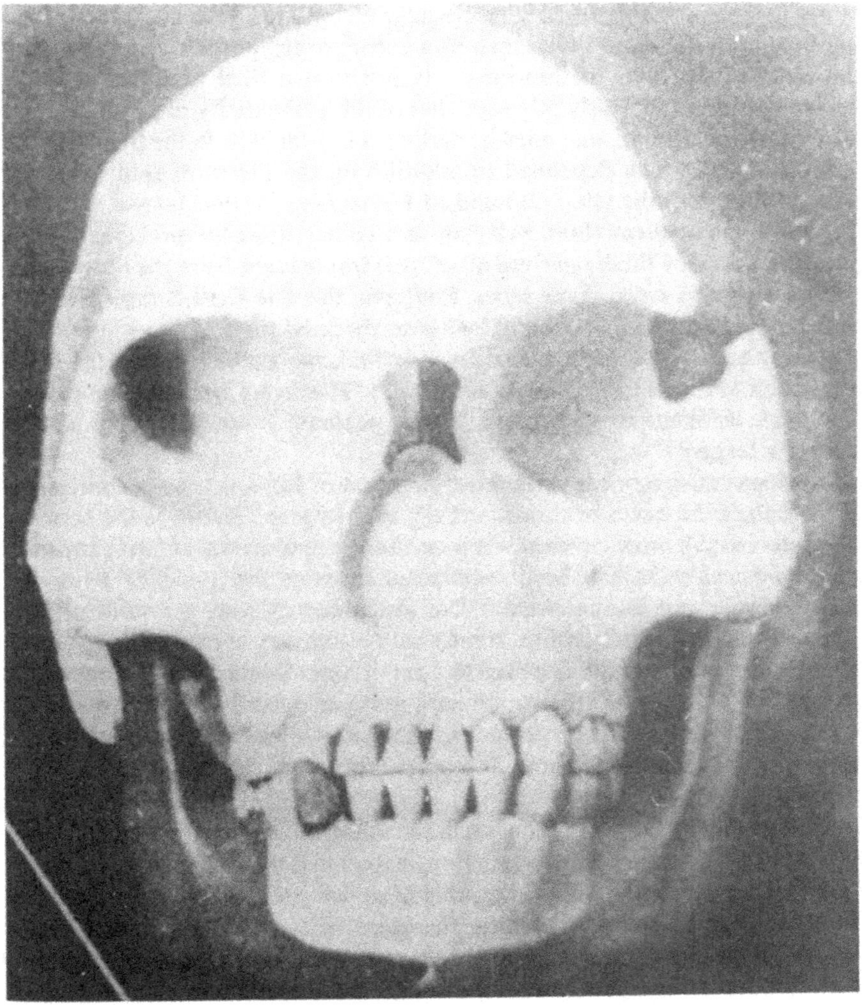

Figure 5. "Piltdown Man," the entirely fabricated falsehood which ideology needed in order to support the thesis of the "pre-Sapiens." It is made from the juxtaposition of a skull of a modern man with a high forehead and a jawbone of a monkey whose canines one can see. (According to M. Boule and H. V. Vallois: *Les Hommes fossiles,* Figure 119.)

of this fossil, sunken by the forger-scholar to a depth of 1.50m. in the gravel of the Ouse River in Sussex. It was necessary to wait until 1954, in order that another English scholar of good faith working in the British Museum, Oakley, might have the idea to determine the quantity of fluorine contained in the two pieces, and to deduce from the difference of the proportions found, the certainty that the specimen was false; because the said jawbone and the skull do not belong to the same individual, as a consequence of their not containing the same proportions of fluorine.[34] He put thus a final period to a bitter debate which lasted nearly 50 years, that of the authenticity of Piltdown, and also struck in so doing, one must underline, a mortal blow to the theory of the "pre-Sapiens," which depended in addition on the pieces of skulls without faces of Swanscombe (1935-36) and of Fontéchévade (1947)—two such unsatisfactory specimens (how well that fact comes from the previous Vallois passage), that they finally derived all of their importance from the only apparently convincing piece of the series, Piltdown; this one has a complete face, a high forehead of "Homo sapiens" without the least trace of the supraorbital protuberance, so characteristic of Neanderthal; more evolved than the latter and indigenous to Europe, a true ancestor of "Homo europeus," of an extraction quite different from Negroid "Homo sapiens" from whence he comes; alas it's a forgery.[35]

X-ray spectrometry has confirmed the fraud of Piltdown, by permitting to bring to light the traces of chromium salt used to give a patina to the bones.[36] The facts are still more comical when one knows that several identifications of morphological traits had been established between the fossils of Piltdown, Fontéchévade and Swanscombe: "The resemblances with the skull of Piltdown, brought to light by Keith, appear on the contrary to have to be retained. The English author had concluded from it that Swanscombe Man was a descendant of that of Piltdown, already more evolved in the Homo sapiens sense. This hypothesis is incorrect, since we now know that it's Swanscombe Man who is the most ancient. The relationship between the two is no less evident."[37]

Concerning the Fontéchévade fossil, the same authors write: "The forehead of the Fontéchévade men was therefore shaped like that of modern man and quite different from that of Neanderthal Man. Here still the resemblance with Piltdown Man is obvious, because the piece of the forehead which corresponds to the second discovery of this layer is itself also missing a bulge, and its profile superimposes almost exactly with that of the Fontéchévade piece."[38]

In reality the "modern" qualities of this fossil are simply imagined by the scholars, instead of being actual morphological traits as Bernard Vandermeersch states: "The piece discovered in the Fontéchévade cave in Charente is represented by a part of the cranial arch whose morphology would be, according to H.V. Vallois, more modern than that of contemporary fossils, particularly for the frontal region. It is unfortunately very incomplete and bears no characteristic structure. The "modern" traits brought to light do not therefore result from direct observations, but they are inferred by the proposed reconstruction and have often been contested."[39]

If "Homo sapiens" were indigenous to Europe, it would be possible to follow his evolution on the spot from his supposed ancestors of the Mindel-

Riss interglacial stage, who would have lived 350,000 years ago, up to his descendant, the Cro-Magnon of the Solutrean Period, who lived 20,000 years ago. But, nothing has been able to fill, to this day, this paleontological void.

The "pre-Sapiens" vanished without leaving any lineage after 350,000 years and it will be necessary to wait for the beginning of Würm, about 80,000 years, in order to see the Neanderthal "appear"; who will disappear abruptly within 40,000 years, without leaving any lineage. This at the moment when "Homo sapiens," in this case the Grimaldian Negroid, is going to enter Europe, 20,000 years before the appearance (by mutation probably of the Negroid) of the first traces of Cro-Magnon, the ancestor of the present European.

The fossil discovered by Henri de Lumeley and named, "Tautavel Man" brings no new element to the thesis of the "pre-Sapiens." It was dated by the method of amino acids (J. Bada) and by that of uranium (K. Furekian).[40] The Tayacian and Acheulean created deposits containing the fossils would probably have an age between 320,000 (soil G) and 220,000 years (soil F).[41]

This man, as his inventor seems to think, would be an intermediary between "Homo erectus" (Pithecanthropus) and Neanderthal Man. He presents a prominent supraorbital bulge, so characteristic of Neanderthal, with a cranial capacity inferior to that of the latter.

Another fact merits mention; the industries associated with "pre-Sapiens" are characteristic of "Homo erectus" and, a supreme contradiction, more primitive than that of Neanderthal Man, the Mousterian. Actually, we have just seen that Tautavel Man is associated with a Tayacian industry and of the middle Acheulean Period; likewise, the Fontéchévade industry is Tayacian and that of Swanscombe, Acheulean.

So many facts often left in darkness have led paleontologists like Vandermeersch to reject the thesis of the "pre-Sapiens."

The period of evolution considered goes from the Mindel-Riss to the Riss-Würm. Vandermeersch considers that it is not tenable that during a lapse of time of 250,000 years, the Neanderthal Man and the "pre-Sapiens" could evolve separately, in the same European region, each one accentuating his specific traits, without any cross-breeding; whereas on the contrary it would have to occur and attenuate the differences, given that the "specific barrier" did not play a role: there was interbreeding, because Neanderthal is only a sub-species of "Homo sapiens." Likewise, the cultural barrier couldn't have played a part, because one finds the two sub-species, the so-called "pre-Sapiens" and Neanderthal, associated with the same Acheulean and Tayacian industries.

We recall even that the classic Mousterian industry of the Neanderthal is clearly and paradoxically more evolved than those above, attributed to "pre-Sapiens." So that at the colloquium of 1969, on the appearance of modern man, organized by UNESCO, they had taken care, as far as I remember, to disassociate cultural evolution (industry) and morphological evolution, this namely in order to eliminate the insurmountable rock which has just been raised: How can a being more primitive morphologically and physically, the Neanderthal, in this case, be responsible for an industry, and consequently for a material culture more advanced, more perfected than that of a being more evolved, such as the "pre-Sapiens."

The study of the skull of Biache-Saint-Vaast, a new pre-Neanderthalian, recently discovered in the north of France, led Vandermeersch to the conclusion that Swanscombe, Fontéchévade and all the other fossils found in Europe before the appearance of "Homo sapiens," about 37,000 years ago in that region, all belong to the neanderthalian lineage.

Let's say that to this lineage belong equally, according to Vallois himself, Ehringsdorf Man, the bony head no. 1 of Saccopastore, the Steinheim skull . . .[42] and Heidelberg Man.

According to Vandermeersch, with "the skull of Biache, the distance which would separate pre-Neandertalians and pre-Sapiens, is considerably reduced. Of all the pre-Neanderthalians, this is the one which approaches Swanscombe Man the most. All the more because the region of the Biache skull which presents the most acknowledged neanderthalian characteristics is the mastoid region which is not preserved on the Swanscombe skull. The Swanscombe skull appears more modern, one should say, more archanthropic, because it is older, nearer the origin of the race, therefore less specialized in the neanderthalian sense. It's a question of a general law of evolution."

Thus, the Archanthropics, having come very probably from Africa, would have begun (during the Mindel-Riss interglacial stage) to take on individual characteristics of the neanderthalian type, by virtue of the very same climatic conditions, of the paleo-environment, generally speaking. At the beginning of the Riss-Würm glacial period 80,000 years ago the evolutionary process which was to come to a dead end with Neanderthal was complete and the European neanderthal population stayed homogeneous during all of Würm I and II, that is practically from − 80,000 years to − 40,000 years.

These facts led Vandermeersch to conclude that Neanderthal alone is specifically European and that the origin of "Homo sapiens" is to be sought elsewhere, in the Orient and more precisely in Palestine, even if he does not explicitly give precise details about the latter.[43]

It is not possible that Neanderthal resulted, as one has just said, from a progressive adaptation of the African "Homo erectus" in Europe during the Riss-Würm interglacial stage, and that he emigrated later toward the other continents where he died out without leaving any descendants, contrary to what Vandermeersch thinks. If it were really like that, prehistoric archeology will have to prove that the European neanderthalian fossils are older than those found on the other continents where this species would have come later, as a migrant. But, one is far from being able to peremptorily make such a statement.

Broken Hill Man (Rhodesia or Zimbabwe Man) is a neanderthalian fossil, in certain respects more primitive than the European skull of La Chapelle-aux-Saints, which it unmistakably resembles (Figure 6).

I was not far from adopting the point of view above, but the fact that the African neanderthaloid of Broken Hill, dated from 110,000 years by the amino acid method, may be older than those of Europe or, in any case, of a comparable antiquity appears to question things again; now it is no longer absurd to suppose that even Neanderthal Man could have come from Africa.

The oldest neanderthalian fossils of Europe scarcely seem to date back beyond Interstadial Würm I/II (− 80,000 years).

Since dating by radiocarbon, we know now that Negroid "Homo sapiens sapiens" with a very voluminous skull going to 1500 cm^3 on the average, if not more, lived in southern Africa between − 50,000 and − 100,000 years and that they were probably the ones which are called the first mine operators in the world: the iron mines of Swaziland, cited in the first chapter. The fossils of these "Homo sapiens" are represented by the voluminous skull of Boskop, the incomplete head of Florisbad (a part of the skull and the face) and the bony head of Cape Flats.[44] Thus the most voluminous fossil skulls found to this day are those of these Negroids of southern Africa, contrary to the calculations of the authors of *Race et Intelligence*, a work which I will talk about again later on.

The Florisbad fossil is dated moreover from 41,000 years; it is therefore older than all the European "Homo sapiens sapiens" and from the other continents, dated by a method of absolute chronology, without biased interpretation.

Finally, the oriental origin of "Homo sapiens," as Vandermeersch declares, is today scientifically untenable.

In fact, Vandermeersch takes up the idea of H.V. Vallois who, following Keith and McCown, studied the Neanderthalians of Palestine and concluded that these fossils probably are not the direct ancestors of the Upper Paleolithic men, but that their existence "indicates that the transformation of Neanderthal Man into modern man, if it did not happen in Europe, had to be able to happen elsewhere. This is a conclusion of extreme importance."[45] Vandermeersch himself had recognized that there existed a grave difficulty of a chronological order, which unfortunately continues to exist: in fact, in order for the above hypothesis to be acceptable, these fossils would have to belong, at least, to Riss or to Riss-Würm. But, we know now that this is not the case. The radiocarbon and amino acid datings made for this region agree and give an age which varies between 37,000 and 53,000 years B.C.[46] Therefore, these supposed ancestors of "Homo sapiens" are indeed more recent than African

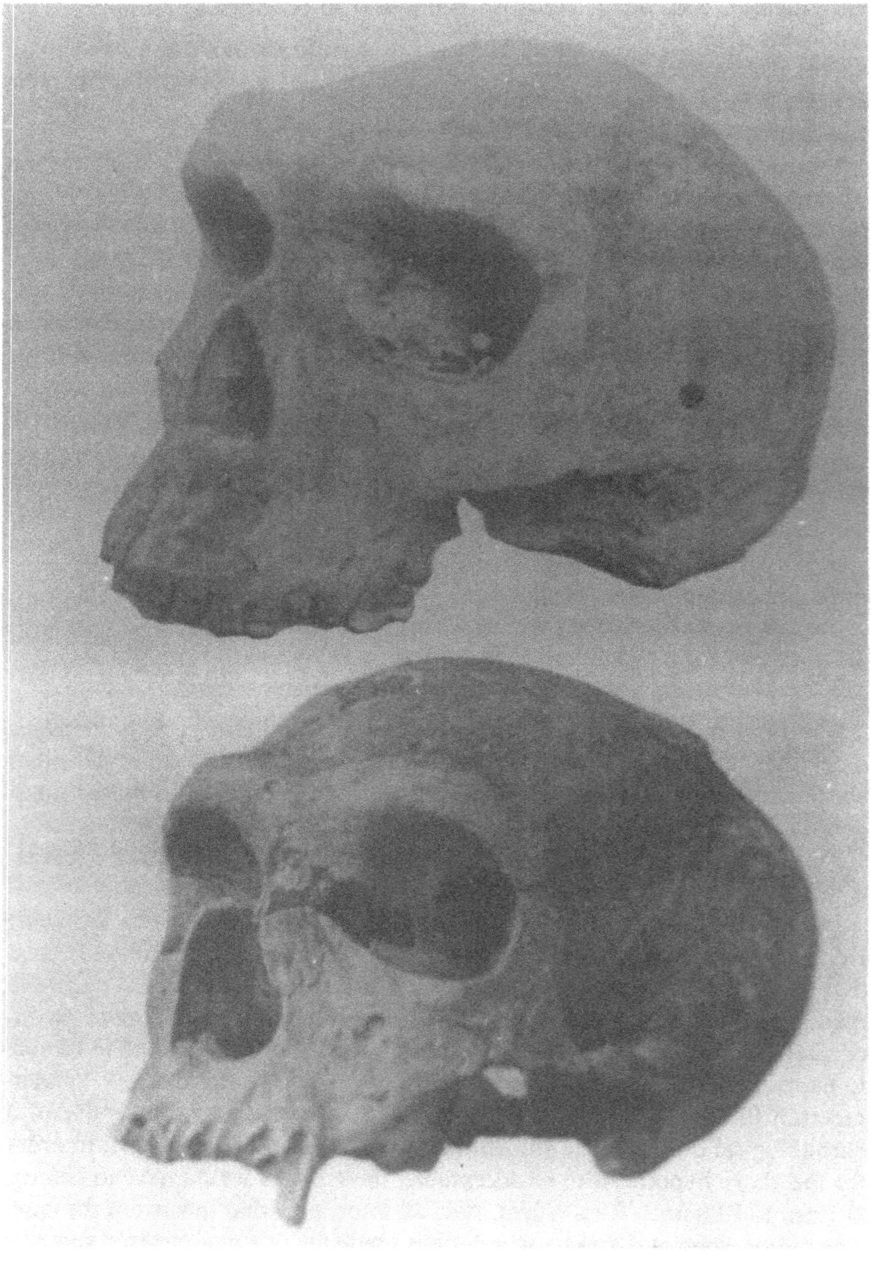

Figure 6. Skulls of Broken Hill (top) and La Chapelle-aux-Saints (bottom); $^3/_4$ view, almost from the same angle, to facilitate comparisons. (According to M. Boule and H.V. Vallois: *Les Hommes fossiles*, Figure 282.)

"Homo sapiens sapiens" which appeared at least 150,000 years ago (skull of Omo I, Omo II; Kanjera Man).[47]

Before drawing all the consequences of anteriority from the African "Homo sapiens sapiens" which compared to all the other "Homo sapiens sapiens" which appeared on the other continents, let's insist on the fact that the "evolved Neanderthalians" of Qafza (− 37,000 years) are strictly contemporaries of European "Homo sapiens" and cannot therefore be the ancestors of this latter one. B. Vandermeersch writes, in his report presented at the Paris Colloquium of 1969, that layer XVII containing the three skeletons which he discovered equally contain traces of coal and ashes in such an abundance that their color is "an even deep grey." But, in these conditions, it is absolutely possible to carry out a radiometric dating on the said ashes. Has it ever been attempted?[48] M. Ottieno of Kenya and I represented the African continent at the Paris Colloquium and the ideas which I had developed then against the polycentric and differentiation thesis, from "Homo erectus" on, are the ones which I develop here.[49]

The Neanderthalians of Palestine and Iraq are consequently only dead ends, too recent, and are not at the origin of any species of "Homo sapiens sapiens." Endocranial molds made of these fossils would permit one to better understand the still enormous distance which separates them from "Homo sapiens sapiens." But one has neglected until now to make such molds and to study them, although I posed the question at the Paris Colloquium of 1969. If modern man was not born in Europe, well then he's going to be born in Palestine, in accordance with sacred scripture, these eminent anthropologists seem to say to themselves in their subconscious!

Irony of ironies, Palestine seems to be a paleontological vacuum during the period corresponding to the appearance of "Homo sapiens sapiens." One will have to wait for the Mesolithic Age, around − 8,000 or − 10,000, in order for him to manifest himself there in the form of a Negroid: the Natufian of Miss Garrod is, all ideology put aside, the first "Homo sapiens sapiens" population of that region. The vacuum which exists between him and the Neanderthalians evolved from Qafza is not, to this day, filled in by prehistoric archeology. But, at almost the same time, a Negroid culture called Capsian, characterized by little blades in the shape of a crescent, extended from Kenya to Tunisia and to Palestine. This was the epoch of the Negroids of the Capsian culture. In Africa, this Capsian culture was immediately preceded by that of the Ibero-Maurusian which disappeared ten thousand years ago, without leaving any descendants. There exists no demonstrable link between Ibero-Maurusian Man and the Guanches of the Canary Islands of protohistory. A vacuum of 8000 years, which nobody has dreamed of filling in, separates them: the Guanches, who practiced mummification, and who were more or less impregnated with the Punic culture, must be considered as a simple branch of the current Berbers who are, to be sure, descendants of the European leucoderms called Sea Peoples, in the Egyptian texts, and who invaded Egypt in the XIXth dynasty (1300 B.C.), that precisely of the Ramessids. Conquered, they were pushed back to the west of the Nile delta, from whence they scattered progressively to the Atlantic, through Cyrenaica, from the Nasamonians to the Getulians of the Moroccan South.

As paradoxical as it may be, the thesis of the polycentric origin of humanity, that which proceeds from common sense, at first sight, does not withstand the analysis of facts, especially chronological facts. That's why on adopting it, even scholars of the calibre of Andor Thoma are led to explain human evolution backwards. Thoma, who adopts the views of Vandermeersch of the men of Palestine, writes: "The Qafza VI skull recently described by H.V. Vallois and B. Vandermeersch is the most archaic representative of the western Neanthropics."[50] Thus the hypotheses of Keith and McCown, taken up by Vallois and Vandermeersch, become a certitude, commented on by Thoma and the other polycentrics. Thoma does not hesitate to compare the infant skull aged one and a half of *Starocelia*, found in Crimea and of the Aurignacian type according to Guerassimov,[51] to the Neanderthalians of Palestine. One can state in a few words, that the sub-orbital protuberance so prominent in the Qafza Men and the exaggerated width of the nasal orifice,[52] in short, the primitive and almost bestial aspect of the Palestine Men, which should eliminate all possibility of direct comparison with "Homo sapiens sapiens" is unconsciously toned down in his reproduction of the article and it suffices to refer to Figure 250 of H.V. Vallois in order to realize it. For Thoma, Qafza and Starocelia are the proto-Cro-Magnons, descending from Paleanthropics such as Steinheim and Swanscombe, which would date from more than 200,000 years. Their descendants are the Cro-Magnons of Europe and of North Africa; these later ones "on colonizing Africa, were rapidly "negroidized" under the effect of high selective pressure exercised by the new environment, because the alveolar prognathism indicated, the considerable width of the nose, the shape of the relatively low and very long neuroskull are already typically negroid."[53]

A. Thoma describes thus the morphological traits of a series of skeletons dating from the final Paleolithic Period (10,000 to 12,000 years B.C.) and discovered in Nubia, when studied by J.E. Anderson.

For Guerassimov, the child of Starocelia is a typically Negroid "Sapiens sapiens."

Let's add that the dimensions and the shape of its forehead forbid classing it among the Neanderthalians, even evolved ones.

Still according to Thoma, the evolutionary passage from the paleanthropic phase to the neanthropic phase must have been accomplished in at least three geographic centers: In Indonesia and in Australia, 600,000 years ago, during the archanthropic phase, for the individualization of the australoid branch of humanity. In Siberia for the mongoloid phylum, 80,000 years ago, while the separation of the Europoids and the Negroids did not happen until the neanthropic phase, around 12,000 years ago, according to what precedes.

For Thoma, the study which he made on the resemblances between the digito-palmar skin grooves concerning the "five" great races confirms particularly the recent separation of the Negroid and the Europoid; we would say of the Grimaldian and the Cro-Magnon. If this latter fact is paleontologically true, it came about in a way contrary to the process which Thoma supposes, in the south of France, in any case in southern Europe, and not in Africa, and this between −40,000 and −20,000 years, that is during the interval which separates the arrival in Europe of the Man of Grimaldi—Negroid migrant having probably come through Gilbraltar—from Cro-Magnon Man of the Solutrean Period. These "homo sapiens," having entered Europe, have no need of the Men of Qafza in order to exist, because they precede them or at the very least are contemporaneous, as the radiometric datings carried out on the sites prove.

Let's say also the immunological data have come to confirm the hypothesis of a recent separation of Black and White, of the Negroid and the Caucasoid,[54] although this latter term is improper, because the Caucasus is by no means the cradle of the white race (Figure 7).

According to J. Ruffie, citing Nei Masatoshi and A.R. Roycoudhury, this separation of racial groups is probably more remote. These authors begin with several sets of about ten blood markers in order to study the inter and intragroup genetic differences between Negroid, Caucasoid and Mongoloid populations.

"They define the correlation coefficients which permit dating, more or less approximately, at what moment these groups separated from each other. The Negroid became entirely independent some 120,000 years ago, whereas Mongoloids and Caucasoids would have separated only 55,000 years ago."[55]

Even if 55,000 years seem too early an age for the formation of the Caucasoid and Mongoloid branches, account taken of the pre-historic data, 120,000 years corresponds well with the appearance of the first African Negroid "Homo sapiens sapiens" in the valley of Omo and in Kanjera.

According to Thoma, "The current Australoids can be connected to the pithecanthropus of Java by the medium of the Ngandong Men in Java (the beginning of the Upper Pleistocene Period, around 150,000 years)."[56] The Australian site of Kow Swanif (8000 years B.C.) produced about twenty skeletons which would correspond morphologically to the population of Ngandong and which supply the proof of existence of an Australian phylum.

At the Paris Colloquium in 1969, the same inclination had emerged, the need to individualize the Australoid phylum too much in order to make a sub-humanity of it, destined perhaps to disappear. Dr. L.S.B. Leakey, address-

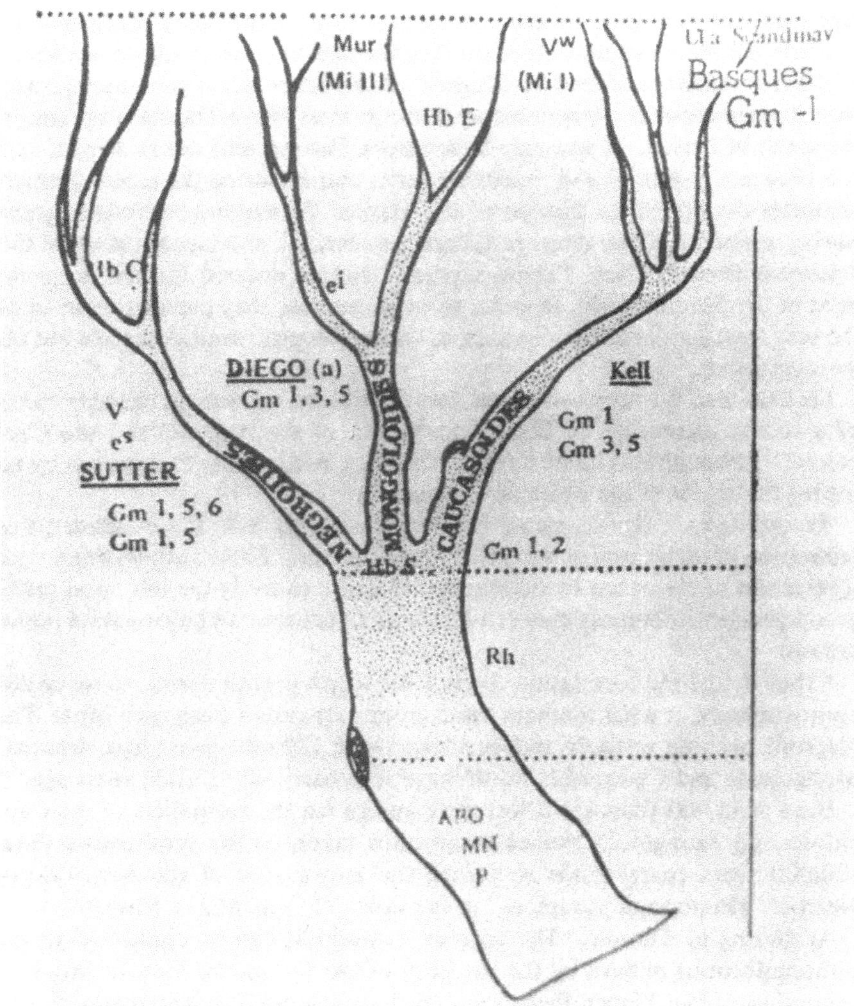

Figure 7. Racial differentiation according to data of hemotypology. There exists, in short, racial markers significant enough which would permit identifying the ancient Egyptians, if they were not already. The three factors: Sutter (Negroid), Diego (Mongoloid), and Kell (Caucasoid) are underlined by us in the diagram. (J. Ruffie: *De la biologie à la culture,* p. 395.)

ing the colloquium, which was in plenary session to adopt the conclusions, said that what they were in the act of doing contained nothing scientific and he asked that the indicated paragraph be suppressed from the final text, which was done.

Another great scholar told me: "Psychically, I don't know, but morphologically, the Australians are distinct from contemporary man."

Nevertheless, the Australians are from "Homo sapiens sapiens" in the strict sense of the word and do not constitute a distinct branch. Their intellectual capacities have been tested and one knows that their performances are indeed identical to those of modern man.

They are not of an insular origin. They arrived in their current localities, in Australia, by navigation from the Asian continent, around 30,000 years ago.[57]

According to Thoma, Mongoloid fossils which are known only in the recent Würm Glacier (around 20,000 years ago) of southern Siberia (Atontova Gora, Malta, Bouriet), where they are accompanied by human figurations of the Mongoloid type, would result from a neanthropization of the Neanderthal of the Near East, when Siberia was habitable up to 61° north latitude. The author bases his reasoning on the fact that the paleosiberian fossils and the Mongoloids in a general way, like the Neanderthalians, have no canine fossa but they have high, large and rounded orbits. But the same author, in the same article, describes the Neanderthalians of the Near East as having precisely a canine fossa and being able from that fact to be proto-Cro-Magnons.

Still according to Thoma, it is only in the Neolithic Period, 6,000 years ago, that the Mongoloids are in constant selective avantage in the environment of origin. Consequently, one must expect that the Mongoloid traits be found again in the numerous Asian populations not descended from the Mongoloid phylum.

Espousing the point of view of W.W. Howells according to which evolution always contains a certain part of anagenesis (that is to say improvement without the possibility of diversification) and a certain part of cladogenesis (that is to say the birth of several branches of which only one is advanced to perfection), Andor Thoma claims that the most probable hypothesis for human evolution is polycentrism, which one must not confuse with polyphyly.

According to this latter point of view, a species can be born of several other species belonging to families or to different genera: thus they assumed at the beginning of the century, that Whites descend from the chimpanzee, Blacks from the gorilla and Orientals from the orangutan. The three human races would thus respectively descend from three different genera: "Pan, Goullael, Pongo." This was in order to be able to say: I, the Caucasoid, I come from the chimpanzee, I have nothing to do with the Black who comes from the gorilla or with the Oriental who comes from the orangutan, although we are all three humans! It was a question of finding, at all cost, a difference of origin capable of justifying a racial hierarchization. It is H.V. Vallois who demonstrated in 1929 the impossibility of polyphyly.[58] Thoma shows that polycentrism originated with Th. Mollison of Munich, in 1931, and was developed consequently by Weidenreich in 1943. He proceeds: "The conception of human evolution of F. Weidenreich was examined in depth by Sir A. Keith then modernized by Professor C. Coon in 1962, in an authoritative work.[59] But these authors scarcely took into consideration the possibility of prehistoric migrations. This omission seemed inadmissible to a great many prehistorians as well as to myself. As of 1962,[60] I have developed another polycentric outline of human evolution."[61]

Thus, for Thoma and the tenants of the polycentric thesis, modern man was born several times, from different paleanthropics, in remote places, of the ancient world, in the Upper Pleistocene Period. Then, by secondary characteristics, he adapted to the local environment always varied, always different, from one center to the other, and thus necessarily experienced a cladogenetic evolution. This hypothesis is also one of common sense; it forces itself, at first glance, upon good sense with a virtually compelling necessity!

However, it is false, and an objective analysis of the facts compels one to reject it. If it were true, the American continent, which is as old as the other continents—the African and European in particular—and which extends from the South Pole to the North Pole, which experienced consequently all the climatic transitions, should also be a multi-center of the birth of humanity, as well at the stage of Australopithicus and "Homo erectus" as at that of "homo sapiens."

But, we know that it is nothing of the kind. There exists no indigenous fossil man from America: this continent was inhabited from Asia, by the Bering Strait. All scholars are in agreement on this fact.

The polycentric hypothesis leads to an insurmountable contradiction which consists of assuming that the children were born before the parents who begot them. It's this fundamental contradiction which one sees throughout all the reasoning of A. Thoma who, however, deployed a remarkable effort of erudition in order to rejuvenate and to adapt the polycentric thesis. He had pointed out in particular the fact that authors like Keith and Coon were neglecting migratory currents and that this rendered their conception at least partially inadmissible.

For A. Thoma, one has seen, it is at the neanthropic stage that Africa is inhabited, late, from Europe: ". . . they are migrant Cro-Magnons who, on colonizing Africa, around − 10,000, would quickly be negroidized after a strong pressure of genetic selection".

One would not know how better to take liberties, especially with chronological facts.

If the polycentric hypothesis were valid, one would have to be able to find, somewhere in the rest of the world, at least one single center of birth of "Homo erectus" or "Homo sapiens sapiens," respectively more ancient than the African centers. But, the chronological data compels us, in the case of the polycentric hypothesis, to admit that the supposed ancestors of the Africans, in this case the Cro-Magnons of A. Thoma, were born well after their "African sons," and better still, that they descend, in all probability, from their supposed sons, by mutation of the Grimaldian Negroid. A. Thoma passed over this latter one completely in silence throughout his whole development, while tacitly likening him, perhaps, to Cro-Magnon, as is the practice at the present time, especially with the French ideologists.

The African "Homo sapiens sapiens" is confirmed (as one has seen above) with the skull of Omo I, in particular, at least 150,000 years ago; Richard Leakey explained to me, in May, 1977 in Nairobi, how these fossils were dated. They are buried in layers of the middle African Pleistocene Period, in a region where the stratigraphy has not been disturbed by tectonic movements. A piece of coal found a distance one third the depth of the fossils has rendered an age higher than 50,000 years; by extrapolation, by multiplying this age by three, one thus finds the average age of the fossils; dating by the uranium/thorium method confirmed this result by yielding 130,000 years.[62]

This specimen of Omo I is to be brought nearer just as Dr. Leakey did with Kanjera Man, a "homo sapiens sapiens"[63] of the Middle Pleistocene Period which he had discovered in 1933.

A conference assembled at Cambridge had then concluded that in spite of their antiquity, the fossils of Kanjera Man scarcely differ from current man.[64] At the time, following criticism of the British geologist, P. Boswell, a certain doubt hovered over the age of these fossils. Now these doubts are raised and we know that it's a question of a specimen of "homo sapiens sapiens" without a sub-orbital protuberance of any kind, with a forehead of modern man.

But even if he were correct and these fossils dated only from 60,000 years, they would still be the oldest in the world of their species.

We know on the other hand, that around 30,000 years ago, the most ancient iron mine in the world was worked in South Africa, in Swaziland, for the extraction of hematite, red ocher, by a man who could only have been a "Homo sapiens sapiens." The mine contained 23,000 stone tools whose analysis will permit one to state precisely the type of man responsible for this working, because one knows or supposes that Neanderthal Man also covered his body with red ocher. A block of hematite extracted from this mine rested on a piece of coal, which, dated by Yale University, gave an age of 29,000 years.[65]

These are the facts for Black Africa. Let's now follow closely the chronology of the appearance of "Homo sapiens sapiens" on the other continents.

In Europe, we have already seen, the first "Homo sapiens sapiens" is the migrant Negroid, responsible for the Aurignacian industry. Now the chronological facts of Africa relating to the antiquity of "Homo sapiens sapiens" on this continent allow one to imagine that the Grimaldian Man left Africa and that he entered Europe by the Iberian Pensinsula and not by the Orient. He left all along the way still visible traces of stone wall paintings which are lacking on all the other alleged routes.

His arrival in Europe is dated with carbon 14 by Professor H.L. Movius, Jr.[66]

The excavations undertaken from 1958 to 1964, at the Pataud shelter (Les Eyzies, Dordogne) under the aegis of the Musée de l'Homme (Paris) on the one hand and of the Peabody Museum of Harvard University on the other hand, led to the discovery of 14 archeological layers. These levels, the majority of which have been dated with radiocarbon, are listed in the note below.[67] The dates obtained are spaced out between 34,000 BP, either around 32,000 BC for the layer forming the base of the old Aurignacian Period, and 21,940 BP or 19,990 BC for the proto-Magdalenian.

Layer I of the Solutrean in the same cave did not furnish any samples capable of dating, but in west Langerie-Haute, a bordering stratum, layer 31, which would be a layer equivalent to Solutrean I of the Pataud shelter, has given a date (20,890 BP ± 300 or 18,940 BC) which is in excellent accord with the preceding dates and confirms the anteriority of Grimaldi with regard to Cro-Magnon because, one must recall, this latter is correctly Solutrean Man.

In la Quina (Gardes, Charente), the recent Mousterian gave the date of 35,250 BP ± 350 or 33,300 BC,[68] which fits in well with the old Aurignacian Period and illustrates the remark of Boule and Vallois according to which, stratigraphically, nothing separates the Negroid Aurignacian race of Grimaldi, from the Mousterian: "It is none the less true in any case, that the Negroid skeletons (of Grimaldi) date back to the beginnings of the reindeer age, to a time which borders on the Mousterian, if it doesn't become confused with the latter. This fact must not be lost sight of."[69]

For F. Bordes, Aurignacian man is not originally from Europe. He is an invader who arrived with his industry ready made: "One thing seems probable, it's that the Aurignacian industry arrived in France fully developed, and if certain of its tools (streamlined) are found there in the Qunia type Mousterian, and even sooner, it does not seem to have any possibility of evolution there on the Aurignacian locality. They have clearly the impression, for once, of an invasion coming from the east."[70] In fact, the expansion of the Aurignacian Period was made from west to east and not the contrary, as all the above-mentioned facts confirm.

F. Bordes thinks that the truly indigenous industry of Europe of the Upper Paleolithic Period is the Old Perigordian, characterized by the so-called

Châtelperron point. It would probably be derived (that is to say, evolved), from the Mousterian Period of the Acheulean type B tradition immediately preceding Würm II. It would thus probably date from the end of the inter-stadial Würm II/III. It is particularly known since the excavations of A. Leroi-Gourhan and F. Bordes himself.[71]

Bordes notes that this industry is interstratified with the Aurignacian Period in at least two sites (Piage and Roc de Combe).

What is there to say if not that it is difficult to distinguish the two industries which were considered as two aspects of the Aurignacian, as is stated above.

It is also as problematic to individualize the perigordian industry as to establish its anteriority in regards to the Aurignacian; in fact, hasn't F. Bordes just told us that the streamlined tools of the Aurignacian Period are found in the Quina type Mousterian Period, dated as one has seen from 35,000 years BP, and even sooner? No dating with absolute chronology has yet permitted establishing definitely this anteriority of the Perigordian, if indeed it is distinct from the Aurignacian, which has several aspects of which one could be Perigordian I, as was admitted at the beginning, and which has an incomparable extension higher than the Perigordian, as we are going to see.

Movius is of this opinion when he writes, with a great deal of politeness: "The following C14 dates, relative to layers of Perigordian I in France, suggest that this last industry was probably, at least in part, contemporaneous with the lower part of the Aurignacian Period of the Pataud shelter and of other localities."[72]

The anthropological identity of this hypothetical native of Europe, which would probably be inserted between the final Mousterian period and the Aurignacian Period and who would be the one responsible for Perigordian I, is still more mysterious and constitutes an almost unsolvable problem of prehistoric archeology. In fact, Madame D. de Sonneville-Bordes notes that: "since the very ancient discovery (1909) of the Man of le Roc de Combe-Capelle, Dordogne, the southwest region of France, has unfortunately not delivered human remains attributable to the lower Perigordian Period"[73] and that currently one is reduced to conjectures as to the man responsible for the industry of this name. Just as we have already said, the Grimaldian Negroid responsible for the Aurignacian industry being manifestly an invader, as F. Bordes recognizes himself, one is tempted to associate the Man of le Roc de Combe Capelle with the Perigordian I industry, who would then be the true native of Europe, the indigenous race of Europe; a race which could have been able to be born and to develop right there, independent of all foreign stock and especially of Grimaldian African Negroid stock, between the middle Paleolithic and the upper Paleolithic Periods, from "pre-Sapiens" Europeans on. Pure gratuitous and ideological speculation which *not* the least fact of prehistoric archeology supports, has resulted in what has been said above.

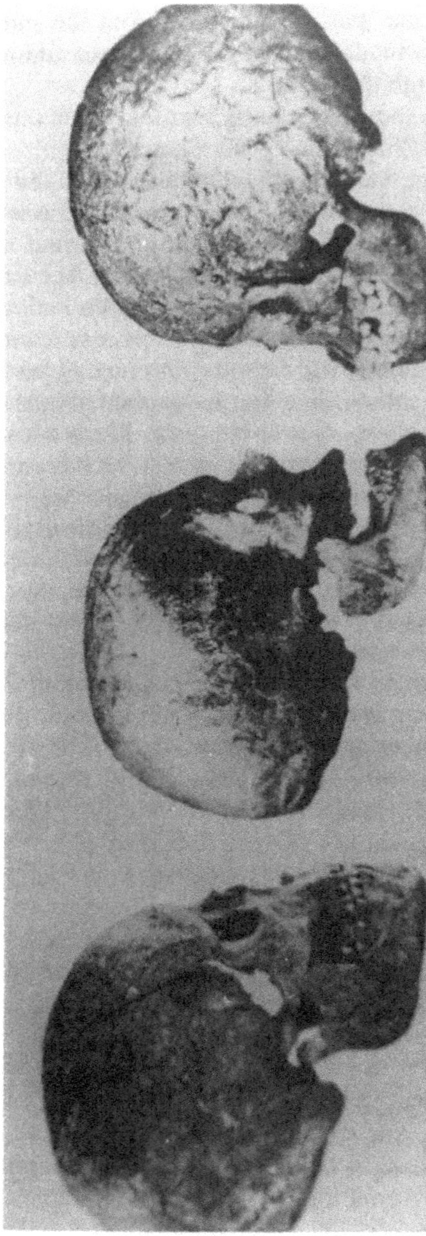

Figure 8. Here are the three skulls of Combe Capelle (left), Cro-Magnon (center) and Grimaldi (right) seen from the same angle. Compare the prognathism of the two Negroids (Combe Capelle and Grimaldi) to the orthognathism of Cro-Magnon in the center. (Mounting by the author.) Certain specialists even think that the Man of Combe Capelle could be an imitation sold to the German museum by the provider, Hauser: (See F. Lévèque and B. Vandermeersch, in *La Recherche*, no. 119, op. cit., p. 244).

To say that the Man of Combe Capelle is a Europoid, is to forget his profound morphological similarity with the Negroid of Grimaldi, in particular his sub-nasal prognathism (Figure 8). Those who seek to class him in the Cro-Magnon series are obliged to postulate an extreme variability of this type. To put it another way, they are modifying the criteria to the point where they no longer characterize anything.

The description of Boule and Vallois is revealing enough and shows that we are indeed in the presence of a characteristic Negroid type: "The skull of Combe Capelle, first described by Klaatch, who made a new species (Homo aurignacensis), has been, since, the object of numerous anthropological studies. Moschi found in him Australoid characteristics because of his strong superciliary arches. According to Giuffria-Ruggeri, this skull is more dolichocephalic, more raised, more prognathous, more platyrhine, and thus presents Ethiopic similarities."[74] He would gladly call him Homo preaethiopicus. Mendes Correa shares this opinion.[75]

We are thus in the presence of a Negroid specimen, who in addition was found at the bottom of the Aurignacian site, but in conditions which leave too much to be desired; actually, this fossil was discovered at a time when prehistoric scientific archeology was in limbo (1909), not by a professional, but by a dealer in antiquities who was the provider of the Berlin Museum, to which he sold it. This specimen, which his very inventors named "Homo aurignacensis," couldn't possibly be older than the industry in which it was found. The estimates which made it date back to 50,000 years were not supported by any scientific data. They wanted to age it sufficiently in order to be able to make of it a native "Homo europeus," predecessor of the Grimaldian Negroid invader: now, it behooves us to recognize that it is not distinct from this latter and that the dating of the Aurignacian industry by carbon 14 assigns a more precise age of around 32,000 years. Besides, the method of dating by amino acids of J. Bada, which is actually not destructive, is very applicable to this fossil and could contribute precious complementary information, just like dating by C14 with accelerator.

One could justly expect that the so-called lower Perigordian industry, created by a hypothetical native of Europe, would cover this whole continent; nothing of the kind, this role will be vested in the Aurignacian industry of the Grimaldian Negroid invader. At the IXth UISPP Congress of Nice, symposium XVI, devoted to the Aurignacian in Europe, showed that this continent was literally covered by different general aspects of the Aurignacian Period, while the Solutrean, attributed to a true Cro-Magnon who will not appear until 20,000 years later, is absolutely non-existent.[76]

According to this study, the Aurignacian Period is present in France; in the entire basin of the Upper-Danube in Austria (Joachim Hahn), with 19 sites indexed, among which are the famous village of Willendorf, Vogelherd, Kleineofnet, Gopfelstein, etc.; in Slovakia (Ladislav Banesz); in North

Rumania (M. Bitiri) and in Banat (F. Mogosamu); in Poland (Elzbieta Sachse-Kozlowska); in Moravia (Karel Voloch); in the Balkans (Janusz Kozlowski); in eastern Europe (G.P. Grigoriev, text missing); in Belgium (Marcel Otte); in Bosnia (Djuro Basler) and even in the Near East, where they uncovered a pre-Aurignacian industry (Ladislav Banesz). We have already spoken about the African Aurignacian Period, whose age will have to be restudied using methods of absolute chronology.

Let's add the Aurignacian Period of Crimea, and that of Irkoutsk, near lake Baïkal in southern Siberia, discovered by the late Professor Guerassimov, a scholar of exceptional objectivity; and finally the Aurignacian Period of Grimaldi and that of Java.

Although the Aurignacian culture preceded by nearly 20,000 years that of Cro-Magnon Man of the Solutrean Period, and although no confusion is possible between the two physical types respectively responsible for these industries, the western ideologists, French in particular, do not hesitate now to liken the Negroid of Grimaldi to a Cro-Magnon, or else, to pass over him completely in silence, by presenting the Cro-Magnon as the very first "Homo sapiens sapiens" of Europe. These are gross falsifications of that type, straining to explain human evolution backwards by purely ideological prejudices, which finally kill the intellectual appetite of the young generation, repulsed by the destruction of the meaning of facts.

The list of works, all French, which attempt to remodel the skull of the Negroid of Grimaldi in order to try to make it orthognathic like Cro-Magnon, or else the reconstruction of its teeth for the same reasons grows longer from day to day, as the note below proves.[77]

All of these works are fallacious for many reasons:

1. Pressure from the burial material which would have deformed the face of true Cro-Magnons in order to give them a Negroid appearance by making an accidental prognathism appear, would surely not have left the skulls of the subjects unharmed: but the skulls are absolutely unharmed.
2. On the other hand, the most typical Cro-Magnon lived in the same Cave of the Children where De Villeneuve discovered him at the same time as the Grimaldi, but at different levels. How did this specimen and all the other Cro-Magnons who are similar to him miraculously escape the deforming effect of the materials?
3. The most grave is that these studies are silent on all the other specific morphological differences between the Negroid and the Cro-Magnon. The osteology of Grimaldi is typically Nigritic. On the other hand, Boule and Vallois note that "the nose, depressed at the root is very broad (platyrrhinian). The floor of the nasal fossae is connected to the anterior surface of the maxillary by a groove on each side of the nasal spine, as with Blacks, instead of being bordered by a sharp edge as with the white races. The canine fossae are deep."[78]

Concerning dentition, the same authors write: "All the rear upper molars have four well developed denticles; even the last, which in the civilized races, has only three. All the lower molars have five very distinct denticles, even the second and third which ordinarily have only four in the white races. . . .The mandible is strong, the body is very thick; the ascending branches are broad and low. The chin is not very prominent; a strong alveolar prognathism, mutually related to the upper prognathism, gives him a pronounced receding appearance. . . .The majority of these facial and skull traits are, if not Nigritic, at least Negroid."[79]

When one compares the dimensions of the bones of their limbs, one sees that they had very long legs in proportion to the thighs and the fore-arm very long in proportion to the arms; that their lower limb was extremely developed in length in relation to the upper limb. But, such proportions reproduce, while being exaggerated, the characteristics which Blacks exhibit today.[80]

On the other hand, the Aurignacian art faithfully reproduced the physical type of the race, not only that of the typical African woman, but also that of the man: there exists in this regard a very characteristic Negroid head in the Museum of Saint-Germaine-en-Laye, and about whom one almost never speaks (Figures 9 to 12).

Finally, those two individuals preserved in the Museum of Monaco, a woman and a child, have respective heights of 1.60m and 1.56m which do not permit having an accurate picture of the actual height of the race of Grimaldi (Figure 13). For that purpose it would have been necessary to fall upon an adult male subject.

Likewise, for M.M. Guerassimov,[81] the Grimaldian, the Man of Combe Capelle are plainly "Homo sapiens" Negroids. The Man of Predmost, which he considers as a cross-breed of Neanderthal Man and "Homo sapiens" could only be an Australoid "Homo sapiens sapiens," because at that late epoch of the Upper Paleolithic Period, every trace of Neanderthal Man seemed to have already disappeared. This man has every appearance of a true Negroid, although Vallois tries to class him among the Cro-Magnons. One could say as much about the Man of Brno: Predmost and Brno seem to descend in a direct line from the above mentioned Aurignacians of this same region of the Danube and central Europe.

Guerassimov also thinks that the Grimaldian is a Negroid invader and certainly not a native of Europe; he writes: "It is quite clear that the man of the Upper Paleolithic Period penetrated into the territory of western Europe, while already possessing diverse variants of culture and specific traits of the lower "Homo sapiens," and while showing more or less equatorial traits. This complex pseudo-Negroid shows himself in an agreement with the specific traits, not only of a physiognomical order, but of a temperamental order."

The mutation of the Negroid into the Cro-Magnon did not take place in a

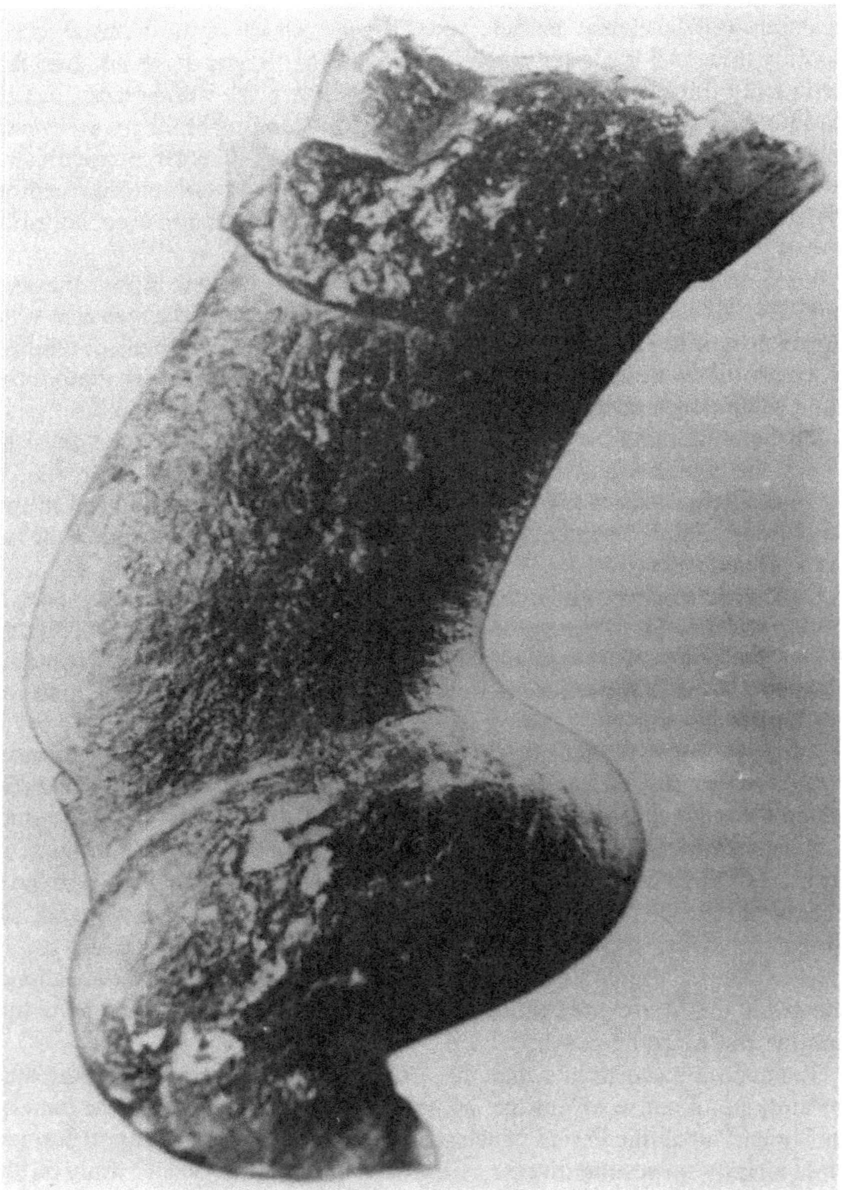

Figure 9. Negroid Aurignacian art of the Upper European Paleolithic Period: Headless Venus of Sireuil, Dordogne. Notice the typically Negroid pelvis. (Musée des Antiquités nationales, Saint-Germain-en-Laye.)

Figure 10. Paleolithic art (aurignacio-perigordian): Venus of Willendorf. Notice the typically African hair-style. (Musée d'Histoire naturelle, Vienna).

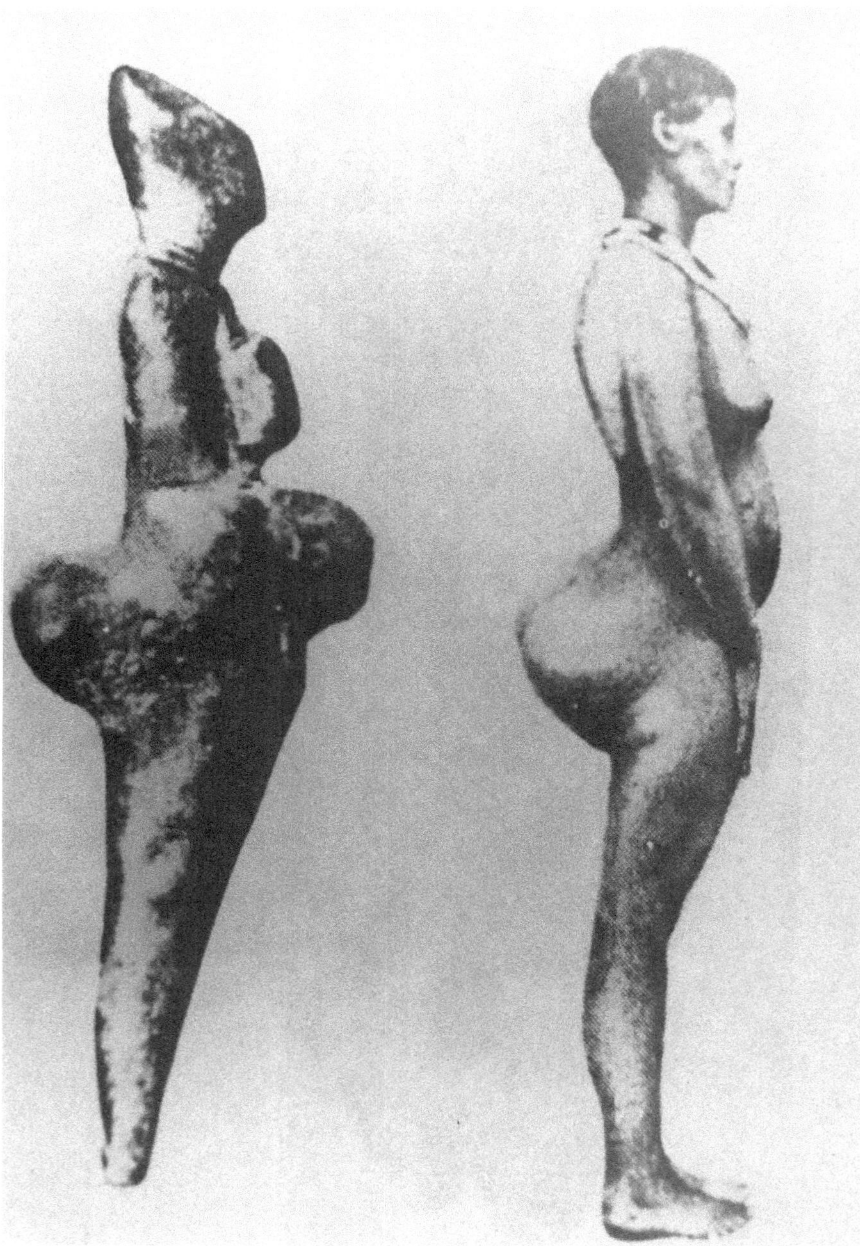

Figure 11. The shape of a statuette or an Aurignacian Venus, compared to that of the famous Hottentot Venus (mould on the right), who lived in France between the two world wars. (According to M. Boule and H.V. Vallois: *Les Hommes fossiles,* p. 325.)

Figure 12. Aurignacian Negroid art: Negroid head preserved at the Musée de Saint-Germain-en-Laye. (Musée des Antiquités nationales, Saint-Germain-en-Laye.)

day! There was a long transition period of more than 15,000 years, corresponding to the appearance of several intermediary types between the Negroid and the Europoid, without there being able to be a question of crossbreeding. Specifically, the osteology of all early Cro-Magnons is Negroid, which seems normal.

In fact, the Negroid osteology developed in a savannah paleo-environment, where the giraffe appeared. This osteology took time to adapt to the hunched up cave life in Europe, during the glacial era, in other words, to pass from a life in the open air to a virtually subterranean life. The Negroid proportions of the initial Grimaldian type will be progressively disarranged. Also, Guerassimov notes: "The classic Cro-magnons can only be called Europoids conditionally.

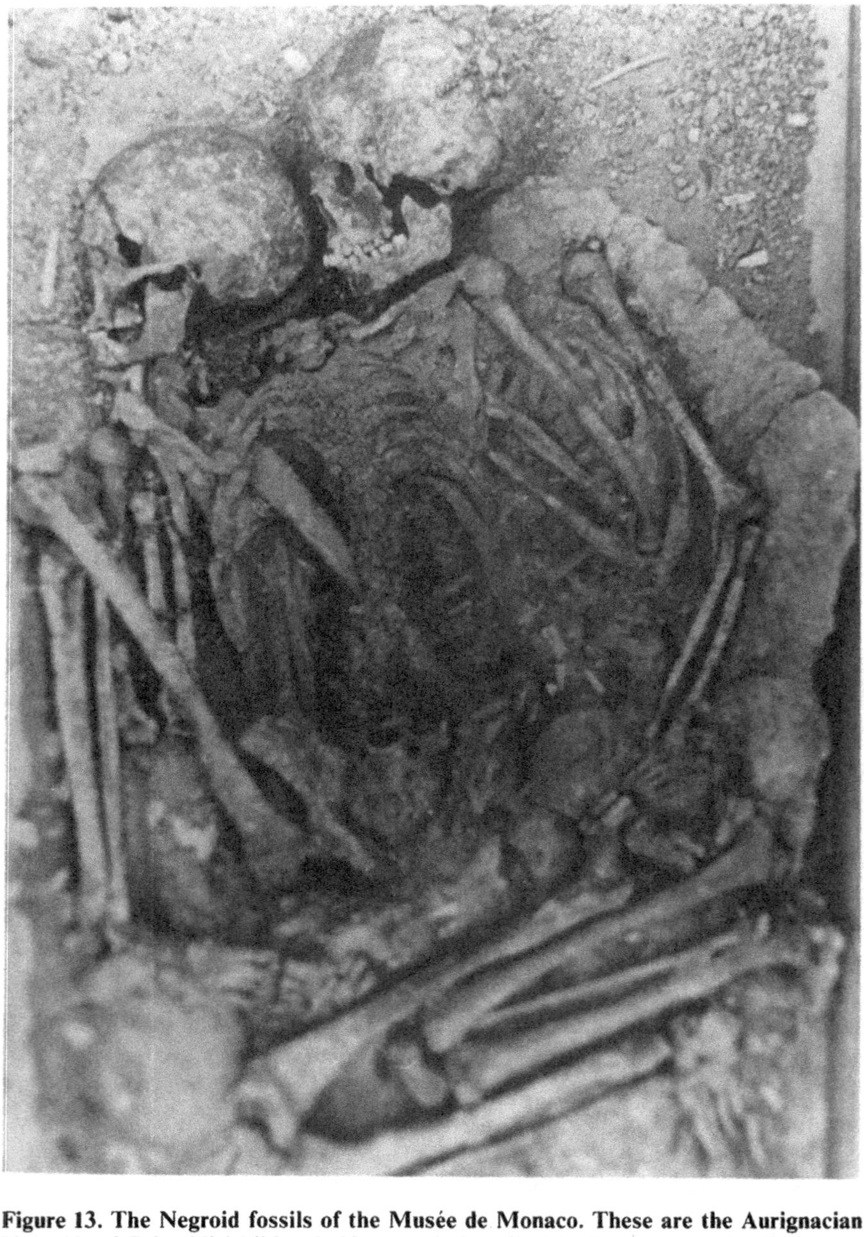

Figure 13. The Negroid fossils of the Musée de Monaco. These are the Aurignacian Negroids of Grimaldi (child and old woman), described by R. Verneaux, M. Boule and H.V. Vallois. Why would the pressure of the materials which supposedly made them prognathous have miraculously spared the skulls, which are intact, although being no more strong than the bones of the jaws and face? (Musée d'Anthropologie préhistorique de la Principauté de Monaco: Subjects of Grimaldi, Cave of the Children, Italian Liguria, "Homo sapiens" fossil of the Upper Paleolithic Period.)

The dimensions of their bodies are nearer Negroids, in addition, physiognomically, numerous are those who have a high forehead and faintly evident eyebrows, a very noticeable prognathism, and consequently a *prokhélie* (protrusion) of the lips. These peculiarities of the equatorial type are manifested more clearly with the women."

Finally, the author, although he is a Russian, shows in turn that the area of expansion of the Negroids extended from western Europe to Lake Baïkal, in Siberia, passing by Crimea and the Don basin: he's the same one who discovered the Aurignician industry of Siberia, near Lake Baïkal, this very industry which A. Thoma speaks about in his article.[82] He continues: "The complex of 'Negroidity,' although expressed in another form, is especially very clear in the skeletons of Grimaldi. This specific equatorial complex is expressed in a particularly precise manner in the skeleton of the 'Maquina Gora' on the Don River. The skull of this man cannot practically be distinguished from the skulls of the present-day Papuans, either by descriptive indications or by measurement data. The skeleton of Combe Capelle is also expressive although it possesses different characteristics, those of the Australoid type."

It is interesting to notice that the fossil of Combe Capelle which they would like to make the ancestor of the Europoids, is described here as an Australoid, especially if one recalls that A. Thoma would like to make the Australoids descend from the archanthropics; one sees how untenable this latter point of view is. At present, the very recent nature of the formation of the Australian branch is practically demonstrated.[83]

But Guerassimov continues: "The most 'sapiential' skull, linked to the Mousterian industry was discovered in the USSR, in Crimea, near the city of Bakhclussarai, in the shelter of Starocelia. The skeleton of a child, evidently buried, has been discovered at the site. The stratigraphic data are impeccable, and the belonging of the burial to the Mousterian era is indisputable. The skeleton belongs to a child of one year and a half to two years of age. The skull is virtually intact (it has been able to be restored). Archeologically speaking, it is a final Mousterian. The characteristics of 'Homo sapiens' have the traits of the equatorial type."

They discovered, on the other hand, bones belonging to an adult woman of the Mousterian period. The author analyzes the fossils in the following terms: "The degree of development of the chin protuberance attests to the presence of 'Homo sapiens' entirely developed. The morphology of the child's skull and the fragment of the adult woman's maxilla permit one to suppose that these findings establish the nearly final stage of the formation of ancient Homo sapiens' in his specific equatorial variant near the Man of 'Maquina Gora' on the Don. The findings of Starocelia permit assigning the formation of "ancient Homo sapiens to the middle Mousterian."

It results from what precedes that the most ancient "Homo sapiens" of Europe, up to the confines of Asia, are Negroids, if one sticks to an objective analysis of the facts. If we pass to Asia, the old Asia of the orientalists, what astonishes is contrary to all expectations; the extremely recent appearance of "Homo sapiens sapiens." The carbon 14 analysis carried out by the Chinese themselves permitted establishing that Ziyang Man—whom the scholars' estimates made date back one hundred thousand years—dates from 7,500 ± 130 BP or 5,550 BC. Likewise, the man of the upper cave of Zhoukoudian, to whom the specialists attributed equally an age of one hundred thousand years, dates from 18,865 ± 420 BP or 16,915 BC.[84] Weidenreich studied succinctly the fossils of this upper cave of the shelter where Peking Man was discovered. He finds that one of the skulls, very dolichocephalic, shows similarities which are both Cro-magnoid and Mongoloid and would be by this fact, for the author, the primitive type of the Mongol. The two other feminine skulls studied ressemble, one the Melanesian type of New Guinea, the other the modern Eskimo type. Weidenreich thinks that the above mentioned dolichocephalic skull could be a very remote precursor of the current Chinese. But, observes Vallois, "these (the current Chinese) appear only a good deal later and in a sudden fashion, with all their anthropological characteristics already well indicated. It is thus that the Neolithics of the Yang-Shaw epoch, with polychrome pottery, dating from round 5,000 years ago and whose skulls have been collected by Andersson in Kansu and in Ho-nan and studied by Black, already belong to a type essentially similar to that of the Chinese of the North."[85]

All of the prehistoric Japanese sites, except perhaps one in the south, are of the Holocene Age. Matsumoto has exhumed Neolithic skeletons which would ressemble rather the Ainu, and men of the recent Paleolithic Period and of the European Neolithic Period.[86]

So therefore, all the customary orientalist chronology crumbles with the advent of radiometric methods of dating. Here, by way of summary, are the dates of the appearance of "Homo sapiens sapiens" in the different known centers of the world:

- Black Africa, Omo I and Kanjera, 150,000 years ago.
- Invasion of Europe by the Grimaldian Negroid having come from Africa, 33,000 years ago.
- First Cro-Magnon in Europe, 20,000 years ago (in order to remain within fully verified dates).
- Arrival of the Australians in Australia, 30 to 20,000 years ago.
- Appearance of the first paleosiberian (according to Thoma), 20,000 years ago.
- The first "Homo sapiens" of China, 17,000 years B.C.
- The appearance of the present Chinese type, around 6,000 years B.C.
- The appearance of the Japanese type: Neolithic, perhaps around 5 or 4,000 years B.C.

One can grasp now the impossibility of the polycentric thesis. The appearance of "Homo sapiens sapiens" in the different hypothetical centers would obviously have to be contemporaneous; certain of these centers would even have to be older than that of Africa in order to better bring out the independence of this polycentric genesis in regard to Africa: nothing of the kind. All the pretended centers of appearance of modern man are more recent than that of Africa and thus can be explained from Africa, by a connection more or less direct as a result of migration and geographic differentiation, coming from adaptation to the paleo-environment. Therefore, what surprises is not the independence of the centers, but their necessary liaison with Africa in order to be scientifically explainable. One can now measure all that cannot be accepted in the revised and improved polycentric thesis by Thoma, following Keith and Coon.

The races which the fact of white peopling would condemn to disappearance become living fossils, derived from Archanthropics: this would be the case of the Bushmen and Australians, especially all "Homo sapiens sapiens," having absolutely the same intellectual capacities as all other races, when they did not degenerate individually, as a result of chronic malnutrition.

Australia did not witness the birth of "Homo sapiens," he arrived there by navigation 30,000 years ago. Therefore, the idea of a formation, on the spot, of an Australian type independent of these invaders who were supposed to be a branch of the Aurignacians of Asia, is indefensible.

Negroids survived everywhere, in Europe, until the Neolithic Period: Spain, Portugal, Belgium, the Balkans, etc. We have seen that in the upper and recent Paleolithic Period, they were already in Siberia, in China (upper cave of Zhoukoudian, see above) and this, before the birth even of the Chinese and Japanese type; they probably coexisted thus in the far east with a Cro-magnon type more or less mongolized, in the same cave of Zhoukoudian (see above). One could not better outline the conditions of a cross-breeding (between Negroid and mongolized Cro-magnoid) in a definite paleo-environment; cross-breeding being able to lead ultimately to the formation of the recent branches of humanity: Orientals (Japanese and Chinese), Semites (Arabs and Jews in another geographical context). The formation of the semite branch is found between the Vth and IVth millennia. It concerns an actual cross-breeding between White (non-mongolized Cro-Magnon) and Black on the threshold of the historical era.[87]

In the Ryad Museum, in Saudia Arabia, one can see the reproduction of stone paintings showing the Negroid type which inhabited the Arabian peninsula in the Neolithic Period and who cross-bred progressively with white-skinned elements, migrating from the northeast, to finally produce the Arab type. Until the Sabean era, 1,000 years B.C., this cross-breeding still was not completed in the South (Figures 14 to 16).

Figure 14. Engraving from the Arabian Desert. There exists in the Ryad Museum more typical reproductions of the black populations of the prehistory of the Arabian Peninsula, populations whose fusion with white-skinned elements explains in large measure the birth of the semite branch. (L. Frobenius: *Ekade Ektab, Die afrikanischen Felsbilder,*Akademische Druck u. Verlagsanstalt, Graz, Autriche, 1963, p. 49, fig. 63)

Figure 15. This byzantine icon of the XIth century A.D. shows that up to that still recent time, the remembrance of black Egypt had not yet been erased from the memory of the people: it concerns that famous scene where Abraham, whom one distinguishes by his halo of sanctity, is presented with Sarah, his wife, before the black pharaoh . . . the contrast of the colors is more striking in the original than in this black and white reproduction. There is no possible confusion, the pharaoh and the dignitaries of his court are Blacks, Abraham and Sarah are white-skinned. (Reproduction of the *Octateuch,* folio 35, in J. Devisse: *L'Image du Noir dans l'art occidental,*vol. II, offprint, Office du Livre, Fribourg, Switzerland, fig. 72, p. 102)

Figure 16. The Hebrews in Egypt: the first two individuals on the right are Blacks, these are the Egyptians, those who follow, are Hebrews bearing tribute. One well sees the difference between the two communities during this era. In the reproductions in the academic manuals, the two Blacks, the Egyptians, are generally omitted. (K.R. Lepsius: Denkmäler aus Aegyptien und Aethiopien, vol. III and IV, ed. Belles-Lettres, Geneva, 1972, part II, p. 133.)

No brachycephalic race could have been formed before the Mesolithic Period, that is to say before 10,000 years ago. We can therefore distinguish the dolichocephalic races of the Upper Paleolithic Period:

- Negroid of Africa (Omo I, Kanjera: 150,000 years ago.
- Grimaldian Negroid (Europe): 33,000 years ago.
- Cro-Magnon: 20,000 years ago.
- Paleosiberian: 20,000 years ago.

The recent brachycephalic races which appeared in the Neolithic Period are yellow-skinned:

- Chinese, Japanese: 6,000 years ago.
- Semites (Accadian, Arab, Jew): 5,000 years ago.

The mutation of the Grimaldian Negroid into the Cro-Magnon, having become a virtually obvious fact for all scientists whom ideological prejudices do not shackle, molecular biology now tries to explore the process in the laboratory.

Thus, at the Bichat Conferences of 1976, a round table directed by Professor B. Prunieras was devoted to the phenomenon, that is to the study of the depigmentation of the Black leading to the white-skinned type.

A renowned white American biochemist has just proposed a new explanation of the same fact, based on the biosynthesis of vitamin D under the influence of ultra-violet rays.

The correlation between the color of the skin and the latitude of origin of the populations is a fact, plausible but not demonstrated. Its interpretation by a selection/adaptation process remains a hypothesis.

Europe did not see the birth of "Homo sapiens sapiens," he came as a migrant in the form of a Negroid. The mutation of the latter into a Cro-magnoid compels recognition more and more as a necessity, but the intimate process of this mutation is not yet totally outlined, far from it. Molecular biology has just introduced the problem.

In the first edition of *Nations Nègres et Culture*, in 1954 (p. 180 of the current paperback edition) I had stated as an hypothesis that the yellow race probably was the result of a cross-breeding of Black and White in a cold climate, perhaps near the end of the Upper Paleolithic Period. This idea is largely shared today by the Japanese scholars and researchers. A Japanese scientist, Doctor Takano, M.D., head of the Dermatology Division of Hammatsu Red Cross Hospital, has just developed it in a work in Japanese published in 1977 and which he had the kindness to offer me when in 1979, making a short stay in Dakar, he visited my laboratory with a group of Japanese scientists.

The author upholds in short that first humanity is Black; Black gives birth to White and the cross-breeding of these two races (Black and White) gives birth to the Yellow: These three stages constitute the very title of the book, in Japanese, as he explained it to me.

Let's say a few words about a book published in 1977 and entitled *Race et Intelligence*, by Jean-Pierre Hébert (Editions Copernic Factuelles, Paris).

I will limit myself to calling attention only to the inaccuracy of the basic facts on which the structure rests.

The authors recall the thesis of Coon according to which "the transformation erectus-sapiens would have taken place in Europe, around 200,000 years ago, well before the African sapiens appears" (p. 44) and they recall that A. Thoma has qualified "the work of Coon as an authoritative work" (p. 44).

To sustain this idea, the conservative anthropologists have stopped at nothing: they did not hesitate to fabricate a forgery (Piltdown Man, which the authors of this book pass over completely and modestly in silence) in order to lead the scientific world into error for a half century.

The motivations which they try today to attribute to this scholarly forger appear quite unacceptable to us. Thus the theory of the European pre-Sapiens rests on a deception, and since the masterpiece has been revealed as an imitation, intentionally forged, the thesis has lost all of its stability.

A scholar like Carleton S. Coon does not hesitate to write a paragraph like the one which follows in which all the dates, without exception, are false, radically false, just as the chronological analysis of the facts has just proven to us. He writes: "The most ancient skulls known of 'Homo sapiens,' probably both feminine, are those of Swanscombe and Steinheim, of the Mindel-Riss interglacial period, dated today from between 470,000 and 300,000 years old. In North Africa, the most ancient 'Homo sapiens' are between 100,000 and 47,000 years old, in east Africa between 60,000 and 30,000 yeears old, and in Java, Sarawak and in China not more than 40,000 years old."[88]

What can one call "Homo sapiens" in North Africa 100,000 years ago? In Java the presence of an Aurignacian industry would connect "Homo sapiens sapiens" to the same Negroid origin.

The tendency is very strong with the ideologists, to touch up the facts. Thus another English scientist of a world-wide reputation, Sir Cyril Burt, did not hesitate to falsify the results of supposed experiments bearing on the I.Q.'s of homozygous and heterozygous twins. According to him, the correlation between the I.Q.'s of twins reared separately would be 0.771, accuracy being moved to the third decimal. Likewise, for the twins reared together, the correlation is still of 0.944. A priori, such a constancy of this proportion to the third decimal seems astonishing. A verification undertaken by J. Kamin, professor of psychology at Princeton University and by A. Clarke, of Hull University, proved that it was question of a fraud comparable in scope to that of Piltdown Man, in an attempt to prove the innateness of intelligence and the inferiority of certain races.[89]

The authors of this book are not naive; they have read entirely the article of A. Thoma, therefore they know perfectly well that the expression "authoritative work" which Thoma uses, put back into its context, is not a compliment: it is the customary precaution which an author takes before demolishing the opposing thesis. Thoma, all the while being devoted to the polycentric thesis, avoids falling into the same trap as Coon who, in order to safeguard the individuality of the European race, rejects any notion of migration. But Thoma sinks no less into insurmountable difficulties, as we have demonstrated, because polycentrism, the common sense thesis, is scientifically untenable today.

We will not alter our views with regard to precise chronological data already presented and to so many other facts which compel us to renounce polycentrism at the stage of "Homo erectus".

Thoma, in order to defend polycentrism, uses the method of Penrose in order to calculate the distances between builds of different races, and he finds that the Oriental is nearer to Neanderthal Man than to Cro-Magnon; ideology must truly have flown somewhat to the aid of the author in order for him to find more distance between two "Homo sapiens" than between one of these (the Oriental) and "Homo 'faber'" (that is, the Neanderthal) when one knows the profound morphological difference which exists between Neanderthal and "Sapiens." "The distance of builds between these two human variants (Paleosiberian and Neanderthalian) is in effect inferior to that which separates Paleosiberians and Cro-Magnons: Neanderthalians and Cro-Magnons are still more far apart."[90]

Coon, Thoma and all the polycentrists evade the major difficulty which consists in knowing where European "Homo sapiens" disappeared, for 250,000 years, the lapse of time which separates their hypothetical appearance in Europe and the Man of Grimaldi, the first true "Homo sapiens sapiens" to have appeared on the European continent. In fact, the pretended European "Homo sapiens" vanished without leaving any descendants during this entire period: why don't the polycentrists discuss this question honestly, if they wish to make a scientific study? No, there is a consensus: they know that the difficulty is insurmountable, they pretend not to see it and nobody raises the question. They will please refer to the developments which we have outlined in our study of this problem.

The authors of this book have a knack for duping the reader, as one has seen regarding the expression "authoritative work," deliberately interpreted in an erroneous and misleading sense. In face, they write: "A skull discovered in Vértesszöllös, studied by Professor Thoma, is some 500,000 years old. This man knew how to make fire and his cranial capacity attained 1400 cc." Professor Thoma concluded that it's a question of "Homo sapiens." "The intelligent man, 'Homo sapiens' would therefore have appeared in Europe a very long time ago."[91] Here, one approaches the fraud, because he does not give the reader any means of guessing that all of these figures (500,000 years, 1400 cc) are purely imaginary.

In fact, it concerns an occipital, found in Hungary in 1966-1967 and associated with fauna of the Middle Pleistocene Period, and whose morphological type is very debatable: the volume of the skull is not measured since it doesn't exist: it is deduced by conjecture. That's why this fossil almost escaped unnoticed at the UNESCO Colloquium of 1969. In order to give it a particular significance, it was necessary to ardently want to; the mere fact that Thoma classes it in the same series as Heidelberg Man (Mauer jawbone), which is a "Homo erectus," proves this fully.

"Fragmentary fossils cause the existence of a western phylum to be seen imperfectly, more uncertain than the two preceding ones: (Mauer?)—Vértesszöllös—Swanscombe—Fontéchévade—(Quinzano?)—Proto-Cro-Magnon of the Starocelia type—Qafza. . . ."[92] Clearly from all that precedes, this passage by Thoma is quite incoherent, in any case inconsistent. The fossil in question is without face, forehead, without a single characteristic trait which permits classifying it, sanely, among the "Sapiens." And always the same question! What could have become of his descendants for 500,000 years? And Thoma, aware of this abyss, even if he doesn't say so, uses such hesitant terms, that one sees clearly that he does not believe a great deal in what he writes in the paragraph cited above: "Fragmentary fossils cause the existence of a western phylum to be seen imperfectly, more uncertain than the two preceding ones. . . ."

One has just observed: in order to build the theory of the pre-Sapiens, our authors dispassionately transform the hesitation of Thoma into a virtual certainty.

If one wishes to know the truth concerning the age of the occipital of Vértesszöllös, it would suffice to date it by the amino acid method, which is not at all destructive.

Finally, the thesis of the pre-"Sapiens," in order to be credible, would have to be able to be applied to the antiquity of "Homo sapiens" on the other continents, in Asia in particular. It's for that reason that the authors of this book, relying on joyful stratigraphic estimations which permit aging the fossils at will, write: "In Asia . . . the first Sapiens known appeared 150,000 years ago in the province of Szechuan in Tze-Yang."[93] That's false: this fossil, dated with C14 by the Chinese themselves, only revealed an age of 7,500 years ± 130. It corresponds therefore to the African Neolithic man.

But the authors continue: "The cranial capacity of this man is of 1210cc. He is therefore less precocious and with a smaller brain than the Man of Vértesszöllös (1400cc, 500,000 years ago.)"[94]

Here the fraud is evident. The man of Vértesszöllös, pure poetic fiction as for his cranial volume and his age, becomes a tangible, objective reality, which they compare with an Asiatic type of equally false age.

The authors pursue this masquerade: "He (the man of Liu-Kiang) . . . lived 100,000 years ago."[95] This is all just as false: this fossil, dated equally by the Chinese themselves, revealed an age of 16,915 years ± 420. Thus, the theory of the pre-Sapiens crumbles, as I have demonstrated above. The differentiation of the races is a geographic phenomenon which, in the empire of physical factors, took place after the appearance of "Homo sapiens sapiens," which is an African Negroid, and not at the stage of "Homo erectus" as the western ideologists have wished.

Let's get to the point of the analysis of racial differences. They come under the heading of the senses and have no demonstrable value: everybody states that the phenotype of a Black Man is not that of a Swede. Therefore, they create irksome verbiage, of scientific appearance, on indexing all the true or supposed racial differences which can exist in the different domains; a certain blood group is more frequent with Blacks than with Nordics . . . So what? Is this an indicator of intellectual aptitudes?

The Germans, also, searched for the "blue blood" which was to distinguish them from "the degenerate French," from the "Welsh." A young German, 16 years of age, wounded during the Second World War, preferred to die rather than "permit them to transfuse into him the impure blood of a Welshman," who gave his blood; he thanked him nevertheless, twisted and died. An admirable sonnet was dedicated to him in the *Mercure de France* of that time.

The work of J.P. Hebert studies "the HLA system and its polymorphism, in the different races" (p. 95) then "the pressure of the right hand and the pressure of the left hand, in Whites, Blacks, American Indians and the fellahs of Kargh (Egypt)" (p. 98).

This is the kind of absurd filler intended only to condition the layman, who has the impression of reading a scientific work.

To list the anatomical differences between the races, which are essentially different in appearance, has no scientific significance. It would be necessary to succeed in demonstrating that these anatomical differences correspond to hierarchical differences in the sense of humanization: if the authors succeeded in doing it, they would no longer be masked authors, entrenched behind anonymity; they would be raised to the dignity of "masked sorcerers," of great miracle workers.

This remark is particularly true for the so-called anatomical differences found between the brains of different races, although it may be necessary to distinguish the reality from the subtle fraud.

It has been proven for a long time that all races of "Homo sapiens" have exactly the same cerebral morphology. The big difference between "Homo erectus" and "Homo sapiens sapiens," or between Neanderthal Man and "Homo sapiens sapiens," is less a case of the brain weight than the absence of the lobe of the forebrain in Neanderthal Man.

Molecular biology has just taught us that at the individual level, there exist no two identical human brains, and it is this polymorphism which is the essence of chance in the human species or its power of adaptation; but these individual differences, such as the lines of the hand, do not initiate any racial hierarchization.

As we have seen above, it would be necessary therefore to find, at the level of the brain in general and of the forebrain in particular, a hierarchical difference between races and in particular between Black and White, but this is material for another discussion! And also in this case, quite simply, these facts are cited only to lead the layman astray, when they are not indeed false.

"In the arrangement and the degree of complexity of the interneuronal connections of the frontal lobe, one can present the primitive characteristics of the Australians, for example, and the pedomorphism of the Sanides" (Korsan, p. 113). A pure grotesque joke, this bit of imaginative fiction, in the sense that it concerns people whose native land has been confiscated and whom they want to condemn to disappearance, like fossilized beings.

Each difference at the level of the brain can have only an individual significance, never racial; to write, after a few plausible measurements, of "well chosen types," that there is such and such a specific difference of weight, of morphology (convolutions, between races, in particular between Black and White) reveals scientific fraud. These measurements would be valid only if they were made by teams of mixed scholars (White, Black, Yellow) of equal competence, choosing duly their specimen from equally educated racial milieux and enjoying the same social standing.

Otherwise, take a homogeneous team of Blacks or of Orientals, working on White subjects, and all the results cited in this book will be reversed, or at least put in question. Isn't it bold to use the anatomy of an alcoholic and degenerate Black Kenyan in order to prove the inferiority of Blacks, as did Dr. Vint, of the Medical Research Laboratory of Nairobi? "The brains which he examined come actually, for a large number of them, from autopsies of sick people, of persons suffering from cirrhosis in particular" (p. 115).

It is at the cost of similar manipulations that one has been able to align the imaginary differences cited in this book; for who is the western researcher who has access to the brains of healthy subjects of other races?

According to the racial origin of the team which proceeds with the research, the superior race is Nordic, Germanic, Anglo-saxon, or Celtic . . .

Thus, Brigham's research (1923), bearing on 2 million Americans, decides for the average score of intelligence on the native subjects of England (let's say the WASP,)[96] with an average of 14.87, then come the natives of Scotland, of the Low Countries, of Germany, of Denmark, etc. The Mediterraneans and the Slavs appear at the end, the French do not appear (p. 160). And one knows that an American law, not yet rescinded, the "Immigration Act," strangely limits immigration to the United States of Europeans native to the regions situated to the south of the Loire River. So that the anonymous authors of

Race et Intelligence would experience serious difficulties if they wished to emigrate to the United States: they know that they have no place in the Germanic Valhalla, where they are considered descendants of prehistoric Negroids who stayed in the South of Europe. Thus the term "nordism" used by the authors is only a euphemism, which does not give enough account of the feeling of Germanic superiority before which "celtism" appears only as a sorry reaction growing out of a inferiority complex.

A team of Blacks possessed of the same partiality would begin its measurements with the tiny brain of Descartes (the size of an apple), in spite of its numerous convolutions, and so forth . . .

At present the Orientals, in particular the Japanese, make their proof in the scientific manner, in spite of the supposed inferiority of their cranial measurements. Racism in this regard tends to become insipid. That's why it takes more and more a bipolar character Black/White. At the last cabinet meeting of July, 1979, the French government assigned to itself as an objective to overtake Japan.

Blacks, in history, subjugated the White race for three thousand years. Visit the tomb of Ramses III, if you dare to interpret correctly the reality of the mural paintings. Today, Blacks are on the eve of a new departure, after having been, in turn, sold by the pound by the West.[97] So much the better for the racists, if they find that they are the most intelligent; what then do they worry about (Figures 17, 15)?

The book poses the problem of cross-breeding: is this a positive or negative factor in the order of historical evolution? History has already answered the question. All the Semites, Arabs and Jews, as well as the near totality of Latino-Americans are from the cross-breeding of Blacks and Whites: every prejudice and every complex put aside, this cross-breeding is still visible in the eyes, lips, nails, hair, in the majority of Jews.[98]

The Orientals, and the Japanese particularly, are also of mixed blood and their own scientists today recognize this important fact.[99]

Beside the racist ideologists, there are impartial scholars who promote human knowledge in this very delicate domain of physical anthropology, and the list would be too long to present: A. Jacquard, F. Jacob, Boas, Montagu, J. Ruffie . . .

A. Jacquard states that to "identify intelligence and IQ is as ridiculous as confusing rectal temperature and health"[100] and he adds: "The true problem is to understand why certain people raise this question. Their true objective is to justify social inequalities using so-called natural inequalities."[101]

We have just recalled that the Egyptians were Blacks of the type of all the native people of tropical Africa (see Figure 17). That is particularly true when it concerns Ramses II, his father Seti I and Thutmose III.

The three mummies of these pharaohs being well preserved, in the Cairo Museum, I had the opportunity, at the time of the preparation for the Cairo

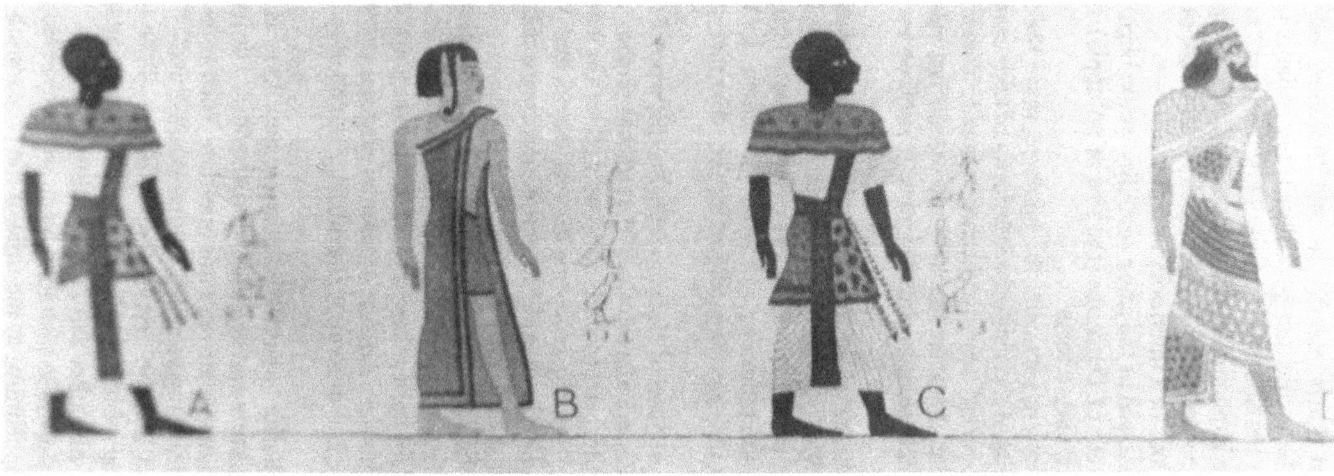

Figure 17. This painting from the tomb of Ramses III (1200 BC) shows that the Egyptians saw themselves as Blacks, and painted themselves as such without possible confusion with the Indo-Europeans or the Semites. It is a representation of the races in their most minute differences, which insures the accuracy of the colors. Throughout their entire history, the Egyptians never entertained the fantasy of portraying themselves by types B or D.

A) The Egyptian seen by himself, blacktype
B) The "Indo-European"
C) The other Blacks of Africa
D) The Semite

(K.R. Lepsius: Denkmäler aus Aegypten und Aethiopien, Ergänzungsband, plate 48.)

Colloquium on the ethnos of the ancient Egyptians, under the aegis of UNESCO, to ask for a mm^2 of skin of each one in order to analyze the percentage of melanin and consequently, to determine the pigmentation. This is absolutely possible.[102] Alas, the authorization to take the samples was never given, so that my analyses in this domain rest on the Egyptian mummies from the Musée de l'Homme.

Although the notion of race is very relative, molecular biology has revealed racial markers, factors all but restricted to each racial group: The Diego factor with the Orientals, the Kell factor with the Whites and the Sutter and Gm6 factors with the Blacks.[103]

Science can therefore, through research of the Sutter and Gm6 factors and through analysis of the percentage of melanin, determine with precision the race of Ramses II, by the most objective means.

At the time of its stay in Paris, they felt it necessary to study the inhaled dust in the abdomen of the mummy and to make analyses of organic debris and blood. But it seems that they decided, on principle, to carry out all but those analyses which would have been able to direct us validly concerning the race of the mummy, because of their preoccupation with keeping the body intact.

In this case, let no one appear to tell us that Ramses II was leucoderm and red-haired. Ramses II was not leucoderm and could have been even less red-haired, because he reigned over a people who instantly massacred red-haired people as soon as they met them, even in the street; these people were considered as strange beings, unhealthy, bearers of bad luck and unfit for life.[104] How could one find again the hair color of an old man 90 years old? The fifty renowned Parisian laboratories which studied the mummy taught us that it had nicotine in the intestines, but, out of a so-called respect for the intactness of the body, they could only determine its race by the structure of a single hair! Let them compare that structure to that of a hair of a present day Nubian of Upper Egypt with blue-black colored skin, before concluding!

These few lines show that the determination of the race of Ramses II, to which they have just proceeded in Paris, has no scientific value. It is surely not conclusive. Today still, even after the radiation which turned the mummy yellow (which was actually black before the operation, as I can state), one can still determine the percentage of melanin in the skin, through results of deterioration of this melanin which lasts even, on animal fossils, for millions of years. Hasn't anyone wondered if it really concerns the same mummy discovered by Maspero?

Ramses II is black. Let's let him sleep in his black skin, for eternity.[105]

The mother of Ramses II was a princess of the royal family and his father, Seti I, was compelled to share the throne with him while he was still a child, because in the eyes of the Egyptian traditionalists he represented legitimacy.[106]

Finally, on another level, a major discovery is constituted by the nicotine found in the abdomen of Ramses II; in fact, if tobacco is really a plant of

American origin, as R. Mauny and A.L. Guyot[107] claim, it would surely be necessary to acknowledge maritime relations between pharaonic Egypt and pre-Columbian America from the XIXth dynasty and perhaps before. One could not overestimate the importance of this fact, which we had already suggested in *l'Afrique Noire précoloniale* (pp. 156-157) and in *l'Antiquité africaine par l'image.*

On the other hand, it is remarkable that the snobbism of the young Senegalese woman of today, with the use of "xeesal" (or kheesal-"lightening of the color of the skin" by means of different cosmetics), may have permitted the solving of an enigma four thousand years old: the fact that the middle-class Egyptian woman sometimes may have a complexion lighter than that of the man in the representations on monuments; this was only the result of an affectation absent in the man. The idle middle-class urban woman, of Dakar or Saint Louis, with her neo-antique Egyptian hairdo, is in the act of reproducing before our very eyes the exact profile of the pharaonic Egyptian woman.

NOTES

1. Jacques Ruffie: *De la biologie à la culture*, Flammarion,Paris, 1976, pp. 392-393.
2. See Figure 7.
3. The business street where there are a majority of Lebanese-Syrian immigrants.
4. See chapters 16 and 17, Figure 75.
5. See pp. 405ff.
6. See chapters 5 to 13.
7. A countryside set apart for geological core samples in the Strait of Gibraltar and in the two trenches encircling Sicily would permit dating the marine carbonated sediments with C14 and determining the age of these depressions. The same procedure would permit stating precisely the date of the formation of the Nile delta. The isotopic analysis ($^{18}O/^{16}O$) would tend to prove that the depression of Gibraltar is relatively ancient (Duplessy). But that does not prevent the existence of a chain of islands. On the other hand, one has known since the congress of Nice of the U.I.S.P.P. (1976) that the first navigations date back to the Upper Paleolithic period, 20 to 30,000 years ago. The example of the inhabiting of Australia is now convincing.
8. Cheikh Anta Diop: "L'apparition de l'Homo sapiens," in *Bulletin de l'IFAN*, vol. XXXII, series B, no. 3, Dakar, 1970, p. 627. See also H. Alimen: *Préhistoire de l'Afrique*, ed. Boubée & Cie., Paris, 1955. We are of the opinion of Léo Frobenius, who thinks that a part, at the very least, of this art is from the Upper Paleolithic period and the research by Africans will have to proceed to confirm this important opinion. Notice Frobenius' explanation: "No province of images inscribed on rocks is as extensive and as fertile in specimen as South Africa. The number of images which one finds between Zambezi and the Cape on one hand, between the mountains which border the southwest of Africa and those of the east, on the other hand, greatly excede the entirety of all the other works of prehistoric times and of the earliest historic times worldwide. They have tried to explain this by saying that the images inscribed on stones of South Africa have an ethnographic significance, that they were all executed during a recent epoch by the Bushmen, and that consequently they have not been exposed to the damage of the centuries. This theory which emanates from a naive enthusiasm of conquest cannot withstand an in depth examination. The engravings of South Africa, executed with great care, are true artistic marvels. The contours of the antelopes, of the hippopotami, of the rhinoceros are engraved so minutely, the folds of the skin, covered or not with fur, so skilfully

worked, that the relief almost gives the impression of colored works. The color of the stone (basalt, diabase diorite) is uniform in the worked and unworked places. This proves their extraordinary age. By their technique, these stone engraved images have much in common with the desert Nubian style and with the most ancient and the most recent styles of the Saharan Atlas Mts. Their art renders them unique. At Klerksdorp and at the Orange River, they have occasionally unearthed stone tools of a typically Capsian style. They can find no relationship between the style of these engraved works and that of the paintings. These two styles are foreign to each other. Now and then they have found engravings underneath the paintings." (Léo Frobenius: *Histoire de la civilisation africaine*, translated from German by Dr. H. Back and D. Ermont, Gallimard, Paris, 1952 (3rd ed.), pp. 50-52).

9. Museum of Monoco (see Figure 13).

10. Ch. A. Diop: op. cit., pp. 623-641.

11. Kim Marshall: "The Desegregation of a Boston Classroom," in *Learning*, August-September 1975, p. 38.

12. Asiatic invaders from the east.

13. K.R. Lepsius: *Denkmäler aus Aegypten und Aethiopien.*

14. Kennst du das Land, wo die Zitronen blühn,
Im dunkeln Laub die Gold-Orangen glühn,
Ein sanfter Wind vom blauen Himmel weht,
Die Myrte still und hoch der Lorbeer steht,
Kennst du es wohl?
Dahin! Dahin!
Möcht ich mit dir, o mein Geliebter, ziehn.

(Goethe: *Gedichte*, Reclam, Stuttgart, 1978, p. 88.)

15. Marija Gimbutas: *Gods and Goddesses of Old Europe 7000-3500 BC: Myths, Legends and Cult Images*, Thaures and Hudson, 1974. See also the article by the same author in the review *La Recherche* no. 87, March, 1978, pp. 228-235.

16. Marcellin Boule and Henri V. Vallois: *Les Hommes fossiles*, Masson, Paris, 1952 (4th ed.), p. 378.

17. M. Gimbutas: in review *La Recherche*, op. cit., p. 234.

18. M. Gimbutas assumes that this chariot could well be a borrowing made by the hypothetical Kurgans from the Mesopotamians, which implies an oriental cultural influence not negligible from this epoch onward, on Europe.

19. What does this vague term mean?

20. *La Recherche*, op. cit., p. 234.

21. Ibid. p. 229.

22. Charles Mugler: *Dictionnaire archéologique des techniques*, vol. II, Ed. de l'Accueil, Paris, 1964, p. 682.

23. Raymond Furon: *Manuel de Préhistoire générale*, Payot, Paris, 1958 (4th ed.), p. 374.

24. R. Furon: op. cit., p. 375 (citing Ch. Autran: *Mithra Zoroastre et la préhistoire aryennne du christianisme*, Payot, Paris, 1935). See also Cheikh Anta Diop: *Nations nègres et Culture*, Présence Africaine, Paris, 1954 (reissued in paperback, 1979, pp. 119-120) and *L'Antiquité africaine par l'image*, no. 145-146 of the series "Notes africaines," I.F.A.N., Dakar, 1976, Figure 54, p. 38, Figure 63, p. 42, and map, p. 43, concerning the black virgins.

25. K. Schreiner: *Crania Norvegica*, II, Institutet for sammenlignende Kulturforskning, ser. B XXXVI, 1946.

26. M. Boule and H.V. Vallois: op. cit., p. 238.

27. Ibid. pp. 385-386.

28. M. Gimbutas: in *La Recherche*, op. cit., p. 235.

29. See note 22 above.

30. H.L. Movius, Jr. (Peabody Museum, Harvard University, Cambridge): "Radiocarbon Dating of the Upper Paleolithic Sequence at the Pataud Shelter (Les Eyzies, Dordogne, France)" in *L'Origine de l'homme moderne*, Colloque de Paris, 1969, ed. Unesco, Paris, 1972, pp. 253ff.

31. René Verneaux: *Les Origines de l'humanité*, F. Riedder & Cie., Paris, 1926.

32. The "fossil of Piltdown" was discovered in 1912 by the British geologist Charles Dawson and studied mainly by Smith Woodward, Elliot Smith, A. Keith, and other scholars.

33. Marcellin Boule and Henri V. Vallois: *Les Hommes fossiles*, Masson et Cie, Paris, 1952 (4th ed.), p. 193.

34. Contrary to the conclusion of Vallois citing however, the same authors as we: Oakley and Hoskins (Henri V. Vallois: op. cit., pp. 182, 183, 191).

35. K.P. Oakley: "Analytic Methods of dating bones," Report of the British Association for the Advancement of Science, meeting at Oxford, 1954.

36. J.S. Weiner: *The Piltdown Forgery*, Oxford University Press, 1955.

37. M. Boule and H.V. Vallois: op. cit., p. 196.

38. Ibid., pp. 198-199.

39. *La Recherche*, no. 91, 1978, p. 695.

40. Datations absolues et analyses isotopiques en préhistoire. Méthodes et limites", pre-printing in IXth Congress U.I.S.P.P., colloquium I, Nice, 1976, edited by the C.N.R.S., under the direction of J. Labeyrie and C. Lalou; see pp. 46ff.

41. IXth congress U.I.S.P.P., the tour book guide A5 Pyrénées-Nice, 1976, p. 72 and following. Since, one has aged this fossil to 500,000 years, using estimates, which change nothing. Gamma ray dating, according to the new method of Yuji Yokoyame and Huu-Van Nguyen, provides nothing new and just permits supposing that the age is higher than 200,000 years (*Le Monde*, April 25, 1981, p. 16). Likewise, too much uncertainty surrounds the recently discovered fossil in Petralona, in Greece. Even if it were a true "erectus" dating from 700,000 years ago, that would not change anything in the much more ancient African data. But no radiometric dating. The skull gathered by peasants was not found in the "original position." The archaism of the teeth, alone, would have permitted attributing by calculation an age of 700,000 years to it. But these teeth, gathered independently of the fossil, are probably those of a bear, to certain specialists. The proportion of fluorine is indispensable.

42. M. Boule and H.V. Vallois, *op. cit.*, pp. 169-178.

43. "There would be therefore in Europe only one sole lineage, that of the Neanderthalians, which ended at the end of the Mousterian Period. The "pre-Sapiens" line, that which led to modern man, would be looked for in other regions. It's that one which gave, in particular, the Cro-Magnons which one saw appear in Europe around −37,000 and about whose oriental origin one now knows." Bernard Vandermeersch in *La Recherche*, no. 91, 1978, p. 696.

44. M. Boule and H.V. Vallois: *op. cit.*, pp. 477-484. The three reconstructions of the cranial volume of Boskop give respectively 1830 cm^3 (Haughton), 1950cm^3 (Broom), 1717 cm^3 (Pycraft).

45. M. Boule and H.V. Vallois: op. cit., p. 395.

46. "The amino acid racemization ages listed in Table 3 for Skhul and Tabuzs are consistent with radiocarboon dates and other age estimates for these sites. Oakley lists A.2 dates on charcoal of 39,700 ± 800 years (Gr N - 2534) for Tabun Layer B and 40,900 ± 1000 (Gr N - 2729) for Tabun Layer C. Faunal bone from lower Layer C gives an amino acid age of 44,000 years." Jeffrey L. Bada, in IXth Congress U.I.S.P.P., Colloquium I, preprinting, p. 51.

47. *L'Origine de d'homme moderne*, Paris Colloquium, 1969, Unesco, 1972. Communications of L.S.B. Leakey: "Homo sapens in the Middle Pleistocene and the evidence of Homo sapiens evolution," p. 25 and following: M.H. Day: "The Omo human skeleton remains," p. 31.

48. Cheikh Anta Diop: "L'apparition de l'Homo sapiens," in *Bulletin de l'IFAN*, vol. XXXII, series B. no. 3, Dakar, 1970, p. 625.

49. *L'Origine de l'homme moderne*, op. cit., p. 217.

50. Andor Thoma: "L'origine de l'homme moderne et de ses races," in *La Recherche*, no. 55, August, 1975, p. 334.

51. See below.

52. A. Thoma: op. cit., p. 335.

53. Ibid. The prognathism and the width of the nostrils are controlled by the same gene.

54. C. Petit and E. Zuckerkandl: *Evolution génétique des populations. Evolution moléculaire*, Herman, Paris, 1976, p. 178.

55. J. Ruffie: *De la biologie à la culture*, Flammarion, op. cit., p. 398.

56. A. Thoma: op cit.

57. IXth Congress U.I.S.P.P., Colloquium XXII: the South Sea Islands Prehistory. Message of A.J. Mortlock: "Thermoluminescence. Dating of objects and materials from the South Pacific region," preprinting, p. 187.

58. H.V. Vallois: *L'Anthropologie*, 1929, pp. 39, 77.

59. C. Coon: *The Origin of Races*, Knopf, New York, 1962.

60. A. Thoma: Revue *Anthropologia Hungarica*, no. 5, 1962, pp. 1-111.

61. A. Thoma: Revue *La Recherche*, op. cit., p. 332.

62. Yves Coppens, F. Clark Howell, Glynn L. Isaac, and Richard E.F. Leakey: "Earliest Man and Environment in the Lake Rudolf Basin," in *Prehistoric Archeology and Ecology Series*, Karl W. Butzer and Leslie G. Freeman, eds., pp. 19-20.

63. See *Nature*, July 20, 1969.

64. H.V. Vallois: op. cit., p. 464; see also "Early Human Remains in East Africa," in *Man*, April 1933.

65. Ch. A. Diop: op. cit., pp. 627-628.

66. H.L. Movius, Jr.: op. cit., pp. 253ff.

67. The following table is taken from the article of H.L. Movius, Jr., op. cit., pp. 258-259. The abbreviation *BC* means "before Christ" (av. J.-C.), just as *BP* means "before present" (before the present, that is to say, 1950 taken as the zero year).

- Layer 14 (Base Aurignacian): more than 7m deep, 34,000 BP or 32050 ± 675 BC.
- Layer 13 (Base Aurignacian): no date.
- Layer 12 (Base Aurignacian): 32,250 BP ± 500 or 30,300 BC.
- Layer 11 (Base Aurignacian): 32,600 BP ± 800 or 30,650 BC.
- Layer 7 (Intermediate Aurignacian): 32,800 BP ± 500 or 30,850 BC.
- Layer 5 (Perigordian IV): 27,900 BP ± 260 or 25,950 BC.
- Layer 4 (Noaillian or Perigordian Vc): 27,060 BP ± 370 or 25,110 BC.
- Layer 3 (Perigordian VI): 23,010 BP ± 170 or 21,060 BC.
- Layer 2 (Proto-Magdalenian): 21,940 BP ± 250 or 19,990 BC.

68. GrN -2526, according to Vogel and Waterbolk, in H.L. Movius, Jr: op. cit., p. 259.

69. M. Boule and H.V. Vallois: op. cit., p. 297.

70. F. Bordes, in *L'Origine de l'homme moderne*, op. cit., p. 211ff.

71. F. Bordes: op. cit., p. 214. Ch. A. Diop: op. cit., p. 631.

72. H.L. Movius, Jr.: op. cit., p. 259 note I. Reindeer Cave (Arcy-sur-Cure), GrN - 1,736: 33,720 BP ± 410 or 31,770 BC; GrN - 1742: 33,860 BP ± 250 or 31,910 BC. These samples were collected at level VIII, which was from Perigordian I.

73. D. De Sonneville-Bordes: "Environment and culture of man of the Old Perigordian Period in the southwest of France. Collected data," in *L'Origine de l'homme moderne*, op. cit., p. 141ff.

74. Otherwise stated Negroid (underlined by the author).

75. M. Boule annd H.V. Vallois: op. cit., p. 311.

76. IXth Congress U.I.S.P.P., Colloquium XVI: The Aurignacian in Europe. Direction Janusz Kozlowski, Nice, 1976, preprinting. Finally, the recent discovery of the Neanderthalian of Saint-Césaire singularly confirms our point of view as to the nonexistence of a "Homo sapiens sapiens" native of Europe and before the Grimaldian Negroid. This Neanderthalian who lived only 35,000 years ago is found associated with the most typical forms of the castelperronian industry, of which he is the true inventor. A cross-breeding with "Homo sapiens" becomes probable: Brno, Predmost.

(François Lévèque and Bernard Vandermeersch, in *La Recherche*, no. 119, February, 1981, p. 242-244.)

77. "Study and assembling of the facial mass of the "Negroid of Grimaldi," by F. Mantelin, University of Paris VII, 1972, p. 71. "Reconstruction of the teeth of the adolescent of Grimaldi," doctorate in dental surgery, Max Banti, University of Paris VII, 1969. Magazine articles: P. Legoux: "Odontological study of the race of Grimaldi," in *Bull, du Musée d'anthropologie préhistorique de Monoco*, no. 10, 1963, pp. 63-121. L. Barral and R.P. Charles: "New anthropometric data and precision on the systematic resemblances of the negroids of Grimaldi," ibid. no. 10, 1963, pp. 123-139. G. Olivier and F. Mantelin: "New reconstruction of the skull of the adolescent of Grimaldi", ibid., no. 19, 1973-1974, pp. 67-82.

78. M. Boule and H.V. Vallois: op. cit., p. 301.

79. Ibid., p. 301.

80. Ibid., pp. 299-300.

81. *L'Origine de l'homme moderne*, op. cit., p. 287ff. See also Ch. A. Diop: op. cit., p. 636ff.

82. *La Recherche*, no. 55, August 1975.

83. See *La Recherche*, no. 108, February 1980.

84. Magazine *Archeologia*, no. 123, October 1978, p. 14. See also Kia Lan-Po: *La Caverne de l'Homme de Pekin*, Peoples' Republic of China Publishing House, 1st ed., 1978, p. 2.

85. M. Boule and H.V. Vallois: op. cit., p. 405.

86. Ibid., p. 406.

87. Cheikh Anta Diop: "Genetic relationship of the pharaonic Egyptian and the Negro-African languages," I.F.A.N., Dakar, 1977, p. XXIX-XXXVII.

88. Review *La Recherche* no. 89, May 1978, p. 447.

89. Review *Raison Présente* no. 53, p. 135-136. Dossier prepared by Georges Chappaz, Jean-Paul Coste, France Chappaz.

90. A. Thoma, in *La Recherche* op. cit., p. 333. Nothing is more contrary to the truth than the statement according to which the "theory of Coon has almost been officially accepted by the anthropologists assembled by Unesco in 1969 in Paris" (*Race et Intelligence*, p. 45): and that "the polycentric theory is now winning over the majority of the votes among the specialists, as the Paris colloquium on the origins of 'Homo sapiens' demonstrated" (p. 88). Actually, the majority of the participants at this colloquium are not to be confused with the majority of all of the specialists absent and with contrary opinions. Everything depends on the organizers and on the manner of invitation. Numerous specialists did not wish to participate in this colloquium for diverse reasons.

91. J.P. Hebert: *Race et Intelligence*, ed. Copernic Factuelles, Paris, 1977, p. 90.

92. A. Thoma, in *L'Origine de l'homme moderne*, op. cit., p. 84.

93. *Race et Intelligence*, op. cit., p. 91.

94. Ibid., p. 91.

95. Ibid., p. 91.

96. WASP: White Anglo-Saxon Protestant.

97. In the last century black children were sold by the pound in America.

98. Ch. A. Diop: *Parenté génétique de l'Egyptien pharaonique et des langues Négro-Africaines*, op. cit., chapter "Processus de semitisation".

99. Nobuo Takano, M.D. See above, p. 80.

100. *Le Monde*, February 4-5, 1979, p. 2.

101. Ibid.

102. Ch. A. Diop: "Pigmentation des anciens Egyptiens. Test par la mélanine," in *Bulletin de l'I.F.A.N.*, vol. XXXV, series B, no. 3, July 1973, pp. 515-531.

103. C. Petit and Zuckerkandl: op. cit., p. 190-191. See Figure 7.

104. A regrettable prejudice, certainly, which Montesquieu already cited, but which leaves no doubt about the fact that the people who behaved in this way were not white-skinned.

105. See Cheikh Anta Diop: *L'Antiquité africaine par l'image*, op. cit., p. 28, Figures 40 and 41.
106. Gaston Maspero: *Histoire ancienne des peuples d'Orient*, 12th, ed., Hachette, Paris, 1917, p. 259.
107. R. Mauny: *Tableau géographique de l'Ouest africain au moyen age,* I.F.A.N., Dakar, 1961, p. 59. A.L. Guyot: *Origine des plantes cultivées,* series "Que sais-je?" P.U.F., Paris, 1942, p. 69.

Dr. Diop being given his itinerary by Dean Lawrence Carter Sr. at Paschal Brothers Motor Hotel, Atlanta, Georgia. Also pictured are Dr. Edward F. Taylor to the right and Dr. Charles Finch. Photo: Larry Williams.

FURTHER CONVERSATIONS WITH THE PHARAOH

Charles S. Finch

Central to the ideology of the ancient Kamite religion was the divine principle in man as personified by the pharaoh. More than God's representative on earth, the pharaoh was he in whom the divine spark, present in every person, shone the brightest. Indeed, the Egyptians had a word for it, "wr" or "ur," which could mean both "great god" and "great man." A pharaoh-to-be underwent many arduous years of education, training, and fortifying of his mind and spirit. His character and intellect were tempered like fine steel because in him was invested the strength and vitality of the nation. Under the best circumstances, the Kamite pharaohs achieved something close to a complete unity of the self and could justly be said to be the human counterpart of heaven. In our own time a rare individual emerges now and again whose life and character seem to echo the lost "pharaonic principle." Such a man is Cheikh Anta Diop.

Two-and-a-half years ago an interview was published in the pages of the *Journal of African Civilizations* which was the fruit of my first encounter with Cheikh Anta Diop. My recent meeting with him marked the fourth such encounter and I had the good fortune to engage in a series of conversations with him over a period of 10 days in Dakar, Senegal in October 1985. Each successive encounter with Professor Diop has served to deepen my inestimable regard for his intellect and character. Though I have studied many of his works, including the most recent, *Civilization ou Barbarie*, I have come to the conclusion that the sum of his published works does not begin to exhaust his knowledge. Most of what he knows is still in his head. But Professor Diop is no ivory-tower intellectual. He has been a political activist his entire adult life, in France and in Senegal. He has worked out a theoretical model for the political, economic, and social reconstruction of Africa and has seen many of the programs and projects he has advocated over the last 30 years become public policy in his own country.

With the publication of *Civilization ou Barbarie* his place as a world historian seems assured. Posterity will undoubtedly place him in the company of Herodotus, Manetho, and Ibn Khaldun as an historian whose work not only changed the way we look at history but made history itself. Like all great historians, Professor Diop has turned his attention to a searching examination of historical principles, what he calls "the motor of history." His work perfectly exemplifies the dictum of Ivan Van Sertima that "what happened 10 minutes ago or 10,000 years ago occupies the same space in consciousness."

For Professor Diop, history is at the very core of life and to lose one's historical memory is to lose one's soul. When we have no history we have no sense of self. In the Diopian scheme, three factors constitute a culture: the historic factor, the psychic factor, and the linguistic factor, and they are all of a piece. To change one is to change them all.

As a summation of his life's work, Professor Diop has achieved a perspective of world history which demands a rewriting of that history in its entirety. It was Napoleon who called history a set of lies mutually agreed upon, and certainly the conventional history we are taught is but a shadow-play offered to the world as substantial reality. For example, the most conventional history will concede is that the Mediterranean world and Western Asia in some vague way felt the "influence" of ancient Egypt, whereas recent Afro-centric historiography from the publication of *Stolen Legacy* to that of *Civilization ou Barbarie*, makes clear that these cultures took the *essentials* of their civilizations from Egypt. In particular, Greek civilization, the spark that lit all later European civilization, took what Egypt offered, swallowed it whole, but only imperfectly digested it. There is no phase of Greek civilized life—religion, science, philosophy, state organization—that was not heavily influenced by Egypt. It might well be asked why the worthy Macedonian, Alexander, the greatest standard-bearer of Greek culture in the ancient world, chose to make Egypt the capital and jewel of his empire, why he undertook a perilous journey across Egypt's western desert to the Oasis of Amen to have himself declared the son of Amen? Indeed, Professsor Diop maintains that Alexander, and the later Roman Caesars, learned statecraft, particularly the organization and administration of a large multinational empire, by studying and copying Egyptian models. It might also be asked why the flower of Greek science bloomed *not* in Athens or anywhere else on the Greek mainland, but in Alexandria in Egypt? How many of the great Alexandrian scientists were actually Greeks? It now appears that Euclid, the famous geometrician, was an Egyptian with a Greek name. Moreover, Greek tradition tells us that almost all of the important Greek philosophers from Thales and Pythagoras down through Plato were trained in Egypt. In the legend of Danaus and his fifty daughters, Greek mythology points clearly to Egypt as the original home of Greek culture. Finally, as Professor Diop demonstrates in *Civilization ou Barbarie*, even the canons of Greek sculpture and architecture are derived from Egyptian models: the prototypes of the famous Doric columns are to be found in the colonnades of the magnificent Ipet-isut, the great Temple of Apt at Luxor built for the second time at least in 1700 B.C. Unless we take the new view of history as exemplified by Professor Diop's work, the true sources of history and world civilization in the Nile Valley are veiled behind so-called classical Greek culture.

A similar veil is thrown over the history of Western religions by the persistent focusing on Palestine as the cradle of these religions. This has ceased to be tenable. The figure of Moses offers a typical example of the obscurantism associated with this subject. When discussing Moses in the course of our conversations, Professor Diop and I both agreed that an Egyptian princess of the blood would never undertake to adopt a non-Egyptian child of humble origins any more than the First Lady would if a Black child from the slums of Washington, D.C. were laid at the doorstep of the White House. As an historical character, Moses can only be identified with Osarsiph, an Egyptian priest of Ra, who took up the part of a group of Egyptian outcasts and led them out of Egypt. Moreover, Professor Diop agrees that the people of the Exodus, whoever they were and to the extent that such a thing was an actual historical occurrence, must have had Egyptian, or a dialect of it, as their primary language. If, for the sake of argument, we accept the Biblical captivity in Egypt of 400 years, those proto-Hebrews would have lost whatever language they brought with them into Egypt by the end of the second generation. Hebrew did not emerge as a formal, written language until the 10th century B.C., three to four centuries *after* the Exodus. As a group, these people would have been speaking Egyptian, or a form of it, and their educated class would have been reading, writing, *and* thinking in Egyptian. This fact alone puts an entirely different color on Biblical history as we know it.

Professor Diop's early struggles are very revealing in the anecdotes he relates of his student days. In the early 1950's, he had the "temerity" to register for a course in Egyptian hieroglyphics in Paris. "I noticed," he says, "that whenever a Black showed the slightest interest in things Egyptian, Whites would actually begin to tremble. I was sitting in the hieroglyphics class in which there was one other student, a Frenchwoman, and when the professor instructed her to go up to the board to write a passage in hieroglyphics, she would erase it almost as fast as she wrote so that I couldn't copy what she had written. Not a single person in all of France ever encouraged me in my researches and the more I pursued them, the more uncomfortable and hostile they became, even issuing vague threats against my future teaching career. But I didn't care. I was an angry young man then and the more I was resisted the more determined and stubborn I became."

There was one brief encounter in Professor Diop's early student life that more than any other single incident reveals the often uncanny, even prophetic, twists and turns of history. In the midst of his researches into the African origin of Egyptian civilization he met just one man who applauded him, encouraged him, and offered him support, a man who in a few short years after that brief meeting in Paris was to meet a sudden and untimely death. That man was apparently none other than George G.M. James, author of *Stolen Legacy*.

My conversations with Professor Diop were carried out on four different afternoons in his home. My intent in this second interview was to make it a sequel to the first while taking pains to introduce topics not touched upon in the earlier interview. It was as if we were picking up on strands of an earlier conversation and continuing our train of thought. I was, however, much more relaxed in doing this interview and more confident of the result because Professor Diop and I were, by then, more familiar with one another, I had been present at a number of his lectures and seminars, I had read more of his more recent published work, and in general I was more conversant with the body of his ideas than I was on that first occasion.

Professor Diop does have one important desideratum that has yet to be fulfilled. He desires a forum or colloquium somewhere in which an extensive and exhaustive discussion, analysis, and clarification of his ideas can be carried out. He feels that his work and ideas have not had the proper feedback, examination, and testing necessary to properly validate them despite their ever-widening reception (as an aside, Sudanese scholars are now pressing for a translation of his books into Arabic). He makes no claims, implicitly or otherwise, for infallibility; he is entirely receptive to honest, thoughtful clarifications of his theories. His is a search for truth, not the establishment of a new orthodoxy. It is to be hoped that somewhere in the world such a forum can be summoned in his lifetime, as a testament to Cheikh Anta Diop the man as well as to the mental and spiritual labors of the entire African world.

INTERVIEW WITH CHEIKH ANTA DIOP

JAC: Dr. Diop, over two years ago, in August of 1983, the *Journal of African Civilizations* conducted an interview with you.

DIOP: I remember it very well.

JAC: Can you tell us a little about your new areas of research since that interview?

DIOP: I have continued to work in the same direction. In particular, in the field of linguistics I have worked to make more systematic the relationship between Ancient Egyptian and African languages. I have worked quite a bit in this area. In other fields as well I have found a certain number of important things. You know, the fields of African research are almost virgin land. One has but to lean in any direction to make new discoveries. Which is why I would very much like now to make way for others. I would like to work with an interdisciplinary team, to indicate the direction research should take because no one person can exhaust the material; to organize the work to be done rather than try to exhaust the subject matter myself.

This interview took place in Dr. Diop's home in Dakar, Senegal, on November 1, 1985.

JAC: You visited the United States for the first time in April of 1985 as the guest and honoree of Morehouse College, in Atlanta, Georgia. What were your impressions of that visit?

DIOP: I was very much impressed . . . by my contact with the black American community and with Americans in general. I discovered many things of which I was totally ignorant. As I said in the United States, I feel very strongly that this was a sort of pilgrimage for me. I think that all thinking Africans who go to America are, in one way or another, on a pilgrimage. I said before I left that I was going to find half of my family in America. It was just that. We are beginning to feel in a most vital way this biological kinship which ties us to America, the umbilical cord has not been cut. And this is very important. These relations must become much closer in the future. I believe that all of what lies in our common future is in this perspective. America is uniquely brought closer to Africa by historical ties. I was especially aware of this on American soil.

JAC: In *Civilisation ou Barbarie*, you devoted two important chapters to the discussion of prehistory. What is the importance of prehistory for the study of African history?

DIOP: It is the foundation, it is the point of departure without which all other studies—even African history—are left hanging in mid-air. If you are to discover the intelligibility of the facts, you must follow their evolution in the right direction, you do not swim upstream. You must also begin at the source. Prehistory is the point of departure. The separation of man and animal took place in Africa and not elsewhere. I have seen grotesque attempts in recent publications where they have brought out a jawbone which dates from 40 million years ago in an effort to again question the African origins of humanity. It is completely ridiculous. A monkey's jawbone dating from 45 million years ago cannot raise questions about the African origins of humanity. We are talking about the separation of man from animal and that process was completed in Africa, we have all the specimens.

So, it is from that point that you must start to understand all the rest of evolution: how Africa was peopled, first; how the first men born in Africa confronted nature, how they took on the challenges of nature to create civilization; how this civilization spread across the continent of Africa toward other continents; and how the world was peopled. That is the first step to complete and it will condition all the rest. It is when this phase of humanity has been committed to memory that what comes after is understood. It is for this reason that prehistory is of particular importance, and African prehistory is not only important for African history but for all of world history, because it allows each continent to know how it was peopled, all ideology put aside.

JAC: The study of African cultural history appears to be developing increasing scientific complexity. What do you think of this and what scientific disciplines do you think future historians will have to master?

DIOP: Unfortunately, the historian today must be many-sided, mastering most of the scientific disciplines which now come into the study of the past and this is impossible. But what is clear is that the historian's educational background must be vast and profound. It would be tedious to enumerate the different scientific disciplines it would be necessary to master to be able, for example, to be really productive in the field of historical investigation. I think that the way to overcome this difficulty is to create teams which would integrate scientists from the various disciplines so as to respond to the necessities of a collective work.

JAC: In *Civilisation ou Barbarie* you touched upon many areas that deal with the influence of Egypt on world history. Please discuss what the Greek world owed Ancient Egypt.

DIOP: Greece owes everything to Egypt. Egypt was teacher to Greece in its infancy. The Greeks themselves, their most eminent scholars, admitted it. Listen, one crucial idea must be kept in mind: if the Greeks had their own special genius, an autonomous thinking which would have enabled them to create civilization ex nihilo, it would have been done before they met the Egyptians. This is fundamental. But Greece never philosophizes before it encounters Egypt. Greece does not develop the slightest nuance of scientific thought before it encounters Egypt. Go back to the 8th century, go back to the 9th century, even in the Aegean epoch there had already been contact with the Egyptians. But the Greeks were too barbaric to assimilate and retain the Egyptian influences.

Egypt brought writing to Greece during the Mycenaean epoch, across the Minoan world, across Crete. But after the destruction of Crete by the explosion of the island of Santorin, all the elements of civilization which were to pass into the Mycenaean world were not preserved, and in the Greek Middle Ages, after the arrival of (these eastern influences), all this was lost. There is no writing in the tomb of Agamemnon, just formulas, accounts which the scribes brought in (from the Minoan world) on what were called tablets of the Mycenaean epoch in the Linear B script. But the Linear B script was lost during the Greek Middle Ages which means that the civilization, the state of Greek society was such that it was unable to support writing. A second contribution from Egypt was required before the Greeks were to awaken to civilization. So, the crucial question to pose is: Where is Greek thought before the encounter with Egypt? Where is Greek science before the encounter with Egypt? Where is Greek philosophy before the encounter with Egypt? If the question is posed from this angle you have the answer. Here is a people who were to invent everything, but who invented nothing which was not initiated in Egypt at the level of her greatest thinkers.

It was Thales who began the cycle by going to Egypt and he admits it. He then told Pythagoras who followed in his footsteps. And we know that all the Greek thinkers, even those who never went to Egypt, made up the trip to give themselves some importance. So, it is out of this contact that what is called Greek thought was born. Egypt was, therefore, preceptor to Greece and the Greeks themselves recognized this. I have already cited for you the passage from St. Clement of Alexandria in Stromateis which says that a book of a thousand pages would not be sufficient to cite the names of his Greek compatriots who have used and abused Egyptian thought and science. That says it all. The Greeks themselves admit it. Egypt was their teacher and that is why, to the Greeks, all non-Greeks were barbarians except the Egyptians. Those who had given them all the elements of civilization could not be considered barbaric in their eyes. The Greeks always admitted, quite humbly, that the elements of civilization came to them from Egypt and not elsewhere.

It is Western ideology which has tried in vain to obscure this thesis. In any case, the important thing to bear in mind is that if there had been an autonomous Greek thought, it would have been expressed before their encounter with Egypt, in both mathematics and the exact sciences, and in philosophy. But Greece does not develop a philosophy until its exposure to the Egyptians. It does not practice the sciences until it has been exposed to the Egyptians. And we know that Greek tradition, Greek society resisted this scientific and philosophical thinking. The proof is that all the adherents of this new ideology, of this new thought were persecuted. Socrates was persecuted. He committed suicide, he brought an end to his life. Plato, Aristotle, Anaxagoras, all narrowly escaped death, as well. In fact, in ancient times, there was no state more hostile toward science and philosophy than Greece. Yet another inconsistency. There was a veritable antipathy between Greek tradition and scientific development, between Greek tradition and philosophical thought and this must not be forgotten. Science and philosophy were born into and protected, however, by the power of the Egyptian state. There was no antipathy between the state and scientific development, there was no antipathy between philosophy and the state in Egypt. It was the contrary in Greece.

JAC: What can you say about the impact of Egypt on the revealed religions of the world, that is to say, the Jewish religion, the Christian religion, and the Islamic religion?

DIOP: Once again, Egypt is the beginning of everything. Akhenaten's monotheistic thinking precedes Moses, so it precedes all Judaism, if we put aside all legend. If we search written history proven by documents in chronological order, Egyptian monotheism precedes all the other monotheistic religions which have existed since, in this case, Judaism, Christianity, and Islam. The revealed religions borrowed from this Egyptian thought.

If you go into the tomb of the father of Ramses II, Seti I, I reproduced this representation of hell. The dead crosses a bridge which is suspended over hell. In Egyptian mythology, in black African thought, this concept of heaven and hell precedes the birth of all the religions we call revealed. The first man to say that God is one, and that his power is incompatible with an image, the first to affirm the oneness of God, the purest monotheism invented, was instituted by a black man, Akhenaten. He is the first prophet.

African scholars must revise the erroneous elements of what has been taught them in the schools, even as to the history of religions. Akhenaten has clearly been put aside and is not considered to be the first of the prophets, this is no more than an exercise, a racist attitude. It has nothing to do with anything certain.

All this demonstrates that history was taught by men like you and I with all their weaknesses, and that we must radically revise all the errors which have been taught and with which the cultural awareness of our students, our generation, our children and our people has been obscured.

JAC: There seems to be a lot of ambiguity or uncertainty in the literature of Egyptology on the date when Egypt truly emerges in world history as a unified culture and nation. Will you discuss what is known as the short chronology as against the long chronology? Which is more valid?

DIOP: What is certain is that in 4236 BC Egypt had already invented a calendar the periodicity of which is 1,460 years. That is a mathematical fact. This data was established by Meyer and is considered to be one of the surest dates in all of the history of mankind because it was not determined on the basis of vague conjecture. It was established based on facts which we know to be founded on the periodicity of the Egyptian calendar of 1,460 years. That is to say, based on the heliacal rising of Sothis or Sirius and the sun.

Now, this is a trap. We must no longer say below (that is, north of) the latitude of Memphis, it's wrong. In no text are we told that it was below the latitude of Memphis that this phenomenon (the heliacal rising) was observed. It could not have been observed below the latitude of Memphis because the rising of the Nile cannot even be seen below the latitude of Memphis. [The beginning of the Egyptian calendar, at 4236 BC, is tied to the simultaneous heliacal rising of Sirius and the beginning of the Nile flood, around June 21 —Ed.] This phenomenon had to have been observed in the interior, at a place where the river was much more engorged, where the swelling was much more easily visible. All of this is part of the succession of distortions which have completely altered the teaching of history and the truth. We must come back to that. So, this calendar date, which corresponds to the beginning of the Egyptian calendar, is the oldest in the world. How many years did it take to make such observations, to put in place such a calendar? I have said in my published works what the significance of this calendar is. It is too long to take up again in such a short interview. It is enough to refer to what we all have written about the calendar. But the question is: How was the Egyptian in 4236 BC able to accomplish this project? How long did it take? Certainly not less than 5,000 years. And that takes us back almost as far as 8,000 or 10,000 years, which is squarely in the Neolithic period. And this is precisely in accordance with what we know about the origin of humanity.

Egyptian civilization goes far back in "prehistoric" antiquity. If man as we know him was born in the region around Kenya (to the exclusion of all other regions) some 120,000 years ago, and if he began to colonize the Nile Valley from the area of the Great Lakes and on into Egypt, then there is nothing strange about the fact that there should already be an established civilization in this valley dating to 10,000 years ago. All of which will explain the precocity of this civilization at a time when the rest of the world was in barbarism. Egypt was the first to emerge, all ideology put aside. It is not possible—it clashes with chronology—to establish a parallel between Mesopotamia and Egypt, even though the first Mesopotamian civilizations were black. Elam and Susa, it must not be forgotten that these were black cities. But the movement was out of Egypt, the Egyptian influence spread through all of western Asia. It was much later, compared to Egyptian history, that these regions, that this black world was also to emerge to civilization.

JAC: Let us turn now to the difficult subject of race. There seems to be a growing consensus or idea in the literature of anthropology that there is no such thing as race. One consequence of this thinking is the idea that black people in India, Asia and the Pacific Islands who have almost the identical physical characteristics as Africans—that is, black skin, kinky hair, full lips, broad noses, etc.—are said to be totally unrelated to Africans. Please discuss this.

DIOP: You know, if we could get the Europeans into the trap where we would say to them "Prove to us that you are whites," we could drive them to distraction.

The Europeans, all the Occidentals say there is no race. But they know very well what a white man is, they know very well what a yellow man is. But we don't know what a black man is. Can they be serious when the black man was the first to exist on earth? It is the ideology which has been developed to destroy the cultural consciousness of the colonized, dominated people that we are. We now know how the white man was formed, he was the most recent. He developed beginning in the Soluturean period, from 20,000 years ago. He was born of the mutation of a black man.

A racial classification is given to a group of individuals who share a certain number of anthropological traits, which is necessary so that they not be confused with others. There are two aspects which must be distinguished, the phenotypical and the genotypical. I have frequently elaborated on these two aspects.

If we speak only of the genotype, I can find a black who, at the level of his chromosomes, is closer to a Swede than Peter Botha is. But what counts in reality is the phenotype. It is the physical appearance which counts. This black, even if on the level of his cells he is closer to a Swede than Peter Botha, when he is in South Africa he will live in Soweto. Throughout history, it has always been the phenotype which has been at issue, we mustn't lose sight of this fact. The phenotype is a reality, physical appearance is a reality. And this appearance corresponds to something which makes us say that Europe is peopled by white people, Africa is peopled by black people, and Asia is peopled by yellow people. It is these relationships which have played a role in history.

Now, every time these relationships are not favorable to the Western cultures, an effort is made to undermine the cultural consciousness of Africans by telling them, "We don't even know what a race is." What that means is that they do not know what a black man is; they do know what a white man is, they do know what a yellow man is. Despite the fact that the white race and the yellow race are derivatives of the black which, itself, was the first to exist as a human race, now we do not want to know what it is. If Africans fall into that trap, they'll be going around in circles. They must understand the trap, understand the stakes. There is the phenotype and, on the level of molecular biology, the genotype. Someone is always trying to drown a fish. They will tell you that race does not exist until there is a hereditary disease, then race will reappear. They will tell you that sickle cell anemia appears only in blacks, but if there is no race . . .? They use the same molecular biology to explain the flaws in blacks. All of this is fraught with ideology and is not reliable.

On the other hand, in the case of thalassemia, the disease which strikes inhabitants of the northern Mediterranean, instead of saying it is a disease which affects whites they will say that it affects the inhabitants of the region around the Mediterranean which is a euphemism and, again, is unreliable information. So, race, even though it is a relative notion, corresponds to something which allows us to situate individuals in their sociogeographic cradle, so to speak, and to distinguish them one from another. At the level of their phenotype we are able to follow their historical relationships. It is the phenotype which has given us so much difficulty throughout history, so it is this which must be considered in these relations. It exists, is a reality and cannot be repudiated.

What must now be done is to educate the cultural consiousness so that we no longer see in a being anything other than his humanness, plainly and simply, separated from all ethnicity. But we are not yet at that point. In our world, we see first only what is different from us, we see only the phenotype in our social relations, in our historical relations, in our human relations. The proof: in South Africa what is happening? There is no race? They are in the process of destroying one while they say it does not exist.

There it is, all the hypocrisy of international political and social relations. There is no race? That is what they are destroying. Why is it the blacks do not want apartheid? What is this? All of humanity's historical and social relations, from the beginning of time right up to the 19th century, were ethnic relations founded on phenotype. No other explanation will make sense of the movement of history if we make an abstraction of this view. Throughout history, there have always been ethnic confrontations, assimilations, and destruction. And now humanity is thinking about how it can find another road. But humanity has been governed essentially in its development by these ethnic confrontations.

JAC: From time to time, one hears the comment from blacks that learning about Egyptian or Ethiopian history is fine but why is it important today? What has it to do with worldwide problems of blacks today?

DIOP: It is the knowledge of Egyptian history which allows us to know what our ancestors did on this earth. We have been brainwashed. Do not forget that we have become an amnesic people from the sole fact that for almost 2,000 years, in differing degrees, we have been dominated. There was a reversal of the situation in Egypt with the arrival of the Persians, as you know. After the Persians there were the Greeks, then the Romans, then the Arabs. And the domination continues. The historic consciousness of African peoples has dimmed and we have become progressively an amnesic people, cut off from our history. We must restore the historical awareness of the African peoples, and Afro-Americans. And this restoration will come through a knowledge of Egyptian history which is the first manifestation of culture in Africa. The first African experience was that of Egypt. That is why, if we are to return to the source culturally, it must be at the foundation of our humanities. We must teach it systematically and show *all* that our people contributed to other peoples of the world before passing the torch.

JAC: What are the plans of Cheikh Anta Diop for the foreseeable future?

DIOP: We must continue. First, we must have a heightened awareness of the nature of the work to be done, of the effort to be undertaken. I believe this is the most important thing. To know what is to be done has nothing to do with the brevity of human life. To solve problems by organizing the work. It is not possible, in the space of one human life, to solve all the problems posed by our cultural birth. But I believe that now the African peoples throughout the world are sufficiently aware, sensitive to the task to be undertaken and that is a great step. What is important is the organization of the work.

As I have often said, we must be very severe with ourselves. We must be armed to the teeth with science to go to reconquer our cultural inheritance. This is the task which awaits the future generation. As long as I live, I will assist in the formation of interdisciplinary teams for the pursuit of this task here as well as in America.

INTERVIEW WITH CHEIKH ANTA DIOP

Shawna Moore

BBB: In the preface of your book *The African Origin of Civilization,* you state: "The history of Black Africa will remain suspended in air and cannot be correctly written until African historians dare to connect it with the history of Egypt." Could you elaborate on this point in the context of what you further discuss regarding the development of "A body of African human sciences," pointing out some of the vital questions that these sciences should address?

DIOP: This idea follows the proposition that ancient Egyptian culture enjoys a position vis-à-vis present day African cultures analogous to the role which Greco-Latin culture plays in regard to contemporary western culture. Could you imagine a western scholar researching in western history *without* referring to Greco-Latin culture? Could his work be considered as scientific? The same applies to African scholars in respect to ancient Egypt. This is why I say that as long as we ignore ancient Egyptian culture, the oldest evidence of an African civilization, we will be unable to create anything in the domain of the social sciences that could be considered as scientific. It is only by a systematic reference to Egypt that we can introduce a true historical dimension to the social sciences, whether the field be linguistics or any other. For instance, why not replace the study of Roman law in our law schools with the study of Egyptian jurisprudence?

The same applies to philosophy. Ancient Egypt was at the origin of an elaborate philosophical system, and not a mere cosmogony as most still hold.

I consider culture as a rampart which protects a people, a collectivity. Culture must above all play a protective role; it must ensure the *cohesion* of the group. Following this line of thinking, the vital function of a body of African human sciences is to develop this sense of collective belonging through a reinforcement of culture. This can be done by developing the linguistic factor, by restablishing the historical consciousness of African and black peoples so as to arrive at a common feeling of belonging to the same cultural and historical past. Once this is attained, it would become more difficult to 'divide and rule' and to oppose African communities, one against the other. My feeling is that such is the role of a new body of African human sciences, provided it does not depart from a strictly *scientific* terrain. This is most important; never to depart from the path of science.

This interview originally appeared in *Black Books Bulletin,* vol. 4, no. 4 (pp. 30-37).

BBB: In 1954 *Stolen Legacy* appeared by George G.M. James, who affirmed that Greek philosophy was borrowed from the system of "mysteries" developed by the Egyptians. Is there a connection between the mysteries that James writes about in *Stolen Legacy* and the African human sciences you speak of?

DIOP: If you go back to my works, especially *Black Nations and Culture,*[1] you will definitely see the connection. Unfortunately, I had no knowledge of James' work when I was doing my major research work on ancient Egypt in the early 50's. But if you look at both books closely, you will see the relationship between them. Both our works agree that ancient Egypt was the scientific cradle from which emerged, much later on, the scientific contributions of the Greeks. Of that, there's no doubt. In fact, we know of many cases where Greek scholars actually invented fictitious trips to Egypt so as to gain scientific legitimacy, much in the same way as some of our brothers today do in regards to Europe. The 'mysteries' James refers to deal with the elaborate system of initiation whereby the Egyptians transmitted knowledge. It would be too lengthy to get into that. . . .

BBB: You point out the necessity of research teams working on many of the ideas you have advanced. Would you elaborate on this necessity and speak specifically to the kinds of skills African researchers need to pursue some of the questions you raise?

DIOP: The work I undertook in the early 1950's was actually the work of a generation of scholars, as I was soon to realize. What I mean is that so many disciplines had to be mastered that no one person could possibly hope to succeed on his own. For instance, I had started attacking the problem of ancient Egypt and its relationship to the rest of Africa via linguistics and history. But it was soon apparent that I would have to master various other fields, such as ethnology, anthropology and so on. Consequently, I was led to tackle biochemistry, physics, mathematics, philosophy, etc. I also had to learn the ancient Egyptian language to communicate with them without intermediaries, such as translators. So you see what I mean . . . We must stop being dilettantes, dabbling here and there, and become well-trained, *pluridisciplinary specialists!* We need a new division of labor among our researchers. Those who may not be able to master several disciplines at a time must at least master one of them—but completely. That's the least we can expect from serious scientific researchers today. Scientific cadres of the black world must cultivate competence.

BBB: You talk a great deal about the Aryans. Specifically what is an Aryan and what is your hypothesis concerning their origin?

DIOP: By 'Aryan' I was designating the early white inhabitants of what I call the 'Northern Cradle'—that is, northern Europe. Within this context, the term *Aryan* is devoid of the racist connotation given it by people such as Hitler. By 'Aryan' I mean the original white tribes of northern Europe who spoke what is known as 'Indo-European' languages and whose dispersal began after the 2nd millennium B.C. We know these original white populations under the generic term of *Aryan*. So, as employed in my works, the term *Aryan* has nothing to do with either racial purity or any other racist-intended notions. The reason I have used the term frequently in my works, rather than the term 'Indo-European' commonly used by European scholars, is because *Indo-European* has a purely linguistic connotation. Not being a racist, I don't hesitate to use the term 'Aryan' when I intend to designate these original white populations ancestral to the present day Europeans. Just as I freely use the term 'Negro' in my works, I feel equally at ease using the term 'Aryan.'

As to the origin of the Aryan people . . . We see them appear suddenly around 1500 B.C., with a branch invading India and another branch progresssively occupying eastern Mediterranean Europe. Traditionally, it was thought that these populations came from the Eurasian steppes and were sort of Asian migrants. Now we can categorically affirm that *white Europeans originated in Europe itself and that their origin can be found nowhere else than in black populations which migrated from Africa into Europe tens of thousands of years ago.* As to exactly how a white race developed out of these black European populations is still scientifically obscure, but there is no doubt that such was the case. If not, how else to explain the origin of the whites?

We know that mankind originated in Africa and that this mankind, as I have discussed elsewhere in my works, was deeply pigmented or black-skinned. No serious scientist would contest that today. It would seem that among some of those Upper Paleolithic black populations which had ventured far north towards the Baltic Sea during the warm period, definite biological changes took place leading to the appearance of 'Alpine' and 'Nordic' white types. At any rate, *as far as science knows today, before 20,000 B.C. there were no whites in existence.* Yellows appeared even later, around 10-15,000 B.C. Today, science can rely on irrefutable material evidence to illustrate these facts.

BBB: You speak of two races—the Aryans and the Africans. Could you elaborate on this in terms of the place a race theory has in the global struggle of Aryans to continue their efforts to conquer the world?

DIOP: Racially speaking, I have used terms such as 'Negro,' and 'black'—but not 'African'—to signify race. Africa is a purely geographical delimitation. Now, are you talking about struggles between black and white peoples in contemporary or ancient times?

BBB: From ancient times right down to our epoch.

DIOP: It is delicate to use the term 'Aryan' in this wide context. Nevertheless, if we analyze things with an unbiased mind, we find that up to a certain epoch the entire planet was inhabited solely by the black populations. Considering that mankind developed in Africa and that this first mankind was black-skinned, blacks had to be at the origin of the world's first civilizations. Their domination extended over the entire globe. The overall supremacy of the blacks extended right down to the Assyrian period. As of 750 B.C., this supremacy was definitely on the wane. This was the epoch when the 25th Sudanese Dynasty was making strenuous efforts to maintain Egyptian supremacy against the terrible blows of the Assyrians. We know that it failed, and that in 633 B.C., Thebes was sacked. Following the Assyrians, around 525 B.C., Egypt was occupied by the Persians of Cambyses. As you know, Cambyses set fire to all the temples of Egypt, took slaves and sacked Egypt. Cambyses' slogan was: 'Trample all that made the grandeur of Egypt.' Now, from this we shouldn't infer that Cambyses' invasion was tantamount to a racial war, yet we detect quite clearly a peculiar determination on the part of the Persians to diminish and humiliate the representatives of the oldest and most venerable civilization.

When we talk of racism in antiquity, it is important to understand that racism as we know it today could not have been *expressed* in the same way vis-à-vis blacks, for the simple reason that it was the blacks who had monopolized technical, cultural and industrial know-how. The other races had to pattern their technological, cultural and religious development after the accomplishments of Egyptian technology, science, culture and arts. The Greeks were forced to come humbly and drink at the fountain of Egyptian culture. Therefore, the respect paid the black man at that time was immense. Of course, we witness the inordinate hatred of the Assyrians, but look at the devotion shown by Alexander towards Egypt and Egyptian culture! After conquering the entire eastern Mediterranean basin, Alexander went as far as to set up the capital of the empire *in Egypt,* not in continental Greece or Macedonia. Don't you find that strange? It would be like France setting up its capital in Dakar, rather than Paris, after having achieved its colonial empire. Alexander's decision is indicative of the cultural ascendancy exercised by Egypt over non-black peoples, even at a time when she had already lost her national sovereignty. Helenistic civilization was indebted to Egypt beyond measure. It was to Egypt that all of the Greek scientists of the Helenistic period came in search of knowledge. Hence, racism in the modern sense of the word could not have been exercised by whites against blacks in the same way during antiquity.

The problem is complex since we find at the end of the Alexandrian period, and more specifically at the end of the Greek occupation of Egypt, decidedly racist discriminatory practices were enforced against Egyptian blacks in their own home. Such a phenomenon became all the more explicit with the Roman invasion and occupation of Egypt and North Africa. I must say that there was definitely a racist approach of Romans and post-Alexandrian Greeks. This racists outlook translated itself in clearly *racial discriminatory practices* of various sorts . . . Egyptians were even barred from entering Alexandria and living in certain residential areas. Residential segregation existed at the time predicated along racial lines. Both Greeks and Romans enforced it against the Egyptians. This is made explicit in the colonial legislation of the epoch. *Racism therefore existed in antiquity.* From the Greco-Roman period right down to the Middle Ages we can document its progression. We all know the rest.

BBB: In a booklet entitled *The Cress Theory of Color Confrontation and Racism* (1970), Dr. Frances Cress Welsing has argued that the origin of racism must be found in the awareness by whites of their minority status and melanic deficiency as compared to the dark-skinned majority of mankind. What is your opinion?

DIOP: There is absolutely no doubt that the white race which appeared for the first time during the Upper Paleolithic—around 20,000 B.C.—was the product of a process of depigmentation. [The date is much earlier—about 30,000 B.C.; later works by Diop and others correct this—Ed.] Of course, it would be difficult, if not impossible, to provide exact data on the numerical proportion of these proto-whites to their black ancestors at that period in Europe. However, there can be no doubt that the cultural outlook of these proto-whites was eventually conditioned during the glacial epoch by the extremely harsh conditions of their 'Northern Cradle' until the moment of their migratory movements towards the southern areas around 1500 B.C. Molded by their environmental cradle, these early nomadic whites undoubtedly developed a social consciousness typical of the hostile environment to which they were confined for a long period. Xenophobia was one of the traits of this social consciousness, Patriarchal hierarchization another. Now, if we try to delve deeper into the psychic makeup of individual consciousness, and extend it we tend to agree with Dr. Welsing. Nevertheless, we must be careful because when we deal in this abstract realm, the realm of individual consciousness, and extend it over such a long period of time for which we have no documented data, a great amount of caution is in order. I think what Dr. Welsing has accurately assessed is that at the origin of racism we are to find a definite defensive reflex. I believe racism to be a reaction of fear, more often than not unavowed. The racist is someone who feels threatened by something or someone he does not and cannot control. This feeling of anxiety and fear in face of an uncontrollable foreign element is most certainly an essential feature of racism both in ancient and modern times.

It is possible that the early whites were conscious of being a minority group and that they isolated themselves in a reflex of ethnic self-perpetuation. This is a *possibility*, not a certainty. However, such might have been the origin of later theories of racial purity. By counterdistinction, we have no evidence that blacks in ancient times and right down to the medieval epoch developed any such behavioral attitudes in their relationship to other races. I feel this needs to be studied carefully. What I find remarkable is that in the individual attitude of blacks towards other races there's a difference of approach. Blacks are not racists. Blacks are not afraid of ethnic contacts. *Whites are!* I think that much of racism stems from that fear. Is it an inherited trait of the nomadic life of the primitive Aryan? I don't know. Is it a biological or other type of instinct? I don't know either. What is quite evident, however, is that *xenophobia* is definitely an entrenched trait of European cultures from way back. I think even European scholars would agree with me on this. In fact, as it turns out, one of the weaknesses of black civilization, particularly during medieval times, was the openess, the cosmopolitanism of these societies. The medieval black kingdoms were open to peoples of all horizons. And today, one of the basic weaknesses of African societies is that they still maintain this inherited cosmopolitan trait. Nationalism in Africa emerged as a purely defensive reflex. Narrow nationalism, xenophobia, exclusion of foreigners, has never been a policy of African cultures. We always find it associated with Indo-European cultures.

BBB: In your work, *Black Nations and Culture* (1955), you proved that ancient Egypt was black. Since then, have you done any additional research to enhance your earlier demonstrations?

DIOP: Of course. I have done extensive research work over the years on this particular aspect of African history and have made my findings public. I may refer you to the Final Report of the crucial Unesco Symposium on "The Peopling of Ancient Egypt and the Deciphering of the Meroitic Script," held in Cairo from 28 January to 3 February 1974.[2] It would be too long to go into the results of my most recent researches, but they are available for the most part in the publications of the Fundamental Institute of Black Africa (IFAN).[3] As you will see, particularly in the UNESCO report, my conclusions have gained wide acceptance in international scientific circles. The Unesco Symposium, as you know, brought together at my request the most reputed specialists and Egyptologists of the world.

BBB: In a work done by an African scholar in this country, *The Destruction of Black Civilization*, Dr. Chancellor Williams talks extensively about how Blacks lost their civilization. What is your assessment of some of the factors which caused Blacks to lose their civilization?

DIOP: We must delimit definite historical epochs and isolate for each epoch and civilization in question the reasons for its downfall. We have seen how the first civilizations developed by mankind,—and of which Egypt was the towering giant,—eventually crumbled under the repeated assaults and invasions of Indo-European elements. As a result, the ancient Egyptians were practically reduced to a near-animal level with wide-ranging migrations set in motion. This was not only the case of Egypt but of other black societies of that epoch. Similar events occurred over and again, throughout the centuries leading up to the Middle Ages. If we are to isolate the one element common to each of these occurrences of black downfall, then, I would not hesitate to say that that element is *the loss of national sovereignty.*

The internal weaknesses in the makeup of a society that favors the loss of its national sovereignty once under attack is a very complex subject of analysis. Precisely, the work I am presently undertaking deals with this subject. Evidently, it is not the type of subject which can be detailed in an interview. . . . Nevertheless, I can already tell you that if in spite of the many calamitous destructions, invasions, assaults, slave-trade and conquests inflicted upon the ancient and medieval black world, blacks have maintained the basic features of their civilization, it is becaue the internal makeup of ancient black societies, with all of its deficiencies, was perfectly valid. It was valid because it served the most essential function which a culture must serve, and by that I mean *survival!* What else has saved black people, if it's not the *ensemble* of political, economic and cultural institutions developed by black civilization throughout the ages? No doubt, in terms of material and technological progress, the overthrow of successive black civilizations caused immense setbacks. Yet, we are still here and, what's more, still able to have the determination to stage a comeback in modern times, in spite of the destructions, the enslavement, the lies, the scholarly falsifications . . . What accounts for this determination other than the validity of our common cultural and historical legacy? I think you see what I mean! The loss of national sovereignty is, in each case studied, the cause of the downfall of ancient and medieval black civilizations. That's the way I see it.

BBB: But what about the internal weaknesses of these black civilizations themselves as a factor of their own downfall?

DIOP: The internal weaknesses of any given society serve to justify the victory of any enemy over that society, only *after* conquest has been achieved. The Roman empire was overthrown by culturally and technologically inferior barbarians; the Hellenistic Greeks themselves were conquered by the Romans; the medieval Arabs and the Huns conquered European civilizations; Hitlerian Germany conquered the equally industrial nations of Europe and nearly pulverized England; victorious Germany was in turn conquered. . . . I can cite numerous examples of the sort. If internal weaknesses are the ultimate cause for the downfall of a civilization, then all living societies are susceptible to being conquered.

The internal weaknesses of a society lead to revolution and social change at a given point. As such, these weaknesses can also be seen as a factor conditioning progress inasmuch as they lead to social changes. In my works, particularly *Pre-colonial Black Africa* (1960),[4] I have detailed a good deal of the social weaknesses of ancient African states and societies. Luckily, such weaknesses existed, if not these societies would have remained unchanged. As we know, it is impossible for societies to remain unchanged over the ages. A 'perfect society,' that is, a society without weaknesses, would be a perfectly *immobile* society. Internal contradictions are at the base of profound societal changes. When we talk about internal weaknesses what we actually mean are social contradictions. Again I say that luckily ancient black societies presented such conflictual elements. On the other hand, the way a society goes about transmitting knowledge, for example, is fundamental to the development of its technology and crucial to its overall expansion. In this respect, the system of initiation whereby knowledge is transmitted in African societies is typically Egyptian. Yet, this system which is generalized in African societies is *not* the best way to transmit or generalize scientific knowledge. Nor does this system allow for the critical examination of scientific theories. This has been extremely harmful to the technological and social development of traditional black societies. The monopoly of knowledge by a restricted group of religious men has been detrimental to the development of African societies. Even today, in the villages, elders only release on their deathbed, and to a favorite son, part of the knowledge accumulated throughout the centuries. This takes place just before the elder dies. You can imagine the inefficiency and waste involved in such a practice, considering that the old man has already lost a good deal of his mental faculties and can only transmit a confused, disjointed amalgam of directives.

At any rate, I think you'll agree with me that unless you are ready to afford me several hours to explain and document my views on this question, I can't really tackle the problem in an interview. . . .

BBB: You discuss the future organization of Africa being that of the confederation of three areas on the continent which have collegial relationships that will ultimately lead to the development of one unified political system. Please discuss this idea.

DIOP: As you know, I've written a book solely on this question.[5] In my opinion, the stage of micro-states such as could be seen in 19th century Europe, and as seen today in Africa, has become an anachronism. Today, the only viable political solution for Africa is in a continental state. If a continental state cannot be achieved at a first stage, then at least a union of sub-Saharan states must be definitely aimed at as the next step. Why? For the simple reason that in our times a state which cannot control or defend its very atmospheric and cosmic space cannot be considered independent. How can states made up of 200,000 or even several million inhabitants hope to achieve the means by which they could defend and control their cosmic space? At this time, the only viable state is one which can undertake activities in outer space. This is why at present only the Soviet Union, the United States and China can be considered as truly independent states.

My idea of a continental union is a flexible federation which does not stifle national identity, but in which defense, foreign trade and foreign affairs are vested in a continental government. Look what has happened recently in Uganda! All of Africa was humiliated by the Israeli raid, which just goes to show that the independence of African governments is purely symbolic. Anyone can come in and do whatever he wants—in fact, even kidnap a Head of State—and go out scot-free in our present "independent" countries! Only personal, egoistic interests are keeping Africa away from a continental state. At present all we have are unstable regimes, coups, countercoups and a South American type situation. There's no security, either for the individual or the national collective. What's here today might be gone tomorrow in the aftermath of a coup. How can Africa create any permanent institutions or advance technologically in such conditions?

In the near future, when foodstuffs and natural resources will have been exhausted on the surface of the earth, it will be in the deep seas that man will have to look for food and raw materials. How can you ask a country like Gabon inhabited by 200,000 or 400,000 people, or Senegal with its 5 million inhabitants, to dive into the deep oceans for the purpose of feeding the nation and securing the natural resources needed to promote and sustain its material development? It's just like asking a born cripple to compete in the olympic games. Isn't it? Only a continental union can save Africa. In the book I already mentioned you will see that I detail the means whereby such a union could promote the industrial, political, technological and scientific development of African peoples. A lot more needs to be said.

BBB: What are your opinions on the role that blacks in the United States, Caribbean, and South Pacific should play in the context of strengthening the development of the African world against white supremacist domination?

DIOP: The future of blacks all over the world is interconnected. It was so in the past when black civilizations were under serious pressure. It is even more so at present. A continental African state is a prerequisite for the survival of black societies wherever they might be. Black communities must find a way to articulate their historical unity. The ties between black Africans and the blacks of Asia, Oceania, the Caribbean, South America and the United States must be strengthened on a rational basis.

BBB: Would you speak of the current situation in Southern Africa?

DIOP: It is irrational to think that any African, wherever he might be, can make plans for the future as long as the South African problem is not solved. South Africa is the stumbling block in the way of African development. In fact, it has become imperative to liberate South Africa in time so as to avoid a nuclear war. That's the way I see it. To wait is to allow South Africa the time to leisurely develop its nuclear capability. If this is allowed, there will be no equilibrium for their terror and consequently the other African states will be impotent to act. So, in the interests of world peace itself, we must immediately intensify the struggle for the liberation of Southern Africa. Otherwise, whatever political or other projects we might make will have no meaning. The racist regime of South Africa must be liquidated without delay. If not, there will be an atomic war in Africa in the next five to ten years. Within less than 6 years from now, South Africa will have at their disposal a small stockpile of nuclear weapons, enough to create mass panic among Africans. . . .

BBB: As a scientist, what role do you see science and technology playing in the latter part of the 20th century? How will this affect Black people and what should we be doing to prepare?

DIOP: I believe that during this interview I've explicated the overall conditions for the utilization of science and technology. None of this can be achieved without the existence of a *continental* state of Africa, or at least union of sub-Saharan states. The enormous progress of science and technology in the 20th century runs the risk of being turned against the development of Africa and black peoples in general. Science and technology will allow other states to reinforce their power and to be in a better position to continue their domination over the fragmented African states. I'm afraid that in this context, scientific progress, rather than acting in our favor, will work to our detriment, unless we create the social and political conditions for a rational exploitation and utilization of science and technology.

BBB: In much of the western world and especially in the United States, the mass media (radio, television, newspapers and magazines) has had a profoundly negative effect upon Black people. Do you see any ways of combating this?

DIOP: The mass media has a negative effect on *all* peoples. As concerns the effect it has on the blacks in the Americas, I can only hope for an intensification of the cultural contacts between blacks of Africa and those of the Americas. I believe that this is the only way that we can arrive at a cultural renaissance that will profit all of us. Whatever valid cultural achievements are attained in Africa can only have a beneficial effect on the blacks of the Americas. Vice-versa, whatever valid cultural contributions emerge from the blacks in the Americas will also positively affect all other members of the black world. We must support each other to keep from sinking. That's an important fact. Although we belong to different political worlds, we share a common cultural soul. To reinforce this common identity is in itself to fight against the nefarious effects of the mass media.

NOTES

A special thanks to Shawna Maglangbayan and Carlos Moore for their exacting translation and their help in coordination without which this interview would have been impossible.

1. *Nations negres et culture* (Black Nations and Culture), Paris: Presence Africaine, 1955 (10 chapters of this work have been translated in English and compose the greater part of *The African Origin of Civilization: Myth or Reality*, N.Y.: Lawrence Hill, 1974).

2. See: Unesco document SHC-73/CONF.812/4, Paris, June 28, 1974, 37 pp, plus Annexes I-IV.

3. *Pigmentation des anciens Egyptiens. Test par la melanine* (Pigmentation of the Ancient Egyptians. Melanin analysis). Bulletin de l'I.F.A.N., T. XXXV, ser. b. No. 3, Juillet 1973.

4. *L'Afrique noire pre-coloniale* (Pre-colonial Black Africa), Paris: Presence Africaine, 1960 (this work has not as yet been translated into English).

5. *Les fondements culturels, techniques et industriels d'un futur etat federal d'Afrique noire* (The cultural, technical and industrial basis of a future Black African federal state) Paris: Presence Africaine, 1960, revised edition 1974 (this work has not as yet been translated into English).

Selected I.F.A.N. Publications

L'apparition de l'Homo sapiens (The Appearance of Homo sapiens), Bulletin de l'I.F.A.N., T. XX-XII, ser. B. No. 3, 1970.

La metallurgie du fer sous l'ancien Empire egyptien (Iron Mettalurgy during the ancient Egyptian Empire), Bulletin de l'I.F.A.N., T. XXXV, ser. B, No. 3, Juillet 1973.

Introduction a l'etude des migrations en Afrique centrale et occidentale (Introduction to the Study of Migrations in Central and West Africa), Bulletin de l'I.F.A.N., T. XXXV, ser. b, No. 4, 1973.

Pigmentation des anciens Egyptiens. Test par la melanine (Pigmentation of the ancient Egyptians. Melanin analysis), Bulletin de l'I.F.A.N., T. XXXV, ser. B, No. 3, Juillet 1973.

Comment enraciner la Science en Afrique: exemples walaf [Senegal] (How to Implant Science in Africa: wolof examples (Senegal), Bulletin de l'I.F.A.N., T. 37, ser. b, No. 1, Jan. 1975.

Physique nucleaire et chronologie absolue (Nuclear Physics and Absolute Chronology), Bulletin de l'I.F.A.N., T. XXXI, 1974.

INTERVIEWS WITH CHEIKH ANTA DIOP

Carlos Moore

Professor Diop was persuaded to break a 15-year silence to speak to Africa and the world, when he was convinced that Afriscope *is a highly serious-minded and uncompromisingly African organ. Our man, Carlos Moore, assisted by the ever-diligent Shawna, fielded almost a hundred questions.*

—I—
AFRICA'S POLITICAL UNITY

AFRISCOPE: Since the early 1960's the African Continent has shown itself to be coup prone. How do you account for the growing political instability of African regimes?
DIOP: I had foreseen the 'South-Americanization' of the African continent and in my work, *Les Fondaments culturels, techniques et industriels d'un future etat federal d'Afrique noire* (Presence Africaine, 1960), I alluded to this phenomenon. Earlier, in 1956, I also touched on the subject in an article "Alerta sous les tropiques" (*Presence Africaine*, No. 5, Jan. 1956), warning that unless we took care the African continent upon independence would go down the road of 'South-Americanization.' No matter how much one may claim that history doesn't repeat itself, I have nonetheless been haunted by Simon Bolivar's failure to unite the South American continent in a single bloc. It can no longer be denied that Africa is the victim of 'South-Americanization.' That Africa is 'politically unstable' is a fact. We can't even talk anymore about 'balkanization,' since the Balkan regimes are stable, whereas in Africa we have a change of regime almost every week or every month. At any rate, every year. And this instability is growing. . . . .

In my opinion, what has been lacking are national leaderships which could set an example. Had this been the case, military overthrows would have been made much more difficult. At any rate, stability in Africa would have been much greater. Political selfishness is killing Africa; it's the basis of the problem. Once African interests become merely a pretext for individual selfishness, instability necessarily rears its head. When the only organized force,

These interviews originally appeared in *Afriscope*, February 1977 (vol. 7, no. 2).

in the country—the army—ceases to respect the civilians in power, it will seize power for itself.

AFRISCOPE: However, practically, each time the army has seized power, it has perpetrated the same evils it pretended to overthrow. In turn, there is still another coup.

DIOP: Yes, this is true because the army has not in the meanwhile been educated along patriotic and political lines. What generally happens is that the army wakes up one day and discovers that it is merely an instrument of civilians wielding power. Yet, the army also knows that the survival of civilian rule depends on army-backing. The contradiction is solved by a seizure of power. But when the army overthrows civilian rule, without having had any political formation, and when this very army is itself devoid of any profound ideals, the result of army rule cannot be any better than the civilian rule it overthrew. . . . .

AFRISCOPE: The Economic Community of West African States (ECOWAS) is the latest regional attempt at regroupment in black Africa. We have seen at least four other such attempts fail in the past, including the East African Community. Why have all of these projects failed? What chances do you give ECOWAS?

DIOP: Once again we're putting the cart before the horse. We want to create regional economic organizations from which member states can draw maximum benefits, yet we refuse to relinquish even an inch of our respective national sovereignties. There is a serious contradiction here. My opinion is that all such regroupments are bound to fail. In the past, each attempt at regional economic regroupment was shortlived. The reason they have failed and will continue to fail is simple: the links uniting the parties to all such regional agreements have never been irrevocably binding; *nor have the terms of economic cooperation ever been indissoluble.* Moreover, all such attempts at economic regional regroupment have lacked an important and indispensable counterpart: *a supra-national political umbrella, in the sense of an executive organism, able to take political decisions that are binding to all parties.* Consequently, whenever and for whatever reasons one of the parties to the agreement decides to withdraw, the regional grouping starts crumbling. In the absence of a supra-national executive body with full powers, what can prevent a state from pulling out of a regional grouping? In the absence of *irrevocable* commitments, quite naturally involving the partial loss of national sovereignty, what can prevent the party to a regional agreement from withdrawing on a mere whim? . . . . .

To overcome the tremendous obstacles in the way of the economic unification of Africa, decisive political actions are required in the first place. Political unification is a prerequisite. *The rational organization of African economies cannot precede the political* organization of Africa. The elaboration of a rational formular of economic organization must come *after* the creation of a

Carlos Moore (right) interviewing Diop in Dakar, Senegal.

federal political entity. It is only within the framework of such a geo-political entity that a rational economic development and cooperation can be inserted. The inverse leads to the type of results we have witnessed over the years. If, for example, West Africans had the courage of creating a federal political executive entity with full decision powers, and to which West African states would renounce a definite portion of their national sovereignty, then that would be another matter. In that case, the federal executive body could be asked to draw up carefully studied plans for a rational organization of West African economy. The full powers attributed to such an executive body would allow it to take consequential decisions without fearing that the day after one or another head of state would announce: 'I don't like what's happening; I'm leaving.' It's a vicious circle and we must have the courage to face that fact.

AFRISCOPE: How to break out of this vicious circle?

DIOP: In my opinion, the way out of the present deadlock is quite clear. The rational, economic organization of the African continent or any part of it cannot precede a common political organization along regional or continental federal lines. The first step would be to politically organize a geographic entity and, then, within that geographic space proceed to a rational economic organization. The inverse is not possible. Yet, this is what African heads of state have been trying to do from the very beginning. Why? Simply out of selfishness, out of personal and egoistic power interests. Where does

Africa stand in all of this? Selfish African heads of State want to reduce continental and regional exigencies to their own personal and national egoisms. In other words, they latch onto power, have no intention of abandoning it and they talk about creating regional economic interets. However, the defence of power interests is in direct opposition to the avowed wish for regional economic coöperation and unity. It just isn't true that Africa is uppermost in the minds of these heads of state. It is not in the interests of Africa to latch onto power and monopolize it to the extent of refusing to relinquish even a portion of it to a supra-national executive body so as to be able to arrive at an economic union. No one wants to relinquish an iota of national power. That's why all previous regional associations have failed. There's a long list of these and the list is getting even longer. My most sincere wish is that ECOWAS would reverse the trend. But I have no illusions about it. ECOWAS lacks the essential, the one element conditioning its success or failure.

AFRISCOPE: E. Wilmot Blyden in the 1850's, Marcus Garvey in the 1920's and Kwame Nkrumah in the 1960's championed the project of a continental state of Africa. For two decades you have championed the idea yourself. Why, in your opinion, has no African leader taken concrete and decisive steps towards its realization?

DIOP: Whether an African leader has or has not taken concrete steps towards the implementation of this goal, the fact remains that a continental federation is an urgently vital necessity for the totality of African peoples. In my opinion, it is the pre-condition for our collective survival. The more time goes by, the more it will be seen that we must either join in a continental federation or fall into a generalized and endemic state of anarchy. In fact, we have already arrived at that stage. . .

AFRISCOPE: What other concrete intsruments of federal control do you propose for a continental union?

DIOP: The links between a federation of African states should be flexible enough to allow each one breathing space. Each national grouping must be left to enjoy the largest possible internal autonomy. But political and economic life must be rationalized from a federal perspective. A certain number of federal agencies must be created; defence, external trade and foreign affairs must definitely be unified. We need a modern continental army worthy of the name, capable of facing any eventuality, rather than our present armies which are mere auxiliaries to the police force. In fact, our armies were not created with the intent of facing up to any external threat. . . . .

Whereas there would be administrative autonomy of each member state, the Federal umbrella government would be fully in charge of such activities that go beyond the national prerogatives. For instance, in terms of defence, the armed forces would be on a continental basis. The individual states would have a territorial guard. Troops would be based in various African countries, whether Tanzania, Gabon, Algeria or Libya, and officers would equally come from all regions of the continent. That is, officers and troops based in a state would not necessarily be indigenous to that particular country. Along the same lines, federal administrative cadres would be drawn from all areas of the continent and would serve wherever posted. Continental citizenship is a must. No African should need anymore than an I.D. card for travelling to and from any part of the continent.

A federal African state would have to rationalize African economies on a continental basis. External trade would necessarily fall under the attributions of such a state. The general integration of African economy would allow for the global bargaining of all of Africa's commerciable surplus of raw materials at prices advantageous to us, besides providing a very important source of capital accumulation. The development of our countries, the accelerated formation of technological cadres, as well as the transferral of advanced technology become possible in this context through a rationalization of our commerciable surplus on a continental basis. Naturally, whatever is indispensable to the internal functioning of national economies can be left in the hands of local governments, after careful study. As you see, the viability of such a state is certain. In fact, it is the prerequisite for the survival of African peoples. It's the only way out for our countries.

AFRISCOPE: In practical terms, how in your opinion does one go about creating such a state?

DIOP: To begin with, a group of states could already band together in an open federation and actively incite the other states to join. I understand that this is more easily said than done, but a start has to be made somehow, somewhere. I see no other way for such a state than in one, two or three states taking the initiative of surrendering a good part of their own national sovereignty and accepting to be the initial nucleus of an open federation. This demands courage, a lot of courage, political foresight and, above all, a deep profound commitment to Africa as a historical, cultural and political entity.

AFRISCOPE: How would the wielding of political power be organized?

DIOP: A collegial system of political leadership could be envisaged, based on the concept of rotation. For instance, an executive council of the federated states, comprised of the heads of those states, could be set up. The federated states would have to accept a permanent, *irrevocable* transfer of part of their national sovereignty to such an executive council. That is, from the outset, the nucleus of federated states would integrate their defence, economy, external trade, civil service and foreign affairs. These would be prerogatives of the federal executive council. Equally, universities and scientific research centres would be unified and rationalized on a federal basis. The president of such a federation could be elected from within the federal executive council itself. That system could be adopted at a first stage, since continental-wide elections pre-suppose the existence of a continental federation. In as much as the functions of a federal president would be symbolized by a person, such a person could be one of the heads of the federated states. Leadership, however, would be exercised on a collegial basis. Also, the presidency of the federal executive council would be on a rotative basis. Every two, four, or seven years, or whatever the case may be, the presidency would go to one of the heads of the federated states. We need some kind of convenient formula that would ensure stability. In fact, we could even envision a rotative system based on alphabetical order. This would eliminate the type of rivalries that could jeopardize the stable functioning of such a federal state. The important thing is that the federal executive council be a truly democratic and collegial body, open to discussions and thorough analyses of each and every problem that might affect Africa as a whole. However, once decisions have been democratically arrived at by consensus, all federated states should be bound to them. In synthesis, I am in favour of any sort of formula that would allow African peoples and countries to bind together democratically in defence of their common interests and that would ensure their own survival. . . .

AFRISCOPE: On the informal plane, what measures would you suggest for arousing a continental African consciousness?

DIOP: We could go and on. . . . But a practical thing leading to a continental consciousness is inter-African contacts on an informal free and leisurely basis. An aspect of the problem of the unification of the African continent, and which is seldom stressed, deals with an inter-African tourist circuit. A special agency must be created for this purpose. Africans do not know Africa. How can you love a country, or have faith in its destiny, if you don't know it? All the more, how can we love our continent or develop a continental consciousness without knowing it?. . . . .

—II—
OBSTACLES TO EMANCIPATION AND UNITY

AFRISCOPE: The western bloc is setting up South Africa as a permanent white bastion-state enclaved in Africa. The 'bantustan' policy and so-called 'independence' of Transkei are the corollaries to this plot. Isn't the existence of a white South Africa a monumental obstacle in the way of a continental African state?

DIOP: Without a shadow of a doubt. The setting up of a continental African state presupposes the eradication of the South African threat. The establishment of a white state anywhere on the continent of Africa is inconceivable, inadmissible. The whites who are in southern Africa could remain there, but only within the framework of black majority rule. A borderline between a white state and a black state is inconceivable. Sooner or later it will lead to a racial war. . . . . The white South African regime is a permanent danger which should act as a mobilizing force for all Africans. We should have no illusions about this. It is either unity or destruction!

AFRISCOPE: With the active complicity of the West, fascist South Africa is developing its nuclear capability at an alarming speed. This poses the threat of extermination of black peoples. Yet, some African leaders insist that dialogue is the only way of averting that danger.
DIOP: Nothing could be more dangerous than to initiate dialogue with white South Africa, It would merely give her the necessary time to put the finishing touches on her nuclear program. South Africa only believes in one solution and speaks only one language: brute force. Look at Soweto! To the white fascist leaders of South Africa, any black country is Soweto. South Africa is feverishly preparing for a showdown. Pretoria now knows that *any technically organized minority, fully equipped and enjoying a high educational standard can successfully face and repulse by violent means an entire continent which has remained at the level of semi-development.* South Africa is actively working to achieve an equilibrium of terror. Pretoria is going about acquiring the most sophisticated and efficient nuclear weapons, along with the vehicles or systems to deliver them to any point on the African continent.

South Africa is virtually a nuclear power and is preparing to put up a long and terrible resistance to the rest of the continent. Objectively speaking, South Africa does not consider anyone on the African continent as her 'friend.' What we have are these so-called pacifists who are trying to camouflage their cowardice and capitulation by proposing a so-called dialogue with a regime that has vowed to destroy the black man. The policy of dialogue with South Africa, presented to us as the product of political 'realism' can only be judged as political blindness or the surrender of the best interests of African peoples. It takes two to dialogue. South Africa is not seeking dialogue but time; the necessary time to develop her nuclear arsenal. I don't think any African leader ignores this, though some pretend to.

Whereas it was previously believed that Pretoria would fabricate nuclear weapons by 1983, the latest developments force us to drastically revise that prevision. South Africa is now in the position to become a full nuclear power within the next few years at maximum. *If only for this reason, the struggle for the overthrow of white supremacist South Africa must be intensified immediately!* No compromise! No procrastination! The armed struggle in southern Africa must be intensified immediately! It's the only way to avert a nuclear war in Africa in the near future. Once South Africa acquires nuclear weapons, it will be too late. At that time, the African states which are today invoking 'realism' to justify their inaction and capitulation in face of Pretoria will definitely have a good argument to preach permanent peaceful coexistence with the white South African regime. However, what they might not realize is that once South Africa acquires nuclear weapons, a *modus vivendi* will be impossible, no matter how much African states bend over. *Once South Africa acquires nuclear weapons, she will take the offensive. Therein lies the reason why a borderline between a white and black state is impossible on the African continent.* It signifies war sooner or later. South Africa knows it and is preparing for it. . . . .

It is irrational to think that any African, wherever he may be, can make plans for the future as long as the South African threat is not eradicated. South Africa is the stumbling block in the way of African development. In fact, it has become imperative to liberate South Africa in time so as to avert a nuclear war. To wait is to allow South Africa the time to leisurely develop its nuclear capability. If this is allowed, there will be an equilibrium of terror whereby the other African states will be impotent to act. *So, in the interests of world peace itself, we must immediately intensify the struggle for the liberation of southern Africa.* Otherwise, whatever political or other projects we might conceive will be devoid of any meaning. The racist regime of South Africa must be liquidated without delay. *Otherwise, there will be an atomic war in Africa in the next five to ten years.* Already, within less than six years from now, South Africa will dispose of a small stockpile of nuclear weapons; quite enough to create mass panic among Africans. . . . .

AFRISCOPE: Technologically speaking, at what stage of development can South Africa's nuclear capability be assessed now?

DIOP: With the complicity of the West, South Africa has been able to come up with an absolutely revolutionary and efficient method for the separation of isotopes. . . .When first announced, it was believed Pretoria was bluffing. It was no bluff at all! At Velindaba there is a pilot centre where South Africa has been able to experiment with this new method of isotopic separation. She was helped by the German firm, Steag. That centre is now fully operational and can allow Pretoria to assemble the most difficult of atomic bombs; that is, the Uranium-235 bomb. Moreover, South Africa definitely has the know-how of reprocessing spent nuclear reactor fuel (uranium fuel). She can therefore manufacture plutonium atomic bombs. [Spent uranium is the waste from a nuclear power reactor, that when processed through a special reprocessing plant, creates plutonium. It takes about 13 pounds of plutonium to make a small atomic bomb.—Ed.]. Thus, with her present nuclear installation, South Africa can build atomic bombs based on plutonium-239. Furthermore, she will be able to go directly into the U-235 category. This is extremely serious, for unless science comes up with another shortcut, the U-235 bomb is indispensable as a *trigger* for a thermonuclear bomb. What all of this means is that South Africa is not only in possession of advanced nuclear technology, and on the verge of building classical plutonium atomic bombs, but more importantly, very close to the thermonuclear stage!

Right now, South Africa has what we can call a *nuclear capability.* I don't believe she will wait another five, six or ten years to build atomic weapons, considering the mounting political pressures she faces from black Africa. At present, she would have to enlarge the pilot installation she already has, discreetly improve it and make it run day and night to isolate enough U-235 to build the type of bomb acquirable *without* a nuclear plant. It's quite possible that Pretoria already has the data whereby she could manufacture an atomic bomb without the need for a nuclear plant. Needless to say, whenever South Africa does acquire a nuclear plant, her production of fissionable material will have been multiplied by one hundred. Whereas she may now be able to build one or two bombs, with a nuclear plant she will be turning out one hundred bombs instead. There's no doubt about that. The danger is staring us in the eyes. In fact, the situation will be untenable whenever her nuclear plants become operational.

AFRISCOPE: South Africa invaded Angola in 1975. Israel attacked Uganda in 1976. Israel and South Africa are allies; they are both virtual nuclear powers. Shouldn't we read in their actions against Africa an ominous sign of things to come?

DIOP: Concerning South Africa, the dangers are real; there's no question about it. The connivance between South Africa and Israel is really astonishing. One would have thought that a people such as the Israelis, who had suffered from racism in modern times, would have aligned themselves with black people, the veritable historical victims of racism. To my great surprise I realised that something essential was missing in the relationship between black and Israeli peoples. We have seen Israel choose the western camp. Yet, the recent past of the Israeli people would have justified the expectance of their aligning themselves with those who have also suffered as the Israelis, if not more, from the ravages of racism. In other words, we would have expected Israel to have sided with black peoples particularly and the Third World in general. We would have expected a non-expansionist attitude on the part of Israel, which is not the case. We would have expected understanding on the part of Israel, which is not the case. We would have expected sympathy from the Israelis for the cause of the Third World in general, which is not the case. Instead, Israel chose the western camp. . . . .

AFRISCOPE: After Vorster's visit to Israel, are we not to fear that Tel Aviv will help Pretoria develop its nuclear weapons?

DIOP: The Israeli-South African alliance defies the imagination! Against all expectations, Israel has done the unimaginable. From this point on, anything can be expected. We know Israel to be in possession of a small stockpile of operational nuclear weapons and to be a highly advanced technological nation. We're now justified in believing that Israel will put her advanced nuclear technology at the disposal of the fascist South African regime, enabling it to skip the stages in the obtaining of operational nuclear weapons. More specifically, Israel is in the position to help South Africa develop the triggering device for her nuclear weapons. In fact, with Israeli aid, South African atomic scientists and engineers will be able to considerably cut down the period normally necessary for achieving operational nuclear devices. This new alarming development is to be feared. South Africa has the raw materials, advanced technology and the material means to become a nuclear power in a very short period of time. With Israeli aid, that period of time will be even shorter. Moreover, once Pretoria will have received the nuclear plants recently negotiated with France, she will be able to multiply by 100 her nuclear capacity production. As I've said before, I fear South Africa will manufacture nuclear weapons in a record time, thus surprising the entire African continent. Once this becomes a *fait accompli*, the struggle against South Africa will have acquired entirely new and foreboding consequences.

AFRISCOPE: Once South Africa is ready to take the offensive, no doubt using nuclear weapons, isn't it conceivable that Israel would equally join Pretoria in a two-pronged assault against the black continent?

DIOP: South Africa, no doubt, wouldn't hesitate to commit nuclear genocide on the black peoples of Africa. In fact, it's certain that such a plan is in the back of the minds of the white supremacist leaders of that black country. Could we foresee the possibility that Israel, from the Middle East, and South Africa, from the southern tip of the continent, would combine their forces to launch a nuclear attack on black Africa with the aim of exterminating its peoples? An answer to that question is, perforce, hazardous. . . . . Yet, in view of recent events, we must pay the most serious attention to strategic possibilities of that nature. . . . .

AFRISCOPE: Do you think that Israel's position in the Middle East vis-à-vis Arabs is analogous to the position of white South Africa in respect of Africans?

DIOP: Within the Arab world the state of Israel finds itself in an entirely different context. My opinion is that whether one likes it or not, the state of Israel will in the long run be absorbed by the Arab world. True, there is a technological gap between both at present. As long as a portion of the Arab world remains at a nomadic stage, Israeli technology will of course make itself felt. In that context, Israel will continue to appear as a western prolongation in the Middle East. However, Middle Eastern Arab countries will develop technologically, closing the present gap. The state of Israel will then be completely absorbed demographically by the Arab World. Therefore, in the long run, the Arab-Israeli conflict will abate. In fact, if the state of Israel would right now desist from its bellicose attitude and would seek a viable *modus vivendi* with her Arab neighbors, Arab-Israeli peace would come about very quickly. My opinion is that the Arab-Israeli conflict will necessarily evolve in the direction of a peaceful solution acceptable to both parties. This is all the more likely given the historical context underlying the relationship of these two Semitic peoples.

I foresee a time in the near future when the Arab and Israeli ethnic groups which have a very old common historical past in the Middle East, will peacefully resolve their differences. Both peoples belong to the same Semitic branch. The defeat of Israel can already be determined by the geographic context of the Middle East. Israel finds herself too isolated in that region not to ultimately seek a peaceful solution. Arab and Israeli cultures are very close to one another. Such affinities extend into the realm of religion. As we know, the Muslim and Judaic religions emerged from a common source, from practically a common people and from the same geographical area. Eventually, both Semitic groups will again fuse. None of the foregoing considerations apply to South Africa in regards to the rest of Africa.

AFRISCOPE: The aim of Pan-Arabism, as defined by Gamal Abdul Nasser, is the formation of a federation of North African and Asian Arab states as a single political and economic entity. Doesn't that project conflict with that of a federal continental African state?

DIOP: The way I see it is that there already exists a continental African consciousness. For lack of a precise Pan-African project, however, certain North African Arab countries might be tempted to group separately with Asian Arabs. In face of the disunity and uncertainty characteristic of intra-African politics, North African Arab states might indeed be instinctively tempted to seek fusion with their Middle Eastern brethren. Nevertheless, I believe that a continent-wide African consciousness does exist already. When you go to North Africa, to Algeria, Morocco, Egypt, for example, you can detect an African *behaviour*. We can build on this as long as an effort is made to forget many painful things of the past. Africans to the north and south of the continent must think in terms of uniting because it is in their global interests to do so. If we can overcome prejudices and fears through information and open discussion, then the advantages of a continental federal state are apparent. We might nuance our opinion on the steps to be taken towards establishing such a state. To begin with, there could be a federation of the Maghreb (Morocco, Algeria, Tunisia, Libya, Egypt) on the one hand, while on the other, a federation of all the sub-Saharan African countries. A confederation of these two federations could then be envisioned. With time, both entities could fuse so as to arrive at a true continental federal state. This is possible. Hence, the North and the South could be federated independently, then subsequently fused. A lot of effort would have to be expended in destroying prejudices, fears and susceptibilities and creating the basis for a common understanding between North African Arabs and sub-Saharan Africans.

AFRISCOPE: Nevertheless, Arab countries are increasingly forming exclusive organizations of all kinds from which sub-Saharan African states are excluded but which include Asian and North African Arabs. In fact, there are no less than 25 such organizations. The most recently formed are ALECSO (an exclusively Arab Unesco) and CASTARAB (or standing Arab Scientific Conference). Besides, isn't there a discrepancy in North African Arab states being members simultaneously of the Arab League and the O.A.U.?

DIOP: I won't deny that there are great difficulties in bringing Arab North Africa and sub-Saharan Africa together in a federal continental political union. Difficulties do exist. I still continue to believe, however, that an African continental state is vital to the survival of all Africans, to the North and South of the Sahara. Ways and means must be found to overcome the obstacles in its path. . . . .

AFRISCOPE: Supposing the assumption of a common historical destiny between North African and Asian Arabs proves stronger than the pan-African common interests you speak of?

DIOP: If despite goodwill on our part, North African Arabs were to refuse a continental federation, then nothing should stand in the way of the formation of an exclusively sub-Saharan continental federation. However, I feel that if the perspective of a continental federation were clearly defined, backed by a strong sub-Saharan wish in this direction, then North African states would have to reconsider their position on that score, when if prior to that they were thinking along other lines. Should this not be the case, then black Africa couldn't be blamed in the future for grouping along purely sub-Saharan lines. The fault would not be ours. Nevertheless, I think we must push the experience to its logical conclusions. . . . .

AFRISCOPE: Gamal Abdul Nasser's project was that of an "Arab Nation" from the Nile to the Euphrates. Egypt tried to federate with Syria and northern Yemen. Libya has now taken up the project.

DIOP: The very failure of the Egypt/Syria federation shows how difficult it is for African states to look outside of Africa for a federation. In fact, that failure should be a warning; a political federation involving states situated in Africa cannot be extra-African. Nothing prevents North African Arab states, within the context of a continental African state, to maintain cultural contacts with Arabs of Asia, with whom they share a common language. Again, it would be as if black Africans were prevented from establishing close cultural links with blacks of the Americas and the rest of the black world. One thing is to establish cultural ties and another to form a *political* federation. This is absolutely clear. Our objectives must be the creation of an economic and politically federated continent. All Africans who express the desire to build such a federation, irrespective of whether they be from the North or sub-Saharan Africa, must be welcomed on an equal footing. I am convinced that if vigorous propaganda were made in this sense, we would end up with very positive results. . . . .

AFRISCOPE: However, Col. Muammar Qaddafi of Libya and others still agitate along these lines.

DIOP: People must have entire freedom to talk and expound their views even when these ideas are not realizable. My opinion is that too many divergencies exist for such a project to materialize. The concept of an Arab state from the Atlantic to the Persian Gulf is devoid of any economic base, whereas I can very well conceive of North African Arab states joining the rest of Africa to form a viable political economic entity. As I said, membership in such a continental political arrangement should not prevent North African Arabs from continuing to entertain close cultural links with the Arabs of Asia. By the same token, a continental political federation including North African Arabs should in no way prevent black Africans from entertaining the closest cultural links with blacks of the Americas, Oceanic and Asia. It is absolutely indispensable to make the difference between relationships based on a cultural continuum and those based on a geo-political entity. . . . .

AFRISCOPE: Suppose Asian and North African Arabs short-circuited black Africa and agreed to set up what Qaddafi has been agitating for.

DIOP: If that was ever to be the case, then, it would be explicitly clear that a federation with black Africa was being rejected. If we black Africans take steps to include North African Arabs into a continental federation and the latter prefer instead to elaborate organic political ties with Arabs of Asia, this would be tantamount to a rebuff. If north African states, rather than looking to black Africa in a natural partnership, preferred a federation with Asian Arabs extending to the Persian Gulf, *then we would be entirely justified to organize ourselves in an exclusively sub-Saharan federation.* In such an eventuality, no one could accuse sub-Saharan Africans of being guilty of exclusivism, since their appeals to the North would have been refused. However, I do not really envision this being the case. Rather, my feeling is that the necessary ideological and propaganda work in favour of an all inclusive continental federation has to be undertaken as of now.

AFRISCOPE: Many Africans argue that the very cohesion of the Arabs as an ethno-cultural entity would pose the problem of their dominating any confederal arrangement.

DIOP: Sub-Saharan Africans must realize that they have nothing to lose culturally, politically or otherwise in a federation which includes Arab North Africa. Black Africa would not be an appendage of the Arab world in such a federation. There is a distinct African identity which can and ought to be continually developed. In the past 20 years a lot of work has been done in terms of reinforcing the cultural, linguistic and historical identity of African peoples. The black world has reinforced its cultural personality. As a consequence of this development, our cultural, linguistic and historical personality can no longer be strangled in any way by cultural contacts with other peoples. The time has come for us to abandon our complexes and work in favour of a union that is favourable to all Africans. That's the crux of the matter.

In the final analysis, what is really at the core of the controversy of whether North and sub-Saharan Africans can join in a common federation is the question: Are we culturally ready to meet with the Arab world? Are we culturally ready to join in a common federation without surrendering an inch of our cultural, linguistic and historical identity as black Africans? This is the real question. My answer is affirmative. Black Africa has recovered its cultural personality to an extent and vigour which makes it impossible for anyone to strangle it. What remains to be done is the day-to-day work of solidifying and redefining in all areas the contours of this distinct personality. Considering all of the efforts which have been accomplished in sub-Saharan Africa in terms of the restoration of our historical and cultural identity, Africans no longer have to fear being dominated by the Arabs. . . . .

AFRISCOPE: Don't you think that another serious stumbling block in the way of the constitution of a continental state would appear to be the entrenchment of staunchly egoistic neocolonial regimes both in North and sub-Saharan Africa?

DIOP: Definitely. It's obvious that once we eliminate difficulties of a subjective nature—that is, whether North and sub-Saharan Africans do or do not want to federate—there remain the objective obstacles of a political nature. The egoistic nature of certain political regimes, north and south of the Sahara, is such that they are terrified at the idea of a continental African state. The stranglehold of alien economic interests is not foreign to that fear. The neocolonial character of such regimes is therefore an objective factor in the way of constituting a continental federation.

African unity, I feel, will come from the base and develop as an undercurrent to the present political sterility and economic stagnancy rampant on our continent. A feeling of general insecurity, generated by the ineptitude of African regimes in dealing with the most crucial issues—including that of South Africa—will result in the masses entering the picture sooner or later. . . . As generalized insecurity spreads, no African regime will be able to prevent the masses from seeing that the ineptitude of their own governments is linked to this general insecurity. At that point, I feel the masses will find within their own ranks the type of political vanguards, made up of young, altruistic and politically motivated Africans, to unleash a powerful continent-wide movement. This political undercurrent would eventually be forced to sweep away the objective obstacles standing in the way of a continental African federation.

AFRISCOPE: Ideological bloc bi-polarity seems to be installing itself in African politics. What ideological preference, in your view, would the united foreign policy of a continental African state reflect?

DIOP: A continental African state must, of necessity, be non-aligned. Africa then will be a continent *with its own specific political personality.* In time, Africa would have to play a world role. *A continental African state must be an end in itself!* it would even be humiliating to conceive of a continental African state being towed as a vessel by any other state, government or bloc. A continental African state would entertain relations with all other countries on a perfectly equal footing. How else could Africa lift itself to the level of the other powerful states and deal with the rest of the world from a position of true independence?

Today, only three states can be considered as independent: the United States, the Soviet Union, China. These three states are organized on a continental basis. That's no accident. Significantly, Europe is now trying desperately to federate itself into one continental state. Highly industrial and technological European states are trying to elect a pan-European parliament, establish an economic common market, attempting to unify their defence and foreign policies and preaching in favour of the continental federal approach! That's an edifying example for us Africans. I'm even hoping that the European states succeed and thus show the way to Africa, considering that African leaderships tend to ape European initiatives. Since Africa is so prone to imitating Europe for the better or the worse, that's one initiative we can start imitating as of now. For once, it would be a positive imitation! Even Europe is showing the way and attesting to the fact that the 19th century mini-states have become an anachronism in our epoch. A great political future is in store for Europe because all European problems are being seen by European leaderships as *continental* European problems. Why is it any different for Africa? Why should the underdeveloped mini-states be valid for Africa when the super-developed mini-states are invalid for Europe? Only the blindest form of selfishness could restrict the vision of African leaderships to the confines of their mini-states. Even a lucid selfishness would dictate that *the continental solution is the only one. Only this can prevent the voice of Africa from merely being an echo of some other state or bloc.*

—III—
CULTURE, NEGRITUDE, AND THE AFRICAN PERSONALITY

AFRISCOPE: What is the actual mission of culture?
DIOP: Survival and creativity. Man must create to survive. To create he must ensure his survival.

Collective historical consciousness is one of man's chief means of survival and a source of creation. Destroy or stifle it and the chances for the survival of a people become questionable. The cultural personality of Africa is inseparable from the restoration of our collective historical consciousness. Because most people are vaguely conscious of their local historical past they end up flirting with their own past. Most of us are not even equipped to systematically refer to the Nile Valley for an understanding of either the present-day or ancient structures of our societies. Yet, we can make very little headway in understanding our cultures, languages and social structures without a thorough knowledge of the many facets of ancient Egyptian civilization. Ancient black Egypt was in every sense the actual cradle of our cultures.

Without a systematic reference to Egypt, there can be no true cultural renaissance in Africa. Afterall, what is our objective if it is not that of recover-

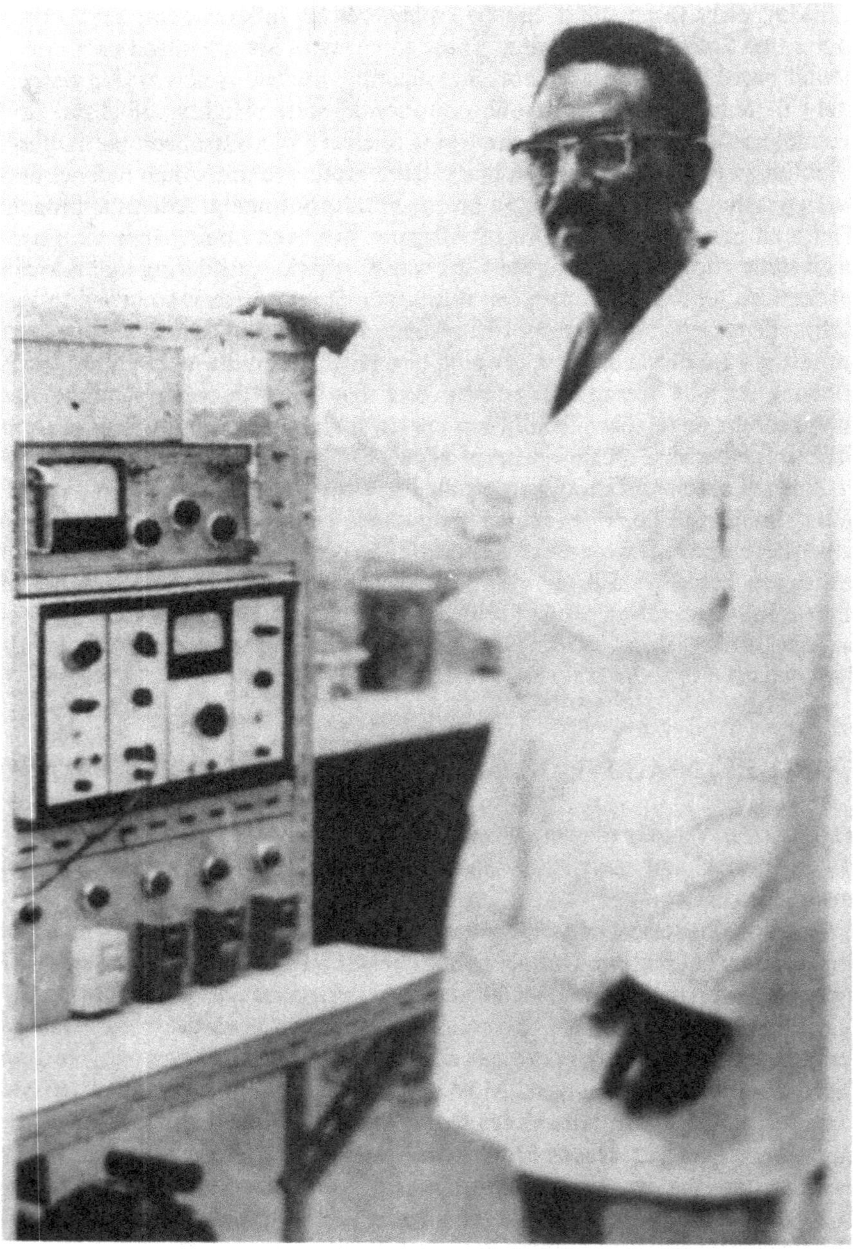

Dr. Diop standing before a machine in his Radio Carbon Laboratory at I.F.A.N. University, Dakar.

ing and promoting the *creativity* of our peoples? Man's mission is *creation.* African renaissance, black renaissance, is inseparable from the restoration of the black world's creativity.

To assume his destiny, man must be a creator irrespective of his race. The loss of our national sovereignty strangled our independent creativity. Today, as black people are slowly recovering their national sovereignty, we are obliged to free ourselves from all forms of cultural alienation. Without that internal recovery and psychic self-appraisal, very little can be accomplished. The recovery of political sovereignty is merely one aspect of the question. Economic sovereignty is another. Psychic autonomy is yet another. All three must combine in a dynamic renovative effort. These are the terms by which I define the African and world black renaissance.

The restoration of the historical consciousness of black and African peoples, with all its implications, necessarily leads to a veritable reversal of perspectives and to a fundamental transformation of our cultural relationship with the rest of the world. Black peoples have been weighed on the scales of history by others and been found wanting.

Yet, once we awaken to the historical realities through a scientific approach to history, we find that the very people who were considered to be historical debtors were actually the historical creditors. From ancient Egypt, from the oldest world civilization, came the scientifiic and technological knowledge, the religious ideas and cultural, artistic contributions which shaped the earliest cultures of the European world. The day when Africans and blacks in general will impose that point of view, a view supported by scientifically verifiable historical data, the self-image of blacks and the warped image that others entertain about blacks will have to undergo a most profound revision. It will mean that an entire vision of the universe will have to be changed. The hour is therefore approaching when other peoples will have to divest themselves, even against their conscious will, of the falsifications and lies that have buried the original and unique contributions of the black man to world history. To that end we must work, fully equipped with the tools of science in every conceivable discipline. We should never lose sight of the fact that the restoration of the cultural personality of African and black peoples in general can only be achieved through *struggle.*

AFRISCOPE: Many people attack Negritude as a deceptive concept. Others defend it as a philosophy of African and black rehabilitation. You are among its critics. Yet, all of your works deal with the historical, cultural and social rehabilitation of the black man. What, then, is your concept of Negritude?

DIOP: I really wouldn't like to get into that! There are just too many emotional and conflicting issues involved. It would be too long to get into such a complex question. . . . .

AFRISCOPE: Precisely, this is why your comments on it are vitually important. It's an important issue.

DIOP: If we want to talk about Negritude, the case of a man like Aime Cesaire must be treated all by itself. Cesaire is an exceptional literary genius. He is undoubtedly one of the greatest creative minds of the black world. He's a man who lives his philosophy. He's a man truly committed to the cause of the black world and to the progress of oppressed mankind. He's an unflinching anti-colonialist. Because of this, Cesaire was practically the only one to have played a decisive and personal role in the mobilization of the black students who were in France during the colonial period. He summoned all of us to our feet in the struggle against the colonial oppressors. At political meetings we were all captivated by Cesaire, his clear thinking and lucid appraisal of the colonial question. Cesaire was always physically present at our meetings, alongside all those who were fighting colonialism. In fact, all of us used to talk about Cesaire, his genius, his sincerity and devotion to the black and anti-colonialist struggle. We weren't talking about Negritude. Cesaire was magnetic, vigorous and poetic. Cesaire created the term *Negritude*, and at the time we devoured his works.

Negritude, as it became known, was originally a West Indian creation; Africans confiscated and monopolized it in post-colonial times! During the post-colonial epoch an entirely different interpretation was given the term Negritude. Under this blanket term a flood of literature emerged, the content of which was clearly deceptive. In fact, as far as I can remember, the term Negritude was only applied to a literary or political current after Jean Paul Sartre's *Black Orpheus* written in 1948. Cesaire coined the term but prior to the publication of Sartre's book I knew of no political or literary current which went under the name of Negritude. This is an important element. Actually, what was done in the post-colonial epoch was to gather the political anti-colonial black movements and writings of the 1930's and 40's and place them under the blanket term Negritude. This was done only after, and as a consequence of Jean Paul Sartre's theorizations in *Black Orpheus*.

In the 1940's, along with Cesaire, there were men of the caliber of Leon Damas, who was also anti-colonialist. However, Damas' role was smaller than that of Cesaire, who in fact dwarfed everyone else with his intense commitment and action against colonialism. At that time there were other black intellectuals in Paris who were defending the colonial status quo with philosophical arguments. Their writings were indigestible to the mass of black students in Paris at that time. The difficulty today when evoking Negritude resides in the fact that certain people use Cesaire as a cover to fend off attacks from those who consider the post-colonial utilization of Negritude as an obvious imposture. This is why all discussions on Negritude must begin with a separate appraisal of Ceasire, the man, the literary genius, the clairvoyant political agitator and determined anti-colonialist. All of us who knew Cesaire during those years and who have continued to relate to him since then have an immense respect for his work, his integrity and lasting contribution to the emancipation of black people. Cesaire cannot be associated wth anything other than the struggle against colonialism and the emancipation of black people. When I talk about Cesaire, I don't talk about Negritude; I talk about Cesaire, the man I knew and respected, the genius, the fighter. Through his actions and works, Cesaire exercised a personal influence on all those who came into contact with him. He continues to do so today over the younger generation.

Cesaire showed where there was a definite cultural alienation among blacks, more pronounced in the West Indies than in Africa, which required special attention in the struggle against colonialism. His aim therefore was to recover the lost cultural personality of colonized black societies. He attempted this through poetry. Hence, he extolled the psychic factor as a necessary component of a new African cultural personality and national consciousness. Let's say he rediscovered, or introduced, the psychic and cultural factor into the struggle of black peoples to regain their national sovereignty usurped by colonialism. Cesaire thus wrote about how the black world lives, feels and suffers. He attached importance to the differential psychology of Africans, blacks, as opposed to Europeans. The poetry of Cesaire, his literary creation, centered on the convulsions of the 'black soul' when subjected to the oppressive conditions of colonialism. Militant action was attached to the new form of poetry among black intellectuals. Cesaire's poetry was definitely not an abstract literary effort but was rooted in the suffering of Africans, blacks. . . . In a famous line of his extremely sensitive, beautiful, violent *Cahier d'un retour au pays natal,* Cesaire wrote:

> My negritude is not a rock, its deafness hurled against the clamor of the day.
> My negritude is not a film of dead water on the dead eye of the earth.
> My negritude is neither a tower nor a cathedral.
> It plunges into the red flesh of the earth.
> It plunges into the burning flesh of the sky.
> It pierces the opaque prostration by its upright patience.

Published in 1947, these lines were the words of a profoundly committed militant. The man who wrote these lines was loved, respected and revered by all those who dreamt of freedom and independence and were working toward that goal. Jacques Rabemananjara of Madagascar, Leon Damas of Guyana, and many others were among them. They all spoke and wrote in moving terms about the 'black soul' and the suffering of black people. There were many West Indians among them. These militant intellectuals, Africans or West Indians, were therefore talking, writing and acting within the context of the anti-colonial struggle. We weren't talking then about Negritude.

AFRISCOPE: In other words, your scientific researches were spurred by the existence of a colonial order and by the cultural and psychic disorders analyzed by Frantz Fanon?

DIOP: That's correct. But that motivation wasn't called Negritude then. When I started writing *Black Nations and Culture,* I approached the problem of black subjugation from a different perspective than the literary anti-colonialist of the 1940's. Not being a poet, nor a literary man, I did not approach it from the psychic angle which had made Cesaire's poetry such an irresistible and cutting weapon in the awakening of an African anti-colonial consciousness. I realized that the cultural personality of a people, of any people, was made up of three interrelated factors. The *psychic* factor. The *linguistic* factor. The *historical* factor. I didn't invent that notion. Others had outlined it before. I merely saw it to be a fact. Hence, my efforts were geared towards the restoration of the *linguistic* and *historical* personality of black Africans. The poets of what was later called Negritude had emphasized the psychic element which is undoubtedly one of the components of the cultural personality of a people. . . . .

I understood my scientific researches at a time when the prevalent and accepted data concerning the historical past of black societies was a misleading one. My cultural approach was scientific, rather than poetic. Once on scientific terrain I had only objective phenomena to analyze. I realized that out of the three components of the cultural identity of a people, *only two could be apprehended scientifically, i.e. the linguistic and historical factors.* I therefore laboured towards restoring the historical and linguistic personality of black peoples. I also worked towards the restoration of our common historical past by attaching primordial significance to the oldest and most accomplished civilization elaborated by black African peoples: ancient Egypt! Once I had realized that the collective personality, the cultural identify of a people, centered on three components-linguistic, historical annd psychic—I concentrated my scientific efforts along the two lines which could be grasped objectively by scientific research. That has been my approach to the cultural rehabilitation of the black man and of black societies.

AFRISCOPE: The difference, then, in your approach to the rehabilitation of the black man and that of the Negritude poets of the 1940's is in your emphasis on sociology, linguistics and history?

DIOP: Exactly! By describing the political and social structures inherited from our common historical past, and which reflect the conditions in which our ancestors lived, I was able to make a contribution to our rehabilitation. I was not, however, describing any sort of permanent state in man, since human beings are conditioned by their social and physical environment. Once you change the social environment, even a black man who has been conditioned by a communitarian life-style can become the most individualistic and self-centered being. Consequently, my work in history, sociology and linguistics kept to the path of objective verifiable reality. By throwing light on the falsifications to which the historical past of the black man has been subjected, these historical, sociological and linguistic studies serve to reinforce the cultural personality of Africans. The cultural renaissance of our people is inconceivable outside of the restoration of both our historical past and our languages to a privileged position as the vehicles of modern education, technology, science and the creative sensibility of our people.

As long as the historical path linking us to our ancestors is not understood, critically appraised, legitimized, we will be unable to build a new culture. To this end the retrieval of our national languages is foremost.

A systematic policy in favour of their growth, the inclusion of a modern technological and scientific lexicon, can no longer be eluded. The path which leads us to our ancestors and which led our ancestors to us cannot be understood without a systematic reference to ancient Egyptian civilization. In fact, it is impossible to elaborate a new body of social studies without a systematic reference to ancient Egypt. Ancient Egypt plays for Africa and blacks in general the same role which Greco-Latin culture plays for the western world. From the outset, my researches were centred on ancient Egypt, its culture, language, religion and science. I demonstrated the profound links binding the ancient Egyptians to modern black Africans, not only racially and culturally, but also linguistically.

AFRISCOPE: As a literary current, would you say that Negritude has neglected the objective basis of society in favour of the purely subjective world?

DIOP: That's certainly so in the case of post-colonial 'Negritude'! In fact, I see a total incompatibility between the formal defence of African culture on the one hand, and the systematic refusal on the other to adopt concrete measures to develop our national languages. Those who are incapable of solving this problem can do nothing for African culture. They merely embrace African culture to better smother it. Their attitude shows them to be impostors. Take a country like Senegal, for example, where 95% of the population speaks Wolof. How can one understand the fact that some people are panic-stricken when the adoption of Wolof is proposed as the official national language? If the Senegalese people can't be helped to retrieve and develop their linguistic unity *now*, what use is there to talk about defending African culture? In contrast to this, the attitude of someone like Julius Nyerere is consequential. Without rhetorics or fanfare, he elevated Swahili to the status of a national and governmental language.

Flight from one's own language is the quickest shortcut to cultural alienation. For Africa this has been a monumental problem, but it has to be tackled head on. I have attempted to do this in my works and my most thorough contribution on this subject will soon be available *(The Genetic Kinship of*

Pharonic Egyptian and African Languages). Too often we talk about culture without grabbing the cow by the horns, as the saying goes. Why? Simply because we are contented with compromises that avoid the adoption of a radical stance in face of cultural problems. Few of us dare go to the roots of the problem via a scientific approach. As a result, many of those who *talk* about promoting our national languages limit their intent to the domain of folklore. When they want to deal with serious questions, they turn to the languages of. . . . .Europe!

AFRISCOPE: Kwame Nkrumah had opposed his concept of 'African Personality' to the concept of 'Negritude.' Are both concepts antithetical or do they converge anywhere?

DIOP: They converge in the sense that both deal in generalities! We must get down to the facts, to the objective apprehendable realities. When we talk about personality, meaning the personality of collective groups, we can only mean a *cultural personality.* And what is the basis of the cultural personality of a people, African or otherwise, if not a historical, psychic and linguistic self-consciousness? These three elements are the constituent elements of a people's cultural personality or identity. They are not static factors, but factors conditioned by man's social and physical environment. You have already seen my own approach to the problem of restoring the historical foundations of African cultures through scientific research in the fields of history and linguistics. Moreover, you can also see where that approach has also clarified what is called the particular sensibility of the black man, or 'black soul.' I have tried determining the nature of the black particularity in history and to ascertain the way in which the 'black soul' or 'black sensibility' has influenced the material existence and creativity of black peoples by using the *structures* evolved by ancient black societies as a basis. Consequently, I analyzed family structures, clannic and tribal organization and finally the territorial state. These structures are the objective reflection of precise historical conditions and also of what is called the 'black soul.' So, my approach to the 'black soul' has been through history, linguistics and the material structures of ancient black societies. Rather than deal in generalities, we must know what the 'black soul' is because its *our* soul. The way I saw it at the beginning was that Africa's soul had been 'stolen' and could only be retrieved through a scientific approach.

In synthesis, we cannot oppose 'African Personality' to 'Negritude' since both deal with only one of the three components determining the cultural identify of a people. People *live* their culture. The roots of their culture are inseparable from their linguistic structure and historical past. That's the way I approach the question of culture.

—IV—
ETHNICITY AND NATIONAL CONSCIOUSNESS

AFRISCOPE: A constant theme in your works is the emphasis on culture, language and historical consciousness as the kernels of national and continental unity. How do you see the problem of ethnicity, so-called 'tribalism,' in that context?

DIOP: As African societies continue to evolve, tribalism is being superseded everywhere and must progressively die out in the consciousnesss of all Africans. Tribalism is a primary category in the general evolution of a society, following immediately after the state of the *clan*. It belongs therefore to a form of socio-political organization and is observable in the evolution of all human societies. During the pre-colonial era, when large territorial states emerged, tribal organization had already given way to the monarchical phase, this being the next stage of socio-political organization. Colonization and slave trade helped to retribalize Africa.

In the present context of evolution of African societies, tribal consciousness is receding. Africa cannot be built on the basis of a tribal consciousness. Henceforth, larger communities are called for. Detribalization is therefore a progressive process which must be encouraged everywhere. The individual must be encouraged to detach himself from the purely tribal community and become a citizen of a much larger socio-political community. . . . .

AFRISCOPE: However, in many black countries, much of what officially passes for attempts at eradicating 'tribalism' and promoting national consciousness translates itself in reality as being the monopoly of state power by an ethno-cultural and social elite which belongs to an easily identifiable ethnic group.

DIOP: That's true . . . and dangerous! It denotes a form of egoism which is presently blocking the establishment of a federal continental state of Africa. Under no circumstances should an ethnic group be allowed to monopolize power in a country. That's the worst way of going about promoting the fusion of all the ethnic groups within a country. When an ethnic group monopolizes power in order to promote its particular interests, it is working towards a greater retribalization of Africa. This runs counter to the general progress of all African peoples and is detrimental to the best interests of Africa. Wherever such behaviour prevails, it must be unhesitatingly condemned. Whether we realize it or not, we are all part of a larger African human community. We must find the correct way of achieving the fusion of the various tribal individualities within the framework of the larger community. I feel it is in that direction that history has been pointing.

AFRISCOPE: How best to promote a sincere, unselfish fusion of the various ethnic communities?
DIOP: A dynamic utilization of ethnological studies, a constant scientific and frank explanation of the issues involved would be immensely helpful in this regard. Once the various ethnic groups discover how many binding and profound cultural, linguistic, social and historical ties exist between them, psychological barriers would begin to collapse. Ethnic groups often do not realize the extent to which they share kinship with the languages, culture, traditions and historical socio-political structures evolved by communities they have come to view as rivals!

African unity, as I have advocated in all of my works, must be strengthened by all available means of scientific inquiry. When I began studying ethnology I saw it as a sort of weapon to be used on behalf of African unity. In a short study ("Introduction to the Study of Migrations in Central and West Africa. Identification of the Nilotic Cradle of the Senegalese People"), I set out to prove the profound ethnic kinship existing between all of the tribes of the upper Nile (in the area of Nuba, northern Uganda and Lake Albert) and the populations of West Africa and the Equatorial Basin. I analyzed factors such as linguistic structures, clannic names and a variety of other ethnological elements to demonstrate that point. The cultural, sociological and political significance of promoting such studies is self-evident. They reveal the profound kinship binding populations which are presently separated by enormous geographic distances. Conducted among ethnic groups in close proximity to one another, the immediate benefits of such inquiries are obvious.

Ethnic groups tend to see themselves as self-enclosed communities. For example, are the *Luos* of Kenya aware of their close kinship to the *Luos* of Senegal? Prolonged scientific efforts must be made for the various African ethnic groups to discover the profound overall kinship which makes them part of a wider spatial and sociocultural community. In fact, we ourselves individually tend to be ignorant of the ancient bonds of kinship that unite the various ethnic groups living on the continent of Africa. *Rigorous ethnological studies must be promoted and inserted within a new dynamics of unity without resorting to ideological gimmicks.* We must not deviate from the terrain of science. The strength and relevance of ethnological studies of the type I have referred to is to be seen in that what they reveal is factually true.

Ignorance plays a greater role than is commonly thought in the maintenance of a comparementalized tribal consciousness. Believing itself to be a self-enclosed world, the ethnic group which seizes power is bound to pursue its own sectional interests. That's the crux of the matter! Either we close our eyes to these realities because it serves our own particular interests to do so, or we conform our behaviour and thinking to the latest scientific data. The conclusions of rigorous scientific investigations must be integrated into a new type of consciousness. National consciousness does not arise out of a vacuum. Today, political, cultural and national consciousness must be linked to scientific research. *A novel cultural and political function must be assigned to a renovated African ethnology: that of revealing to all African ethnic communities the basis of their common overall kinship.*

AFRISCOPE: What type of political structures favour or retard the growth of national consciousness and inter-ethnic unity?

DIOP: Regardless of the form of organization we seek to achieve, the principle which should guide us must center on the most scrupulous respect for the greatest possible degree of freedom for the various groups. We must avoid solutions based on coercion. *It should be clearly understood that it is in the very interests of the majority of the constituent groups within a federal arrangement that the federal structures themselves not be challenged as such. The permanency of federal structures must be inviolable.* This principle should be upheld whether the case be a national federation like Nigeria, a regional federation, or a continental federation. Once a federal structure is set up, it should become irreversible. Once federal structures are elaborated, confirmed and consolidated, secession of any kind must be prevented.

Secession must be discouraged within the framework of continental, regional or national federal arrangements. However, its counterpart must be the granting of cultural freedom and autonomy to all communities. Africa must be protected against anarchy. No particular group can lastingly profit from it and all groups will permanently lose by it. While Africa must be protected from anarchy, we cannot condone the other extreme which leads to the stifling of the cultural freedom and autonomy of the various communities inhabiting the continent. Each community must be able to enjoy to the fullest a freedom compatible with its desire to fulfill itself culturally and linguistically.

Each ethnic community in Africa once enjoyed a continuous territorial base. Colonialism created a new and difficult situation when it drew arbitrary borders. The independent states have ratified these as intangible. Yet, that situation has segmented many ethnic communities. Take the Hausas, for example. We find them split between French-speaking Niger and English-speaking Nigeria. The Yorubas have suffered a similar fate, split between Nigeria and Benin and so on. How to solve that problem, when to preserve a minimum of peace, the intangibility of border delimitations inherited from colonialism has been upheld as a sacred principle?

As long as continental union is not achieved through a federal arrangement, any modification of the present borders inevitably leads to serious conflicts. *Within the framework of an irreversible regional or continental political and economic federation of African countries, that problem no longer has any reason for existing. In such a context, nothing should prevent the Hausas, Yorubas, etc., from reconstituting their former territorial and cultural base and enjoying the fullest cultural and linguistic autonomy.* If structured irreversibly, regional or continental political and economic federation renders former colonial border demarcations useless. That's the only way to reverse the negative trend introduced by the colonial partition of Africa.

AFRISCOPE: Past conquests and oppression make up for a present situation wherein residual inequalities and unresolved historical conflicts maintain a latent situation of tension within a multi-ethnic context. Often, the ruling group of such societies has emerged from the ethnic community manifestly favoured by the old colonial masters.

DIOP: The problem is quite complex. . . . . *It's a catastrophe to have selfish group interests—whether the group be ethnic or social—masked by a facade of pseudo nationalism! That's a dangerous phenomenon.* A young, dynamic leadership, animated by the purest patriotic motives and sentiments, can bring about viable political structures anywhere in Africa. That's the core of the problem. Only the most patriotic of sentiments and most unselfish of political behaviours can save Africa in this sense. Otherwise, there would be ample room for a terrible pessimism!

AFRISCOPE: In your opinion, where does the right of self-determination start and end in multi-ethnic societies as those characterizing the black world?

DIOP: That right begins wherever the need for a minimum of freedom is not guaranteed. *Each ethnic group should have ample latitude to organize on an autonomous basis. Internal autonomy must be allowed each ethnic group. Each ethnic community should enjoy the freedom to expand and organize itself on a cultural basis. There should be no attempts to stifle an ethnic community under the guise of promoting national union and harmony. African unity should not be a monolithic unity based on a draconian centralism.* Account has to be taken of differences, of inequalities existing between the various ethnic groups. *We must aim at a form of federal structures flexible enough to preserve fundamental freedoms and cultural autonomy, and strong enough to safeguard the interests of the African continent.* This notion applies to federal associations at any level, whether local federations (Nigeria), regional federations or a continental federation.

The right to self-determination ends when it is evident that the result of its exercise will be anarchy. Anarchy must be avoided at all costs. Anarchy is the reference point. The aggressive forces which are working against Africa would like to dissolve African unity. We must fight against the explosive forces of fragmentation. Our attitude must be the inverse of those forces and in favour of a unitary, democratic Africa. I am against tribal breakdown. There must be a link which surpasses the tribal community, uniting all of the ethnic communities within the borders of a constituted state. That link ought to be *national*, with enough elbow room left for each group to fulfill itself.

AFRISCOPE: Looking at things closer, we see that colonial domination implied not only the conquest of tribes but of nations. The latter in most cases were grouped under an umbrella colonial state but continued being nations, even though deprived of their sovereignty. Consequently, decolonization has also had the effect of reactivating a national, as opposed to *tribal*, aspiration among these conquered nations. Are we to view that aspiration as a manifestation of 'tribalism' rather than *nationalism*?

DIOP: Had the evolution of Africa not been arrested by the impact of imperialism, we would undoubtedly have wide multi-national political structures today. The political evolution of the pre-colonial African states was going towards large spatial structures. *If we could bring about a federal state of Africa, that sort of problem would find a convenient solution insasmuch as the present-day political boundaries between states would progressively fade away and become no more than administrative borders.* Their modification would pose less political and/or psychological problems. *A federal state would have the necessary authority to modify borders in conformity with the best interests of present-day Africa within the framework of a federal continental state, nothing would stand in the way of having the great ethnic groups coincide with national, linguistic or territorial structures. Old nations could be restructured along modern lines without that fact being disruptive in the least. In fact, the organization of Africa on a wide scale could be done much more rationally, since the ideal situation would have to have territorial delineations coincide with the great ethnic and linguistic groups of Africa.* This need not degenerate into each miniscule ethnic groups becoming an administrative entity, but the inverse is certainly a rational way of seeing things on a continental scale.

A greater stability would emerge in Africa if administrative delimitations were made to correspond everywhere with large linguistically homogeneous ethnic groupings. This could only be possible in a wide political federation where federal macro-unity would no longer be called into question by any of the constituent groups. *In the final analysis, all present-day ethnic and national conflicts in Africa are rendered possible by the absence of a continental federal state. It is the narrow, straight jacketed framework of our present individualistic states which is at the base of all such conflicts—from border disputes and clashes, ethnic and linguistic rivalries to attempts at secession.*

Without the various linguistic communities having to give up their own languages, a continental language could be quickly adopted by a federal state of Africa. Border demarcations would then amount to no more than administrative delineations which could be easily modified. Take, for instance, the United States. A modification of inter-state borderlines neither creates a state of national emergency nor threatens the executive federal authority. At most, a referendum on the issue would be called for. Hence, the important factor to consider is that any federal arrangement must be flexible and democratic enough to allow the greatest amount of freedom to all the constituent communities.

AFRISCOPE: Do the political and juridical institutions imported wholesale from Europe and imposed on black societies impede, retard or accelerate the

process of national or continental union and socio-cultural democratization?
DIOP: We can't look at the situation in terms of an *impasse.* Precisely, it is in the process of contact with the outside world that we are able to judge the virtues and vitality of African structures. Historical chances brought Europe in contact with Africa. That contact has continued for four centuries now. This necessarily implied profound modifications. Throughout the period of *direct* domination of Africa, Europe administered Africa by its laws. *The paraphernalia of institutions imposed on Africa by Europe did not result in the breakdown of African structures.* Had this been the case, Africa would have been totally broken up. For instance, we would have had a totally new juridical order if African structures had collapsed with the impact of colonial conquest. African structures went underground with the establishment of direct European colonial rule. The flexibility of our pre-colonial structures allowed them to survive to a great extent.

African societies are today assimilating whatever is acceptable of the administrative structures imposed by Europeans. That process is not always visible to the naked eye. African societies were first submerged in their contact with Europe, but are now surfacing again by digesting whatever is valid from the imposed alien structures. Every digestive process implies a process of elimination. Consequently, African societies are at the same time rejecting those elements of the imposed structures which are inimical to their self-assertive development.

The institutional cultural and social organism of African societies did not break up regardless of how violent the impact of the West has been. Proof of the vitality of African structures can be gotten from the difficulty Africa experiences in integrating the imposed alien institutions. That difficulty implies a *resistance.* Africa is at present selecting what to accept and what to reject from the European institutional order. We must pay attention to that process. Depending on the degree of cultural consciousness as well as the political orientation of a given country, the form that digestive process takes may be seen differently. As it obeys one and the same general law, however, the process will on the whole give the same results everywhere. In other words, we have an African organism that accepts from the outside what it deems indispensable for adapting itself to the exigencies of the present world.
AFRISCOPE: Is that to say the future political, juridical and economic institutions of black countries will emerge from a selective fusion of elements coming from two structures which when they met were antithetical?
DIOP: No doubt! I don't believe we can extirpate and reject everything which came from Europe. Nor do I believe that we can re-establish everything from our pre-colonial structures. Neither probability would be realistic. However, if we consider Africa as a living organism, then we must acknowledge that she is engaged in a two-way process of digestion/elimination. Just as any other organism digests a substance and eliminates the toxic wastes, societies func-

tion along similar lines. We shouldn't see this process as one in which African identity is being lost. Rather, we should understand it as a process in which African identity is being *reinforced* through an adaptive selection of foreign elements. Perhaps on the individual level we are not so conscious of the process going on, but it's a reality. Africa has always reacted in this way without ceasing to be Africa. Already, the Africa of today is no longer the Africa which existed before her contact with Europe. Yet, Africa remains essentially herself since she is a living and distinct cultural organism which continues to develop according to her own laws.

AFRISCOPE: In black societies the one-party system has become the most popular political institution borrowed from Europe. How does this square with the need for a general democratization of society? Moreover, how can the single party promote a true national consciousness in situations where it coincides with the monopoly of state affairs by ethno-cultural and social elites?

DIOP: In Africa the creation of political parties along purely ethnic lines is not worthwhile. It must be avoided. In Senegal, for example, that stage has been superseded. Personally, if I were given the choice of either organizing a political party along ethnic lines or staying out of politics altogether, I wouldn't hesitate to choose the latter. Wherever it is done in Africa, I consider it to be a mistake. Possibly, certain countries are still at that stage. However, I would hope that everything be done to supersede that stage as quickly as possible, for nothing positive can come from it.

Concerning the one-party system. If the single party emerged out of the people's desire for it and truly expressed the aspirations of the *entire* country, then there would have been no danger. An oppositional force would have had no grounds to manifest itself in such a case. However, what is counter-productive is to set up a one-party system when 9/10ths of the people in a country are against it, and when monopoly over the state apparatus is the product of a usurpation of power. The state is an instrument of coercion. The usurpation of state power is therefore a sign of ominous intentions. *Wherever one-party rule emerges not out of open elections, but from a usurpation of power, it cannot translate the best interest of the people.*

If the totality of the people and all of the ethnic groups in a country unanimously and through honest elections chose to work within the framework of a single party, there would have been no problems. Whatever conforms to the consent of the freely expressed will of the people is good. But when the single party arises because a political movement has taken advantage of favourable circumstances, to *impose* its will on the entire country, then we are faced with a bad situation. My constant reference point is always *patriotic sentiment* in the building of a unified Africa. Either the leadership at the head of a state is animated by a sincere and profound patriotic sentiment, or it is not. If the leadership fits the first category, it will undoubtedly enjoy the full backing of the people, unless it makes enormous mistakes. Nevertheless, new methods of government must be studied which are designed to increase the participation of the people, even there where sincere patriotic leaderships, enjoying full popular backing, may be in power. Popular consultations have the effect of reinforcing the position of those who have espoused a correct line of action. In such a process, an opposition must be accepted there where necessary. A moment arises when opposition becomes indispensable.

AFRISCOPE: Doesn't the very existence of a one-party system already indicate the intent to liquidate any and all oppositional tendencies?

DIOP: That's undoubtedly so, although we must take into account the various contexts wherein one-party rule has been established. *Experience has overwhelmingly shown that the* one-party system has failed to build the type of Africa we desire. Consequently, we must now direct ourselves to a new formula allowing for a greater amount of freedom for all of the constituent groups of a country.

AFRISCOPE: Does that mean a new system based on several nationalist parties?

DIOP: Yes. The building of Africa must be based on freedom of choice. Only what is built on the basis of freedom is durable. We must gear our policies towards the obtaining of optimum conditions for freedom. If one is right, why be frightened of opposition? To shortcircuit the various political forces in a country by imposing a one-party system is at best naive, for the result is far from conclusive. Only institutions founded on wide consultations, and political action carried out with the greatest respect for Man can be durable. Sometimes it is thought that for the sake of political expediency it is necessary to circumvent other political movements and seize power. But soon it is realized that one has not gotten very far at all!

—V—
AFRICA AND MODERN TECHNOLOGY

AFRISCOPE: In February 1976, 100 black scholars and writers from all over the world gathered in Dakar for a seminar on "African Alternatives." Out of that meeting emerged a Union of African writers and a *World Black Researchers Association* (WBRA). You were elected President of the latter. What are the aims of the WBRA?

DIOP: The World Black Researchers Association, as indicated by black scholars from all over are harnessing their talents towards developmental projects. First, we aim at establishing a list of all black scholars and scientists in the various fields, whether they be in Africa, Asia, Oceania, North and South America, the Caribbean or Europe. Our first objective therefore is to reverse the brain-drain. The WBRA will englobe all of the scientific disciplines, both the natural and social sciences. Consequently, it will comprise two permanent international secretariats, one for the natural sciences and the other for the social sciences. In both domains scholars and scientists of the black world will be asked to direct their efforts towards solving the most vital scientific and sociological problems presently confronting the black world. This approach will further solidify the cultural ties binding all black populations of the globe.

By taking stock of the intellectual and scientific potentials of the black world, this world community will be better able to overcome the obstacles blocking its development at present. Who can deny that of all peoples, blacks have been the greatest victims of aggression, racism and oppression. The consequences of these are seen today in the state of underdevelopment and technical backwardness of black societies. For these reasons, the black peoples of the world have the right to pool their efforts together in defence of their best interests and to struggle against racism and underdevelopment. The founding of the World Black Researchers Association is in itself a manifestation of opposition to racism because science and technology cannot be considered the monopoly of any specific racial group. By creating the WBRA we aim at facilitating the entry of the black world into the era of advanced technology and cultural renovation. Thus from the outset our Association placed particular emphasis on the inclusion of blacks from Australia, Fiji, New Guinea and the rest of the Oceania and other parts of Asia, a zone of the world where black populations find themselves scattered and isolated.

AFRISCOPE: What immediate projects does the WBRA intend to undertake?

DIOP: We intend to hold a preliminary meeting of World Black scholars and scientists in the course of 1977 to prepare our First World Black Congress of Scientists and Researchers, scheduled for 1978. Thereafter, similar congresses will take place periodically, at which time we will assess the progress of research projects and establish new ones according to what has been determined as the most vital problems facing the world black community. The Association is geared towards servicing the sociological and scientific needs of the black world and will be responsive to suggestions and requests emanating from black states which require its services. Our Association must be in the position to promote scientific and sociological research on a large scale. Isolated black researcherrs must be helped to make their particular contributions to the development of our societies.

AFRISCOPE: In September 1976, a meeting of Arab scholars and scientists took place in Rabat, leading to the formation of the standing scientific conference of Arab world (CASTARAB). Is the WBRA similar to CASTARAB?

DIOP: CASTARAB pursues the same aims which motivated the founding of the WBRA in early 1976. The World Black Researchers Association, however, is a *non-governmental* and *non-political* body. From the start it was agreed that ideological conflicts should be banned from the Association. The problems facing the black societies are essentially the same; it's the *approach* to their solution which differs. Ideology intervenes precisely in the approach one takes to the solution of problems. Yet, if scientists and scholars do not depart from purely scientific lines, they are bound to adopt a similar approach in solving identical problems. Were our organization to be governmental there would be too many cleavages. Scholars and scientists would end up battling each other in defence of the political options held by their respective governments, rather than seeking universal scientific solutions to the problems besetting the world black community. Our Association is not political; it is purely scientific. The conclusions of our research projects will be made available to *any* black state. We intend to harness the scientific potential and creativity of the black world and place it at the disposal of all black states without distinction. Uppermost in our minds is the welfare of black populations of the world black community. Creativity is a vital function of any people and our Association aims at developing creativity in the black world. This is a commendable objective which in no way can be called racist or political.

AFRISCOPE: Is the creation of advanced centers of technology one of the aims of the World Black Researchers Association?

DIOP: The World Black Researchers Association will eventually have to tackle problems of that type. Specialized scientific commissions will be created to evaluate such problems and submit detailed reports on them. We will be organizing seminars along those lines. Their aim will be to present viable alternatives so that Africa in particular and black countries in general be advised on these problems. This is why we saw the necessity of grouping the scholars and scientists of the black world as a first step towards the above aims. Researchers must issue pertinent warnings so that indispensable solutions be undertaken in time.

Even before the convening of the First World Congress of Black Researchers, it is essential to emphasize the importance of federal centers of advanced technology. We cannot envision the creation of such centers for every small territory. However, those African countries which have the means must immediately undertake the creation of such centers to enable the assembling of technicians from all horizons. The solution to the problem of technological transferal is to be found in federal centers of advanced technology. We cannot adopt a chaotic or short-sighted approach. Neither can we depend on foreign 'technological philantropy.' It is up to us to determine which branches of technology are indispensable for the insertion of our continent into the world of modern technology. The next step is logically to introduce these without delay. If nothing else, the swift accomplishments of South Africa in the nuclear realm should incite us to instant action.

Those African states which have a technological capability should immediately undertake the creation of higher technological centers. Even if understaffed at the outset, they would eventually attract the necessary technicians. When African universities were first created, they too faced the problem of being understaffed. The situation was remedied rather quickly. The same would apply to advanced centers of technology. Actually, we were so accustomed to rushing to Europe for higher education at that time that many people even opposed the idea of creating African universities!

It is absolutely indispensable at this point to transfer advanced technology to Africa. *The transferal of advanced technology is inseparable from the creation of higher technology centers.* The latter will allow Africans to master the most sophisticated technology of our epoch. The first step is to assess which advanced technological fields are to have priority in this transferal. And even if at the outset these centers are under-utilized, in due course they will be fully serviceable.

AFRISCOPE: Could you give an example?

DIOP: Let's take Nigeria for example. Already having a technological capability, Nigeria should not delay in creating a nuclear center. (In fact, I think something to that effect is in the making). Zaire too has an equivalent technological capability. She already has a small reactor and could develop her own nuclear industry. I hope this will be the case so that Africans can assemble in those states which are presently capable of sustaining advanced technological centers. In spite of the technical difficulties involved, Africa should orient itself towards 'breeder' reactors with a policy of burying the waste material from its power plants rather than dumping it into the ocean. The seismic stability of large regions of Africa allows for burying the waste material which, thus far, is the best solution until science finds a better method of waste disposal.

Eventually, other sub-Saharan African states, such as Angola and Mozambique, may be in a position similar to Zaire and Nigeria. Algeria and Morocco are also capable of developing pilot centers of advanced technology, Egypt too, but her demographic problems make things difficult. A country like Libya can be important in this sense, being underpopulated while having abundant means at her disposal. Libya could thus sustain such a center. There must be *continental* centers, aimed at servicing Africa as a whole. In other words, we should not aim at multiplying the same centers but of diversifying them according to an order of technological priorities. Otherwise, we will end up having a situation whereby the various centers will be competing with one another and vying for the monopoly of technicians and advanced technological know-how. A disastrous reversed mini brain-drain would result. Specialists of a given field would rather be employed in a particular center, regardless of its location on the continent, which specialized in their specific field.

AFRISCOPE: Which branches should have priority in your opinion?

DIOP: All of the basic fields of advanced technology should be covered. For instance, we have the very serious problem of the depletion of conventional sources of energy. As a result, everyone now sees thermonuclear fusion as the next stage. *It's vital for Africa to create a pilot center of thermonuclear fusion.*

The worldwide research being undertaken in this domain will soon fall under a cloak of secrecy. The more the industrial nations progress in this field the more they will be reluctant to share their discoveries. However, at present we are still in the position to assess what is happening in this field. Consequently, Africa must create her own pilot center for thermonuclear fusion now. This will allow Africa to have technicians with a level of qualification compatible with present international standards. Africa must stop waiting for the results of research work undertaken elsewhere and contenting itself with merely importing already-made equipment and the alien know-how for its functioning. At the beginning, African research centers would undoubtedly need foreign technicians. But progressively Africans formed these centers and who will have achieved the highest qualifications, would be in charge of them. At that point, they could take the initiative of defining their own research projects and make their own contributions in the field of advanced technology.

Once thermonuclear fusion is domesticated as a source of industrial energy, it will cause the greatest revolution in history. Nothing will be comparable. We will have entered the era of unlimited energy. We are actually at the threshold of the era of energy abundance. Energy produced by thermonuclear fusion will surpass all other sources of energy used till now. All other sources of energy will in due course become peripheral. We can only talk of a post-nuclear era in terms of an era in which the dominant form of energy will be derived from thermonuclear fusion. Solar energy could become a secondary source of energy for Africa's needs. At present, solar energy merely serves an auxiliary function.

One of Africa's natural endowments is her immense hydro-electric potential. The hydraulic power of the African continent must be harnessed *now* with the ulterior objective of setting up thermonuclear fusion centres. Enormous quantities of electricity are indeed needed to extract deuterium (heavy hydrogen) from seawater by way of electrolysis. Deuterium is needed to feed a thermonuclear plant. For that process to be profitable, electricity of hydraulic origin must be employed. The *immediate* development of our continental hydraulic resources is therefore a sure way of establishing one of the bases for the near future when thermonuclear fusion will be the chief source of energy. A rational approach would be to start equipping our natural hydraulic sources with the type of facilities required. We must begin taming our rivers, because *Africa must be present as of now in the race towards the exploitation of thermonuclear fusion as a source of energy.*

AFRISCOPE: What are the prospects for Africa's development in the nuclear field?

DIOP: In the preface to my book, *Nuclear Physics and Absolute Chronology,* I explained that considering the political balkanization of Africa, small states such as Senegal could not hope to be present in the domain of high energy. For example, it is quite difficult and expensive to build powerful installations, whether it be a nuclear plant or a high energy nuclear research accelerator as the one used in Battavia (USA), or as that set up by the European Centre for Nuclear Research (CERN) in Switzerland by all West European states. That type of particle accelerator develops energy up to 400 billion electrovolts. It costs more than half of the national annual budget of Senegal. How do you expect a small African country to equip itself with such installations isolatedly? If we are to be present in the domain of high energy, we need federal regroupments which can pool their resources together. The expense of such equipment compels a cooperative effort in terms of national resources for the creation of large research centers. There are some countries in Africa which could, on their own, be present in that domain; Nigeria, Zaire, Algeria, Morocco and, eventually, countries such as Angola and Mozambique. These nations are in the position to equip themselves with modern installations for advanced research. That is, equipment designed for basic research purposes in the domain of high energy, such as breaking up nuclear and determining various aspects of the behaviour of matter.

TWO INTERVIEWS WITH CHEIKH ANTA DIOP

In the opening interview, excerpted from Listervelt Middleton's discussion with Dr. Diop on a South Carolina television program, Diop repeats some of the points made in the lectures we have selected for publication in this volume. We have thus deleted some of his responses. His comments, however, on the incomplete development of Neanderthal man and the clash between "monogenetic" and "polygenetic" theories of man's origin are expressed here with such clarity and force as to justify a certain degree of overlapping. The second interview was conducted by the Nile Valley Executive Committee —Ed.

INTERVIEW I:

MIDDLETON: Dr. Diop, what can you tell us about the evolution of mankind and where Black men fit into that scheme?
DIOP: We are able to say scientifically today, with certainty, that mankind was born in Africa within the region of Kenya and around the area that comprises Ethiopia and Tanzania, dispersing along a north-south axis all the way to South Africa. It is clear that any humanity that had its birth in that region would not have survived without pigmentation. Nature doesn't do anything by chance. It's for that reason that humanity of the subequatorial region was given melanin to protect its skin. It is clear, with certainty, that the first man had to be a black man. It is only after that race of man left Africa to people other parts of the world, which had different climatic phenomena, that man changed—had a different look. Nature created six specimens of man before we got to man as we know him today. According to the scientific information we have now, it appears that the first three species never acquired the potential for leaving their own area. They never had the potential to expand or leave Africa. Three others did leave Africa. The fourth and fifth species disappeared. What remains is man as we know him today—the sixth species.

The fifth species did not have a forehead (Slide 1). The eyes are situated very closely. It's very important because the brain inside the fifth species was very different from man's brain as we know it today. In studying its brain anatomically, it is known that it [Neanderthal Man] did not have the anterior lobe of the brain. That is the major difference between *Homo Sapiens-Sapiens* (which is what we are) and the fifth species. The fifth species was never able to transcend nature and create works of Art.

Dr. Diop and Interpreter Mrs. Elizabeth Clement listen as Listervelt Middleton directs question to Diop. Photo: Larry Williams.

Grimaldi Man

It was from 40,000 to 20,000 years ago that Grimaldi man left Africa to go into Europe at the time of the last glaciation. The climate of Europe was extremely cold. It was much colder than it is now. During this period of some 20,000 years, he underwent an adaptation to become what we know as white man. It is very clear to all the scientists involved in this field, even if they are only able to say it among themselves, and not in public, that the man we know eventually to be a white man evolved from a black man over a period of 20,000 years, a conclusion that rests totally on scientific data. That is the conclusion we must come to. If Grimaldi man had never left Africa to people other parts of the world, and if those people in other parts of the world, in different climates, had not gone through the process of adaptation to become what they are in various regions of the world, all men would be homogeneous. All men would be Black. If that man had not left Africa, the rest of the world would have remained a desert. It never would have been peopled. And so, to

answer precisely your first question, "To what extent did Blacks figure in the origin of man?" the answer is . . . the first man was Black. It was he who gave birth to the other races of the world!
MIDDLETON: Why was it not possible for mankind to have been born in many parts of the earth?
DIOP: When human anthropology had not quite evolved to the extent it has now, there were theories that kept clashing with each other. There was the theory I just explained that man was born in one place and became different as he peopled other parts of the world. That theory had its defenders. This is called the Monogenetic Theory which theorizes that there was one source for the origin of mankind. The Second theory is the Polygenetic theory which contends that man was born in Africa, Europe and also in Asia. In other words, that there were several locations in the world where mankind has its origin. And it is that that explains their differences. The Polygenetic theory made a certain amount of sense. Not that it made good sense. But it made a certain amount of sense. It explains that there are different peoples in different parts of the world with different characteristics. There were two things that made this theory fall apart. The first is that *nature never strikes twice in its evolution. It doesn't ever hit the same place two times. Nature doesn't create the same being twice. In the animal kingdom throughout the evolution of animals, a being was created that either disappeared, or changed somewhat, or a completely new being was created . . . but never the same being twice.* Remaining strictly scientific, it doesn't make common sense to say that man was created twice. It is in the region of Kenya where we find all the most ancient evolutionary information. It's for this reason that scientists are now able to say, with certainty, that man could have been created only one time. All fossils that have been found outside of Africa have been found, under close analysis, to be much much later than those found in Africa. No other continent in the world has a complete series of fossils indicating the six specimens. The three specimens that represent the very beginning of mankind cannot be found in Europe, they cannot be found in Asia, and of course cannot be found in America. They never left Africa! The complete set remains in Africa. The accumulation of the best information now makes it very clear that mankind had its origin in Africa!

The only specimen that appears in America is that of Homo Sapiens-Sapiens. America was peopled through the Bering Straits at the end of the final glaciation. It is for that reason that we only find Homo Sapiens-Sapiens in America. In Asia we have Homo Erectus, the Neanderthal man and Homo Sapiens. In Europe we have the same, Homo Erectus, Neanderthal man and Homo Sapiens. From Africa some of these left by the Isthmus of Suez to go into Asia and eastern Europe and some by the Straits of Gibraltar up into the north, up into Europe.

The polygenetic theorists tried to establish a hierarchy of races and to

Listervelt Middleton interviewing Diop for South Carolina television.

indicate that some races are inferior to others. But if man has the same origin, then there can be no intellectual hierarchy, because all the races, the three races of the world, would have the same intellectual history. If the three races had had different origins then one could say that they had different intellectual capacities, having had different histories. The Polygenetic theory is essential to defending the notion that there are inequalities among the races. It is for this reason that it has been defended so vigorously by people. But science has without question set it aside!

The Monogenetic theory will support the notion that, because our origins are the same, we have the same intellectual capacities. By saying that, I'm not saying that Blacks are superior to whites. That would also be false. No Race is superior to any other! All races have the same intellectual capacity! The anterior lobe is the same for all the races. Studies of the anatomy of the brain have been numerous and very extensive here in America, Africa, Europe, and everywhere in the world. In no way have any significant difference been found to indicate an anatomical difference in the brains of the various races. Certainly not in the case of the forefront of the brain. All biologists and scientists who are aware of this information know that there is no longer any question as to which is the superior race. It is, however possible, that one race can dominate the other temporarily. In antiquity it was Blacks who dominated! That is perhaps not the case now.

This is a picture of the Piltdown man [see earlier lecture—Ed.] and it is to demonstrate to you the lengths to which certain Anthropologists have gone to establish their theory. The Piltdown man was created by a British Geologist in 1912 by the name of Downson. He fabricated, piece by piece, this fake fossil. He excavated in Sussex, England. Like modern man he had eyes and he has the forehead, as modern man does. You can see that in his lower teeth the mandible is that of a monkey. Its canine teeth are that of a monkey. From this fabrication grew a theory called the Pre-Sapien theory which was manufactured to establish that this man (Piltdown man) was the predecessor of modern man. That he was in fact born in Europe and especially in England. There are American Anthropologists who took this theory as their own and defended it. We know today it is false. In France there were also anthropologists who defended the theory. We learned that it was false through an English anthropologist, who analyzed it and discovered that it was in fact a fake. It was in 1955, working at the British Museum, a Professor Oakley analyzed this fossil and discovered that it was false. But you see for 50 years the damage had already been done! For 50 years this was the theory that created the clash between the Polygenetic and Monogenetic theories. So we must give credit to those scientists who are working with a clear head and a clear objective spirit. We must recognize them as we go along, as we must note Professor Oakley in this case.

MIDDLETON: What did ancient writers have to say about who the ancient Egyptians were?

DIOP: All the writers of Ancient Greece and Rome agreed that the Egyptians of their epoch, of their time, were black. And these were the Egyptians towards the end of the great Egyptian civilization. In speaking of the Greeks, we are in the fifth century before Christ and fourth century after Christ. For 900 years the Greeks were constant witnesses to the fact that the Egyptians were Black. So they would be considered Black from their origin, from the beginning, all the way to the end of their civilization!

MIDDLETON: Why is Egypt so crucial to Black people today? What is at stake?

DIOP: Because Egyptian civilization played the same role for Africa that Greco-Roman civilization played for Western civilization. If we are to create a body of social sciences, then we must take Egypt as a point of departure. It is the only way to reconcile African Civilization with history.

MIDDLETON: What will you say to the parent who is content with his or her child learning only European or White history?

DIOP: It is fine to learn the history of others but you must learn your own history first. A people who lose their historical memory becomes a very fragile people. They regress. It is historical memory that permits them to be a strong people! Even in the disapora these ties *must* remain! This can help us to make our lives better in the countries where we live. The fullness of our culture will help us to find the fraternity among races that we must have in this world.

INTERVIEW II: NILE VALLEY EXECUTIVE COMMITTEE INTERVIEWS DIOP

ROBERT BELCHER: How close is the correlation between cranial capacity and intelligence?

DIOP: There is some relative relationship between cranial capacity and intelligence if we look at the evolution of the first three species of mankind. These three never achieved the potential to leave Africa. In looking at Australopithecus Robustus, Australopithecus Gracile, Homo Habilis and Homo Erectus we see that the intellectual capacity for these four specimens increases as they evolve. The cranial capacity increases. Intelligence increased as the cranial volume increased. But for the last two specimens this rule has not been verified. The fifth specimen that followed was Neanderthal man—we call him *Homo Sapiens*. He had no forehead. It was as if his eyes were placed high in his forehead. Neanderthal man already had the cranial capacity of *Homo Sapiens-Sapiens*. He had a cranial capacity of 1,450 cubic centimeters. He had the same cranial capacity that man has today, whether he is black, white, or yellow. But with less intelligence. Intelligence has not only to do with cranial capacity, but with the convolutions of the brain. We may take the example of Descartes. When Descartes died his brain was taken out and was dissected and analyzed. His brain was about the size of a pear. And Descartes was a genius. He was a white man, not a black man. He was a genius and he had a brain about the size of a pear. But his brain was very convoluted. There were lots of loops and turns and it was very dense in that way, which density extends the surface area of the cerebral cortex. Some scientists have tried to prove that the average European brain is larger than that of the average African. But the largest skulls we have been able to find up to this point do not belong to whites but to Blacks. You take a Bushman skull—the very first Bushman skull of South Africa. These are the largest in volume that we have found on the earth. These are the first skulls that were 1,750 cubic centimeters. In the Upper Paleolithic, the first *Homo Sapiens Sapiens* appeared and they were those who had the 1,750 cubic centimeter cranial capacity. We never found anything like that in Europe. Nor in Asia or anywhere else. After this race degenerated, they moved into the Kalahari Desert, where they are now. They can be seen even today. So it is obvious that the larger size of the brain is not to be equated with greater intelligence. If it were true it would be blacks who had higher intelligence because it has been found that some Blacks have a larger cranial capacity. But it [the correlation] is not true. Moreover, they have also tried to link intelligence with the structure of the brain, tried to find some significant anatomical difference to make some relationship to the intelligence factor between blacks and whites. Biologists and all the scientists and all the anatomists know that all this research has ended in absolutely nothing. No result has been found that could be of any value. All efforts to establish that the I.Q. of blacks is lower than that of whites have been failures.

Nile Valley Executive Committee and Presenters (seated left to right): Dr. Walter Palmer, Morris Brown College; Ms. Thurya Wingate, the Bennu Study Group; Larry Williams, Chairman, Public Relations Nile Valley Conference and Co-Convenor of Bennu; Dean Lawrence E. Carter Sr. Martin Luther King, Jr. International Chapel, Morehouse College; Dr. Mwalimu Imara, Morehouse School of Medicine; Professor Ivan Van Sertima, Editor, Journal of African Civilizations; Dr. Charles S. Finch, Morehouse School of Medicine; Askia M. Toure, Facilities Chairman, Nile Valley Conference; Dr. Asa G. Hilliard III, Georgia State University; Mr. Tony Warner, Transportation Chairman of the Nile Valley Conference and Co-founder of Lady Prep. Non-Committee Presenters (standing left to right): Locksley Geohaghen; Prof. James G. Spady, Runoko Rashidi, Prof. Beatrice Lumpkin, Darryl Prevost, Hunter H. Adams III, Dr. Na'im Akbar, Dr. Bruce Williams, Prof. Jan Carew, Dr. John Pappademos and Attorney Legrand H. Clegg II. Photo: Jim Alexander.

The results were falsified, in the same way as the Piltdown man was fabricated. You know that Cyril Burt, an English psychologist, falsified all the information he studied concerning cranial capacity. So it is that those conservative scientists, when they find they can't do anything on purely scientific grounds, begin to fabricate theories to lead mankind down a false trail. It is only after his death did we learn of the fabrication! If what he said was true about the Japanese having a relatively small cranial capacity, we know that they are just as intelligent as others, because now we see that the West is trying very hard to keep up with them.

So, in summary, I can say that all studies to make a hierarchy of intelligence among the races have been failures. The truth is, man has the same origin. His adaptation to different climates does not permit a hierarchy of intelligence. Only superficial changes of appearances have occurred. All races have the same intellectual capacity.

ASA G. HILLIARD III: Looking in retrospect and prospect, where do you feel the priority areas of investigation are now?

DIOP: We must address ourselves to all of the disciplines of the human sciences. As a priority, we must consolidate those results that are available and already established. *It's high time we learn that other people not teach us about Africa anymore.* We must be able in a very short time, to seek out the materials, study them and interpret them. It's high time we organize a team of African and African-American paleontologists and pre-historians who would be able to go, for instance, to Kenya in the region where man was born to conduct research and to obtain artifacts and documents, to study them in an independent manner. Conclusions must be reached to show the scientific community so that that community would be able to come and look at the documents and refute them, if they want to or if they can. This is possible. Even now, it's possible to do it. We have people who can do it, but they are scattered throughout the world. If we make an effort to regroup, we can have a minimum number of people to form a team. It's in this direction that our research must go. I can tell you that my laboratory was doing Radiocarbon dating until now. But it has just established a Department of Potassium Argon Dating. It's that method that made it possible to date all the fossils that were found in the region of Kenya.

My intention is to make it possible that all the fossils found in Africa be dated in Africa without going outside of Africa. Except, in the case where Afro-Americans want to do the work, we can let them bring the fossils to the United States. This is already something that is very precise, that can be done. The team of paleontologists that would go on a dig over in Africa, in the field, should include archaeologists for the Upper Paleolithic period. We have such archaeologists at the University of Dakar. At the IFAN in Dakar we have a team of young paleontologists who would be able to be a part of such a team. If you know here of archaeologists in the U. S. who are very well trained, then we can envisage a joint venture of those paleontologists with Senegalese archaeologists.

As far as paleontology is concerned, we must have medical doctors who would specialize in that field. It's a training that could be acquired very easily and very fast because they already have the basic training, of looking at the human body, and looking at fossils. The separation is not that great. I know personally the whole administrative body of the Leakey Institute in Nairobi. I'm sure that if an Afro-American medical doctor wanted to volunteer to do an internship in order to get involved in human paleontology, there would be no problem. I could recommend that person personally. He would be accepted. In fact, to tell you all of my thoughts, I must say that we don't just need one person. The more we have the better. It's not a saturated field. I can recommend two, three, or more people to go and have some training in Kenya and I'm sure that they would be welcomed. They would make available to them all the documentation that Professor Leakey found and it will be possible to do that within the framework of the team that I was talking about earlier. I think that someone like Dr. Finch and all the other medical doctors that I don't know, who may be here right now, would be most welcome. I think we really have to establish such a team. So that they would be able to take charge of scientific production in that particular field. This would cover the whole period of Pre-history and Human Paleontology in what deals with the appearance of man.

Another problem would be that of Egyptology. The first battle in this field has been won. We had to prove that the Ancient Egyptians were a black people. Now, nobody can dispute that fact in any serious manner! People can silence all this or not talk about it, but no serious scientist can now say it's not the truth. It's no longer possible to see anybody develop a positive thesis to counter that fact. So now we have to go to the second step. We have to rethink the whole of Egyptian history in the framework or mind of the African spirit that gave it its birth. Because the whole of Egyptian history seems to be very fragmented, dispersed, like a disjointed body, because it was seen and interpreted by a thought system that was foreign. It is high time that we reinterpret the whole of these facts.

Where is the problem in this field? The materials that comes from the digs that have already been done are in the different European museums. This is a damage that can never be undone. The criteria of choice, of what had to be kept and what had to be destroyed, those criteria were established by foreign minds whose interest it was to whiten the Egyptian Civilization. Hundreds and thousands of mummies have been destroyed. All the mummies that had distinct African features were put aside and classified as being foreign and they took the ones that looked more white and said they were the authentic ones in Egypt. Yet when they themselves described those mummies, they had to admit that they were Black. But they have tried to take the foreign types

Dr. Diop being presented Nile Valley Conference Memorabilia by Mr. Larry Williams on behalf of the Bennu Study Group and the Nile Valley Executive Committee. Pictured to Diop's right are Lawrence E. Carter, Dr. Walter Palmer, Dr. Mwalimu Imara and Askia M. Toure. To Diop's left are Charles S. Finch, Dr. Asa G. Hilliard III and Thurya Wingate. Photo: Larry Williams.

that lived in Egypt at the time and make people believe that those foreign types were the actual Egyptians. All that failed. What they have destroyed we cannot bring back anymore. But what we can do is have access to the storage of the museums. It's difficult but not impossible. Nobody has the right to stop a scientist from going to the storage of a museum, if it has something he needs to look at and study. They should not hide things that exist. If we want to know what they have stored, we can look at the book of entries of the museums and demand to look at the different pieces.

ASKIA M. TOURE': May I interrupt for a moment? I have some information on this point. There is a European woman, a scientist in England, who is dissecting mummies. She has a great number of mummies that she is taking apart and experimenting on them. Right now at this moment! Her name is Rosalie Davies. Her dissecting of the mummies would be the equivalent of

[Africans] digging up the bodies of George Washington, Thomas Jefferson and Abraham Lincoln (American Presidents) and experimenting on them in Nigeria.

DIOP: This is related to the third point I want to make. I myself have studied the mummies, as you know, in the Museum of Man. These are mummies that Mariette brought from digs in the Egyptian Delta. I was surprised to know that such studies were not done before me. And I was absolutely certain that these studies had to have been done. It was impossible that I could be the first to be doing them. To establish that the Egyptians had Melanin in their skins, nothing is more simple. I even invented an apparatus, a chemical process, for determining the amount of melanin in the skin. I think that since then, the Americans have devised an apparatus that performs a similar function.

If we had grouped our numerous capacities together, we could have done similar things. In the last seven years, I am certain that we are doing the same research, step by step, inch by inch. *Note that the Western world is frightened and scared to death.* These are the last tremors. They now know that they can't have fun by just telling us any old thing. They know that African-Americans are capable of refuting information that is not scientific. We can make these teams that we need. We must have in these teams archaeologists. We are talking about those specializing in the Prehistoric period, the Historic period from 4,000 B.C. right up to the end of the Egyptian Civilization. This would lead us inevitably to creating our own museums, a museum at Morehouse. There would be the museum at Harvard University. We will have agreements with the countries in which these digs will be conducted, to know which artifacts we have left there to be analyzed and those artifacts that have been taken out. We can establish the collections and have good records of what is contained in them. That team needs to be established as soon as possible. This would be a team of African and African-Americans putting together all the abilities or capabilities we are able to find.

DIOP: That team may have more problems working in the field. (jokingly). Egypt couldn't keep us from doing these things. In passing through normal procedures, Egypt couldn't forbid us from doing this. They can't work with Belgians, Roumanians and people all over the world and refuse to allow Africans to do the same thing. But we musn't wait until things are made easy for us. We cannot expect that this will be made easy for us. This team has to undertake the rewriting and re-interpretation of all of Egyptian history including the re-translation of the Ancient texts. There are extraordinary things, incredible things, not yet fully understood, in these texts.

ASA G. HILLIARD III: How old is the Sphinx? According to John G. Jackson, there was an inscription in a temple near the Sphinx, adjoining it, which is kept in the Bulac Museum in Cairo, which says, that the Sphinx received repairs in the age of one of these Pharoahs such as Cephren instead of having been built in the time of Cephren.

DIOP: When we talk about the Sphinx, we say that we think it is the image of the Pharoah Cephren. The real name is Khafre. If you look into the books I have written under this image, you will see that I use the conditional context, that it *could be* the image of Khafre. But we don't know with any certainty.

To return to my discussion of the second team. We have access to these documents that already exist. We must re-read them with our own interests in mind, throughout the world, in all of the museums, from the Oriental Institute at the University of Chicago to the Louvre in Paris and the Metropolitan Museum in New York. We must get into the storage of all of these museums and study these pieces ourselves and re-interpret them to the extent that it is possible. I have a feeling that there will be quite a number of surprises in that effort.

We must organize at the same time, as quickly as possible, to create our own museums, our own storage facilities, our own documents. Then we will be the ones who produce science in the most fundamental sense. This is equally as valuable for the Pre-historic team as for the team that will be involved with the history of Egypt (kmt). So as not to separate our efforts, the second team will be composed of African specialists in the human sciences to better interpret the information found concerning Egypt's place in history. There will be those people who are familiar with those African facts who can establish the necessary relationships between the findings of the Egyptian archaeologists. Later on, when we've made good progress, then we can divide into a number of different specialists. These two teams seem to me basic. This must be done as soon as possible.

DR. WALTER PALMER: The other day, you were speaking on the "sons of light"—the Mysteries System of Egypt. I want to follow up on that. Could you expand on that? What did the Egyptians assume regarding the psychology of man or the way men learn or think specifically? Would you, from your study of linguistic patterns in Egypt, give any significant insight into this pattern of thought? In your studies, have you discerned any special methods of teaching by the Egyptians that the scholars of that time described? You mentioned the Pan African organizations and the need for Pan-African organizations of the African continent, would you comment on the need for Pan-African reorganization and development in light of the blacks in North and South America?

DIOP: As I was saying yesterday, the notion of education for the Egyptians was very elitist. It was also complete and complex. All of Egyptian education, psychologically speaking, was directed to the strengthening or the fortification of the Soul. It was as though they were trying to create supermen, not in the German or Nietzchean sense, but the person that would lead them had to be superhuman. They had to have souls that were indestructible, very, very strong. This was the goal of their education. The criteria for selection, before they were allowed into initiation, and the testing of candidates for initiation, was to weed out or find those that were basically indestructible. To find those who had souls or abilities that were certainly not average. They were looking for the gifted. If the character of the soul was positive, for example, it was possible to see how strong these people were, how strong were their souls. It was possible then to choose them in order to find the level that they should reach. According to the different characters of people, there were levels that could not be surpassed, that's how you will find the different levels such as the "Sons of Light".

The Egyptians had a real global conception of the Universe in general. The last meaning they gave to things, which was a symbolic meaning, was not meant for everybody to understand or bear the weight of. There was a hierarchy and yet it was a very democratic society, much more than people think. Egypt was a country of law. It has been recorded that workers could sue ministers and governors before the law. That shows the level of democracy that existed in Egypt at the time. I could have given you several examples of this. If I have time later, I will. It was a democratic society, but it was elitist.

The ideas that Egyptians had of the world are reflected by platoism. In fact, for the Egyptians, the universe was governed by the number and this is linked with the discovery of the calendar. As soon as the fourth millinium before Christ, every 1460 years, the same phenomenon will reappear. That was the way of establishing the most general law of the universe, it is the periodicity of the celestial phenomenon, the stars and planets. That was the best way of demonstrating that the universe is governed by the number. That is an idea that 4,000 years later the Greeks would take. As I told you, the Greeks did not exist [as a nation] when those laws were discovered. I could have given you many more examples on the significance and importance of Egyptian Science. That science was so important and so profound that human beings had to be tested to see if they could receive it or not, or were worthy to receive it, and once they received it, they wanted to know what they would do with that knowledge.

Now to deal with the last part of your question, Pan-Africanism is a Black American notion. It came from here. You see the kinship. Let's exchange a few ideas. African-Americans must help us create a strong African state adaptable to the conditions of the 20th and 21st centuries. We have two images or pictures that we see before us. We see South America and the United States. South America missed its opportunity for unification at the time of Simon Bolivar and has been underdeveloped for two centuries.

The United States was successful in its federation, which explains its political and economic health. You must help us to realize, to make, side by side, elbow to elbow, a strong African State! Everything that African leaders refute about the notion of federation is said out of egoism and nothing else. Even one who is selfish and egotistic, but is clear-headed at the same time, would have to be in favor of federation.

I think, as I said and as I would say to the students tomorrow, the particular situation of the Black minority in America today constitutes a potential force that is extraordinary and will manifest itself in the future. Here my ideas are very clear. I'm certain, even on an international level, "He who wins Africa wins the world". I cannot see how America will win Africa without going through the channel of Black America. What Americans must understand is that the only Ambassador you can have to capture the ear of Africa are Black Ambassadors. They must pass through you. I'm speaking of Ambassadors in the larger sense, not diplomatic Ambassadors. You are the obligatory Intermediary! America will understand very quickly that it is only through you that they will have what they want. It lies in you, all the potential that Africa has. They cannot have access to it without you. So they must look again with different eyes at the Black minority in this country. It is only under that condition that Black Americans will be the force in the sense that Martin Luther King envisioned. An integrated and harmonious community. It can be done in the spirit of Martin Luther King. It is in complete, total respect for African and American laws that I see how Africa can be a force behind you which can help you realize total integration and do that very quickly. You as a minority in the most developed nation in the world, can aid Africa to survive by helping it to understand those things that will adapt it to its future needs. It's not a question of your ceasing to be American. You are American. But you are Americans of African ancestry as whites are Americans of European ancestry. On the basis of culture, the cultural ties, the umbilical cord that ties us can never be cut. And it is on the basis of that cultural kinship, that you have an official nationality or citizenship, a cultural citizenship, and Africa is open to you. You will be welcomed in Africa.

We have to do all of this work with a total respect for the different laws, we do not want to indulge in any subversive actions. All we want to do is respect each other's laws and that would also be within the spirit of what Martin Luther King, Jr. preached. All that I have just said is really in conformity with the interests of the whole of America and our own African interests. I think that a common future is open to us and that is what we have to work on together. So, it has a double aspect, one that is cultural and one that is social, not to speak of the political aspect. A more concrete formulation of all this has to be worked out, but those are the general ideas I have at this point. Since I have to speak to the freshmen the day after tomorrow, it's in this vein that I'm going to talk to them, without emphasizing the political aspects of all this. I just want to make them aware that Africa is the land of their ancestors. I would like to help them to place themselves in a better manner within the whole world situation. To place themselves in relation to the whole of the American nation by law and by fact. Also to show them all the things that are waiting for them in Africa in the land of their ancestors so that they can see

Dr. Diop issues challenge as Dr. Mwalimu Imara of Morehouse Medical School (right) and Dr. Asa G. Hilliard III (far right) look on.
Photo: Larry Williams.

that the future is not blank for them and that if they see life from that perspective, they will have much more to do than most of the other children of their generation. I will also show them, in passing, that they are the builders of nations though they are not aware of it. That the nation builder is sleeping in each of them, I will like to awaken it. I would also like to help them to awaken the creator that is sleeping in them. I have the feeling that all the children that are passing in front of us, including this small baby who is right here, has a creator sleeping in it. Education must awaken that creator. It all depends on how education is carried out. If the objectives are well accepted, the program of learning and also the method of teaching, the pedagogical effort, will come from that situation. That is the message that I have for them since you are their instructors.

ASKIA M. TOURE': Have you investigated the Kemetic use of the pineal gland or third eye in the development of spiritual consciousness? How was this related to the Egyptian mystery system?

DIOP: The problem posed by modern man, the pursuit of a science without conscience—this was not the credo of the Egyptian priests. That is why the selection was so vigorous. The Egyptian ideal was transformed by the western people later on. We see that when the Greeks came to Egypt for initiation they went through the same process. To illustrate my idea, let us take the case of Pythagorus. When he came to Egypt, he had a lot of problems. He was sent to Egypt with a letter of recommendation. He was sent to Amasis, who was king of Egypt at the time. Amasis sent him to the priests of Memphis who said they gracefully declined the offer. That's how we can see the Egyptian mind working, because what they told him was that they didn't know very much about all these sciences and he could go somewhere else to really procure this knowledge he wanted. He went to Heliopolis. The priests of Heliopolis said the same thing and sent him to Thebes. When he got to Thebes, to discourage him they made him do the most menial task that had no meaning at all. They made him dig very big holes. When he dug them they asked him to fill the holes back up again. Pythagorus had no choice but to do as he was asked. Finally, because he was obedient, the priests decided that they would at last help him to learn something. You know the conditions of the initiation. Your hair had to be shaved and all kinds of things. He had also to write a thesis at the end of his studies in the Egyptian language and those were the conditions of initiation. If you take the writings of Strabo, Plato and Eudoxus they were all initiated in Heliopolis and remained there for 13 years. Here again it is proven that the Egyptians initiated Plato and Eudoxus in a very partial, limited manner. If I had the time I would have given you many more details into the psychological methods the Egyptians used and also on the practical methodology of learning and the homework, the kinds of assignments, that the students had to do. They had to write on terracotta slates. There are many,

many, texts in the Egyptian literature which give you an idea of the importance the Egyptians found in the strengthening of the soul and in particular, the souls of the leaders.

LARRY WILLIAMS: Could you give us insight into the research and work of the Congolese Egyptologist Theophile Obenga?

DIOP: Theophile Obenga has just written a book on the Bantu. He's just been named the President of the Center For Bantu Studies, which is in Libraville in Gabon. . . . I spent two days in Brazzaville with Obenga just before I came here. The book about the Bantu came out a week ago. But he just recently published a book about the Congolese basin. And another book called the New History which is smaller and older.

LARRY WILLIAMS: Dr. Diop, could you give us some information on the Ethiopian playwright Tsegaye Gabre-Medhin? What type of work is he engaged in presently?

DIOP: He's working on a dissertation with me on Egyptian theater. It is a very advanced dissertation and it will tell us a lot of things. He has also made a film based solely on texts that came from the Egyptians. These are plays that they staged right in the Pavilion and on the stairs of the temple. In the very beginning it was the Pharoah, himself, who played the role of Osiris. It was this theater that later gave birth to Greek theatre. So now we have a very clear kinship or relationship with the Greek Tragedy, Dionysus. It is a replica of the play Osiris. Dionysus is Osiris! Dionysus was at the origin of Greek Theatre. This is what Tsegaye is working on now with me. He has written to me that he is going to finish. It's scholars like Tsegaye, who have an international reputation, who have been spared, in spite of problems with the current regime. But he will finish soon. Speaking about film, all of Egyptian history has been so terribly misrepresented, especially by Americans, who are responsible for the great films on the Egyptian era. It is now America's responsibility to provide an antidote to clear the record.

There was a very important Colloqium in Nairobi on the relationship of Nations and Ethnicity and the birth of Nations in Africa. For a week or so they telegraphed or called me. They were insistent that I come. It was done in cooperation with the UN University in Tokyo. Tsegaye was there. But because I had to come here too, I couldn't see him. But he's very active. He still works. It's a question of the problem of communications. The regime that is there now is a regime that is not for the people, but for itself.

It's the same problem you see from one part of Africa to the other. Leaders of the African states are afraid that the people will communicate with one another, that information will be passed. There are a few exceptions to that rule. I'm in the opposition party in Senegal. Senegal is perhaps one country where you can say there is a little more freedom than there is in other places. I can go from one place to the other. Again this is not a freedom we were given. It is freedom that we took. We paid for this freedom. For thirty years I have

paid with my own self. I nearly died in prison as you know. Things like that are no longer possible in Senegal.
LARRY WILLIAMS: Dr. Diop, tell us what happened to your plane as you were on your way to the Nile Valley Conference in September 1985?
DIOP: Let's not dramatize this thing. We'll now talk about the facts. I'm going to tell you about what happened during the trip. Facts only! We must remember during that time we were unable to communicate because everytime I picked up the telephone the line was cut quickly. I tried for an hour to reach Dr. Finch. Everytime I would dial the phone, pick up the phone, a female voice would respond. As soon as I would say Dakar and my name the line was cut! The same thing on this side. Everytime you would call, as soon as I picked up the phone, the line was cut. From some point or other our communication was tampered with. I think it came from my side. But, in any case, it was tampered with the very night I was to take the plane. The plane was to depart at one o'clock a.m. At midnight I was ready and then I got a telephone call from Professor Leonard Jeffries. I said to him "Call Dr. Finch. Tell him I did everything that I could, to get on that plane, but I couldn't. I will tell you this quickly before someone cuts the line. I'm going to the airport to catch the plane. Someone has to go to New York to meet me. Jeffries said that his father lived near the airport in New York. Jeffries said he would go to New York and spend the night with his father, so that he would be there to receive me in the event someone else couldn't be there. I got on the plane. The plane took off. It was a Pan Am plane, a Boeing 747. It was booked to full capacity. When we took off I don't know what happened. It was as if the plane was about to break. But the pilot kept going. It went up and all the baggage and everything fell from the racks. We put everything back. After an hour and a half the speed of a Boeing is about 1,000 kilometers an hour. So for an hour and a half we were in the air. We were about to go to sleep and then we were awakened. We were told to take the baggage from the storage compartment overhead. Put them under our knees and to secure or brace ourselves and that we would have to go back to Dakar. It was some small thing to repair and we couldn't go to New York. So we went back. Everyone on board was very upset. We knew it wasn't normal. It was something very extraordinary. We arrived in Dakar. The airport in Dakar had been alerted. Everyone in the airport had stayed there to await the return of the airplane. Fire extinguishers and fire trucks were there all along the runway to put out any fire in the event the plane would explode. The firemen were there. The plane landed in more or less in this fashion. It bounced. The pilot was an expert. He was an American pilot. Everyone applauded wildly when we landed! It was not over yet. We were asked to wait. We think the doors were jammed by the heat. We couldn't open them right away. So to distract us, we were told stories about this and that. We were told the plane was doing this or that. After almost 30 minutes, they opened the doors. We had to leave the plane by the front.

The back of the plane was very, very hot! The firemen had completely encircled the plane and set up barriers so as to isolate it from the rest of the airport. Upon landing the captain informed us that four tires had blown out. When the plane was still in the air, the four tires exploded. In the cockpit they know which instruments work and do not work. That's how they knew that the tires were no longer working. We landed in Dakar and were told it would take at least 24 hours to fix what was wrong. We waited until five in the morning to see if they would be able to fix the plane. It was too serious and they could not repair it. Then the airline personnel took us to the Novatel Hotel in Dakar. So I stayed at the hotel too, so as not to miss word that the plane had been repaired. But I didn't get a message. I stayed there all day long. They didn't finish the repairs. We had three talks in Atlanta in mind. I was to arrive in New York in the morning, take another plane to Atlanta and in the afternoon I was to speak about the Colloqium in Cairo. Of course, that we couldn't do. We got the impression, it was clear, that they wouldn't be able to do the repairs very soon and that they were just trying to soothe us. I wanted them to endorse my ticket so that I could take the plane that would leave Dakar at midnight to arrive in Paris and take another plane to New York. Then I still would have been in time for the conference. They were about to do it for me and for another African who asked the same thing. They were about to do it. Then from higher up the decision came that they couldn't do it. Because if they did it for us, they would have to do it for the others. By that time I hadn't slept for two days. When the members of my party learned that this accident had almost killed me and found I was at the hotel, they came to get me. It was as though they realized that one day I might not be among them. They were completely against my traveling again. They said to me, "We have to really see why this happened before you travel again." That is exactly what happened.

NOTE

The transcripts of these interviews were prepared by Larry Williams. The first interview, conducted by Listervelt Middleton of South Carolina television, was translated by Elizabeth Clement. The interview with the Nile Valley Executive Committee was translated by Elizabeth Clement and Irene d'Almeida.

Towards unity and reconciliation—The spirit of Diop at the Third Annual Ancient Kemetic Studies Conference held by the Association for the Study of Classical African Civilization (March 20-23, 1986): Ivan Van Sertima (front left), Yosef ben Jochannan (front right), and Leonard Jeffries Jr. (back). Photo: Jim Belfon.

Diop in America

Through recent anthropological discoveries, science has substantially established that the cradle of humanity is Africa. The earliest creatures who passed the divide between animal and man seem to have first emerged in East and South Africa. Professor Raymond Dart described this historical epoch as the moment when man "trembled on the brink of humanity." A million years later in the same place some men of South Africa are again "trembling on the brink of humanity"; but instead of advancing from pre-human to human, they are reversing the process and are travelling backward in time from human to pre-human.

—Dr. Martin Luther King, Jr. appeals for sanctions against South Africa jointly with Chief Albert J. Lutuli on Human Rights Day, December 10, 1962

Dean Carter holding discussions with Dr. Diop at the home of Dr. Charles Finch, who held a private dinner in Dr. Diop's honor. Dean Carter is dean of the Martin Luther King, Jr. International Chapel at Morehouse College, where Dr. Diop gave most of his lectures in America. Morehouse Photo.

Letters of Invitation to Diop

Dear Dr. Diop:

My letter comes in support of the invitation you are receiving from Dr. Hugh M. Gloster, President of Morehouse College and Mr. Andrew Young, Mayor of the City of Atlanta, Georgia, U.S.A. Mr. John Cox, Vice President of Delta Airlines, has announced that Delta is establishing a direct Atlanta-to-Paris route and the inaugural flight is scheduled for April 1, 1985. Mr. Cox has agreed to book you as a complimentary passenger on the Delta Flight #21 that leaves Paris on April 2 at 1225 and arrives in Atlanta at 1440. As our esteemed guest, all of your expenses would be paid in addition to a suitable honorarium.

As the Dean of the Martin Luther King, Jr. International Chapel, I once again look forward to your coming to this historic house to inaugurate your introduction to the United States of America.

With every high hope, I remain,

Yours sincerely,

Lawrence Edward Carter
Dean, Morehouse College

Dear Dr. Diop:

This letter comes inviting you to Morehouse College and the City of Atlanta, Georgia for the April 4, 1985 commemoration events of the assassination of Dr. Martin Luther King, Jr. From Morehouse College Dr. King launched his humanitarian pilgrimage to create the beloved community.

Your scholarly program emphasizing the cultural unity of Africa needs to be heard in the United States and needs the support of Dr. King's name to help bring about mental shifts in the minds of African-Americans.

Highlights of your visit would include an address to the National Association for Equal Opportunity in Higher Education (NAFEO), an organization of all the presidents of the Black colleges in the United States, in Washington, D.C. on April 3; an address to the all-college Morehouse Assembly—where there will be 2,500 persons on hand—in Atlanta on April 4; and the seat of honor at the annual Drum Major banquet given by the Southern Christian Leadership Conference (S.C.L.C.), the organization founded by Dr. King, also on April 4.

Dr. Diop confers with Dr. Hugh M. Gloster, President of Morehouse College. Photo: Jim Alexander.

It is a fact that your work, Dr. Diop, like the life and work of Dr. King, has had a profound impact on the consciousness of African people all over the world. That your first visit to these shores should take place in Atlanta under the auspices of a King commemoration, we think is a fitting testament to you and to Dr. King. We hope that you can accept this heartfelt invitation to join us in Atlanta on April 1.

Very respectfully,

Hugh M. Gloster
President, Morehouse College

Dear Dr. Diop:

I am pleased that you have been invited to come to the United States in April of 1985, and I want to assure you that you will certainly be welcome in Atlanta.

April 4 is the anniversary of the assassination of Dr. Martin Luther King, Jr., and a variety of activities will take place around that date to commemorate Dr. King's life and the movement he led. Many of these activities are planned in Atlanta where Dr. King was born and raised and which was the headquarters of the movement he launched.

Your presence in this country during this period would be very appropriate, because so many people here can benefit from your knowledge and scholarship as we celebrate the work and teachings of a great leader who is honored in Africa, the United States and throughout the world.

I therefore hope that you will be able to share your own thought, which has had a profound impact on the consciousness of African peoples everywhere, by accepting the invitation to be here in April.

Sincerely,

Andrew Young
Mayor, City of Atlanta

Diop in Mayor Young's Office.

CHEIKH ANTA DIOP'S FIRST VISIT TO THE UNITED STATES

—Hosted by Morehouse College—

Lawrence Edward Carter, Sr.

Cheikh Anta Diop does not believe that Martin Luther King Jr.'s dream will be fulfilled in America until African historians dare to connect the history of Black Africa with the history of Egypt.

Tuesday, April 2, 1985, Professor Cheikh Anta Diop, Director of the Radiocarbon Laboratory at the Fundamental Institute of Black Africa (IFAN) at the University of Dakar in Dakar, Senegal, arrived at Atlanta's Hartsfield International Airport on Delta Airlines' inaugural flight from Paris, France, to Atlanta, Georgia. Dr. Diop was the official guest of Morehouse College, the Southern Christian Leadership Conference, the Mayor's Office, the Martin Luther King Jr. Center for Nonviolent Social Change, the Morehouse School of Medicine, and Delta Airlines. The President of Delta Airlines, Mr. Ronald Allen, and Vice President John W. Cox provided Dr. Diop a complimentary roundtrip ticket, medallion class. Both Mr. and Mrs. Allen accompanied Professor Diop from Paris.

Delta also provided Dr. Diop complimentary roundtrip tickets to Washington, D.C., on April 3, 1985, to address the black college and university presidents' annual National Association of Equal Opportunity and Higher Education meeting. His topic was "The New Renaissance: Black Colleges in The Rediscovery of Africa's Contribution to World Civilization." It was at the N.A.F.E.O. meeting that Diop was reunited with his dear friend Dr. Mercer Cook, who translated *The African Origins of Civilization* into English from French. This book has sold over 30,000 copies. Dr. Herman F. Bostick arranged for a French interpreter for the N.A.F.E.O. address.

From April 2nd to April 10th Professor Diop completed a history-making lecture tour which netted him his first honors by the English-speaking world. On April 4th in the Martin Luther King Jr. International Chapel, before over two thousand students, faculty, staff, and citizens of greater Atlanta, President

Dr. Diop in front of Martin Luther King Jr. International Chapel. Left to right: Dr. Edward Taylor (translator) Dr. Lawrence E. Carter Sr. (Dean of the Chapel) Diop (in center) Professor Ivan Van Sertima and Dr. Hugh Gloster (President of Morehouse College). Photo: Larry Williams.

Hugh M. Gloster conferred upon him the honorary degree of Doctor of Humane Letters. Other guests on program were Mrs. Coretta Scott King, Mayor Andrew Young, Dr. Joseph Lowery, Ms. Ellen Stewart, Dr. Ivan Van Sertima, Dr. Alton Hornsby, Dr. Charles Finch, Dean Lawrence Edward Carter, and the Morehouse College Glee Club. That evening Dr. Joseph E. Lowery presented Dr. Diop the first African Heritage Award of S.C.L.C. Both honors acknowledged Professor Diop's distinction in physics, history, anthropology, sociology, linguistics, and politics, but most of all his discoveries as an Egyptologist and authority on ancient Africa.

With 24-hour police escorts and protection provided by the Mayor's Office, the convenience of a newly remodeled presidential suite at Paschal's Motor Hotel, and a team of four professional French and Walaf interpreters—Mrs. Elizabeth M. Clement, Ms. Irene D'Almeida, Dr. Edward F. Taylor, and Mrs. Mary Diallo of Morehouse College—Diop went forth to keep his fifty-three different appointments and speaking engagements at Morehouse College, the Morehouse School of Medicine, Spelman College, the S.C.L.C.'s Drum Major

Dr. Diop descending the steps of City Hall with Dr. Taylor, translator beside him and Dean Carter on lower step (extreme right). Morehouse Photo.

Banquet at the Radisson Hotel, the Washington, D.C., Hilton Hotel, an interview for South Carolina Educational Television, and greetings on Easter Sunday morning at the Central United Methodist Church, where the Rev. Joseph E. Lowery is pastor.

There were well-attended dinners hosted in the homes of Drs. Hugh M. and Beulah Gloster, Dr. and Mrs. Charles S. Finch, and by Dr. and Mrs. Joseph E. Lowery in the Crown Room of the Colony Square Hotel. The Bennu Study Group and the Executive Committee of the Nile Valley Conference sponsored a dinner seminar in the King Chapel Library. Dr. Alton Hornsby and the Morehouse College History Department hosted a faculty luncheon. A second luncheon was hosted by S.C.L.C. at Paschal's Hotel, and a third luncheon was hosted by the National Alliance of Business. Dr. Hugh M. Gloster hosted a welcoming reception in his office for Dr. Diop. Delta Airlines provided a hospitality suite off the International Concourse at the Hartsfield/Atlanta Airport at the time of Dr. Diop's departure for Paris.

Dr. Diop participated in the seventeenth wreath-laying ceremony at the grave of Dr. Martin Luther King Jr. and was taken on a tour of the King Center by Mrs. Coretta Scott King, which was followed by a tour of the

Dr. Diop visiting the Martin Luther King, Jr. Center for Nonviolent Social Change. Pictured from left to right are Dr. Diop, Mrs. Christine King Farris, Mrs. Coretta King, and Dr. Joseph E. Lowery. Photo: Jim Alexander.

S.C.L.C. offices led by Dr. Joseph Lowery. Mayor Andrew Young received Dr. Diop at City Hall, and he and Mrs. Young later presented him the first piece of commissioned art to be given distinguished visitors to the City of Atlanta. There were many gifts from all parts of the city, and tours of the Shrine of the Black Madonna Bookstore, Hakim's Bookstore, Stone Mountain, and the Atlanta University Center. Professor Diop attended the Good Friday Seven Last Words Service and the theatrical musical called "Martin," both sponsored by S.C.L.C. and King Chapel.

The French-trained African physicist gave ten illustrated lectures and addresses by using a series of 19 black-and-white and color slides. His topics were "The Origin of the Ancient Egyptians," "The Significance of Martin Luther King, Jr.," "The Challenge for the Future from the Past," "The Peopling of Ancient Egypt," "The Deciphering of the Meroitic Script," "The Black African as Father of the Human Race," "The Melanin Dosage Test," "The Egyptian Race According to the Classical Authors of Antiquity," "The Egyptians as They Saw Themselves," "Linguistic Affinities Between Hieroglyphics and the Languages of Western Africa," and "The African Human Sciences." For the Senegalese professor, hailed as the world's greatest living historian and as one of the two outstanding black scholars of the 20th century most impact-

Mrs. King discusses a new book, which she published on her late husband. Dr. Diop at right while Dr. Taylor (middle) serves as French interpreter.

ing African thought, "Egyptian antiquity is to African culture what Greco-Roman antiquity is to Western culture. The building up of a corpus of Negro African humanities should be based on this fact."

Diop contends that "as far as science knows today, before 30,000 B.C. there were no whites in existence. Yellow people appeared even later, around 15-20,000 B.C. Today, science can rely on irrefutable material evidence to illustrate these facts."

"Considering that mankind developed in Africa and that this first mankind was black-skinned, blacks had to be at the origin of the world's first civilizations. Their domination extended over the entire globe. The overall supremacy of the blacks extended right down to the Assyrian period."

Diop stated, "The Greeks were forced to come humbly and drink at the fountain of Egyptian culture. Therefore, the respect paid the black man at that time was immense. Of course, we witness the inordinate hatred of the Assyrians, but look at the devotion shown by Alexander towards Egypt and

Left to right: Morehouse President Dr. Gloster, Coretta Scott King, Dr. Diop and Dr. Lawrence Carter Sr. all pose in Mrs. King's office in front of a portrait of the late Dr. King. Morehouse Photo.

Egyptian culture! After conquering the entire eastern Mediterranean basin, Alexander went as far as to set up the capital of the empire in Egypt, not in continental Greece or Macedonia."

"The Egyptian language could not be isolated from the African context, and its origin could not be fully explained in terms of Semitic. It was thus quite normal to expect to find related languages in Africa."

"The African languages constitute one linguistic family as homogenous as that of the Indo-European tongues. Nothing is easier than to set down the rules that allow transfer from a Zulu language (Bantu) to one of these of West Africa (Serer-Walaf, Penl), or even to ancient Egyptian."

Professor Diop pointed to the final report of the crucial UNESCO Symposium on *The Peopling of Ancient Egypt and the Deciphering of the Meroitic Script,* which brought together at his request the most reputed specialists and Egyptologists of the world, held in Cairo from January 28 to February 3, 1974. His conclusions have gained wide acceptance in international scientific circles. From the Cairo Symposium came the call for the history of Africa to be rewritten. Three of the eight volumes are now in print.

Dr. Diop's entire first visit to this country was coordinated by Dr. Lawrence Edward Carter, Dean of the Martin Luther King Jr. International Chapel at Morehouse College.

Citation to Cheikh Anta Diop

Presented by Hugh M. Gloster, President of Morehouse College

King Chapel — 11:00 a.m.
Morehouse College — April 4, 1985

Cheikh Anta Diop:

Man of many talents, you are not limited to one profession. You have climbed to the heights in physics, history, anthropology, sociology, linguistics, and politics. In this period of specialization you are a Renaissance man with an outstanding record of achievement in many fields.

As a young man in Senegal, you demonstrated great genius in physics and went to Paris at the age of 23 to do advanced studies in that field. Within a short time, however, you became interested in studies of the origin of African civilization. Eventually you became convinced that only through restoration of Africa's importance in world history could the cultural shackles of colonialism be removed. Your doctoral dissertation, showing that Egypt was a black African civilization, was rejected but was later published under the title of *Black Nations and Culture* in 1955. This book won wide acclaim, but two additional attempts to receive your doctorate were turned back. Eventually, in 1960, you defended your dissertation, received the degree of Docteur es Lettres, and published *The Cultural Unity of Black Africa* and *Pre-Colonial Black Africa.*

But as a young man you were more than an investigator working in libraries and among ruins; you were also a fearless activist fighting for the liberation of French colonies in Africa. From 1950 to 1953 you were Secretary-General of the Democratic African Assembly, and you helped launch the first Pan-African Student Congress in Paris in 1951. You also participated in the first World Congress of Black Writers and Artists in Paris in 1956 and in the second such Congress in Rome in 1959. After returning to Senegal in 1960, you participated in the first World Black Festival of Arts and Culture held in 1966 in Dakar. In 1974 your principal books were translated into English, and since then you have published two additional books, including *Civilization or Barbarism.*

You are currently Director of the Fundamental Institute of Black Africa at the University of Dakar, you sit on numerous scholarly committees, and you are recognized as one of the outstanding researchers of the world. One writer has hailed you as the "Pharaoh" of African studies.

Dr. Diop in his academic robes before receiving the honorary doctorate from Morehouse. Morehouse Photo.

Dr. Hugh M. Gloster, President of Morehouse College, conferred upon Dr. Cheikh Anta Diop the honorary degree of Doctor of Humane Letters. Dr. Diop is assisted with his hood by Abraham L. Davis, Professor in the Political Science Department at Morehouse. The King Memorial Convocation occurred on April 5, 1985 at 11 a.m. in the great nave of the Martin Luther King, Jr. International Chapel. Morehouse Photo.

Today, as you come to us from Africa to serve as the leading participant in this historic convocation, we greet you as a brother and salute you as follows:

We are brothers, you and I—
You from Dakar, I from Atlanta—.
We are brothers, you and I.
We are brothers, you and I—
You from Senegal, I from
  America—
We are brothers, you and I.

Cheikh Anta Diop, you have proved the contribution of Africa to world civilization, restored the place of Africa in world history, deciphered the Meroitic Script, and established yourself, along with W.E.B. DuBois, as one of the two outstanding black scholars of the 20th century. Because of these contributions, we are pleased to honor you today. Therefore, upon the recommendation of the Faculty and by virtue of the authority vested in me as President by the Board of Trustees of Morehouse College, I hereby confer upon you the honorary degree of Doctor of Humane Letters, with all the rights, privileges, and responsibilities thereunto appertaining.

This report is reprinted from the Morehouse College *Bulletin*, Founders' Day Issue, Winter 1955. Published with permission.

Dr. Diop receiving honorary doctorate at the Martin Luther King Jr. International Chapel, Morehouse College, April 4, 1985. Left to right: Mayor Andrew Young of Atlanta; Dr. Diop; Dr. Hugh M. Gloster, President of Morehouse College; Mrs. Coretta Scott King, President of the Martin Luther King Jr. Center for Nonviolent Social Change, and Dr. Lawrence Edward Carter, Dean of the Martin Luther King Jr. International Chapel. Morehouse Photo.

SPEECH BY CHEIKH ANTA DIOP ON RECEIVING AN HONORARY DOCTORATE FROM MOREHOUSE

I wish to thank you, all of you citizens of Atlanta, for the academic distinction you wish to bestow upon me. And I thank you, not only for myself, but for all of the Senegalese people, and for all of the African people. I wish first to thank Dr. Hugh Gloster, President of Morehouse College. I wish to thank also Mayor Andrew Young for all of his help and consideration. He is not only a great citizen of Atlanta, he is also a great citizen of the Third World. I wish to make that observation, if I am permitted. I wish also to thank Mr. John Cox of Delta Airlines for the assistance they have given us and the opportunity to make this visit possible. I wish also to thank Rev. Joseph Lowery of the Southern Leadership Conference and Dean Lawrence Carter of the Martin Luther King Jr. International Chapel. And to all of the citizens of Atlanta, who have already given us such a warm reception, I wish to say thank you.

Distinguished guests, ladies and gentlemen, Mr. President, my colleagues and friends, I wish to seize this opportunity that has been given me to direct your attention to the gravity of the responsibility which has been entrusted to you—that of the transmission of knowledge to young generations of our community. Looking over history we are quickly drawn to the fact that our nations have declined, and, as a result, our communities. This is intimately tied to national sovereignty and especially to the loss of control of our educational systems which assure the transmission of understanding from generation to generation. The example of the Egyptians is pertinent in this regard. For 3,000 years, from Menes to Cambyses, the Egyptian nation endured, conserving intact its historical memory, thanks to its educational system. In fact, the historical consciousness of a country is the linchpin, that most solid cohesive unit against all forms of aggression that a nation faces. It is the cement which assures national cohesion. The invisible tie which permits a people to distinguish itself from a population. It is also the classical technique of domination, of colonization, throughout history, to destroy and to weaken the historical consciousness of a people who become dominated. All the factors which reinforce that consciousness are taken away, taken out of the instruction so that progressively the dominated nation becomes amnesiac. It loses its historical memory and regresses, becoming an aggregation of individuals who are pliable and totally without any sense of pride. These are the conditions of domination, of permanent domination, that have been created. Intellectual regression and moral regression set in as does doubt and the lack of confidence in one's self. In history, this procedure is classic. Ancient Egypt lived through this situation from 525 B.C. after the Persian conquest.

In fact, Black Egypt lost its independence completely from this date because the Persian occupation was followed by the Greeks and then the Romans. Seven centuries of occupation followed. It took that long for this ancient civilization (the most ancient civilization) to which humanity owes its first progress, to be destroyed. The same Egyptian people who had created this civilization regressed in their own country and fell into mediocrity. Today, African peoples who have just come out of the darkness of colonization are also amnesiac in different degrees and must rediscover their historical memory. There is for us the necessity to organize instruction of history in view of the cultural renaissance. We must reconstruct a new Afro-American cultural personality within the framework of our respective nations. Our history from the beginning of mankind, rediscovered and relived as such, will be the foundation of this new personality. Research in the periods concerned in prehistory and in antiquity have sufficiently advanced to permit a fusion of our programs on the two sides of the Atlantic. Our instruction must take into account all of the new discoveries in this domain. A pedagogical effort must be made to assimilate these indispensable notions of the consciousness of our community. In doing this, we will have contributed significantly to the restitution of our own cultural heritage, to bringing it alive in the consciousness of our people. It is not only a question of programs. It is also, perhaps, a modest way in which to contribute to the harmonious integration of these communities in the cultural fullness of America. Thank you.

This speech was presented to the all-college Morehouse Assembly at the Martin Luther King, Jr. International Chapel on April 4, 1985. The transcript was done by Marva Riffin Carter.

Proclamation

CITY OF ATLANTA

Office of the Mayor

DR. CHEIKH ANTA DIOP, KNOWN AS THE "PHAROAH" OF AFRICAN STUDIES, WAS BORN IN DIOURBEL, SENEGAL ON DECEMBER 29, 1923.

CURRENTLY DIRECTOR OF THE RADIO-CARBON LABORATORY AT THE FUNDAMENTAL INSTITUTE OF BLACK AFRICA AT THE UNIVERSITY OF DAKAR, DIOP SITS ON NUMEROUS INTERNATIONAL SCIENTIFIC COMMITTEES AND HAS ACHIEVED RECOGNITION AS ONE OF THE LEADING HISTORIANS, EGYPTOLOGISTS, LINGUISTS, AND ANTHROPOLOGISTS IN THE WORLD.

IN HIS EARLY 20'S, DIOP SET OUT FOR PARIS TO CONTINUE ADVANCED STUDIES OF THE ORIGIN OF CIVILIZATION IN AFRICA. BECOMING INCREASINGLY ACTIVE IN THE AFRICAN STUDENT MOVEMENTS AGITATING FOR INDEPENDENCE FROM FRENCH COLONIAL RULE. HE BECAME CONVINCED THAT ONLY BY RE-EVALUATING, RE-ASSESSING, AND RESTORING AFRICA'S PLACE IN THE HISTORY OF THE WORLD COULD THE PHYSICAL AND MENTAL SHACKLES OF COLONIALISM BE LIFTED FROM AFRICA.

DURING HIS STUDENT DAYS, DIOP WAS AN AVID POLITICAL ACTIVIST. FROM 1950 TO 1953, HE WAS THE SECRETARY-GENERAL OF THE RASSEMLEMENT DEMOCRATIQUE AFRICAIN AND HELPED LAUNCH THE FIRST PAN-AFRICAN STUDENT CONGRESS IN PARIS IN 1951. HE ALSO PARTICIPATED IN THE FIRST WORLD CONGRESS OF BLACK WRITERS AND ARTISTS HELD IN PARIS IN 1956 AND THE SECOND SUCH CONGRESS HELD IN ROME IN 1959.

ATLANTA IS PROUD OF OUTSTANDING INDIVIDUALS SUCH AS DR. CHEIKH ANTA DIOP AND HIS COUNTLESS CONTRIBUTIONS TO THE GROWTH, SPIRIT AND VITALITY OF THE AFRICAN CULTURE AND IN RECOGNITION THEREOF, I, ANDREW YOUNG, PROCLAIM APRIL 4, 1985, AS

"DR. CHEIKH ANTA DIOP DAY"

ANDREW YOUNG
MAYOR

THE BEGINNINGS OF MAN AND CIVILIZATION

Cheikh Anta Diop

Ladies and Gentlemen, I wish to first thank you today for coming here to hear me speak. I wish to especially thank President Hugh Gloster and all those who participated in organizing this event. Yesterday at a reception, organized by Dr. Gloster at his home, I said that I had come to America to meet with those who are members of my family, that is to say with you all (applause).

In fact, I am convinced that my family has been divided in two and that half of it is here before me now. Just as you Americans go to Africa feel that you are making a pilgrimage to the lands of your ancestors, I too am making a pilgrimage here in America. The most important thing that we have to do by the end of this century is to reconstruct the links that tie us as communities. I subscribe to the teachings of Martin Luther King, Jr. wholeheartedly. They are teachings which are aimed at unifying and reuniting kindred peoples. What I have to say here today is to reinforce the links that unite us and all people across the world and not to weaken them.

To get right to the subject of my speech today, I wish in one hour's time to give you a very clear idea on three points. I want you to leave this room with the conviction that humanity was born and developed in Africa! (Applause). It is this humanity that went out of Africa to populate the other continents of the world! And when it went out, it was differentiated—that is to say it took on different aspects, a different appearance. But we will see that all human beings form one great family and it is only that those human beings changed their appearance as they changed continents. This then will help us to understand that we are one people, an organic unity, and it is this instruction that is important for purposes of identifying us, not for dividing us. The second part of my speech will show you that not only was humanity born in Africa, it was developed there on that continent to create the first of the world's civilizations, which is the Egyptian civilization. As Dr. Finch so eloquently demonstrated, it was obviously a civilization created by Africans, like you and me. It was also this civilization that created medicine, art, and science which was passed on to the Greeks. And we will demonstrate this, remaining always on very solid scientific ground, without any emotional element involved. I wish to especially remind you that humanity must reunite around the availability

The above was delivered as a lecture at the Martin Luther King, Jr. International Chapel, Morehouse College, on April 6, 1985. The transcript of this lecture was prepared by Larry Williams. Translation by Elizabeth Clement, Irene d'Almeida, Dr. Edward F. Taylor, and Mary Diallo.

of such facts. It is that which will endure. In the final part of my speech, I will remind you of the conditions in which Africa lost its historical initiative and fell into servitude even unto this time. It lost its historical memory to such an extent that its sons dispersed throughout the world, or those who stayed where they were, no longer remember this history and that their civilization had done anything. This instruction will permit Africans and African-Americans to find once again the historical memory that we have lost and to find the fullness of our culture. It will also give us greater strength with which to confront others, confident in ourselves. I think that it is on this foundation that the integration of communities can be achieved in a lasting way. Not only here in America but also in Africa and everywhere in the world. This is what we are concerned with today. I am certain this conforms with the message that was left to us by Martin Luther King, Jr. (applause).

We will now go to the first point of my speech. I would like to remind you of another fact. Nature could have presented itself in an opposite way. Humanity could just as easily have been born not in Africa, but in Europe. If this had been the case, the first man would have been pale of skin, that is to say white. And if man had gone from Europe to Africa in the conditions of prehistoric life, that man would have either darkened in Africa or disappeared. But nature doesn't ever do anything strictly by chance. The color Black acts as a protection of the organism. If man was first born in Africa and had not been Black, he would not have survived! We know scientifically that ultraviolet rays would have destroyed the human organism in the equatorial regions, if this organism had not been protected by Black pigmentation, that is by Melanin. That is obviously why man first born in Africa was black, that's all. It is not something we need to be necessarily proud of, it is simply fact. We should consider it only as a fact, scientifically substantiated. And we should say to ourselves that the contrary could just as easily have occurred.

But if, because of the way we have been educated, we reject this idea and try to find another origin for mankind, facts will become incomprehensible and scientific explanations no longer possible. Ideological facts have done a great deal of harm to the work of science. There are those minds that are unable, because of their education, and training, to believe that we did not pass from black to white. These people hold these ideas that bear no relationship to what science can demonstrate.

We can fix the origins of humanity at 5.5 million years ago. This humanity comprised six specimens. The first five have disappeared completely, what remains is the sixth. The sixth specimen which survived is man as we know it, called *Homo Sapiens-Sapiens* and that man is black, white or yellow. The first 3 specimens of humanity had very difficult names to remember. I won't cite them but in discussion you can make reference to them. I will say simply to you that the first three specimens of humanity were born in Africa and became extinct in Africa. They never arrived at a potential for expansion and never left the continent of Africa. The three others did leave Africa. Among

1. Homo Erectus.

these three others, there are two that are closely identified, and I will speak about them later during the slide-projection portion of my lecture. But as I've said, the three final specimens did leave Africa. The first which we call *Homo Erectus* went into Europe 400,000 years ago, he went into Asia 500,000 years ago. He left Africa by means of the Straits of Gilbraltar or the Isthmus of Suez. He was followed by what we call Neanderthal man and then followed by *Homo Sapiens-Sapiens*. We can establish that 120,000 years ago this later man, like you and me, existed in Africa. He was *only* in Africa for a very long time, and not on any other continent. He lived in Africa at least until 40,000 years ago before he left Africa. During this time no other part of the world was populated by man like us. And if this man had stayed in Africa, and not gone to other continents, the rest of the world would not have been peopled. It would be desert. Mankind would not be of many races, man would simply be Black and homogeneous—one color only.

So you see that race is simply a matter of climate. 400,000 years ago this man left Africa (Homo Erectus) (Slide 1.). He gave birth eventually to man as we know him and later in Europe to that man we call white. At that time the climate in Europe was very different from what we know it now. It was before and during the final glaciation. It was so cold in Europe that it was not possible to live on the open ground, it was necessary to live in caves. It was, therefore, impossible to create a kind of civilization, that we know was created in Africa, under these living conditions, it was simply impossible and this fact will explain why Africa was ahead of the civilizations of Europe. Adapting itself to these new conditions that were excessive, very crude, facing these conditions, man became over a period, a different man, the man we call Cromagnon man. The notions of race are difficult for me to engage in but I am obliged to, in order to explain these facts as we know them. At this stage of my speech, I would like to explain by means of slides how man developed in Africa and how he changed over the centuries. This period I have talked about in such a short time goes from about 5,500,000 to 20,000 years ago. So I am going to show you the slide projections so that the ideas can become clear to you. This is the first inhabitant of Europe, *Grimaldi* man. He came to Europe 40,000 years ago (Slide 2, middle). I am not talking about *Homo Erectus*, which came before him and disappeared. I am strictly speaking about the species that is called *Homo Sapiens-Sapiens*. So it is this skull that represents the man who first lived in Europe. Between 40,000 to 20,000 years it changed and gave birth to this skull (Slide 2, left). This is the Cromagnon man. So for 40,000 years, it's only Grimaldi man that existed throughout the world. You can see the morphological features are such that the jaws are protruding. That is a specific African feature. It changes to the other picture that you see now (Slide 2, right). You can see also that this is a *Homo Sapiens-Sapiens*. Look at the forehead which is very large and also the eyes. Essentially, it's the same man,—you can see the eyes and forehead. Here I have shown you the skull of modern African man and you can see that the kinship, the resemblance is striking and that the African man is no different from the first man that inhabited Europe. You can also see that the form, the shape of the cranium, is the same. I've just shown you *Homo Sapiens-Sapiens*.

Here I would like to draw your attention to Piltdown man (Slide 3). The forehead is much bigger and look also at the eyes. The skull is a fossil which

---

Editor's Note: The quality of several of the slides used in the Diop lecture was affected by the need to duplicate these urgently during his brief visit to the United States.

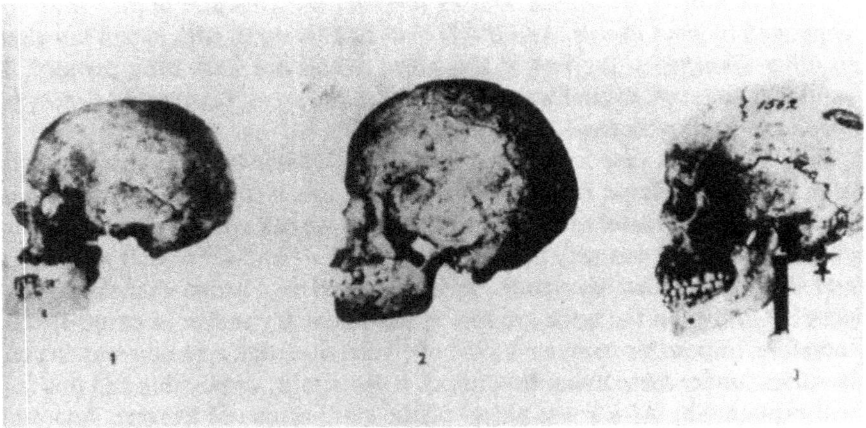

2. Cro-Magnon Man (left), Grimaldi Skull (middle), Modern Sudanese (right).

has been falsified (fabricated). It was made up by a British geologist in 1912. He buried the skull in the sands of Sussex, England. For 50 years the scientific community was divided into two groups. One of these groups defended this fabricated fossil and called it the Piltdown man. And this has given birth to the theory of the Pre-Sapien. All that was done with the intention of demonstrating that the first man was born in Europe and not in Africa! So you can see then that all these fabricators were doing were putting forth value judgments and emotional ideas instead of scientific fact. They committed real crimes against science and humanity. The only passion that must fire the researcher is the passion for scientific truth! But we have scientists who are of good faith and some we have who are also scientists of bad faith. In 1954 another British scientist, Professor Oakley, who is at the British Museum, proved that this fossil was not a real one, but totally fabricated. The upper part of the cranium belongs to a man like you and me.

The lower jaw is that of a monkey of the Orangutang family. You can see the canines of the monkey. During our question and answer period I can tell you, if you want to know it, how Professor Oakley was able to show this skull was counterfeit. So we must also honor and recognize the scientists who are of good faith like Professor Oakley. It's because of scientists of good faith like him and many others that science can progress. All the scientists of the world must be united around the idea of finding the scientific truth and nothing else! This closes the first period of the history of humanity. It lasted about 5.5 million years. During all that time it was Africa that peopled, not only the African continent, but the rest of the world and also exported all its inventions and all its industries to the rest of the world.

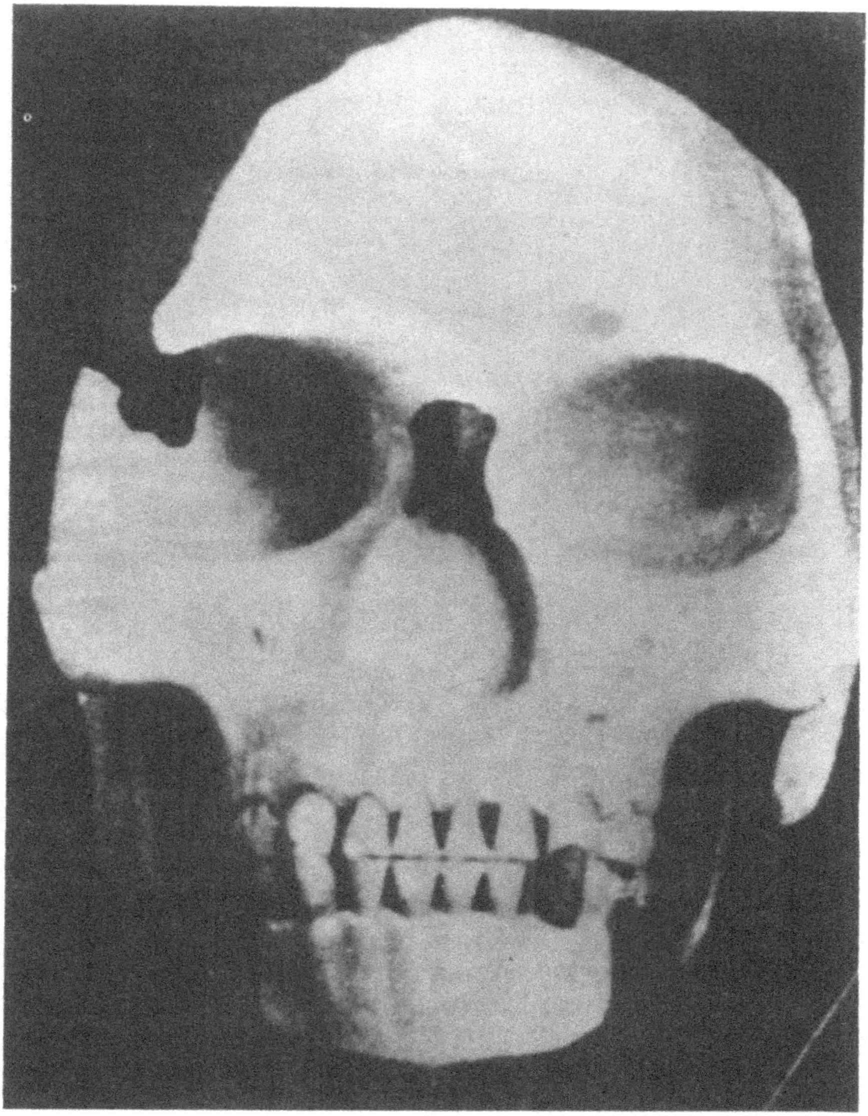

3. Piltdown Man.

Nile Valley

If I had a map of the Nile Valley you would have seen that humanity that was born in Kenya went down to the Nile Valley to create there the first

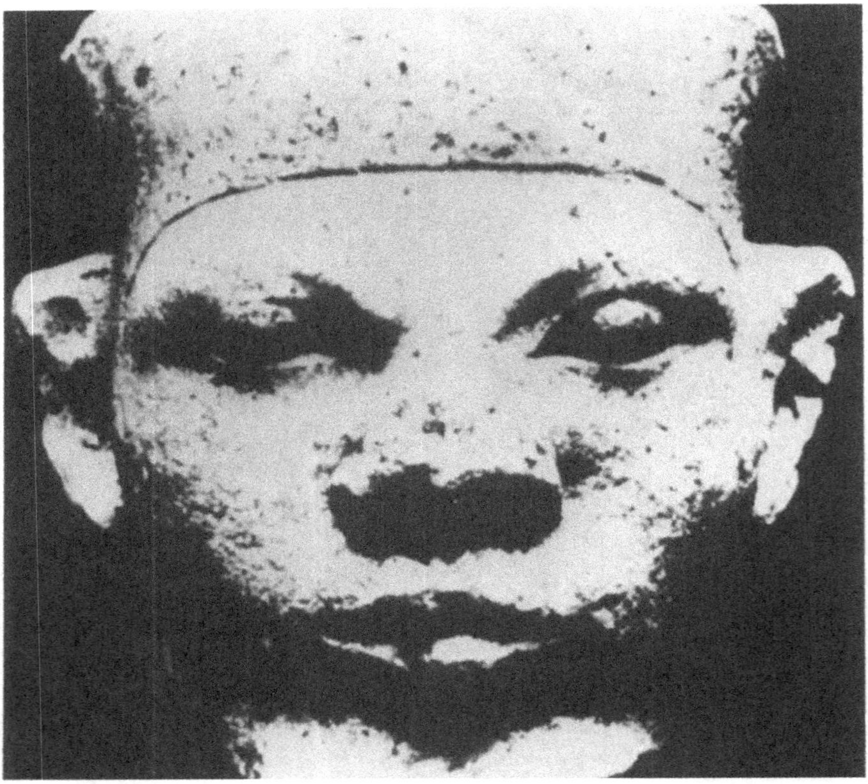

4. Menes/Narmer.

African civilization. When you have a map of Africa you can see that humanity came to life, was born, at the source of the Nile Valley in the region of the great lakes. If you follow the valley of that river this humanity went to the lower valley and created there the Egyptian Civilization. If what I told you on the origins of the first man is true, then the civilization could only have been created by the people who were there before other men were created. Before the very existence of other races!

Later, I am going to illustrate to you, to show you, that during the prehistoric and historic times, all the times I have been covering, the people who created the Egyptian civilization were Black people like you and me. Here again we don't necessarily have to be proud of this. Because, as I told you, Europe was slowed down by glaciation—it was frozen! It was impossible for them to progress because of the glaciation. They were stopped in their development. The glaciation stopped about 12,000 years ago. It's only at that time that European expansion will start whereas, in Africa, it had started a

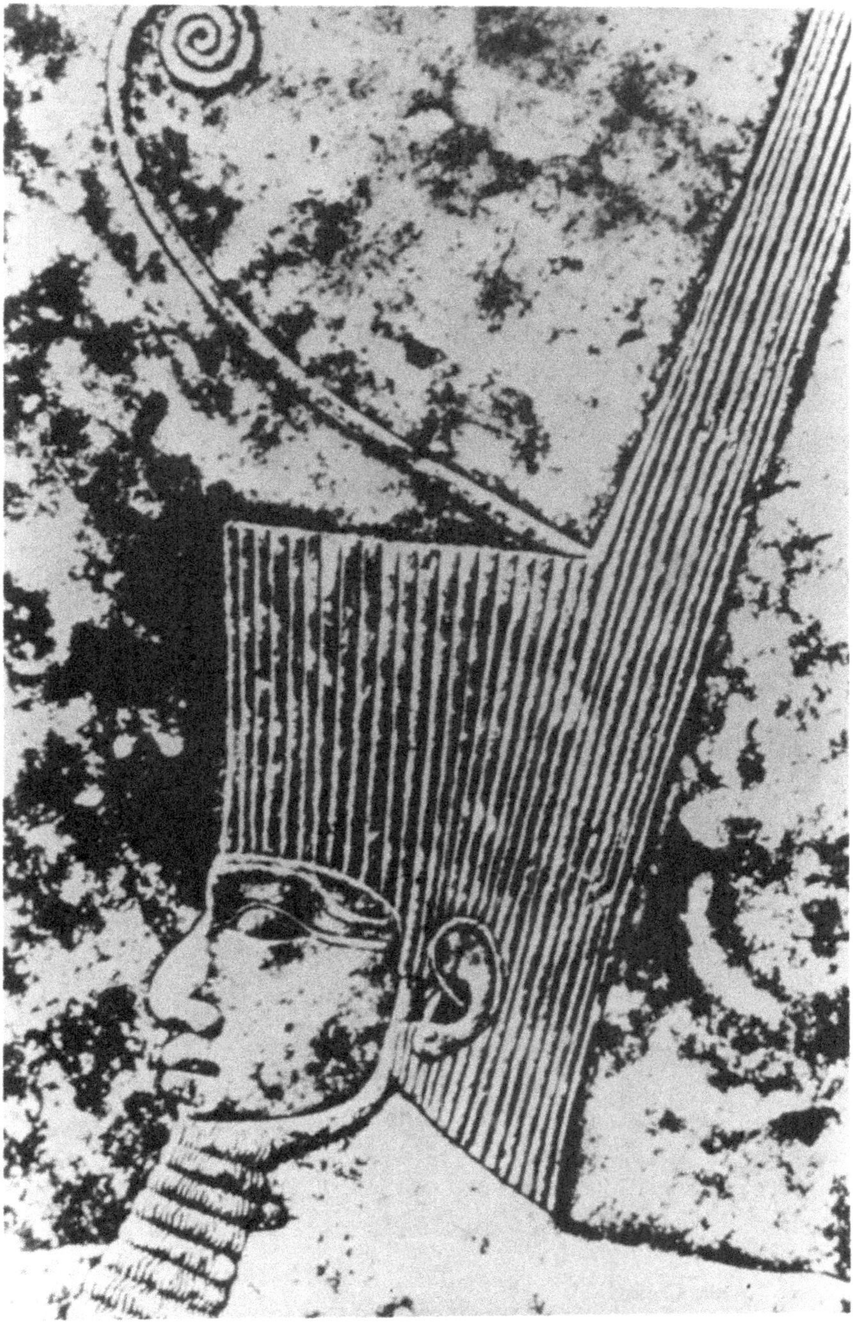

5. Zoser—Red Crown.

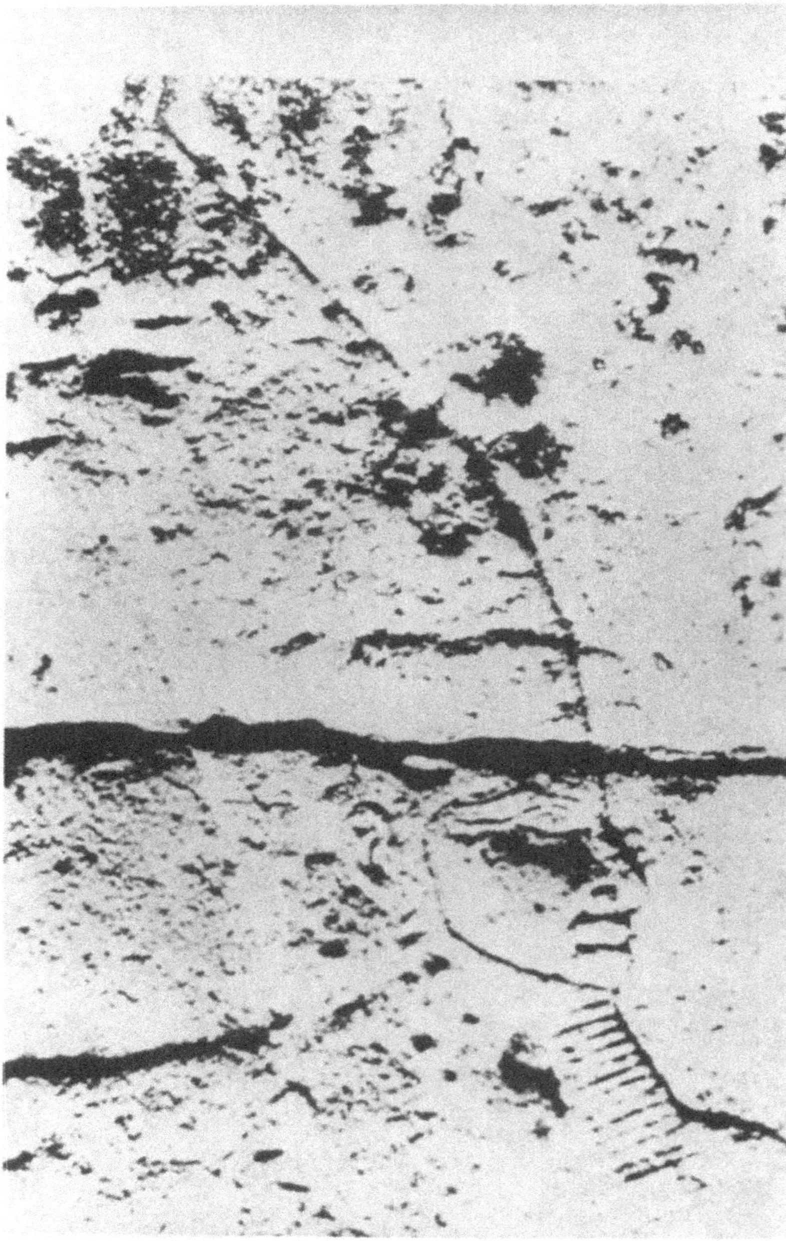

6. Zoser—White Crown.

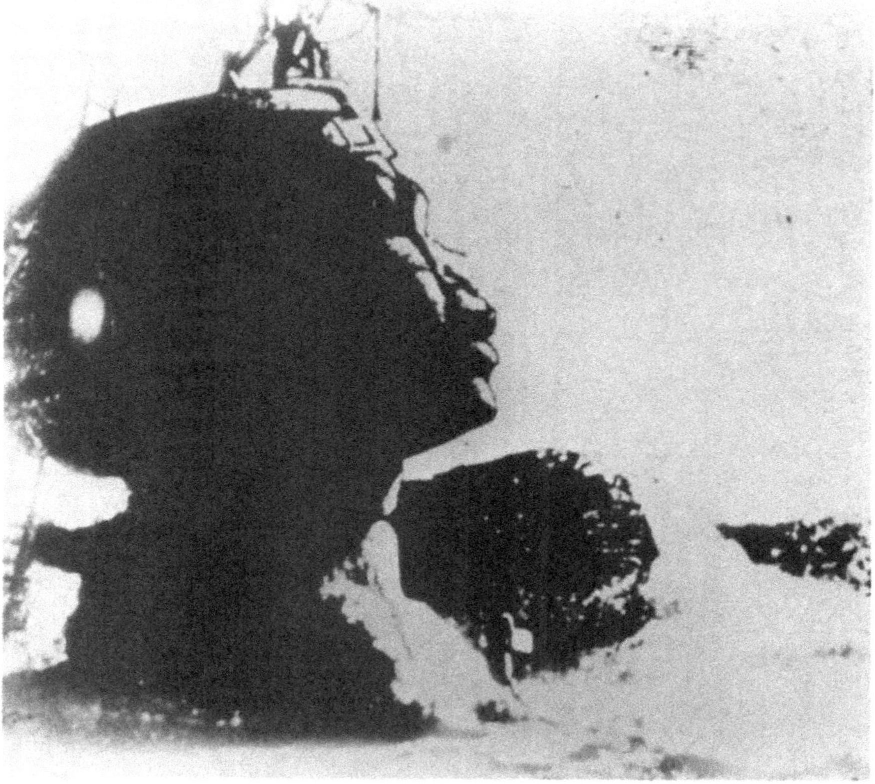

7. Sphinx.

very long time ago. For instance, we know that 17,000 years ago the people on the African continent had started the domestication of plants. If I had more time, I would have shown you in detail how the Nile Valley had been responsible for the beginnings of specialization. I would have shown you how it was indispensable for that specialization to have invented geometry and the other sciences. All I would like for you to know, is that, as early as the third dynasty (that is 2,878 B.C.) all the technological elements of the Egyptian civilization were already in place, then perpetuated themselves until the later period. In order to save time and allow you to ask questions, I'm going to show you the slides and in doing so, I'm going to explain to you, to show you, how these people were in Africa and also how they created their science.

This (Slide 4) is the first King of the world. It is the first Pharoah who unified the Nile Valley from Upper and Lower Egypt. It's King Narmer or Menes, if you like. You can see that his features are typically African. And so

8. Amenhotep I.

that should help us to rectify the notion whereby people thought that the first Egyptians were white and that the Blacks came along later on. That is not true. (Slide 5.) Here you have Pharoah Zoser, here again he has typically African features. Here he is wearing the red crown of lower Egypt. It is during his reign that the scientist Imhotep lived. Under Zoser all the elements of the Egyptian sciences were already there, as early as 2,878 B.C. in the 3rd dynasty.

Here you see (Slide 6) the same Pharoah represented a little clearer with the same typically African features with the white crown of upper Egypt.

Here is the Sphinx (Slide 7). This is represented in the 4th Dynasty approximately 2,600 B.C. Pharoah Chephren perhaps, is represented here. The people you see there on the tops were part of a scientific mission which accompanied Napoleon to Egypt at the end of the nineteenth century. They left that profile of the Sphinx. You can see that it is different from the profile of the sphinx that we know of today, because erosion had already taken its effect over 1 or 2 centuries. But you can see again, that this profile is typically African. So you can see that the Pharoahs that built the pyramids were Africans like you and me. We know that the nose of the Sphinx fell to the ground and was collected and is now in the British museum. Egypt could very well ask to have it returned, to put it back in place. But then the Sphinx would perhaps have a face that is typically African, and we may not want to see that (laughter).

This is Amenhotep I (Slide 8). Dr. Finch and the Executive committee of the Nile Valley Conference are right. We must change completely the names given to the Pharoahs. This Greek appellation doesn't mean anything according to the Egyptian terminology. But that would take an independent and considerable effort in itself. And if I use those Egyptian names you would probably not recognize them. So I use them only from time to time when that name is recognizable. This is then, Amenhotep I. You see that he is represented here in his natural color, which is Black. And also with his kinky hair. He's like us, and African. And these are the great builders of historic Egypt. And it is these Pharoahs that conquered all of Western Asia and were part of the first Egyptian imperialists. When we get to Thutmore III, who was part of the same dynasty, we will see that Egypt had conquered 111 states in Western Asia and the eastern Mediterranean.

This is the mother of the Pharoah you have just seen. This is Queen Ahmose-Nefertari (Slide 9). The fact that there are many colors demonstrates that the colors are real as opposed to symbolic. These are not symbolic colors. What is Black is Black. [Elsewhere in this lecture, Dr. Diop deals with the use of red as a ceremonial color in ancient Egyptian painting—Ed.] What is red is red. What is Blue is Blue (Applause) So you have an African woman like all the Africans. Towards the end of one of the most glorious of the Egyptian dynasties this figure was completely erased from our historical memory. If we

9. Ahmose-Nefertari.

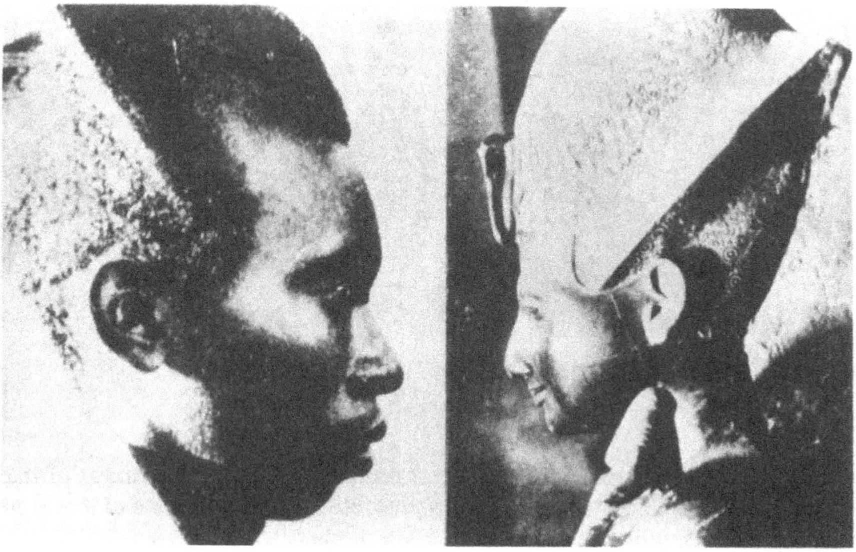

10. Ramses II.

had illustrated our history books with figures like this, our historic memory would have endured (applause). But from the time of colonization, we couldn't fit this into our educational system. Our educational system was in the hands of the colonizers who taught us in the place of these historical truths, a fictitious history,—a falsified or counterfeited history, which led us to doubt ourselves and to believe finally that we never did anything in the world because our true past has been erased or taken away. Here we have Rameses II (Slide 10), one of the most well known of the Egyptian Pharoahs. It is very frequently asked why did he wear this Bronze helmet to go into war and his kinky hair is represented on the bronze helmet, but you perhaps cannot see it. One question frequently asked is, why did his helmet have this bizarre form? Why didn't he have, for example, a helmet like Pericles? All these enigmas were explained by Africans. You see that the African experience enlightened the Egyptian experience—it sheds light on the Egyptian experience. You can't separate these two. It is for this reason that we cannot create a court or body of human sciences if we cut it off from African reality. You can see that this hair-do is very similar to the helmet worn by Rameses II. If you are Eurocentric in your orientation, you will not find this reality in Africa, which explains this Egyptian fact.

Here you have a representation of all of the races such as they were known in Egypt (Slide 11, Races of Man)—we are at 1200 years B.C. that means 3000 years before this time. The Egyptian artist represents here the general type of

11. Races of Egypt (see p. 210 for details).

the Egyptian people of that day. Here is represented all the Egyptians of that day. The Egyptian artists of that time represented Egyptian people of that time like this (points to first man on right). They represented all Europeans like this (points to second man). All the other Africans, in the interior of the continent, were represented in this way (points to man on left). All of the semites, the arabs of Eastern Asia, were represented in this way (points to extreme right). So you can see that these Egyptians were never to be confused with the Europeans! They were never confused with the Semites! And they were never differentiated from the other Africans (applause). This also demonstrates that the colors are real, that Black is Black. What is white is white. What is green is green and so on. So you see the Egyptians were never differentiated from the Africans! This is also confirmed in the language of the Pharoahs. As Dr. Finch will often tell you, the strongest term that exists in *Pharoanic* language to say black is what the Egyptians used to indicate themselves. It's the term *Kemit* (KMT) that they used in talking about themselves, they said Black! In reality, the term is even stronger than that and they used it to indicate themselves. The Egyptians never, never used in any text the word Black to designate whites. The Egyptians called themselves Hamitu which means the man, par excellence. They use the term Nehesu to designate the other populations in the interior of Africa. The Egyptologists translate the term Nehesu as Black. And that is wrong. It is a falsification, it doesn't mean black and that must be known. In the same way that the Romans used the term "barbarian" to distinguish themselves from the germanic races, so the Egyptians in the same way, used a term of civilization to distinguish themselves from the Nubians without ever any indication of color. The only term they used for themselves to indicate black, they also used for these people. Everytime that you see the term *Nehesu* translated as Black it is a falsification. Egyptologists often do it but they know that it is not correct.

12. Menuhotep I.

13. Osiris.

This is Mentuhotep I (Slide 12), the founder of the eleventh Dynasty. The city of Thebes, for a thousand years, worshipped him as a cult-figure. These are the builders of Egyptian civilization, men like you and I.

This is the God of the Egyptian People. (Slide 13-Osiris) These are people that represented their gods in black and in dark black. All of their gods were represented as Black! This throne is the first throne that existed in the history of religion. You must imagine then the germanic people representing their gods with the same color. In Egypt, all the divinities were represented in Black, as OSIRIS is here *The Black One*, the Goddess Hathor was called the Black woman (Slide 13A). The Goddess Isis is a greek word. The real word for Isis in Pharoanic language is *Auset* which means Black woman. A Black woman completely Black (Slide 13B). *[Editor's note: The slides of Hathor and Isis were not shown in the original lecture but are inserted for the reader's benefit.]*

All the Gods were black. It is this Pharoah (Slide 14), Akhnaten, who created the first monotheistic religion. Moses didn't exist yet. Aknaten was the first to say that God is a spirit and was not created and should not be represented by images. It is the purest monotheism represented in religious history.

He is here with the Queen Nefertiti and you see that she is an African like the King, and African like us. They had six daughters. One of the daughters is in the king's hand and the other is on the shoulder of the king and the other is in the lap of her mother. I blew this figure up so that you could see it (Slide 15). You can see there how she is typically African. You see that the daughter of the first prophet of the world had the features typically African like all of the young women in this room. If this Egyptian princess had thick lips it's because she sucked her thumb. The Egyptologists say that. You see again the typical African Hairdo, it's the totemic hairdo. And this reshaping of the head is similar to the reshaping of the head of the Mangbetu tribe of central Africa. In the discussion ask me why the Pharoahs painted themselves in a red color. I am showing you here Egyptians represented in their natural color and not painted in the color red which is used for ceremonial occasions. This is why you can often see a pharoah in two colors, black his natural color, and also the ceremonial red color.

Here I have taken the pictures published by Professor Van Sertima (Slide 16). Here on the right side is Queen Tiye. She was the mother of Pharoah Akhnaten, the first prophet in the whole world. The one that said that God is one, is an African like you and me. And this is his mother, who is also a typically African woman. This woman had a very, very important role in the diplomacy of the 18th Dynasty. At that time all the little kings of western Asia would write letters to this African woman to ask her to intercede with her son so that they could be in his good books.

Here you can also see again, the daughters of the pharoah and you can see that the features are typically African (Slide 17). They could not be better

14. Akhnaten.

represented. It's not enough to suck your thumbs to have those kind of lips (laughter). Here also you can see Queen Nefertiti and you can tell that she is a real African woman! I must stress again, that those pharoahs have contributed to the greatness of Egypt. I showed you the very first king in this Egyptian world—he was black. I showed you the builders of the pyramids—they were

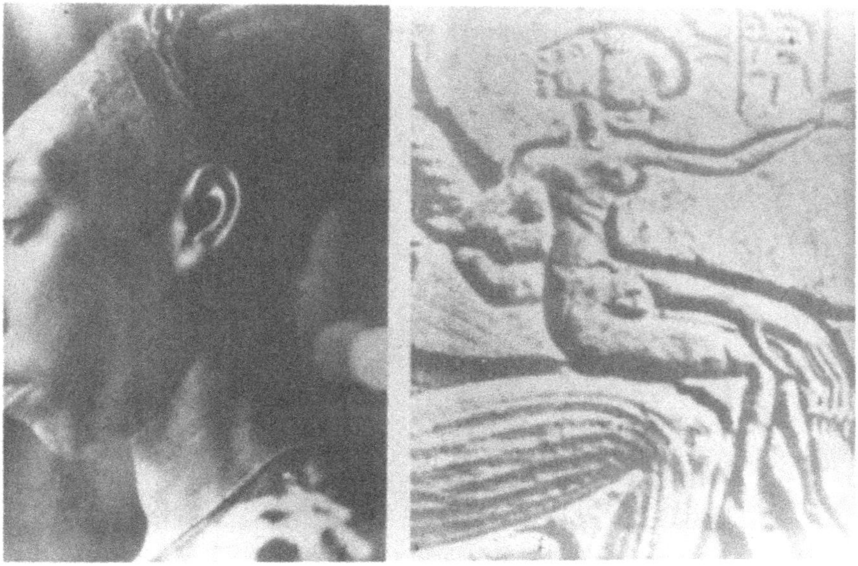

15. Daughter of Akhnaten & African Woman (Note headshape).

black! Before then I showed you the Pharoah Akhnaten. The first one who spoke about monotheism. I showed you Rameses II who is the best known Pharoah in the whole of Egypt and you can tell that all of them are Africans, like you and me. We've been moving through Egyptian History, from the origins to the New Empire.

After the New Empire Egypt will decline. The highest point of Egyptian history was the 19th Dynasty of Rameses II. Then they will have a renaissance with the Ethiopian Kings. Then we enter the Saite period and the end of the Egyptian Empire as a sovereign power with the occupation of the country by Cambyses, the king of the Persians. Here I want to tell you that people say that the picture in the middle is a representation of the real Black person. You can see it on the tomb of Prime minister Horembeb. I put it right in the middle of a picture of an Egyptian woman and a modern Senegalese woman (Slide 18, left hand side). There is no more difference between those peasants and the Egyptian woman and the Senegalese woman. It's just a difference of class. It's not an ethnic difference. These old peasant women don't have any time to look after their beauty.

This little girl is an Egyptian (Slide 19). You can see her totemic hairdo. She predates Moses. Her totemic hairdo shows that the hairdos of Africa go back a very long time. This little girl now could really be taken for an African girl. The African girls are even less typical, in a sense, in that Egyptian picture. Let's suppose that a researcher wants to study African totemism. If you cut

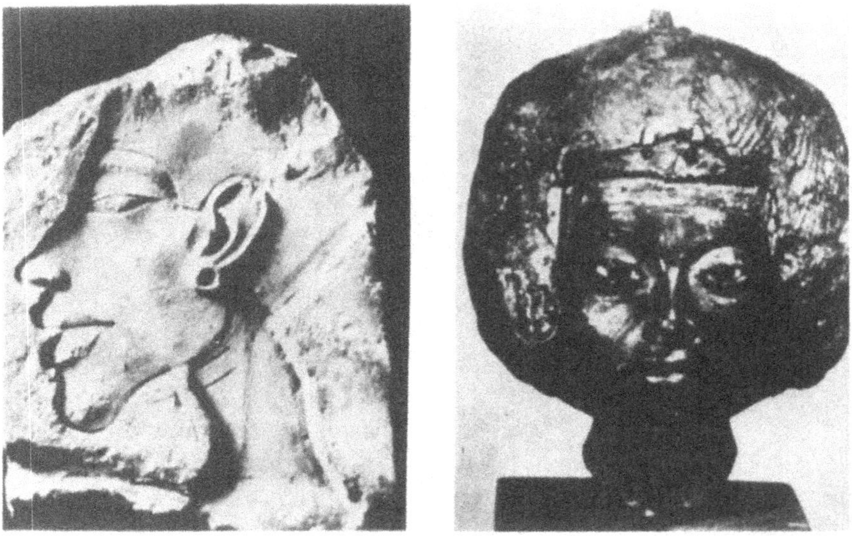

16. Akhnaten and Queen Tiye.

yourself off from this reality, you leave behind you 5,000 years of history. You will not be able to support your theory with real facts. It's the study of Egyptian antiquity which makes it possible for us, whether we are here in the U. S. or in Africa, to re-introduce the historical dimension, to take into account the time factor in research. That is why I say that in order to reconcile African civilization with history we have to go back to Egypt. It's only in that way that we can build a core body of human sciences!

Here Egypt comes into contact for the first time with Indoeuropeans during the period of invasions by Indoeuropeans (Slide 20). This is 1,300 B.C. This is in the beginning of the first dynasty. These pictures are on the tomb of the first pharoah of the first dynasty. His name is pharoah Horemheb. Look at the way the Egyptians represented the European features when they saw them. Look at the nose, the forehead, the eyes, the chin, the hair. Then you have the woman behind them and the child on the shoulders of the mother and, behind them, you have the whole people. Those are tribes who had attacked Egypt and were defeated. There were thousands of prisoners who were branded with an iron, with a letter, that meant that they were slaves. They were distributed around, in the different temples in Egypt. They were transformed into farmers. From the 19th Dynasty, in virtually each Egyptian family, there was a foreign slave. Usually they were European slaves from Greece, Sicily, Sidon, Athens, etc. We also have to say that there were black slaves also. The Egyptians sometimes had Nubian slaves who were the same color as the Egyptians, but were nonetheless slaves. That also existed, but in virtually all the Egyptian families there

17. Daughters of Akhnaten and Nefertiti.

were white slaves. It is in that manner that Egypt started to have mixed races. This is even a clearer picture of the face of one of the slaves (Slide 21). The hands are in shackles. And the one behind has raised its hands to request pardon. In all of Egyptian history there is no profile of any pharoah that is like this one.

Here you see again the semites, all of them, taken in the form of slaves—captives (Slide 22). There was never any Pharoah that had this profile either! You see that Egyptian civilization was not a western civilization and it was not

18. Senegalese & Egyptian Woman.

a semitic civilization. Establishing these historical truths renders a great service to humanity so that they can fraternize on a ground based on truth. It is not meant to destroy the brotherhood of humanity.

This is the first representation, in the history of religion, of hell and heaven (Slide 23). We are at 1,300 B.C. This is in the tomb of the father of Rameses II. The old testament didn't exist yet. Moses didn't exist yet. And here are the flames of hell. There are the doors of hell and the guards of the doors of hell. This is death, a woman. The solid ground on which death walks stops there on the upper left and is taken up on the upper right. Paradise is beyond that and the dead person must cross this bridge. This bridge is suspended over nothing. The bridge is actually a serpent, a monster. This is his head high up here and then it makes these curls and comes down and goes up again, making more curls and then it stops on the other side. It is on this bridge that the dead person must walk, on this moving bridge, to arrive at paradise. That dead person is only sustained on the bridge by the quality of his life. After he is judged, he presents himself before this monster and tries to cross. If he did in life more good than he did harm, he will cross with no problem and enter paradise. In the opposite case, he quickly falls to hell and is taken in by the gate keepers. So the notion of heaven and hell, the notion of the immortality of the Soul, was invented by Egypt from the old dynasty. All of these ideas are typically African. It's only in the second century before Christ that the old testament of Judaism adopted definitively the idea of hell and the beyond. This was almost 3,000 years after Egypt.

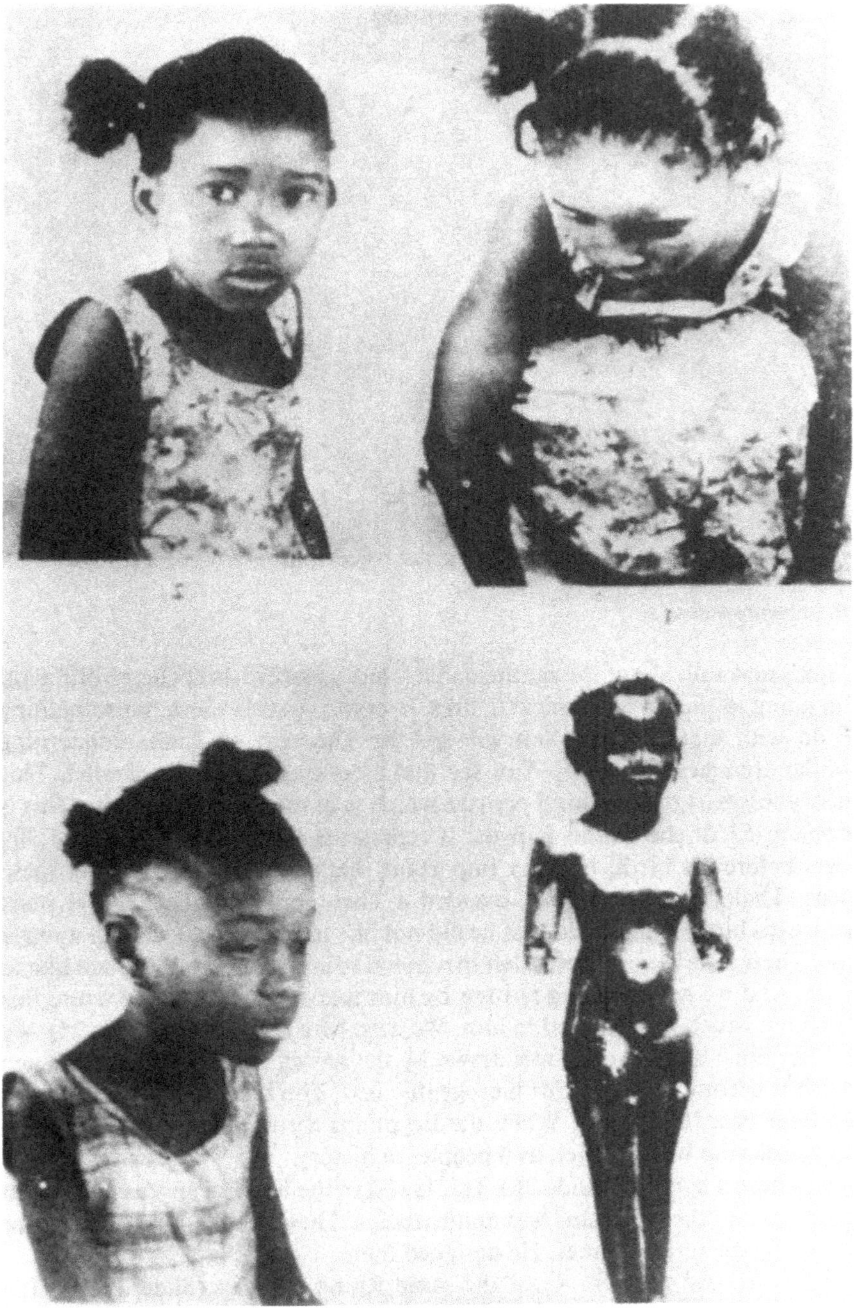

19. Egyptian Girls & African Girls. Egyptian Girl in Lower Right.

20. Indoeuropeans.

Let's now talk about the mathematical and scientific importance of Egypt. I'm going to show a few typical figures. Everyone in this room has something to do with mathematics. You will see the Theorem of Thales concerning similar triangles (Slide 24). You see that sides and bases are parallel. This theory was part of the Rhind papyus, which is in the British museum. This is problem 53 of the Rhind Papyus. It represents the Thales Theorem 1,300 years before his birth! It's very important that we knock down all of these ideas. Thales could not have invented a Theorem that existed 1,300 years before his birth. Thales said that he did not like to write. He never left a single line. There is, however, a letter left to a friend which said that he did not like to write. And we have nothing written by him that indicates that he wrote this Theorem which is attributed to him. We have here a Trapezoid (Slide 25). We did not draw this figure. It was drawn by the scribe, Ahmes, 4,000 years ago and it is accompanied by this hierogyphic text. You see there the small base, the large base, the height. When the Egyptians arrived at this mathematics, the Greeks did not exist yet, as a people, in history.

You have a pyramid (Slide 26). This is still in the Rhind Papyrus and it also indicates that the Egyptians had mathematics. These are figures that were not copied by the scribe Ahmes. He designed them.

Here we have problem 49 of the same Rhind Papyrus (Slide 27). It's the problem of the quadrature of the circle. It's a classical mathematical problem.

The solution for finding the rectangle was solved by the Egyptians. Slide 27

21. Slave of Egyptians.

shows the solution for the Quadrature of a circle and for finding the volume of a rectangle.

Here is another papyrus, called the Moscow Papyrus (Slide 28). It's problem number 14 which asked for the volume of the trunk of a pyramid. It's a very difficult problem which involves mathematical expression that you cannot arrive at by empirical data. It's only with a theoretical approach that you can reach that kind of result.

Here we are speaking of the tomb of Zoser (Slide 29). You can look at the architecture. I've shown you this Pharoah of the third dynasty and I told you all the elements of Egyptian technology were already in place. This architecture is taken to have grown up spontaneously at the time of the third dynasty. It's the beginning of their great stone architecture. That was 2,400 years before the Greek Panthenon.

QUESTION & ANSWER PERIOD

Q: Is it possible to pinpoint the time in history when the truth about the beginning of world civilization was falsified and what was the motivation behind that falsification?

A: It's around 1,525 B.C. that Egypt was conquered by Cambyses, the Persian King. The command that Cambyses gave was to destroy everything that revealed the greatness of Egypt. The temples were torn down and the libraries were destroyed. After Cambyses, Alexander the great conquered the Egyptians. This was the Hellenistic period. The Romans came and drove the Greeks out of Egypt. For seven centuries the Egyptian population, which remained in the valley, were overwhelmed in an unprecedented fashion. The Greek population crumbled under the weight of the Romans. Education regressed. Egypt was no longer the master of its own education system, and that is fundamental. It is for that reason that Egypt regressed. Here we have a school and I can come and talk to you, transfer information when we feel that it is important to do that. From the moment that Egypt was occupied by foreigners, that became impossible. It took away all the local, popular initiative. For generation after generation, the people regressed in their knowledge. And this is how your historical memory is lost, little by little.

Cambyses also destroyed all of the Egyptian intelligentsia. The Egyptian priests fled to western Asia. They were the highest order of scientists and men of knowledge. And this is the process by which historical memory was lost and the people regressed. When Africa was dominated in modern times by slavery . . . when western civilization came here by way of the Atlantic ocean . . . they began to reduce the African population to slavery. This continued, as you know, right up into the nineteenth century. Africa was completely disorganized. Certain populations were exported. But what must be known is that those who stayed where they were, were just as unhappy as those who left. We often don't know that. These people were made very much like beasts, the people who stayed, and they regressed. The essential social cell was destroyed. There was no longer any education. Insecurity would not permit it. And in the same way those who came and conquered Africa made a new history for Africa.

Take a symbolic example. I spoke to you of the mission made by Napoleon in the 19th century. One of the scientists contemporary with Napoleon, Count Volney, was a member of that expedition. He visited Egypt during the time of Napoleon and cried. He cried when he found out that the Egyptians were black and that blacks had created the Egyptian civilization. He was indignant to find that those people who were slaves during that period had once given to the world a great civilization. It is clear that he was well before his time. It was not possible during that time to speak with this kind of truth.

We cease to know our own history. It takes only one generation for a hole to be found in the transmission of one's history. This is how, to various degrees, we have come to doubt ourselves. The philosophy of the colonizer was to make it very clear that the colonized people could do nothing for themselves without the assistance of the colonizing people.

Q: I noticed you were an activist in the Pan-African Student Congress. What do you see of interest in the establishment of such an organization?

A: I think that in facing what we now have in Africa, Pan-Africanism has renewed possibilities. After 20 years of independence, we find everywhere in Africa great difficulty and failure. The states that we inherited from the colonialists are not capable of meeting the challenges of the 20th and 21st centuries. Only an African federation will permit us to have viable states. I would like to direct you to the fact that the United States already has a federation of states. The same is true of the Union of Soviet Socialist Republics. Ideology set aside, it is the federal structure of the state that allows us to live in the 20th or 21st century. If we don't do it in this way, I'm afraid that Africa will fall. That's why I wrote the book *Black Africa*. It deals with the theory of federation. I'm a believer in African federation.

Q: Dr. Frances Cress Welsing has stated that whites are genetically albinos. Is it true that white people are albino genetic mutations of the Black race?

A: The one thing we cannot say is that the populations that left Africa left because they were trying to flee the effects of the sun. In the conditions of prehistoric times the sun was a blessing. The region of the great lakes was practically an earthly paradise. There was much food. Life was abundant there. Man could gather fruit. The prehistoric migration out of Africa must not be considered as a time when they fled. It was not even a migration on a large scale. If, after every 25 years, at the beginning of a generation, one moved 25 kilometers looking in one direction or another for nourishment, at the end of 10,000 years these very small movements (25 kilometers per generation for 10,000 years) would take Africans as far as China, in the Far East. It's frequently these imperceptible movements . . . when you arrive at Gilbraltar you will see Europe on the other side. Even those people in prehistoric times could go there and see Europe on the other side. It's only 15 kilometers across the water from Gilbraltar to Europe. It is now established that navigation existed in the Paleolithic era. We now know that as early as 30,000 years ago, as opposed to 20,000 years ago as was previously believed, man was able to cross the water. It's for just this reason that the first Australopithecus population set themselves up. It's this different kind of movement that took man up into Europe. The question that we can ask and the question which is more troubling is, "Why did the African man leave the sun to go to an area that was so much colder?" It's with this notion of small or imperceptible movements, that we see how man went up into Europe. Some of them went and stayed and were unable to come back. Because they stayed, they sought refuge in the caves. We know the road they chose because traces are still there. So what Welsing said and what she said about race is true. Blacks gave birth to whites by a process of mutation. And of the Blacks that did arrive in Europe, many of them did not survive because of the process of natural selection. Those that did survive were adapted to the climate and were, therefore, transformed or changed. This is what I mean when I say that whites are the product of Blacks. We have to say it without any prejudice and we must say it with no other preoccupation. We must remain faithful to science and fact. To say this simply to explain the process by which races were differentiated would be correct. The thought that they fled from the sun cannot be maintained as a viable theory.

Q: Were the Ice Ages a result of the collision of asteroids or planetary bodies?

A: No one can confirm that the fall of asteroids (and we have seen meteors fall that date back to the age when dinosaurs lived) caused it. We thought that the abrupt disappearance of the dinosaurs is the result of a meteor which fell, a very substantial meteor, which transformed the climatic conditions of the earth and that it was no longer biologically compatible with the make-up of these enormous animals. The final glaciation existed for at least 100,000 years from 80,000 B.C. to 10,000 B.C. This is very well known in prehistoric archaeology. But no one is aware of any meteor having fallen that would explain this glaciation. Glaciation is a cyclical phenomenon. This earth has known four of them. The last one is the one about which I spoke. We wonder now if we are not in the beginning of another such period, and if it is a period in which the earth will become warmer or colder. But no one can say with any great authority. The accurate study of changing atmospheric phenomena is one of the most difficult. It would require all of the technological power of the

United States, all the computers, rockets and satellites to arrive at making enduring studies.

Q: I would like to know if you would agree that in America, educational institutions should begin by teaching of Egypt from the standpoint of Noah's son Ham?

A: I am in complete agreement, and before I leave Morehouse, I would like to express certain concrete ideas about how we should instruct ourselves in our own history.

CHEIKH ANTA DIOP IN AMERICA: AN OVERVIEW

Larry Williams

The arrival of Dr. Cheikh Anta Diop on the shores of America was the realization of a dream that had germinated in the hearts and minds of African Americans ever since the publication of *The Cultural Unity of Black Africa* (1962) and *The African Origin of Civilization: Myth or Reality?* (1974) in the English speaking world. Dr. Diop's pilgrimage to the U.S. was borne on the steel-etched backs of numerous cooperative efforts. These efforts brought together a diverse array of African-Americans.

Where did the idea of bringing Dr. Diop to Atlanta originate? What process was set in motion for African-Americans to learn of his research into the African contribution to world civilization? The history of the idea started over two years ago. In 1983, the Bennu Study Group composed of Larry Williams, Thurya Wingate, Charles S. Finch, Robert Belcher, Askia M. Toure, Dr. Asa G. Hilliard III, Charlyn A. Harper and Dr. Walter Palmer were discussing the possibility of taking on the task of organizing a Nile Valley Conference in Atlanta. Its purpose was to put ancient Egypt into its proper place as an African civilization. The discussion took place in the home of Ms. Thurya Wingate. Later, the Nile Valley Executive Committee was organized to make the effort a reality.[1]

Then, as fate would have it, Dr. Charles S. Finch had to travel to Senegal to conduct medical research. The Bennu Study Group dreamed of his meeting with Dr. Cheikh Anta Diop in Dakar, Senegal. Events seemed to be controlled by the spirits of the griots of African history, J.A. Rogers, F.H. Hammurabi, Leo Hansberry, Carter G. Woodson, George G.M. James, W.E.B. DuBois, etc. Then Professor Jan Carew was invited to speak at Georgia State University through the efforts of Dr. Asa G. Hilliard III. His presentation was titled, "The Indian and African Presence in the Americas: Some Aspects of Historical Distortion." It was part of a lecture series organized by the Center for Cross-Cultural Education. After speaking there, Professor Carew gave an informal chat to the Bennu Study Group. He was informed of the goal of Bennu to host the Nile Valley Conference and to bring Dr. Cheikh Anta Diop to America to address the conference. Professor Carew suggested that he send a letter of introduction to Dr. Diop, his friend, for Dr. Charles Finch. The ice was broken. Dr. Finch met, interviewed Dr. Diop, who enthusiastically agreed to come to America to address the conference.

The branches of the African grapevine reached far and wide as word spread throughout America, England, and the Caribbean that Dr. Diop would be

Dr. Diop (center) answers questions from the Bennu Study Group. To his right are Irene D'Almeida (interpreter) Elizabeth Clement (interpreter) Robert Belcher. To his left are Dr. Carter and Dr. Asa Hilliard III. Photo: Larry Williams.

present at the Nile Valley Conference. Numerous networks were formed around the U.S., as African and African-Americans worked hand in hand to make the Diop visit a living reality. The Amenta Research Group in Los Angeles, California, immediately financed Dr. Diop's trip and was the west coast nerve center of the Nile Valley Conference. Bob Law of the radio program *Night Talk* on WRRL in New York City was instrumental in granting the Bennu Study Group air time to discuss the conference and the work of Dr. Diop. To communicate directly with Dr. Diop in both French and Wolof, the services of Ms. Irene D' Almeida and Mrs. Elizabeth Clement, both outstanding translators, were retained. They were the translators of Dr. Diop's paper "The African Contribution To World Civilization," which was later published in the *Nile Valley Civilizations* issue of the *Journal of African Civilizations.* The paper was read by Professor Ivan Van Sertima at the Nile Valley Conference and was broadcast on February 24, 1985 on KPFK Radio in North Hollywood through the efforts of Kwaku Lynn. Mayor Andrew Young of Atlanta, Georgia, provided the services of his staff and was keenly interested in Dr. Diop's trip to America.

As September, the month of the Nile Valley Conference, approached, the Morehouse School of Medicine, the Bennu Study Group and the Martin Luther King, Jr. International Chapel worked feverishy to finalize arrangements for Diop's visit. Diop, however, did not arrive because of problems wth his flight (which are explained elsewhere in this issue). Nevertheless, the forces that sought to bring Dr. Diop to America were not discouraged. In January 1985, Professor Ivan Van Sertima and Charles S. Finch attended a conference in London, England, featuring Dr. Diop. Negotiations were resumed and he reiterated his commitment to speak in America. Morehouse College was instrumental in providing the dynamics that brought him eventually to America. Morehouse College of Atlanta University Complex has an important place in African-American History. It is the location where W.E.B. DuBois founded and edited *Phylon*: *The Atlanta University Review Of Race And Culture* (1944); wrote *Souls Of Black Folk* (1903), *The Philadelphia Negro* (1899), *Black Reconstruction* (1935), *Black Folk Then and Now* (1939), and *Dusk of Dawn* (1940). DuBois was Chairman of the Department of Sociology and Professor of Economics and History at Morehouse. It was while DuBois was at Atlanta University that he called for a One Hundred Year Study Of The African-American and launched work on the *Encyclopedia Of the Negro.* On June 2, 1943 it was Paul Robeson who received an Honorary Doctor of Humane Letters from Morehouse College and delivered the Commencement Address.

Also the private papers of the great African-American historian George Washington Williams are housed in the library at the Atlanta University Center. It was also at the Atlanta University Center that Sterling Brown taught English in 1935. It was the Rev. John Dawson Gordon, valedictorian of his class at Morehouse, who became Assistant President General and personal assistant to the honorable Marcus M. Garvey. Historically, it is important that a black institution was the site where a man of Dr. Diop's stature came to speak. Africans have been honored at Morehouse College in the past. President Kenneth Kaunda of Zambia and President Robert Mugabe of Zimbabwe have been given honorary degrees there. Even the City of Atlanta has been the scene where Marcus M. Garvey spoke at the Big Bethel A.M.E. church in 1917. Gammon Seminary was the location of the All Africa Congress in 1895 where Edward Wilmot Blyden of Liberia spoke. Haile Selassie of Ethiopia also visited the city. Atlanta has a strong historical link to the dream of Africa. It was the location of the Afro-American Steamship And Mercantile Company which was prominent in the emigration schemes of Bishop Henry McNeal Turner. It was on Haynes Street near the Martin Luther King Center where in 1890 over one thousand black Atlantans awaited journeying to Savannah, Georgia to emigrate to Africa.

After over two years of relentless efforts, Dr. Cheikh Anta Diop arrived at Atlanta's Hartsfield International Airport on Delta Airlines on Tuesday, April 2, 1985. Dr. Diop was the official guest of Morehouse College, the Southern Christian Leadership Conference, the Mayor's Office, the Martin Luther King, Jr. Center For Non-Violent Social Change, the Morehouse School of Medicine and Delta Airlines. Upon arrival he was greeted by representatives from Morehouse College, the S.C.L.C. and the Executive Committee of the Nile Valley Conference. After formal greetings were exchanged he was taken to Paschal's Motor Hotel (scene of many strategy sessions during the Civil Rights Movement) to be briefed on his itinerary.

On April 3, 1985, Diop flew to Washington, D.C. to address the black college and university presidents at the annual meeting of the National Association Of Equal Opportunity And Higher Education. Diop held the audience spellbound. His topic was "The New Renaissance: Black Colleges In the Rediscovery Of Africa's Contribution To World Civilization." Ancient Egypt was the focal point. Diop spoke of the need for black colleges and universities to boldly take up the challenge of giving Egypt its proper place as an African civilization and indeed the mother of western civilization. His message signaled the disintegration of age-old myths that Europe was the center of world civilization.

It was appropriate that Diop's first address was to N.A.F.E.O. in Washington, D.C. because Washington is home of Carter G. Woodson's pioneering work in African-American history and of the work of both Leo Hansberry and Chancellor Williams at Howard University. As Diop lectured, the spirit of Hansberry and Woodson were present. One wonders what his impressions may have been, had he examined the private papers of Hansberry housed at Howard. It was Hansberry who gave inspiration and counsel to many African students in the Americas.[2] For over fifty years, unrecognized and ridiculed,

Dr. Diop receives Drum Major Award from Southern Christian Leadership Conference. Comedian Dick Gregory on left. Dr. Joseph Lowery of S.C.L.C. on right. Dick Gregory presided at the Annual Drum Major Banquet sponsored by S.C.L.C. and Dr. Diop was recipient of their first African Heritage Award.

they too had belabored the same points that Diop addressed. Leo Hansberry was responsible for the establishment of African Studies in American Colleges and Universities. While in Washington, D.C., Dr. Diop was reunited with his lifelong friend Dr. Mercer Cook who translated *The African Origin Of Civilization: Myth Or Reality?* into English.[3]

From April 2nd to April 10th, Professor Diop completed a history-making lecture tour, during which he was honored for the first time by the English-speaking world. On April 4, 1985, in the Martin Luther King, Jr. International Chapel, before over two thousand students, faculty, staff and citizens of greater Atlanta, President Hugh M. Gloster conferred upon him the honorary degree of Doctor of Humane Letters. In his honorary degree citation, President Gloster said, "Cheikh Anta Diop. . . man of many talents, you are not limited to one profession. You have climbed to the heights in physics, history, anthropology, sociology, linguistics and politics. In this period of specialization, you are a Renaissance man with an outstanding record of achievement in many fields."

Other guests on the program were Mrs. Coretta Scott King, Mayor Andrew Young, Dr. Joseph Lowery, Mrs. Ellen Steward, Professor Ivan Van Sertima, Dr. Alton Hornsby, Dr. Charles S. Finch, Dean Lawrence E. Carter and the Morehouse Glee Club. That evening Dr. Joseph E. Lowery presented Dr. Diop the first African Heritage Award of S.C.L.C. for his discoveries as an Egyptologist and an authority on Ancient Africa. Dr. Diop was accompanied on fifty-three appointments and speaking engagements by translators Mrs. Elizabeth Clement, Ms. Irene D'Almeida, Dr. Edward F. Taylor, and Mrs. Mary Diallo. While in Atlanta he spoke at Morehouse College, the Morehouse School of Medicine and Spelman College. He also granted special interviews to South Carolina Educational T.V. and the Bennu Study Group.

Dr. Diop participated in the seventeenth wreath-laying ceremony at the grave of Dr. Martin Luther King, Jr. and toured the King Center and S.C.L.C. offices. While at the King Center, he was only a few blocks from Younge Street where Bishop Henry McNeal Turner's home was once located. Turner's home was reputed to be a virtual museum of African history. Dr. Diop's visit to the area only heightened its historical importance.

Diop's first U.S. visit was particularly remarkable for the ten illustrated lectures and addresses he gave, using a series of black and white and color slides. Some of his topics were, "The Origin Of The Ancient Egyptians," "The Challenge Of The Future From the Past," "The Black African As Father Of The Human Race," "The Egyptian Race According To The Classical Authors Of Antiquity," "The African Human Sciences," and "The Egyptians As They Saw Themselves."

Diop's visit was a pilgrimage that he felt he had to make. It is now time for the African-American community to heed his message. We must boldly challenge those who would place Ancient Egypt into a white mist overshadowing its role as a great African civilization.

NOTES

1. The Nile Valley Executive Committee was composed of Lawrence Edward Carter, Dean of the Martin Luther King, Jr. International Chapel, Charles S. Finch, Professor Charlyn A. Harper, Atlanta Junior College, Asa G. Hilliard III, Georgia State University, Mwalimu Imara, Morehouse School of Medicine, Dr. Walter Palmer, Morris Brown College, Professor Ivan Van Sertima, Editor of *Journal of African Civilizations*. Askia M. Touré, poet, editor, essayist and activist and Mr. Larry Williams, The Bennu Study Group. There were many others, who gave of their time and effort to make the Nile Valley Conference a success.

2. Mercer Cook is a retired U.S. Ambassador educator, translator, composer. Son of Will Marion Cook (conductor/composer) and Abbie Mitchell (vocalist and actress), Cook has served as United States Ambassador to Niger, Senegal and Gambia. He is the recipient of decorations from the governments of Haiti, Niger, Senegal, France (Palmes Academiques). Author, *Le Noir, Portients Americans, Five French Negro Authors, Militant Black Writers in Africa and U.S.A.* Translator of Senghor, Thiam, Diop and Dia, U.S. Link to Negritude Movement, member of the "Independents," life-long friend of Sterling Brown.

3. Most of his academic life was spent as a teacher at Howard University, but in the 1950s he was a Fullbright scholar in Africa and then taught African history briefly at the New School For Social Research in New York City. His last years were spent in Africa. In 1963, the Nigerian government established the Hansberry College of African Studies as part of the University of Nigeria and Hansberry was appointed Distinguished Professor.

Bibliography

Critical Essays on, and Publications by, Cheikh Anta Diop

Compiled by Larry Williams

Carruthers, Jacob. (1979). "Cheikh Anta Diop: A Man Who Refuses to be Forgotten." Part I. *Black America Newspaper*, June 14-20, pp. 30-31.

Carruthers, Jacob. (1979). "Cheikh Anta Diop: The Man Who Refuses to be Forgotten." Part II. *Black America Newspaper*, June 21-27, pp. 30-34.

Clarke, John Henrik. (1974). "Cheikh Anta Diop And The New Light On African History." *Freedomways*, Vol. 14, No. 4, 4th Quarter.

Diop, Cheikh Anta. "Africa: Cradle of Humanity." In Ivan Van Sertima (Ed.), *Nile Valley Civilizations*. (1985) Journal of African Civilizations, Ltd, Inc. Also, "Africa's Contribution to the Exact Sciences" in the same volume.

Diop, Cheikh Anta. (1974). *The African Origin of Civilization: Myth or Reality?* New York: Lawrence Hill and Company.

Diop, Cheikh Anta. (1956). "Apports et Perspectives Culturels de L'Afrique Noire." *Presence Africaine*, Nos. 8, 9, 10.

Diop, Cheikh Anta. (1955/56). "Alerte Sous Les Tropiques." *Presence Africaine*, Dec./Jan. issue.

Diop, Cheikh Anta. (1978). *Black Africa: The Economic and Cultural Basis For A Federated State*. Connecticut: Lawrence Hill, Co.

Diop, Cheikh Anta. (1957). "Civilization Africaine." *Horizons*, July-August Issue.

Diop, Cheikh Anta. (1975). "Comment en Raciner la Science en Afrique: Examples Walaf [Senegal] (How to Implant Science In Africa: Wolof Examples (Senegal). *Bulletin de L'IFAN*., T.37, Series B, No. 1, January,

Diop, Cheikh Anta. (1978). *The Cultural Unity of Black Africa*. Chicago: Third World Press. (First published, 1959.)

Diop, Cheikh Anta. (1962). "De la pyrite de fer dans la region de Khombole (Thies)." *Notes Africaines*, No. 94, pp. 61-62.

Diop, Cheikh Anta. (1964). "Evolution of The Negro World." *Presence Africaine*, Vol. 23, 3rd Quarter.

Diop, Cheikh Anta. (1948). "Etude de linquistique oulove. Origine de la langue et de La Race Walaf." *Presence Africaine*, No. 4, pp. 672-684.

Diop, Cheikh Anta. (1948). "Etude de linquistique oulove. Origine de la langue et de La Race Walaf." *Presence Africaine*, No. 5, pp. 848-853.

Diop, Cheikh Anta. (N.D.), Histoire Primitive de L'Humanite': Evolution du Monde Noir. *Presence Africaine*.

Diop, Cheikh Anta. (1973). "Introduction a L'etude des Migrations en Afrique Centrale et Occidentale. (Introduction to the Study of Migrations in Central and West Africa), *Bulletin de L'IFAN*, T. XXXV, Series B, No. 4.

Diop, Cheikh Anta. (1960). *L'Afrique Noire Precoloniale*. Paris: Presence Africaine.

Diop, Cheikh Anta. (1970). "L'Apparition de L'Homo Sapiens." (The Appearance of Homo Sapiens). *Bulletin de L'IFAN*, T. XXXII, Series B, No. 3.

Diop, Cheikh Anta. (1973). "La Metallurgie du fer sous l'Ancien Empire Egyptien. (Iron Metallurgy during the Ancient Egyptian Empire). Bulletin de L'IFAN., T. XXXV, Series B, No. 3, Juillet.

Diop, Cheikh Anta. (1953). "La Lutten En Afrique Noire." *La Voix En Afrique Noire."*. Paris.

Diop, Cheikh Anta. (1960). "Les Intellectuals doivent etudier le paśse non pour s'y complaire mais pour y puiser des lecons. *"La Vie Africaine,* No. 6, March/April; pp. 10-11.

Diop, Cheikh Anta. (1973). "L'Unite' Africaine, condition de Survie des peuple Africains. *"Problems Actuels de L'Unite Africaine.* Proceedings of the Algiers Colloqium, March 25-April 12, 1971, pp. 410-417, Algiers: SNED.

Diop, Cheikh Anta. (1979). "Letter To The Editor: Journal of African Civilizations." Journal of African Civilizations. Vol. 1, No. 2, November, p. 97.

Diop, Cheikh Anta. (1955). *Nations Negres Et Culture.* Paris: Presence Africaine.

Diop, Cheikh Anta. (1981). "Origin of the Ancient Egyptians." In G. Mokhtar (Ed.) *General History of Africa II: Ancient Civilizations of Africa.* Berkeley: University of California Press, pp. 27-57.

Diop, Cheikh Anta. (1976). *Parente Genetique de L'Egyptien Pharaonique et des Langues Negro-Africaines.* Dakar: University of Dakar Press.

Diop, Cheikh Anta. (1981). Annex to Chapter 1: Report on the Symposium on "The Peopling of Ancient Egypt and the Deciphering of the Meroitic Script." Cairo, 28 January-3 February '74.

Diop, Cheikh Anta. (1974). "Physique Nucleaire Et Chronologie absolue (Nuclear Physics and Absolute Chronology). Bulletin de L'IFAN. T. XXXI.

Diop, Cheikh Anta. (1973). "Pigmentation of the Ancient Egyptians: Test by Melanin Analysis. "Bulletin de L'institut fondamental D'Afrique Noire, Serie B, Sciences Humaines, Tome XXXV, No. 3, Juillet, 515-530.

Diop, Cheikh Anta. (1948). "Quand pourra-t-on parler d'une Renaissance Africaine? *"Le Musee Vivant,* No. Special, November, 36-37.

Diop, Cheikh Anta. (1974). "Radiocarbon Dates I." *Radiocarbon,* Vol. 16, No. 3, 304-306.

Diop, Cheikh Anta. (1977). "Radiocarbon Dates II." Radiocarbon, Vol. 19.

Diop, Cheikh Anta. (1952). "Vers une ideologie politique en Afrique Noire." *Voix de l'Afrique Noire,* Fevrier, Paris, France.

Finch, Charles S. (1982). "meeting the Pharoah: Conversations with Cheikh Anta Diop." In Ivan Van Sertima (Ed.) *Egypt Revisited. Journal of African Civilizations.*

Jeffries, Leonard. (1982, November). Review of Civilization or Barbarism: The Legacy of Cheikh Anta Diop." *Journal of African Civilizations, 4*(2).

Lam, Aboubarry Moussa. (1984). "A Major Piece of Work: Civilization or Barbarism." *Afrique Histoire,* Vol. 2, No. 1, 35-36.

Moore, Carlos. (1977). "Cheikh Anta Diop: African All-Around Genius: An Interview." *Afriscope Magazine,* Vol. 7, No. 2, February, 4-35.

Moore, Carlos. (1976). "Interview with Dr. Cheikh Anta Diop." *Black Books Bulletin,* Vol. 4, No. 4, 30-37.

Obenga, Theophile. (1970). "Methode et Conception historiques de Cheikh Anta Diop." *Presence Africaine,* No. 74.

Sall, Babacar. (1984). "Civilization or Barbarism by Cheikh Anta Diop: Does This Mark the End of a Debate?" *Afrique Histoire,* Vol. 2, No. 1, 32-34.

Spady, James G. (1979). "Cheikh Anta Diop and Freddie L.X. Thomas: Two Philosophical Prespectives on Pristine Black History. "In Ivan Sertima (Ed.), *Journal of African Civilizations,* Vol. 1, No. 1.

Spady, James G. (1975). "The Cultural Unity of Cheikh Anta Diop: 1948-1964." *Black Books Bulletin*, Vol. 3, 28-25, 80-84.
Spady, James G. (1972). "Negritude, Pan-Banegritude and the Diopian Philosophy of African History." *A Current Bibliography On African Affairs*. January Issue.
Wangara, Harun Kofi. (1974). "African Prespective On History: An Interview with Cheikh Anta Diop." *Black World*, February Issue, 53-61.

APPENDIX:
LETTERS TO THE EDITOR

DIOP TO VAN SERTIMA

The following letter which appears in Vol 1, No. 2 (November 1979) is reprinted for the benefit of readers who would like to follow the discussion but have not seen the earlier correspondence.

Dakar
July 17, 1979

Dear Professor Van Sertima,

I received the issue of your Journal which you were so kind to send. I would like to call your attention to a fact which seems to specifically confirm your ideas on the African presence in pre-Columbian America.

The laboratories of Paris which have just analyzed the mummy of Ramses II have found nicotine (tobacco alkaloid) in his stomach. This nicotine served as treatment against the numerous cavities found in the teeth of the old pharoah.

Interestingly, most scholars support the fact that tobacco is a plant of American origin which had been introduced in Africa at a date that remains to be specified. Raymond Mauny thinks that this introduction could hardly be dated before the 16th century.

The first conclusion that one can obtain from these facts is the following: If tobacco is really a plant of American origin; the nicotine in the stomach of the mummy of Ramses II is irrefutable proof that the contacts between Africa and America go back to at least 1300 years before Christ in the middle of the historical period of Egypt; and many historical facts and pre-Columbian civilizations would find there the beginning of an explanation. You probably are already aware of this fact.

In my next letter, I will send you the details and references needed, but I am going away tomorrow and I wanted to send you this information before my departure. I will be returning to Dakar in three weeks.

In my works entitled "L'Afrique Noire Pre-Coloniale" (Pre-Colonial Black Africa) and "Antiquite Africaine par l'image" (African Antiquity through Images), I dealt with the possibilities of pre-Columbian contacts between Africa and America but it was only a working hypothesis. Thus you can imagine how much pleasure your discoveries gave me, because of the conclusive evidence they constitute for historical science. All my congratulations!

It should be noted that the analysis carried out on the mummy of Ramses II has a tendentious aspect that I have taken upon myself to refute in the chapter of a general work which is about to be published. In effect, the authors wanted discreetly to "whiten" the mummy. They have tried vainly to present Ramses II as white skinned.

Sincerely yours,

Cheikh Anta Diop
Director, Radio Carbon Laboratories
Ifan Institute, University of Dakar

VAN SERTIMA TO DIOP
(Reply to letter published in Vol. 1, No. 2 issue)

Dr. Cheikh Anta Diop,
Directeur du Laboratoire
du Radiocarbone
IFAN Universite
Dakar, SENEGAL.

August 22, 1979

Dear Professor Diop,

I was very happy to hear from you and must thank you for your generous praise of my work. I deeply regret that you have not yet seen a copy of *THEY CAME BEFORE COLUMBUS: The African Presence in Ancient America.* I gather from your letter that your comments are based on the Journal I edit and on the postscript to my book published in the first issue.

I had not replied to your letter of July 17 before because I was waiting to receive the details on the tobacco find which you had promised to send me on your return to Dakar. I dispatched a cable to you a day or two ago and am writing you now in the hope that my letter may expedite your response. I await the details of the evidence on tobacco with a great excitement.

The problem of tobacco in the Old and New Worlds is more complex than it would at first appear. I am sending you a photostat of my chapter on the matter — Chapter II "Smoking, Tobacco and Pipes" (p. 207-231) which I hope you will examine closely at your convenience. In this chapter I use primary sources initially examined by Leo Wiener, a Harvard linguist, in the 1920's*, but I subject his source materials to a critical analysis which has led me to very different conclusions. As you will see from my analysis, there is the possibility of both an indigenous American and an indigenous African brand of tobacco. The word "tubbaq" derives from the Syrian word "dubbaq" (viscum, glue) a word

**Africa and the Discovery of America* (Vol. 1-3) 1920-22

that suggests the nature of the substance that issues from the plant. It is mentioned in early Moorish treatises on agriculture. It referred initially, however, to a variety of viscous substances used in fumigation of patients ("smoking out" cures), We do not know exactly when it came to be used for the tobacco plant, as such. It appears that the Africans did have a tobacco plant and added uses — magical, mediative and medicinal — which were later found duplicated in America. There is no evidence that the Africans introduced tobacco into America (as Wiener and his disciples claim) but they certainly introduced certain ritual and medicinal and meditative practices associated with the "tubbaq" or tabaco. The Americans did not have a word for the tobacco plant that was anywhere close to tabaco. They only used the word *tabaco* to refer to the "act of smoking" and the "instrument for smoking" (the pipe) some types of which were introduced by the Africans. Several smoke-words in America, apart from *tabaco,* have great antiquity in Africa (Malinke words like *dyamba, dyemba* and Toma & Bambara words like *duli* which have their variants *nduli* and *luli* in Mende) Wiener mapped the distribution of these words in America in the medieval period with great skill. He was a brilliant linguist but very weak in presentation of his evidence in a logical and analytical manner that would meet our more rigorous standards of scholarship, jumping to conclusions which his evidence could not support.

It is quite possible, as you suggest, that an early visit by Egyptians to America led to the importation of the tobacco plant into Africa and that the African tubbaq is a derivative of the American, borrowed and cultivated in a pre-Columbian period. To establish this, however, one would have to subject the tobacco found in the belly of Ramses II to a chemical, and probably to a botanical, analysis to determine whether it *is* "American" tobacco. The assumption that tobacco is an exclusive American indigene is simply that — an assumption. We are, therefore, in a dilemma unless further revelatory details are forthcoming.

There is no doubt, however, as a result of this find, that the use of tobacco in Africa is of great antiquity and it certainly strengthens the case for the introduction of "smoking practices" and the "smoke-words" associated with those practices, to the American, through later pre-Columbian voyages by Africans. The evidence, therefore, even though it may not be regarded as indisputable proof of a pre--Columbian contact between Africa and America *in the era of the Ramessids,* would place the discussion of tobacco in a revolutionary context and lead to a reexamination of this whole issue, which I would welcome.

By the way, although I have presented evidence in my book for Egypto-Nubian voyages in the first millenium B.C. and Leo Wiener (1920-22) and later Rogers (1942) and Harold Lawrence (1963) etc. have argued (or outlined some of the arguments) for Mandingo voyages in the medieval period (which I also develop in my book) there is evidence for a much earlier contact in the period of the Ramessids, which fits in with this extraordinary find. R. A. Jairazbhoy, in his book *Ancient Egyptians and Chinese in America (1974)* deals with this thesis very persuasively although I have found him to be so radically diffusionist that he ruins his case through over-statement.

I am very keen to continue this correspondence and look forward to hearing from you. With your permission I would like to publish our dialogue in the *Journal of African Civilizations*. I would also like to extend to you from the Directors and Editors of the Journal our very best wishes. We would like to regard you as our Overseas Editor or Editorial Adviser in Africa and would publish anything in this field which you recommend to us. We regard you as the leading light in the world at the moment working for a change of consciousness with regard to the history and culture of African peoples.

Yours, in brotherhood,

Ivan Van Sertima

P.S. A French edition of my book will be available from *EDITIONS FLAMMARION (Paris)* sometime in 1980. In the meantime I am sending an autographed copy of the English edition of the book by separate mail.

EDITOR'S NOTE.

After a long delay and a cable and phone call to Dakar, Senegal, which received no response, my letter of August 22 was followed by a note to Diop in which I offered to withdraw from the debate and let his letter on the subject (published in Vol. 1, No. 2 — November 1979) stand as the last word. It is to this note that Dr. Diop refers when he speaks of my "unilaterally abandoning discussion out of tact" and advises me against "any concession when it is a question of establishing a scientific truth".

DIOP TO VAN SERTIMA

Dakar, November 26, 1979

Dr. Cheikh Anta Diop
Directeur du Laboratoire de Radiocarbone
de l'IFAN,
Universite de Dakar, Senegal

Professor Van Sertima
59 South Adelaide Avenue
Highland Park, New Jersey 08904

Note: (Readers should *not* use this address. Editor left this address in 1984.)

Your two letters are a great reassurance to me because they indicate that we now have young Afro-American scholars of international stature, thoroughly devoted to historic research. I assure you that there was no misunderstanding, you had understood exactly the import of my letter. Your sense of decorum does you credit, but it ought not induce you to unilaterally abandon discussion out of tact, and thereby to sacrifice scientific truth. Once again, this very African comportment delights me and even more gratifying is the concern for precision, conveyed by your last letter. Remember that we are focused on a quest for truth and not on a sacrosanct idol whom we have to avoid debasing. So, there shouldn't be any concession when it is a question of establishing a scientific truth, and I urge you to publish in its entirety your last letter to me, without which, otherwise, this letter would be incomprehensible.

The problem of the origin of tobacco probably is not yet resolved, though authors such as A. L. Guyot, Raymond Mauny, and certainly others rely on a variety of arugments to assert American origin of that plant.[1] Several of these authors are honest scholars, motivated only by the desire to establish a scientific truth, useful to the research on this subject, but others whose ideologies show partiality are prevented from attaining scientific truth in spite of their technical competence; these last often are motivated only by the desire to divest Africa of everything, even of her botanical heritage, if Imay say so. Thus, R. Mauny is committing a subtle error in confusing, in the text which I have cited, the origin of tobacco and the use of the pipe. The comments included

1 Raymond Mauny. Tableau Geographique de l'Quest Africain au Moyen-Age. 1961. Collection "Memoires de l'IFAN" n 61. p. 59:
"Pipes are one of the most useful West African "fossil directors": their presence dates them to a period after 1600 and, in nearly every case in Muslim territory, before 1900. The arrival date of tobacco, an American plant, is in fact well-known: the Tarikh-el-Fettach teaches us that the use of that plant for smoking was introduced to Timbuktu (Tombouctou) between 1594 and 1596, and from 1600 onwards, it was observable on the African coasts."
A. L. Guyot. Origine des Plantes cultivees. 1942. Presses Universitaires de France. Collection que sais-je? p. 69:
"The Pacific coast of South America is another important center of origin for cultivated species: even more than the hot and humid tropical plains. the unscathed slopes of the Andean Cordilleras were, from the outset, inhabited by man. Originating from here are: tobacco, tomatoes, beans, potatoes;...but....."
A. L. Guyot was a professor at L'Ecole Nationale d'Agriculture de Grignon in France in 1942.'

in my first letter, therefore, were intended for these two categories of authors who for diverse reasons postulate South American origin of tobacco. Acceptance of their premise would mean that *if* tobacco really is a plant of American origin, taking into account the presence of nicotine in the stomach of Rameses II, one has to assume that Egypto-American relations existed under the 19th dynasty, 1300 years before Christ.

In fact, nicotine[2] is the principal and specific alkaloid of tobacco. All varieties of tobacco contain it, the percentage varying only with the species. The other alkaloidal plants, such as the sleep-inducing poppy, the coffee-tree, etc., contain other alkaloids, entirely different from nicotine, although capable of producing narcotic effects that are similar or more intense and more toxic to the organism. Therefore, the presence of nicotine necessarily indicates the use of a variety of true tobacco and not simply of a related plant that inappropriately could bear that name. Tobacco must have been used throughout antiquity in human and veterinary medicine, as you have shown, before its use for smoking was practiced.

Modern methods of chemical analysis afford detection of the nicotine molecule when that substance is present in even an infinitesimal quantity; confirmation from the analyses in Paris would prove, therefore, that the Egyptians were familiar with tobacco as early as 1300 B.C., even though they did not smoke it, for one does not find representation of the pipe on the pharaonic monuments. This would disprove the contention that tobacco was introduced in Africa in a post-columbian period. Even if exclusively indigenous to America, tobacco would have been introduced in Africa as early as the 19th Egyptian dynasty, coming after maritime contact; unless one supposes, as others have tried to do, the accidental arrival of the seeds of various plants on the African coasts by means of floatation on the sea's surface and by force of the tides: a hypothesis that is more than hazardous and not a little improbable which we pose only to cover all sides of the question. (See diagram)

2 The chemical formula of nicotone is: $C_{10}H_{14}N_2$ which is diagrammed as follows:

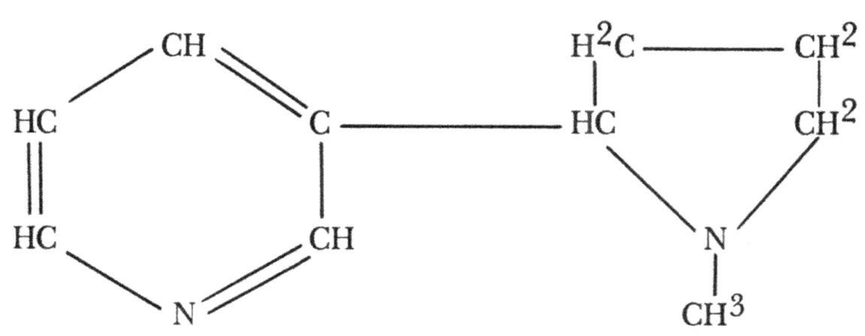

There remains your hypothesis, expressed in your letter of August 22, 1979, namely: an innate origin of tobacco both in Africa and in America; I cannot evaluate this particular proposition at this point in the research. If it were thus, the presence of nicotine in the stomach of Rameses II would not prove pre-columbian, Afro-american contact and you certainly are right in making this very important observation. In this case, there would have been parallel usage of tobacco in Africa and America, and the only new element would be the certainty which we now have of the use of tobacco in Africa as early as the 19th dynasty, therefore, since antiquity.

What remains to be seen now is whether the species that could be considered indigenous to Africa are true tobaccos, containing nicotine, those which you mention in your letter, for example: *dyamba* or *dyemba* in Malinke, etc. Indeed, we have in Walaf (Wolof), a Senegalese language, the same root as in Malinke: *yambass,* designating an alkaloidal plant that is a true drug, even more toxic than nicotine, which is smoked like tobacco. It is an indian hemp, a narcotic plant and a substitute for opium. This plant is being studied by a team in the department of pharmacy of Dakar and I will try to specify the particular alkaloid it contains in another letter.

To my knowledge, the fifty-two Parisian laboratories have not yet published the results of their analyses of the mummy of Rameses II, and it is for this reason that we cannot yet present anything with certainty except the discovery of nicotine: this is certain, because I read it in a publication.[3] As soon as anything new on this subject is published, I will inform you of it.

Please accept my regards, Professor.

Cheikh Anta Diop

(Translated for publication by Rosanne Harris)

3 I will send you the reference later

LETTER BY CHARLES S. FINCH TO CHEIKH ANTA DIOP

Dear Professor Diop:

I was very happy to be able to come to London last January to hear you speak and to make your acquaintance once again. It was more than worth the time and expense to see you, Carlos Moore, and Ivan Van Sertima on the same panel. I was particularly grateful for the two long conversations we had in the Indian restaurant. It gives me great satisfaction to see you and your work acclaimed and studied throughout the English-speaking Black world.

Our private conversations have stimulated me to pursue more deeply and searchingly the topics we discussed over dinner. I have gone back to study both Budge's *Egyptian Hieroglyphic Dictionary* and Sir Alan Gardiner's *Egyptian Grammar.* It is evident that modern Egyptologists, including Gardiner, have adopted the German scheme of transliterating the Egyptian language and alphabet as set forth by Erman and Grapow in the *Wörterbuch der Egyptische Sprach.* Budge, on the other hand, chose to adopt a modified form of the older system of transliteration, one brought into prominence by Samuel Birch among others, but he never explains why the system he adopted is to be preferred over the German one. Budge's *Dictionary* is better suited to someone like myself who is neither a philologist or linguist and I circumvent the fact that he is a little obsolete in this area by interpolating the more modern forms of transliteration as set forth in Gardiner's *Grammar* into the words in Budge's *Dictionary.* As an example, where Budge uses "u" I mentally substitute "w." Where Budge uses "ȧ" I substitute "i" (which is really a consonantal "y"), and so on. So saying, I long ago came to the conclusion that Osiris is really a form of the son of Isis. His name in hieroglyphics employs a seat or throne, which is the ideogram for Isis as "Ast," and the eye which ideogrammatically is "ȧr," or "ir." The "ȧr" or "ir" means "born of, created (of), made (of)" so whether you transliterate Osiris as "Ȧsar" or "Wosir" it still means, hieroglyphically speaking, "born of or created of Ȧst or Isis." Thus, Osiris would appear to be, in one of his earliest forms, a son of Isis and therefore identifiable as an aspect or form of Horus.

I have also come to the conclusion that the Hebrews or Children of Israel who came out of Egypt in the Exodus had to have been speaking Egyptian or a form of Egyptian. Immigrant populations, as a rule, take on the language of the dominant population within a generation or two and the Hebrews would have been sojourning in Egypt for 200-400 years, by their own Old Testament account, perhaps from the time of the Hyksos. It would have been almost impossible for the Hebrews not to have taken on Egyptian as their primary language. Even if they had managed to preserve, against quite formidable odds, something of the earlier Canaanite language that they originally spoke when they entered Egypt, it would have turned into a patois of Egyptian and Canaanite with Egyptian elements predominating. At the time of the Exodus, therefore, they would have been speaking Egyptian or a form of it.

What has really got me going is the analysis you did for me of "Abraham" which you broke down into "ib-ra-em," meaning "in or of the heart of Ra." This same method can be applied to an analysis of the name of the other important early Hebrew patriarchs. "Isaac" is "Ishak" (Arabic) or "Is-ak" (Egyptian). "Is" (Eg) = "tomb, abode, chamber, place;" "ak" = "fire altar, offering by fire, or burnt offering." The biblical Isaac was to be given to God as a burnt offering or offering by fire and the Egyptian form of the name, Is-ak, means "place or chamber of the burnt offering." The biblical Jacob is "Ya-aqab" in Hebrew and Esau in Genesis states that the name Jacob (Ya-aqab) means "twice deceived" or the "double deception" because Esau was twice-deceived by Jacob; once by maneuvering Esau out of his birthright and secondly by tricking Esau out of his father's blessing. "Iu" (Eg) = "deceit or trickery"; "qeb" (Eg) = "double." Iu-qeb = "double deceiver." Additionally, "Iai" or "Ya" (Eg.) = the Ass-god, i.e., he who was identified with Ra because he pulled the boat of the sun (Ra) on its daily circuit in the heavens. "Qeb" (Eg) also means "circuit" so another meaning for Iu-qeb or Ya-qeb (Jacob) is "the circuit of the Sun (Ra as Ass-god). Jacob changed his named to Israel which as the Egyptian "is-ra-er" means "opening to the chamber of Ra." Clearly the Hebrews of the time of Abraham, Isaac, and Jacob were worshippers of the Sun (Ra) as the Ass-god. Additionally, in the geneology of Noah, Shem is the eponymous ancestor of the Semites. Early in their history, the Semitic peoples were nomads and the Egyptian word "shem" or "sem" means "travellers" or "wanderers." Dr. Diop, the Old Testament appears to be a mine of information about Egyptian cosmogony and its earliest books seem to have been given intact to the Hebrews from the Egyptians through Moses.

I am sending you, under a separate cover, a copy of the "Proceedings of the Nile Valley Conference" which is the "Nile Civilizations" issue of the *Journal of African Civilizations*. I look forward to communicating with you again soon.

Mes Meillures Sentiments Fraternels,

Charles S. Finch, M.D.

BIOGRAPHICAL NOTES ON CONTRIBUTORS

CAREW, Jan

Born in Guyana in 1925, he is a novelist, playwright, critic and historian. Presently, he is Professor of African-American and Third World studies at Northwestern University. He has lectured in Race Relations at London University; Third World Literature at Princeton and Rutgers Universities. He is the Director of the Third World Energy Institute, Chairman of the Association of Caribbean Studies, Co-director of the Caribbean Society for Culture and Science, and Head of the Dennis Brutus Defence Committee. His most recent works include a history of Grenada, two novellas for children, and a collection of essays, *Fulcrums of Change.* He is presently collaborating on a book about Dennis Brutus' fight against deportation, and is completing a book on the Afro-American-Seminole Struggle in Florida. His book, *Grenada: The Hour Will Strike Again,* can be ordered through the New York "City Sun" G.P.O. Box 560 New York 11202.

CARTER, Lawrence Edward

Lawrence Edward Carter Sr., Dean of the Martin Luther King, Jr. International Chapel and Professor of Religion at Morehouse College since 1979, has been professionally active as administrator, preacher, teacher, chaplain, pastoral counselor, writer, and Baptist representative in ecumenical councils, both national and international.

Dr. Carter holds the B.A. degree from Virginia College in social science, and the M. Div. degree, and S.T.M. degree and the Ph.D. degree from Boston University in pastoral psychology and counseling. He did further study at Andover Newton Theological School, Ohio State University, Harvard University, and Georgia State University. He holds certifications in multidisciplinary clinical training, clinical pastoral education, community nonviolent training, and is an ordained Baptist minister.

Prior to assuming the Deanship of the King International Chapel, Dr. Carter held positions at Boston University, Harvard University, and Simmons College, as well as ministerial positions with the United Methodists in Stockton, California, the United Presbyterians in Roxbury, Massachusetts, the American Baptists and The United Church of Christ in Boston and Brookline, Massachusetts.

Currently, Professor Carter teaches World Religions, Psychology of Religion, Introduction to Religion and The Life and Thought of Martin Luther King, Jr. at Morehouse College, while administering that institution's programs of religious and cultural affairs. He serves as Chairman of three Morehouse committees. He is a Vice President of the Atlanta United Nations Association; a member of the Board of Governors of the National Council of Churches of Christ, U.S.A., and active in the World Council of Churches on behalf of the National Baptist Convention, U.S.A., Inc. The Dean is also an annual lecturer on Ecumenism for the National Baptist Student Union Retreat and is Dean of the Martin Luther King, Jr. College of Ministers of the International Council of Community Churches. Dr. Carter is a member of the American Academy of Religion, Atlanta Advisory Board for Clergy and Laity Concerned, Omega Psi Phi Fraternity, the National Association for the Advancement of Colored People, and the Atlanta Urban League. His published articles have appeared in *The Journal of The Interdenominational Theological Center, The Expectant, Maroon Tiger, The Journal of Pastoral Care, Daily Free Press,* The Howard University *Journal of Religious Thought, Black Family Magazine, The Oracle, Nexus, Freeing the Spirit, The Pacemaker, Boston University Currents, Morehouse College Bulletin, The Atlanta Inquirer, The Atlanta Constitution, The National Baptist Voice,* Atlanta University's *Phylon,* and *Journal of African Civilizations.*

CLARKE, John Henrik

Editor, writer, historian. His books include: *William Stryon's Nat Turner: Ten Black Writers Respond* (1968), *Malcolm X, The Man and His Time* (1969), *Harlem U.S.A.* (1971), *Marcus Garvey and the Vision of Africa* (1974). Research Director of the First African Heritage Exposition; Associate Editor, *Freedomways Magazine*, Professor of African History and former Chairman, Black and Puerto Rican Studies Department, Hunter College, New York. On Editorial Board of the *Journal of African Civilizations.*

CLEMENT, Elizabeth

Certified interpreter, translator and teacher of French in the Atlanta area.

D'ALMEIDA, Irene

Irene d'Almeida was born in Senegal and raised in Benin. She is a doctoral candidate at Emory University in Atlanta. Her field of study is Comparative Literature, with an emphasis on African literary criticism. She is presently Assistant Professor of French at the University of North Florida in Jacksonville. She translated Chinua Achebe's *Arrow of God* into French.

DIOP, Cheikh Anta

Cheikh Anta Diop was born in Diourbel, Senegal on December 29, 1923. He died in his sleep in Dakar on February 7, 1986. At age 23, he went to Paris to continue advanced studies in physics. Within a very short time, however, he was drawn deeper and deeper into studies of the origin of civilization in Africa. Becoming increasingly active in the African student movements agitating for independence of French colonial possessions, he became convinced that only by re-evaluating and restoring Africa's place in the history of the world could the physical and mental shackles of colonialism be lifted from Africa. His first doctoral dissertation submitted at the University of Paris in 1951—based on the premise that Egypt was a Black African civilization—was rejected. This dissertation was published nevertheless under the title *Nations Negres et Culture* in 1955 and won him wide acclaim. Two additional attempts to have his doctorate granted were turned back until 1960 when he entered his defense session with an array of sociologists, anthropologists, and historians and successfully carried his argument. After nearly a decade, Diop had his 'Docteur es Lettres.' In that same year were published his *L'Unite Culturelle d' Afrique Noire (The Culture Unity of Black Africa)* and *L'Afrique Noire Pre-Coloniale (Precolonial Black Africa).*

During his student days, Diop was an avid political activist. From 1950 to 1953, he was the Secretary-General of the Rassemblement Democratique Africain (RDA) and helped launch the first Pan-African Student Congress in Paris in 1951. He also participated in the 1st World Congress of Black Writers and Artists held in Paris in 1956 and the 2nd such congress held in Rome in 1959. Upon returning to Senegal in 1960, Dr. Diop continued his research. In 1966, the 1st World Black Festival of Arts and Culture held in Dakar, Senegal honored Dr. Diop and Dr. W.E.B. DuBois as the scholars who exerted the greatest influence on Negro thought in the 20th century. In 1974, a breakthrough occurred in the English-speaking world when *The African Origin of Civilization*, a translation and compilation of the first 10 chapters of *Nations Negres* . . . and three chapters from *Anteriorite des Civilizations Noires*, was published. Subsequently, Dr. Diop published two additional books still in French, including his last, *Civilization ou Barbarie (Civilization or Barbarism).*

Dr. Diop was Director of the Radiocarbon laboratory at the Fundamental Institute of Black Africa (IFAN) at the University of Dakar. He sat on numerous international scientific committees and achieved recognition as one of the leading historians, Egyptologists, linguists, and anthropologists in the world. He travelled incessantly, lectured widely, and was cited and quoted voluminously. He was the 'pharaoh' of African studies.

FINCH, Charles S.

Charles S. Finch, M.D. is a board-certified family physician who is currently Assistant Professor of Community Medicine and Family Practice at the Morehouse School of Medicine. Dr. Finch completed his undergraduate training at Yale College, his medical training at Jefferson Medical College, and his Family Medicine Residency at the University of California, Irvine Medical Center. He has worked as an epidemiologist for the Center for Disease Control and was formerly a clinical preceptor at the Duke-Watts Family Medicine Clinic in Durham, North Carolina. He was the founder and chairman of the Raleigh Afro-American Life Focus Project between 1981 and 1982 and is a co-founder and Co-Convener of Bennu, Inc. of Atlanta. He is currently the Associate Editor of the *Journal of African Civilizations* and the author of "The African Background of Medical Science," "The Works of Gerald Massey: Studies in Kamite Origins," and—with Mr. Larry Williams of Bennu, Inc.—the co-author of "The Great Queens of Ethiopia," all published in the *Journal of African Civilizations*. In addition Dr. Finch has visited Senegal, West Africa where he has begun studies on the empirical basis of traditional West African medicine. On his most recent visit, he interviewed Dr. Cheikh Anta Diop, an interview which was published in the re-issue of "Egypt Revisited" edition of the *Journal of African Civilizations*.

HILLIARD, Asa G., III

Asa G. Hilliard is the Fuller E. Calloway Professor of Urban Education at Georgia State University, Atlanta, Georgia. He holds a joint appointment in the Department of Educational Foundations and the Department of Counseling and Psychological Services. Dr. Hilliard served previously as a department chairman and as dean of the School of Education at San Francisco State University. He is a graduate of the University of Denver with a bachelor's degree in psychology, a masters in counseling and guidance and a doctor of education degree in educational psychology. He has had experience as a teacher, administrator, researcher and lecturer throughout the United States and in several foreign countries, including a six-year period of professional service in Liberia, West Africa.

JEFFRIES Jr., Leonard

Dr. Leonard Jeffries Jr. is Professor of Africana Studies and Chairman of the Department of Black Studies at the City College of New York. He is President of the *African Heritage Association* and an Editorial Advisor to the *Journal of African Civilizations*. He has travelled extensively in Africa where he did field research for his doctorate in African Studies and Political Science at Columbia University. He is currently completing a book on the cultural unity of the African Diaspora.

He was Coordinator of the International Conference on Early Civilizations held at City College, New York, in December, 1980. He was also U.S. Coordinator of the Conference on Yoruba Civilization held at the University of Ife, Nigeria. He was initiator and coordinator of the Kinte Library Project of Black Family History in association with Alex Haley and other leading African-American scholars.

MIDDLETON, Listervelt

Producer and host of *For the People*, a television program broadcast statewide over the South Carolina educational television network. Has interviewed many of the Africanist historians and headed the official video-taping crew for the Nile Valley Conference held in Atlanta in 1984. Author of two volumes of poetry: "Fatback and Caviar" and "We Be a Creosote People."

MOORE, Carlos

Charles (Carlos) Moore was born in Camaguey, Cuba. He was educated at the Abraham Lincoln Language College in Havana, Cuba, and received his Ph.D. degree in Ethnology at the University of Paris. He is a political analyst, an ethnologist, and a journalist with an international reputation. As a political analyst, he has written for *Jeune Afrique* in Paris, France.

He has also written for *Afriscope* in Lagos, Nigeria and *Presence Africaine.* As a journalist, he has been a lecturer at the French School of Journalism and has written articles for Nadhatu Ifrigya, Cairo, Egypt and Agence-France-Presse. During 1961-1970 he was a data analyst/translator, Asia-Oceania Division for the Ministry of Foreign Affairs, Havana, Cuba. At the second World Black Festival of Arts and Culture (Festac) in Lagos, Nigeria he was Publicity Officer. He speaks Spanish, French, English, and Portuguese. He is the author of *Fela, Fela: This Bitch of a Life* (Allison & Busby, London, 1982) and *Were Marx and Engels White Racists?* (Third World Press, 1972) Forthcoming in 1986 is Moore's *Castroism and Africa:* 1959-1979.

MOORE, Shawna

Shawna Moore is an editor, translator and photo-journalist. Author of *Garvey, Lumumba and Malcolm X: Black Nationalist Separatists* (Third World Press, 1972). She has served as a translator of a number of interviews with Cheikh Anta Diop, which appeared in *Black Books Bulletin* (1976) and *Afriscope* (1977). As a photo-journalist, her photographs have appeared in numerous publications. Mrs. Moore is the author of the first two chapters of *Fela, Fela: This Bitch of a Life* (Allison & Busby, London, 1982).

PREVOST, Darryl R.

Darryl Prevost is a graduate student in African history and anthropology at the University of California, Berkeley. He has conducted research at many universities in African linguistics, anthropology, history and mathematics. Co-founder of several travel expedition programs at the University of California, served on the African Media and Information Service and the Cimarron Project, Coordinator of the Pan-African Student Collective. Prevost has acted as ambassador of goodwill for the city of Oakland to Oakland's sister-city Sekondi-Takorabi, having travelled through 23 countries in North, East and West Africa. He is presently studying French, Swahili, Twi and other African languages. He has done translations of Diop articles published in the *Bulletin de l'Ifan,* University of Dakar. His translations include:- "The Genetic Kinship of Pharaonic Egyptian and African Languages", "The Appearance of Homo Sapiens", "Iron Metallurgy during the Ancient Egyptian Empire" and many others.

RASHIDI, Runoko

Cultural historian with a special interest in the Kushite nations of antiquity. Founding member of Amenta, 1979. Principal organizer and founding member of the Southern Cradle research organization, 1981. Member of Board of Editors and Board of Directors of the Journal of African Civilizations, 1983. Author of *Kushite Case-Studies* (Los Angeles, 1983). Founder of the African People's Conference, held annually at Compton Community College. 1981 to 1984, African History Specialist for Compton Community College. Participant in the Nile Valley Conference, 1984. Regular contributor to the Journal of African Civilizations; Guest editor of *The African Presence in Early Asia* (April 1985) published by the *Journal of African Civilizations.* Currently History Editor for the National Black Computer Network.

SPADY, James G.

James G. Spady is the author of a recently published book, *Marcus Garvey, Africa And The Universal Negro Improvement Association: A UMUM Perspective on Concentric Activity In the Pan African World,* 1985 (Marcus Garvey Memorial Foundation, P.O. Box 42621, Philadelphia, Pa. 19101-2621).

Spady contributed several entries on Philadelphians to the first comprehensive Black biographical dictionary based on scholarly research, *Dictionary of American Negro Biography,* (W. W. Norton, Inc.) edited by Drs. Rayford W.

Logan and Michael R. Winston. His essay on the surrealistic aesthetic of "Dr. J." appeared in both French and English publications. Other writings by Spady have appeared and been cited in publications in Europe, Canada, Africa, Asia and the Caribbean. They include *The Mainline Times, American Literary Scholarship, Philadelphia Inquirer, The Oracle, Washington Post, Philadelphia Independent, Black Scholar, Germantown Courier, Philadelphia Tribune, Journal of National Medical Association, Africa* (London, England), *Présence Africaine* (Paris, France), *Black Images* (Toronto, Canada), *College Language Association Journal, Washington Star, The Garvey Voice, Black Books Bulletin, Indigene: An Anthology of Future Black Arts* and *Blacks In Science: Ancient and Modern.* He is an Associate Editor of the *Afro-American Journal of Philosophy* and is currently doing a biography of Philly Joe Jones. He recently edited a festschrift, *Cecil B. Moore: A Soldier For Justice,* and wrote the afterword for the 1985 reprint of Druscilla Dunjee Houston's *The Wonderful Ethiopians of the Ancient Cushite Empire.*

TAYLOR, Edward F.

Edward F. Taylor is Chairman of the Modern Foreign Language Department and Associate Professor of French at Morehouse College. He holds the B.A. degree, summa cum laude, from West Virginia State College and earned the M.A. degree from the University of Chicago as a Woodrow Wilson Fellow. Four grants from the Southern Fellowships Fund financed his doctoral study at Northwestern University, where he was awarded the Ph.D. degree. He also studied at the Sorbonne and the Institut de Touraine in France. Dr. Taylor taught previously at North Carolina Central University before assuming a teaching post at Morehouse. He was named an "Outstanding Young Man of America" in 1978.

VAN SERTIMA, Ivan

Ivan Van Sertima was born in Guyana, South America. He was educated at the School of Oriental and African Studies, London University and the Rutgers Graduate School and holds degrees in African Studies, Linguistics and Anthropology.

He is a literary critic, a linguist, and an anthropologist and has made a name in all three fields. As a literary critic, he is the author of *Caribbean Writers*, a collection of critical essays on the Caribbean Novel. He is also the author of several major literary reviews published in Denmark, India, Britain and the United States. He was honored for his work in this field by being asked by the Nobel Committee of the Swedish Academy to nominate candidates for the Nobel Prize in Literature, from 1976-1980. As a linguist, he has published essays on the dialect of the Sea Islands off the Georgia Coast. He is also the compiler of the *Swahili Dictionary of Legal Terms*, based on his fieldwork in Tanzania, East Africa, in 1967. He is the author of *They Came Before Columbus: The African Presence in Ancient America*, which was published by Random House in 1977 and is now in its tenth printing. It was published in French in 1981 and in the same year was awarded the Clarence L. Holte Prize, a prize awarded every two years "for a work of excellence in literature and the humanities relating to the cultural heritage of Africa and the African diaspora."

Professor Van Sertima is an associate professor of African Studies at Rutgers University in New Jersey and editor of the *Journal of African Civilizations*. He was also visiting professor at Princeton University from 1981 to 1983.

WILLIAMS, Larry

Larry Williams is a co-convenor and founding member of the Bennu Study Group of Atlanta, Georgia. He did undergraduate studies at the University of Chicago. He has been a volunteer for the Institute of the Black World. His articles have appeared in *History, The Bible and the Black Man* magazine, the *Atlanta Voice* newspaper, *Return to the Source* magazine, and *Afrika Must Unite: A Journal of Pan-Afrikan Affairs*. He is a frequent lecturer on Marcus Garvey and other subjects in the field of African history.

WILLIAMS-MYERS, A.J.

A.J. Williams-Myers, Associate Professor, Black Studies Department, College of New Paltz, received his Ph.D. from UCLA with the aid of a Ford Foundation Fellowship for Afro-Americans in the Middle East and Africa. He was Professor of African History at Carleton College in Northfield, Minnesota. He has published a number of African-related articles and was the recipient of two summer NEH seminars (NYU, 1957 and Yale, 1980). He is presently doing research into the African presence in the Hudson River Valley.